SECOND EDITION

Writing
for
Career-
Education
Students

WITHDRAWN

SECOND EDITION

Writing for Career-Education Students

Andrew W. Hart

James A. Reinking

St. Martin's Press   New York

Library of Congress Catalog Card Number: 81–51839
Copyright (c) 1982 by St. Martin's Press, Inc.
All Rights Reserved.
Manufactured in the United States of America.
65432
fedcba
For information, write St. Martin's Press, Inc.,
175 Fifth Avenue, New York, N.Y.   10010

ISBN: 0–312–89462–7

ACKNOWLEDGMENTS

ALLSTATE LIFE INSURANCE COMPANY: "Life Insurance: Some Basic Facts You Should Know, 1979."
Reprinted by permission.
AMERICAN CANCER SOCIETY INC.: "What Is Chemotherapy?" reprinted by permission of the
American Cancer Society, Inc.
BARNES & NOBLE BOOKSTORES, INC.: Excerpts from *Webster's Dictionary* sales letter reprinted by
permission of Barnes & Noble Bookstores, Inc.
THE BENDIX CORPORATION: Photograph of the Bendix Sound Level Meter, type 2, model 300
reprinted courtesy of The Bendix Corporation, Environmental & Process Instruments Division.
CHEMICAL AND ENGINEERING NEWS: "Sales by Company Type" reprinted with permission from
Chemical and Engineering News, June 29, 1981, p. 10. Copyright 1981 American Chemical Society.
CHEMICAL ENGINEERING: "Typical Process Flow, Recompression Evaporator (single-stage)," by
permission from *Chemical Engineering*, Feb. 22, 1969. Copyright © 1969.
CITIBANK N.A.: "The Bureaucrat" reprinted by permission of Citibank.
THE EASTERN COMPANY: Hi-tensile Anchor Selection Guide table reprinted with permission of the
Danforth Division of the Eastern Company.
THE EQUITABLE LIFE ASSURANCE SOCIETY OF THE UNITED STATES: "Benefits Paid" used with
the permission of The Equitable Life Assurance Society of the United States.
FAMILY WEEKLY: "Let the Sunshine Do Your Cooking" by Carolyn Jabs, from the June 18, 1978 issue of
Family Weekly. Reprinted by permission of Family Weekly, copyright 1978, 641 Lexington Ave., New
York, N.Y. 10022.
FLOCON PRODUCTS, INC.: Cutaway view of the FloGuard Check Valve reprinted with permission of
the designer and manufacturer, Flocon Products, Inc., Houston, Texas.
HIGH FIDELITY: Excerpt from "Beta/VHS: What's the Difference?" from the January 1981 issue of *High
Fidelity*. All rights reserved.
MACHINE DESIGN: "Beating OSHA to the Punch by Silencing Pneumatic Equipment" reprinted with
permission from *Machine Design*, March 20, 1981, by Penton/IPC, Inc., Cleveland, Ohio.
SIMON & SCHUSTER, INC.: Excerpt from *A Layman's Guide to Psychiatry and Psychoanalysis* by Eric
Berne, copyright © 1947, 1957, 1968 by Eric Berne. Reprinted by permission of Simon & Schuster, a
Division of Gulf & Western Corporation.
WATER POLLUTION CONTROL FEDERATION: "Water-Quality-Related R and D Funding at EPA—
1972-1981" reprinted with permission from the Water Pollution Control Federation.

For Scott

To the Instructor

This second edition of *Writing for Career-Education Students*, like the first, presents a clear, step-by-step introduction to the essentials of practical writing. It is designed for students in vocational and technical programs or for courses enrolling a mixture of vocational and liberal arts students in which a strong emphasis on job-related writing is desired. It may be used for teaching freshman composition. It is also suitable for a one-term course in technical communication.

The second edition offers a number of important improvements over the first. Four new chapters—on abstracts, library research papers, oral reports, and tables, graphs, and illustrations—have been added. The material on business correspondence has been broadened to include a new section on sales letters, as well as guidelines for writing several kinds of memos. Every chapter from the first edition has been thoroughly revised to accommodate the suggestions of instructors using the book. As a result, the second edition has a number of expanded discussions and reorganized presentations. Also in response to instructors' requests, the writing examples now include pieces by professionals along with the ones by students and represent a much broader range of subject matter than those in the first edition. The appendix, completely reorganized and greatly expanded, is now a complete handbook of grammar, usage, and mechanics that includes an exercise for each of its thirty-nine units. Together, these improvements should significantly enhance the usefulness of the text.

Although broader in its coverage, the new edition retains the simple, straightforward organization of its predecessor. Chapter 1 discusses the elements of a paragraph and ways to develop it, and Chapter 2 takes the student step by step through the procedure typically followed in preparing a composition—planning, writing, and revising. These introductory chapters are followed by five chapters on expository writing—comparison, classification, explanation of a process, definition, and description—each illustrated by several examples of student and professional writing. Chapter 8 considers the various kinds of letters and memorandums essential to on-the-job and business-related communication. Chapters 9 through 12 take up more specialized types of communication: proposals, progress reports, investigation or test reports, and abstracts. Chapter 13 deals thoroughly with library research papers: choosing a suitable topic, using the library, taking notes, preparing an outline, and writing and documenting the paper. This chapter is new to the second edition, as are Chapters 14 and 15, which treat oral reports and the preparation of tables, graphs, and illustrations. The text proper concludes with Chapter 16, which discusses the job application letter, personal data sheet or résumé. job interview, and four kinds of postinterview letters. Within each group of chapters, the text progresses from a general to a specialized emphasis and from the classroom to the career.

The Appendix consists of three sections. The first, "Sentence Elements and Types," discusses syntax and the eight parts of speech, offering a "crash course" in traditional grammar but avoiding the excessive complexity and the emphasis on terminology that often merely confuse students. The second section, "Avoiding Common Errors of Usage," is designed to train students' eyes and ears to catch the most common grammatical errors. The final section, "Punctuation and Mechanics," takes up the different marks of punctuation as well as capitalization, abbreviations, numbers, and italics. The exercises in the first section ask students to identify grammatical elements; those in the second section ask them to correct faulty sentences; and those in the third ask them to supply missing punctuation and other mechanical features. A chart inside the back cover of the book lists correction symbols for the instructor's use in marking student papers. The symbols are keyed for student reference to the pertinent discussions in the book.

To a greater degree than comparable texts with which we are familiar, *Writing for Career-Education Students* keeps its sights on what students need to know and *why* they need to know it. In introducing each type of writing, we point out its importance both on the job and in the student's college courses. Directions are presented in an easy-to-follow, step-by-step format—the mode of presentation students encounter most frequently in their technical or vocational courses. The students' writing examples offer realistic, achievable goals and, when compared with the professionally written examples, demonstrate that students can indeed produce first-rate work. The examples represent a range of vocational and general interests and clearly and consistently conform to the patterns of development discussed in the text. The questions accompanying the examples have been designed to underscore important points in the chapter and to reinforce the principles of good writing in general. The suggested writing assignments at the end of each chapter ask students to put these principles into practice in writing of their own.

These features provide a number of benefits. Students readily understand and follow the directions, relate closely to the models, show increased confidence in their own ability, and perceive the value of what they are doing. As a result, they participate more actively in class, put more effort into their assignments, and produce better papers and talks.

Another feature of *Writing for Career-Education Students* is flexibility. We strongly recommend that the chapters on the paragraph and the theme be read first, if only as a general review. Beyond these two chapters, however, the materials in this book can be "mixed and matched" in a number of ways, depending upon the makeup of the class and the course objectives. For example, one instructor might elect to begin with the chapters on expository writing and then proceed to more technical materials, such as business letters and memorandums, reports, and proposals. Another instructor might start with business letters and memorandums, job application letters and personal data sheets, and selected technical reports, then consider types of expository writing, and conclude the course with the library research paper and an oral report based on the paper.

In addition to being suited to the conventional classroom, *Writing for Career-Education Students* is also appropriate for individual study programs in the "open" classroom. The step-by-step approach allows students to proceed at their own pace. When they feel they have mastered a step, they may check with the instructor and then move on to the next step. The variety of writing examples and the large number of suggestions for writing make it possible for the instructor to tailor assignments to the career interests of individual students.

ACKNOWLEDGMENTS

Once again, we are indebted to many people for their encouragement and assistance. First of all, we would like to thank our colleagues at Ferris State College as well as others who have criticized portions of the manuscript, furnished us with writing models, and helped us in many different ways. Special thanks are due John Belanger, who prepared the first draft of the oral reports chapter. We are grateful also to Fred Birkam, Charles Bond, Mary Braun, Ann Breitenwischer, Emma Crystal, Hugh Griffith, Connie Haenlein, Jane Hart, Fred Howting, Robert Large, Elaine Nienhouse, Robert Parsons, Ann Remp, Rex Schuberg, Richard Shaw, Elliott Smith, and Richard Young. The support of Barbara and Gene Bleiler and Steven Reinking was deeply appreciated.

We are particularly grateful also for the perceptive recommendations of the following colleagues who reviewed this edition in manuscript and greatly influenced its final shape: Robert Brien, Madison Area Technical College; Daniel Dalton, John Tyler Community College; Jane Heymann, Mitchell Community College; Louis Janda, Northeast Wisconsin Technical Institute; Valerie Perotti, Hocking Technical Institute; and Arthur Wagner, Macomb Community College.

We are also indebted to the following users of the first edition whose suggestions have been incorporated in this second edition: Arlene Benson, Marshalltown Community College; Jane Bergman, St. Louis Community College at Meramec; David Bloomstrand, Rock Valley College; Kenneth B. Boyer, St. Louis Community College at Florissant Valley; Robert J. Branda, Rock Valley College; David F. Butler, North Country Community College; Alice Chalip, College of Alameda; Marcia S. Carter, Rowan Technical College; Patrick Connolly, Rock Valley College; Barbara Crooker, Northampton County Area Community College; Robert B. Davis, Gavilan Junior College; Joseph F. Dunne, St. Louis Community College at Meramec; Arnold B. Fox, Northern Illinois University; Margaret Gage, Linn-Benton Community College; Barbara Geaither, Malcolm X College; Jeanille Gooch, Utah Technical College; Peggy-Joyce Grable, Walla Walla College; Mary Dell Heathington, Cooke County College; Karen Hess, Normandale Community College; Jane Heymann, Mitchell Community College; Walter E. Johnston, SUNY College of Technology; L. B. Kennelly, North Texas State

University; Beverly Konneker, Southern Illinois University; Greg Larkin, Brigham Young University—Hawaii Campus; Dennis Lynch, Northern Illinois University; Molly Maloney, Lexington Technical Institute; Terence Martin, St. Louis Community College at Meramec; Alice Massey, American River College; Robert E. Mehaffy, American River College; Michael Miller, Longview Community College; Steven Miller, Indiana University—Bloomington; Joseph C. Murphey, Cooke County College; Deirdre Neilen, SUNY Upstate Medical Center; Sylvia Nosworthy, Walla Walla College; Martha L. Peterson, Madison Area Technical College; Dorothy Powell, Roanoke-Chowan Technical College; Donald S. Pratt, Southwestern College; Curt M. Rulon, North Texas State University; Pearl Saunders, St. Louis Community College at Florissant Valley; Timothy L. Seiler, University of Evansville; John A. Shayner, Centenary College; Sarah Smedman, University of North Carolina—Charlotte; Herbert W. Smith, SUNY—Utica/Rome; James R. Sodon, St. Louis Community College at Florissant Valley; Judith Spector, Indiana University/Purdue University at Columbus; Lynne Waldeland, Northern Illinois University; Jeff Walker, Indiana University/Purdue University at Columbus; Garry N. Watkins, Rowan Technical College; Jerry P. Wilkes, Rowan Technical College; and Mary Wilson, Kirkwood Community College.

We also wish to express our appreciation to the thoroughly professional staff of St. Martin's Press, and especially to Tom Broadbent, Nancy Perry, and Charles Thurlow. Finally, our greatest debt is to the many students and organizations whose writing examples and other illustrative materials appear in these pages. Without their help this book would not have been possible.

Andrew W. Hart
James A. Reinking

To the Student

No matter what career you choose, your ability to communicate clearly and effectively will directly affect your success. In the classroom, your instructor will often evaluate your mastery of a subject by the papers and examinations you write. Prospective employers will make judgments about your qualifications and decide whether to offer you an interview on the basis of your application letter and personal data sheet. Once you are on the job, you must be prepared to write clear, accurate reports, instructions, memorandums, and letters and to give effective oral presentations.

There is nothing mysterious about successful on-the-job communication. It does not require a special talent, nor does it depend on inspiration. It is simply a skill, and, like any other skill, it involves a series of steps or procedures that can be learned. Once you are familiar with the steps, the more you practice the easier the task becomes.

Writing for Career-Education Students will acquaint you with the steps involved in successful communication and show you how to apply them to the specific kinds of situations you can expect to face as you pursue your career. The first two chapters, on paragraphs and themes, deal with procedures basic to all successful writing. Chapters 3 through 7 explain the most frequently used types of exposition: comparison, classification, explanation of a process, definition, and description. Chapter 8 discusses letters and memorandums. Chapters 9 through 12 deal with four specialized types of on-the-job writing: proposals, progress reports, investigation reports, and abstracts. Chapters 13 through 15 take up library research reports, oral reports, and the preparation of tables, graphs, and illustrations. Chapter 16, the final chapter, presents detailed suggestions for finding a job: locating job openings, preparing application letters and personal data sheets, handling employment interviews, and writing follow-up letters.

The Appendix reviews the basic elements of grammar, the most common writing errors, and punctuation and mechanics, including capitalization, abbreviations, numbers, and italics. A chart inside the back cover lists the correction symbols that your instructor may use in marking your papers. For your convenience, the symbols are keyed to the specific pages in the book where you can find help in correcting the problems your instructor has pointed out.

This book has several features we hope you will find helpful. It is written in simple, everyday language. Directions are presented in an easy-to-follow, step-by-step format. Above all, the book is written directly to and for you. In the course of your education, you have probably had the unpleasant experience of using textbooks that seemed to be designed more for instructors than for students. In preparing this book, we have tried never to forget that you, after all, are buying the book and paying for the course in which you are using it. Accordingly, we have tried to write the book as directly as possible to you.

Another feature is that a great number of the writing examples have been done by students rather than professional writers. These student examples represent realistic, achievable goals. When you compare them with the professional examples, you will see dramatic evidence that students can indeed do excellent work. We are confident that if you learn to apply the principles presented in the following pages, you can do so, too. Here's wishing you success!

Andrew W. Hart
James A. Reinking

Contents

3 Comparison   41

4 Classification   59

5 Explanation of a Process   75

6 Definition   93

7 Description   110

8 Letters and Memorandums   127

9 Proposals   188

10 Progress Reports 213

11 Investigation Reports 227

15 Tables, Graphs, and Illustrations   322

16 Finding a Job   340

APPENDIX: Grammar, Usage, Punctuation, and Mechanics — 378

Sentence Elements — 379

Avoiding Common Errors of Usage   411

Punctuation and Mechanics   458

SECOND EDITION

Writing for Career-Education Students

1

The Paragraph

Writing is a process of building larger units from smaller ones. That is, the writer uses words to make sentences, sentences to make paragraphs, and paragraphs to make a composition—a letter, report, or college theme. In this book, we deal with words and sentences at appropriate places throughout the text and in the appendix at the end of the book. We will begin our discussion here with the paragraph.

Paragraphs help both you and your readers. Writing a paper of any kind is easier when you can focus on its separate units—the paragraphs—one by one. Your readers also benefit from paragraphing, for they can grasp your main ideas one at a time and follow the progression of ideas throughout the paper in an orderly way.

To understand what is involved in writing a paragraph, you must first be familiar with five basic elements:

1. one central idea
2. topic sentence
3. specific details
4. pattern of development
5. linking devices

In the following sections, we will discuss and illustrate each of these elements.

1

One Central Idea

A paragraph is a group of closely related sentences that develop and clarify *one*, and *only one*, central idea. Carefully select the material you include in each of your paragraphs so that you don't stray from its central idea. Sentences that point in several different directions rather than toward a single idea will only confuse your reader.

Consider the following faulty paragraph.

> As he crosses the parking lot, Dave notices two young men shouting and scuffling. When he opens the door to the athletic complex, he can smell the various refreshments. Once inside the gymnasium, he hears the familiar loud noises of the junior varsity basketball game. While undressing in the varsity locker room, he hears different noises.

What exactly is the writer trying to convey in this paragraph? There is no way of knowing. Each of the four sentences expresses a different idea, and none of them is developed:

1. young men shouting and scuffling
2. smells of the refreshments in the athletic complex
3. noises of the junior varsity basketball game
4. noises in the varsity locker room

For meaningful communication, each of these ideas would have to be fully developed in a separate paragraph.

Each of the following student paragraphs *does* develop and clarify one central idea.

> As he opens the door to the crowded gymnasium, Dave is blasted by the familiar noises of the junior varsity basketball game. Hundreds of voices blend together to form one huge roar, which reaches a peak whenever the home team makes a basket. Suddenly a shrill whistle silences the crowd, and then a stabbing buzzer signals a time out. With a break in the action, the pep band strikes up the school fight song. Trumpets blare to the thumping beat of the bass drum.
>
> While the band is playing, Dave turns and walks toward the varsity locker room, where he is greeted by different noises. The

mumbling and joking of the players mix with the muffled voices of the coaches discussing the game plan in the closed office. The clanging of steel lockers as they are opened and closed blends in. Aerosol cans of skin toughener hiss as the spray is applied to tender feet. Mouse-like squeaks are heard as the nervous players pace the floor. Finally the coaches come out to give their last words of advice and encouragement

Mike Hogan

All the sentences in the first paragraph point toward one idea— the noises in the gym during the junior varsity basketball game. No unrelated details, such as the "smell of the various refreshments," are included. Similarly, all the sentences in the second paragraph point toward a single, but *different,* idea—the noises of the varsity locker room. The writer signals this shift in thought to the reader by beginning a new paragraph.

Topic Sentence

The topic sentence is the most important sentence in a paragraph. Its function is to state clearly the central idea of the paragraph. All the other sentences in the paragraph develop this one idea.

A topic sentence serves two purposes. First, it helps the writer decide what to include in and exclude from the paragraph. Only information that develops or clarifies the idea stated in the topic sentence belongs in the paragraph. Second, the topic sentence helps the reader. By stating the central idea, it eliminates the possibility that the reader will miss the point, and it saves the reader the trouble of having to figure out how the various bits of information in the paragraph are related.

When you formulate a topic sentence, be sure to avoid one that is too broad. The following sentence, for example, encompasses more points than can be meaningfully developed in a single paragraph. You would have to write an article or perhaps even a book to develop the idea it expresses.

There have been great advances in technology in the twentieth century.

Here are two adequate topic sentences.

> The pocket calculator offers a number of advantages over the adding machine.
>
> Frequent headaches may be a warning sign of high blood pressure.

You could develop the first idea by citing, for example, the pocket calculator's low cost, portability, and versatility. The second idea might be developed by indicating the frequency, the location, and the time, particularly early morning, of headaches triggered by high blood pressure.

Because the topic sentence expresses the central idea developed in the paragraph, it should be placed where the reader can spot it easily. Experienced writers, therefore, often start their paragraphs with the topic sentence, and you will probably find it helpful to do the same. Placing the topic sentence at the beginning not only makes the paragraph easier to write but also enables your reader to learn the subject of the paragraph immediately. Examine the following paragraph. The topic sentence is italicized.

> *The nursing station is a hubbub of activity.* Doctors are writing new orders, and their patients' charts are scattered all over the desk. Laboratory and X-ray technicians are explaining results of tests. The pharmacist brings medications and inquires about any new orders for drugs. Inhalation and physical therapists are busy checking charts for their new orders. The dietician asks why a certain patient is not eating the foods he should. Telephones ring and patients' signal lights flash continually. The members of the nursing team, all with their own duties, are trying desperately to keep up with everything that is going on. This pace continues through most of the morning shift.
>
> *Clare Mutter*

Sometimes in order to emphasize the support for the main idea and build gradually to a conclusion, a writer will position the topic sentence at the end of a paragraph. This position can also create suspense as the reader anticipates the summarizing remark. Here is a well-developed paragraph with the topic sentence at the end.

> Most people know that our upper atmosphere has a layer of ozone, a highly reactive special form of oxygen that filters the sun's

ultraviolet radiation. This filtering provides important protection against skin cancer. Harvard scientists have estimated that depleting the ozone layer by 16 percent could result in more than 100,000 additional cases of skin cancer each year. Furthermore, such depletion could seriously reduce the number of phyloplanktons, one-celled organisms that live in the sea and produce most of the world's oxygen. Some scientists even believe that increased ultraviolet radiation might raise the temperature of our lower atmosphere and cause catastrophic weather. *Clearly the ozone layer is important, perhaps vital, to the protection of life on earth.*

Ted VandenHeuvel

All the details lead up to and prepare for the last sentence. At that point, the reader can easily understand why the author of the paragraph considers the ozone layer important.

An experienced writer will occasionally construct a paragraph in which the central idea is only implied. Although such a paragraph has no stated topic sentence, the sentences that make up the paragraph, added together, suggest a single idea which the reader has little difficulty understanding. For example, in the last sample paragraph, an experienced writer might have implied the central idea rather than stating it in a topic sentence. The combination of details—increased skin cancer, fewer phytoplanktons, and increased air temperatures—might have been enough to show that the ozone layer is important to life. However, effective paragraphs without clear topic sentences are hard to write, and even if they are well done, they still make an extra demand on the reader. For the kind of writing you will do in the classroom and on the job, the best advice is to develop your paragraphs from clearly expressed topic sentences.

Specific Details

Most successful paragraphs contain a generous supply of specific details that develop and clarify the idea expressed in the topic sentence. These details may include such things as facts, figures, thoughts, observations, steps, listings, illustrative examples, and personal experiences. Each individual detail is one piece of a larger picture. Separately, the details may mean very little, but when enough of them are grouped together properly, the total picture emerges.

Think back to the paragraph describing the nursing station. The first detail, doctors writing new orders, means little by itself. You begin to sense the activity when you read about the laboratory and X-ray technicians. Then you see the pharmacists, the therapists, and the dietician. Finally, the nurses are described, and you have a total picture of the activity in the nursing station. The details, taken as a unit, have made the picture complete.

Now read the following paragraph and note the difference.

There are two reasons why prices at McDonald's are low. One is that the selection of food is limited. Also the franchise makes a deliberate effort to hold down operating costs.

The problem here is determining what the writer means. This short paragraph begins with an adequate topic sentence, but the writer doesn't develop it sufficiently. Instead of clarifying the main idea, the rest of the paragraph only raises questions. For example, what does the writer mean by a "limited" selection? Are the hamburgers served only with mustard? Or does the writer mean that the chain doesn't sell deli sandwiches and tacos? And what about the meaning of "a deliberate effort to hold down operating costs"? Are workers paid rock-bottom wages? Are utensils and napkins disposable? What about the grade of meat used? Is it some employee's job to rush into the restroom the moment a customer vacates it and make sure the faucets aren't dripping?

The writer may very well know what he or she wants the reader to understand, but the information does not appear in the paragraph. Thus the reader, instead of seeing a clear picture, gets merely a vague impression. This paragraph is obviously underdeveloped—more specific details are needed.

At this point you can see the benefits of supplying plenty of specific details. First, and most important, the reader receives the same message you intended—there is no confusion or misunderstanding. You and your reader connect. Second, specific details make your writing more vivid and interesting. And there is an additional benefit, although it applies more to the writing you do for your courses than to the writing you will do on the job: if you provide enough details to make your ideas really clear, you will seldom have to worry about "getting enough words" for an assigned paper. When you concentrate on giving your reader a complete picture and not just a piece here and there, the length of your paper will usually take care of itself.

Whenever you have a choice, pick a familiar topic to write on. You will then have an adequate supply of details to draw upon and will write with more authority than you could on an unfamiliar topic.

Students often ask, "How long should my paragraphs be?" This question defies easy answer. As a general rule, a paragraph should provide enough supporting details to ensure that the reader grasps the central idea fully. Occasionally one or two sentences will provide enough backup, but usually more are needed.

Readability also plays a role in setting paragraph length. Paragraphs signal natural dividing points, allowing the reader to pause and absorb the material presented up till then. Too little paragraphing can overwhelm the reader with long blocks of material. Too much can create an undesirable choppy effect. To prevent such problems, writers occasionally use two or more paragraphs to develop a single idea, or they combine several short paragraphs into one.

The following one-paragraph excerpts from longer student papers illustrate the use of specific details.

> Hand and foot movements are critical for the snowplow operator. He uses his hands not only to steer but at the same time to raise, lower, and change the angle of the front plow. At certain points, the back plow must also be raised and lowered. Between the plow control movements, the operator's hands are busy shifting his transmission, using turn signals, flipping switches for radios and lights, and sometimes clearing fogged windshields. Meanwhile, his feet move so fast that they might appear blurry to a passenger. They are continually moving from the brakes to the clutch to the accelerator.
>
> *Jim Linscott*

> A program in drafting techniques acquaints students with a number of practical skills. Students first learn basic principles such as lettering, geometric construction, orthographic projection, and dimensioning. They then learn to apply product drafting to surface finish controls, geometric and positional tolerances, sections of parts, symbols used in drawing, and assemblies and subassemblies. During this study of the spatial relationships of lines,

planes, and solids, they learn to solve layout problems by using descriptive geometry and rotational principles. Next they are taught the fundamentals of tool detailing and the basic design of tools, jigs, fixtures, dies, and molds, using standard parts such as clamps, washers, keys, locating pins, and punches. They also gain an insight into the use of drill jigs and milling fixtures, which are drawn as assemblies and then detailed into working drawings.

Richard Johnson

Pattern of Development

Although a well-developed paragraph contains a generous supply of specific details, it is not enough to present them in whatever order they happen to come to mind. Such a helter-skelter approach would make it hard for the reader to grasp the writer's full meaning. There are several common patterns of development a paragraph can follow: the one you use for a particular paragraph will depend upon the purpose of your writing and the nature of your subject.

Five patterns of development are presented below. The first and second are basic; the last three, though listed as separate patterns, are actually special forms of the first or second.

PATTERN NUMBER ONE: GENERAL TO SPECIFIC

The general-to-specific pattern is probably the one used most frequently. The writer begins with a general statement, the topic sentence, and then moves to specific statements that explain or support it. Here is a student paragraph that illustrates this pattern.

My roommate Leonard is the most high-strung person I've ever met. Spending one evening with him is about all that most people can take. At the supper table Leonard constantly drums his fingers on the table top in a staccato beat. Occasionally he stops long enough to gulp down some hunks of food. Those hunks are no doubt well-churned in the most active stomach east of Pocatello. Later, when it's time for a few hands of cards before cracking the books, you'd swear Leonard is shuffling the spots right off the cards. Nobody ever asks to cut the deck when he deals. If I happen to discard casually, Leonard pounces on the card, meticulously arranging it and the whole pile into a neat stack. These nervous mannerisms carry over into his studying. It's a unique experience to watch Leonard pace the floor, abruptly turn, and mumble something like "suburb located right outside city limits, exurb located further out." I can imagine what he's like during an exam. Only when this bundle of nerves winds down and goes to bed does peace come to our room.

Steve Lintemuth

PATTERN NUMBER TWO: SPECIFIC TO GENERAL

A paragraph developed by the specific-to-general pattern presents the specific statements first and then concludes with a general statement, the topic sentence. The following student example illustrates this pattern.

Leslie Jackson has had a number of years' experience as a secretary. Her typing is excellent—65 words a minute—as is her steno. She is neat, punctual, and well organized, and she works well without supervision. When Leslie is given an assignment, she can be counted on to do a topnotch job. Her coworkers look to Leslie for advice, and she never fails to give them the help they need. There is no doubt that Leslie Jackson is well qualified to be an office manager.

Gloria Stillwell

PATTERN NUMBER THREE: TIME SEQUENCE

The time-sequence pattern arranges the events being described in chronological order—that is, the order in which they happen in time. The topic sentence may come first or last, or it may be implied. Here is a student paragraph that illustrates the time-sequence pattern.

I remember well the morning I had my first job interview. Before leaving home, I made certain I was neatly dressed and well groomed. It was a long drive to the interviewer's office, and more than once I thought of being rejected. Then there was the difficult time as I sat in the outer office, nervously waiting my turn. I remember tapping my feet, shifting in the chair, and trying to read several magazines. Finally, my name was called. I swallowed hard and walked stiffly into the office. The interviewer asked many questions, keeping her eyes directly focused on me all the time. After what seemed like hours, she indicated I could report for work the following Monday.

Jane Bleiler

PATTERN NUMBER FOUR: SPACE SEQUENCE

In the space-sequence pattern, specific statements are presented in an orderly arrangement that enables the reader to see how the different items relate to one another physically—that is, in space. For example, if you were describing an object such as a building, you might start at the top and work down to the bottom, describing what you see in that order. On the other hand, you might start at the bottom and work up. This pattern of development offers many possibilities: left to right, right to left, nearby to faraway, faraway to nearby, and so on. Make sure, however, that the particular space sequence you choose is appropriate for the object you are describing. A paragraph arranged by space sequence, like one arranged chronologically, may start or finish with the topic sentence, or it may have an implied topic sentence. The paragraph below illustrates the space-sequence pattern.

The ceramic elf in our family room is quite a sight. The toes of his reddish-brown slippers hang over the mantelshelf. Pudgy, yellow-stockinged legs rise from the slippers and disappear into an olive-green tunic. This jacket, gathered at the waist with a thick brown belt that fits snugly around his roly-poly belly, looks wrinkled and slept in. His short, meaty arms hang comfortably, one hand resting on the knapsack at his side and the other clutching the bowl of an old black pipe. An unkempt, snow-white beard, dotted by occasional snarls, extends from his belt to his lower lip. A button nose, capped with a smudge of gold dust, mischievous black eyes, and an unruly snatch of hair peeking out from under his burnt-orange stocking cap complete Bartholomew's appearance.

Maria Sanchez

PATTERN NUMBER FIVE: ORDER OF CLIMAX

The order-of-climax pattern presents a series of points in a logical progression with the main point coming last. The progression may, for example, be from the least important to the most important, least complex to most complex, or least characteristic to most characteristic. This approach encourages the reader to continue until the end. Once again, the topic sentence may precede or follow the supporting details, or be implied. The following student paragraph illustrates the order-of-climax pattern.

> My wardrobe includes three pairs of Levi's straight-leg jeans. Their tough polyester-cotton fabric, strong stitching, and rivet-reinforced front pockets add up to a garment that easily outlasts any slacks I've ever worn. More important, Levi's are all the rage among young people these days. I can wear them to classes, cookouts, roller skating parties, or any informal occasion at all and be right in style. But above all, it's the look and feel of Levi's that attract me. Trim-legged, snug in the seat, they offer comfort without drooping or bagginess. I'll spend my money on Levi's straight-leg jeans every time.
>
> *Marc O'Leary*

In technical writing, paragraphs are rarely structured by order of climax. Instead, the most important point is presented first, helping to create a straightforward style of writing.

Linking Devices

Now you are familiar with some patterns of development that will give order to your paragraphs as you supply specific details to make the central idea of each paragraph clear to your reader. *Next* you must make sure that the sentences within your paragraphs are linked to one another in ways that make them flow smoothly and enable your reader to follow the progression of thought easily from sentence to sentence. *After all,* you have carefully arranged the sentences in a particular sequence to develop one continuous idea. *That is,* the idea expressed by each sentence is in some way related to the idea in the sentence before it and to the idea in the sentence after it, and they are all related, directly or indirectly, to the central idea expressed in the topic sentence. *Of course,* the relationships among the sentences are clear to you because you wrote the paragraph; *however,* they must also be made clear to your reader. This job is accomplished by the use of linking devices.

LINKING DEVICE NUMBER ONE:
CONNECTING WORDS AND PHRASES

Certain words in the paragraph you just read are italicized. Each of the italicized units is an example of a commonly used connecting word or phrase. Read the paragraph again. Notice how *now, next, after all, that is, of course,* and *however* connect the sentences in the paragraph and relate the ideas they express to one another. To see this clearly, try reading the paragraph aloud with, and then again without, the italicized words and phrases.

Here are some of the most commonly used connecting words and phrases, grouped according to the relationships they show.

SIMILARITY: likewise, similarly

CONTRAST: on the other hand, on the contrary, at the same time, otherwise, however, nevertheless, but, yet, still

RESULT OR EFFECT: since, consequently, accordingly, hence, thus, as a result, therefore, because, if

ADDING IDEAS TOGETHER: first, in the first place, second, and also, furthermore, moreover, too, also, in addition, finally, inconclusion

PROVIDING EMPHASIS OR CLARITY: that is, in other words, again, as a matter of fact, in fact, indeed, nonetheless, besides, although, after all, above all

INDICATING TIME RELATIONSHIP: later, until, while, meanwhile, now, from now on, after, next, afterwards, at times, once, when, then, subsequently

INTRODUCING AN EXAMPLE: for example, for instance, to illustrate

CONCEDING A POINT: of course, granted that, to be sure

The following student example illustrates how connecting words and phrases link the different sentences of a paragraph. The connecting words are italicized.

The psychiatric nurse deals with dangerous mental patients, pathological personalities who have no sense of right or wrong. *For this reason,* she must be on guard at all times; she must, in effect, have eyes in the back of her head. She must *also* have a great deal of self-control. When her patient displays anger and violence, she cannot respond in kind. *On the contrary,* she must be tolerant and understanding. *Furthermore*, she must be able to recognize attempts at deception. *Sometimes* a mentally ill person, just prior to suicide, will act in a completely normal way because he or she has made the decision to die. The nurse must understand this behavior and be alert for any possible attempt.

Peg Feltman

Notice how each sentence is related to the one before it. The connecting words and phrases make the relationships clear, linking the sentences into a continuous unit that can be followed easily.

LINKING DEVICE NUMBER TWO: REPETITION OF WORDS AND PHRASES

Repetition of key words and phrases in several sentences in a paragraph is another way of helping the reader follow the train of thought from sentence to sentence. Read the following student paragraph and notice how the repetition of "college policy" and variations thereon help link the sentences together.

I'm fed up with *college policy*. Many of the rules seem to be roadblocks designed to inconvenience me. For example, I live nineteen miles from campus. When I tried to get a commuter sticker for my car, I was told that *college policy* requires that I live twenty or more miles away in order to qualify for one. To make matters worse, *college policy* prohibits noncommuter students from parking anywhere on campus except in one special lot, which is always full. More than once I've been frantically searching for a parking spot when I should have been in class. And then there's the *school's* tuition *policy*. At our school, students register for the coming term five weeks before it starts. The deadline for paying tuition is exactly three weeks before the term begins. If payment isn't made by then, it's the *policy of the college* to cancel the registration. Last term the tuition check from my parents was delayed in the mail and arrived one day late. As a result, I had to spend three and a half hours re-registering at the start of the term and couldn't get one of my required courses. I think it's high time for the *college* to re-examine some of its *policies*. After all, shouldn't the main *policy* of any *college* be to help, not hinder, its students' efforts to get an education?

Alex Malinowski

**LINKING DEVICE NUMBER THREE:
PRONOUNS AND DEMONSTRATIVE ADJECTIVES**

Pronouns and demonstrative adjectives likewise provide a smooth, easily followed flow of ideas. Pronouns point back to nouns or pronouns that appear earlier in the sentence or in previous sentences. Thus they pull the sentences closer together and help guide the reader along a continuous path. There are four demonstrative adjectives: *this, that, these,* and *those.* All are special adjectives that identify or point out nouns. A word of caution about pronouns: use them carefully and make sure there is no question about which words they refer back to. Notice how the italicized words in the paragraph below link the sentences in a clear pattern that is easy to follow.

There are two kinds of dental mouth mirrors. The first is made of ordinary glass and has a flat reflecting surface. With *this* mirror the dentist sees the patient's teeth just the way the patient sees *them* in a regular looking glass. The second, the magnifying mirror, has a concave surface that makes everything look larger. *This* mirror gives the dentist a better view of the mouth. Both of *these* mirrors have about the same diameter as a 25-cent piece. *They* are securely mounted in circular stainless-steel holders, with the rims equal in depth to the thickness of the mirrors.

Lisa Hines

Conclusion

To test your understanding of paragraphs and to review points that may have slipped to the back of your mind, re-examine several of the sample paragraphs in this chapter, and see whether you can answer the following questions:

1. What is the central idea?
2. Which sentence is the topic sentence?
3. How do the specific details help form a complete picture in the reader's mind?
4. Which pattern of development is used?
5. Which linking devices are used to relate the sentences to one another?

Suggestions for Writing

Write a well-organized paragraph that develops one of the following ideas. Use the method of development you think most appropriate.

1. The one quality most necessary for success in my chosen field is _____.
2. One good example of Americans' tendency to waste is _____.
3. Proper inflation pressure prolongs tire life.
4. To me, the most attractive career would be _____.
5. The best (or worst) thing about fast-food restaurants is _____.
6. The most difficult part of being an X-ray technician or dental hygienist (or substitute another occupation) is _____.
7. The college course I find most useful is _____.
8. The quality I most admire in a person is _____.
9. One reason licensing of auto mechanics is a good (or bad) idea is _____.
10. Fixing a leaky faucet (or substitute another task) is (or is not) a difficult job.
11. Concentration (or substitute your own term here) is an important part of a successful golf game (or substitute your own sport).
12. The primary value of using dental floss regularly is _____.
13. A draftsman must have a good math background.
14. The key to being a successful nurse (or substitute another occupation) is _____.
15. What I most enjoy doing in my spare time is _____.
16. A key punch operator or an auto mechanic (or substitute another occupation) must have great manual dexterity.
17. Sometimes a college student can't help feeling that he or she is regarded as a number, not a person.
18. Apart from physical attractiveness, the most desirable attribute a spouse can have is _____.
19. For spiritual rejuvenation, nothing can beat a country walk on a nice spring day.
20. A recent experience of one of my friends has completely changed his attitude toward the police.
21. My next-door neighbor has a cliché for every occasion.
22. Girls' basketball is a sport whose time has come.
23. Government figures show that the problem of _____ is costly in terms of both dollars and lives and is growing more serious each year.

2
The Theme

In the course for which you are using this book, your instructor will probably ask you to write a number of themes (also known as essays, compositions, or sometimes merely "papers"). Writing themes is good training for many kinds of writing you will have to do in college and on the job. Nevertheless, the announcement that a theme will be due is one that many students dread.

Much of this anxiety stems from the mistaken idea that good themes are dashed off in a burst of inspiration by "born writers." Students themselves often promote this notion by boasting that their best papers were cranked out in an hour or so of spare time. Such claims may be true now and then—and natural ability and even "inspiration" may help. But most successful themes are simply the result of following a systematic, orderly series of steps. When you see a well-written paper, you see only the final product; you don't see the careful step-by-step process the writer used to develop that product.

Since writing is a flexible process, no one fixed order of steps automatically produces a well-written paper. Some experienced writers follow one plan, some another, often combining certain steps as they proceed. Moreover, specialized types of writing, such as those you'll be dealing with later in this book, require special procedures. There is, however, a basic series of steps that you can follow not only for themes but also for most other writing you will do. Once you know these steps, you, too, may wish to combine some of them as you write. For now, however, take the following steps one by one:

1. understanding the assignment
2. choosing your topic
3. analyzing your audience
4. determining your qualifications
5. establishing a specific focus
6. forming your thesis statement
7. brainstorming your topic
8. organizing your information
9. writing the first draft
10. polishing your writing

Each of these steps is discussed below.

Understanding the Assignment

Instructors differ in the assignment of themes. You may be given a specific topic, a choice among several topics, or an entirely free choice. The instructor may also request a certain theme length or leave the length entirely up to you. Whatever the case, be sure you understand the assignment before proceeding any further. Surprisingly, many students overlook this vital first step.

Think of it this way. If your employer asked you for a report on a particular subject (let's say on how working conditions should be improved) and you responded by turning in a report on some entirely different subject (such as how your company could make its advertising more effective) would you expect your employer's approval? Following directions is no less important for writing you do for your classes. Therefore, if you have any questions about the assignment, ask your instructor to clarify it for you then and there. Chances are that the instructor will admire your determination to "get it right."

Choosing Your Topic

If you have been assigned a specific topic and you clearly understand the assignment, you are ready to move on to the next step. However, if you have been given either a limited or free choice of topics, you need to do some careful thinking. Very often, the instructor has the class explore a general subject, through outside reading or classroom discussion or both, and then asks the students to write a paper on any topic related to that general subject.

For example, suppose that your class has been reading or talking about the trend toward shorter work weeks and the increased amount of leisure time that employees will enjoy. The classroom discussion then turns to the ways the new leisure time may be profitably and enjoyably used. Members of the class suggest participation in various hobbies and sports. You are asked to write a two- or three-page paper on a topic of your own choice related to this general subject. You decide to write on some aspect of participation in sports.

Obviously, sports is too large a subject for two or three pages. Even if you narrow the subject to one sport—say, tennis—your subject is too large; whole books are written on tennis. Your problem, in short, is to establish a specific topic that you can deal with thoroughly and interestingly in only two or three pages. If your paper is to be successful, your topic must meet the following requirements:

1. It must be clearly related to the assigned general subject.
2. It must be something you know about (or can learn enough about in the short time you have).
3. It must be limited enough to be adequately developed in the small space you have.
4. It must interest you; if you're bored with your topic, you will write a boring paper.

If you are lucky, a topic that meets all these requirements will occur to you immediately. More often, however, you will arrive at a suitable topic only after some careful consideration and perhaps after jotting down many ideas and then eliminating those that seem least promising.

Occasionally, you may find yourself "blocked"—unable to come up with anything that seems right. This frustrating problem happens to most writers at one time or another. An excellent way to break such a block is to talk the general subject over with classmates, friends, members of your family, or your instructor. Discussion can "open up" a subject, exposing a variety of aspects that might not have occurred to you. Furthermore, knowing how others feel about a subject will sharpen your awareness of how you feel about it.

This increased awareness is perhaps the best way of avoiding what is sometimes called "the terror of the blank page": that feeling you get when you sit, pen in hand, but the right words won't come. The only thoughts that go through your mind are "I don't know what to write about" or "I don't know anything about the subject." Discussion can end all that.

Analyzing Your Audience

All good writing is aimed at some audience—people with whom the writer wishes to communicate. Any audience has certain characteristics that the writer must take into account in order to communicate effectively. Before you start to write, assess your audience carefully, using these questions:

What is their background in the subject?
How much do they already know about it?
What do they want or need to know?
What are their specific interests?

Once you have decided what you will assume about the knowledge and interests of your audience, you can decide how to tailor your writing for that particular group of readers:

What terms will I need to define for them?
What procedures or concepts will they need help in understanding?
How formally or informally should I speak to them?

Suppose that you must write a process explanation for your composition class, and you choose to tell about taking a certain type of X-ray. Your responses to the questions above will determine how you approach this subject. For instance, if you aim your paper at a patient who has never had any X-rays taken, you might first note that taking an X-ray is much like taking a photograph. Then you might explain what the patient would want or need to know about the basic process, including the positioning of the patient's body and the equipment, the safety and reliability of the procedure, and the time involved. You probably would use few technical terms and define those necessary to your explanation. Since a patient might be nervous as well as curious, your tone would probably be reassuring and professional. If, on the other hand, you are adressing fellow radiologic technologists, you might emphasize exposure factors, size of the film, and different views that might be required. This audience would understand technical terms and would know the details of the procedure. You could speak to these readers as colleagues who appreciate clear and precise information.

Just as you would not dial a telephone number at random and then expect to carry on a meaningful conversation, so you should not expect your writing to communicate effectively if you have no audience in mind. When you set out to write something, the audience you address will dictate what you say and how you say it. Their knowledge, their interests, and their level of sophistication must be carefully considered before you start to write.

Determining Your Qualifications

One of the most important keys to writing a successful paper is to choose a topic you are qualified to write on or willing to learn about.

There are three basic qualifications for selecting a topic. The first—and most useful—is *personal participation.* When you write about your own experiences, you already have a variety of beliefs, feelings, and facts to discuss in specific detail. For example, to return to the sports theme, if you don't know a birdie from a bogey, you should not write about golf unless you have the time and interest to learn something about it first. On the other hand, if you played on the high school tennis team for three years, you might consider writing about tennis. When you are interested in your topic, your paper will probably interest your reader. After all, you are writing to communicate, to share your ideas, not merely to complete an assignment.

If you can't write about personal experience, there is a second type of qualification to fall back on, *observation.* You can write about something that you have seen or heard, even though you haven't actually participated in it. Surely there are things you have observed at work, on television, at the movies, in classroom discussions, and at plays, concerts, and athletic events that interest you and that you know a good deal about. One of these might serve as the topic for your paper.

The third type of qualification is *reading.* Anything you have read in trade publications, shop manuals, magazines, technical journals, newspapers, novels, or textbooks can provide interesting material for a paper. (Of course, ideas and facts that you borrow from others must be properly documented; that is, you must tell where you got the material. See pages 285–294. Students seldom rely exclusively on knowledge gained through reading. Instead, they usually combine that knowledge with information obtained through participation and observation.

Keep in mind that the most important person in your life is you. Subjects you are personally well acquainted with and interested in are the ones on which you will write most informatively and interestingly.

Establishing a Specific Focus

The next step is to establish a specific focus for your paper. That is, you must narrow the subject down to a topic that is small enough to develop in detail in the space you have.

Suppose that because of your experience on the high school team you decide to write your sports theme on tennis. Already you have started to focus, since tennis is only one of the many possible sports topics. However, additional focusing will be necessary. Consider, for example, the following aspects that could be included in a paper on tennis:

1. its increasing popularity today
2. major tournaments
3. different court surfaces
4. equipment needed
5. tennis scoring
6. tennis terminology
7. different rackets
8. different grips
9. tennis strategy (singles)
10. tennis strategy (doubles)
11. playing the net
12. topspin strokes
13. backspin strokes
14. different serves
15. return of serve
16. proper body position
17. importance of footwork

18. special shots: the lob
19. special shots: the drop volley
20. special shots: the overhead

This is only a partial list, but it does show the importance of zeroing in. To cover all these aspects in a relatively short paper would be impossible. You would be able to write only one or two sentences about each aspect, and no clear picture of anything would emerge. In addition, the problem of organization would be enormous.

On the other hand, if you focus on *one* aspect of tennis—such as playing better singles—you can develop each of your main points in a paragraph or more. This is what focus is all about. Above all else, it involves saying more about less. It involves concentrating on one aspect of a subject in some depth rather than treating many aspects superficially.

How narrowly and in what direction you focus depends on two factors. First, consider the assigned length of your paper. The shorter the paper, the narrower your focus must be. For a three–hundred–word theme, you might focus on some of the conditioning exercises necessary for a singles player. For a five– to six–hundred–word theme, you might discuss conditioning exercises, concentration, and consistency.

Second, consider the audience you will be writing for. Notice, for example, how the audience would affect the focus for the tennis paper. If you were writing for the beginning player, you might focus on equipment and scoring. For the intermediate player, you might focus on conditioning, concentration, and consistency, and for the advanced player, on special shots. As pointed out earlier, knowing the audience for your writing will help determine what you say and how you say it.

Forming Your Thesis Statement

Now you are ready to develop your thesis statement. This is a statement that tells what the paper will contend, define, describe, or illustrate. Think carefully about the following questions:

What is my purpose in writing?
What audience am I writing for?
How will I organize my information?

Your thesis statement reflects your answers to these questions. Ordinarily, the thesis statement is a single sentence, though occasionally two or more sentences are needed, especially if the paper is long or a single sentence would be clumsy.

You will recall that the topic sentence clearly states the central idea of a paragraph. It also helps you decide what information to include in and exclude from the paragraph. What the topic sentence does for a single paragraph, the thesis statement does for an entire theme.

Because you can't proceed any further without knowing exactly what you hope to accomplish, it is necessary to compose your thesis statement at this point. After all, if you don't know why you are writing the theme, your reader won't either. Spend some time thinking about it. Then, when you have a clear thesis statement in mind, *write it down*. Don't assume you'll keep it in your head; ideas sometimes slip away. In addition, having your thesis statement in written form will make the next two steps—brainstorming and outlining—much easier.

There are two types of thesis statement—specific and general. A specific thesis statement clearly spells out the main points the theme will discuss. Consider this example, which could serve as the thesis statement for the tennis theme:

> Three keys to playing better tennis singles are conditioning, concentration, and consistency.

This specific thesis statement clearly indicates the purpose and scope of the essay, the three areas of emphasis, and the order in which the writer will take them up. Positioned in your opening paragraph, this statement would identify the paper's intended audience (the singles player who knows the game but hopes to become better at it), tell that audience what to expect from the paper, and also help you stay on track as you write.

A general thesis statement presents the writer's topic and purpose but not the points to be discussed. For the tennis theme, a general thesis statement might read as follows:

> If you wish to improve your tennis singles game, there are several ways to go about it.

In this particular case, the general thesis statement is inferior to the specific thesis statement because the reader is given no clues as to what the "several ways" are, and the writer has no guide to follow as he plunges into his topic. With certain kinds of writing, however— process explanations and descriptions of objects, for example—common practice dictates the use of general thesis statements.

> PROCESS EXPLANATION: Caulking a bathtub is a process that involves a few simple steps.
>
> OBJECT DESCRIPTION: A videotape is a magnetic strip on which the sound and picture parts of a telecast are recorded for future broadcast.

A final point about your thesis statement: you may decide to alter it slightly or even change it completely if you run into difficulties developing your paper. If this happens, write out your new thesis statement before you proceed further. Otherwise, you run the risk that your thesis statement will point in one direction and the rest of your theme will go off in another.

Brainstorming Your Topic

Guided by your thesis statement, you are now ready to start brainstorming your topic. Brainstorming involves jotting down everything you might possibly use to develop your paper: facts, ideas, examples, illustrations—in short, the *specific details* that will enable you to communicate your ideas fully and clearly to your reader. (You may wish to review the discussion of specific details on pages 5–8). Jot down your details as they occur to you; the order in which you list them makes no difference at this stage.

Here again is the proposed thesis statement for the tennis paper: *Three keys to playing better tennis singles are conditioning, concentration, and consistency.* Below is a possible list of details you might jot down to develop it:

1. always keep ball in play
2. don't try foolish shots
3. place the ball so opponent runs
4. stay in good condition

5. running
6. jogging
7. skipping rope
8. keeps you on your toes
9. keep your mind only on the game
10. personal distractions
11. courtside distractions
12. temper distractions
13. don't continually drive ball with power
14. two-on-one drill
15. lob ball over their heads
16. return a down-the-line passing shot
17. don't try spectacular overhead
18. chance for opponent to make mistake
19. game of percentages
20. most games are lost, not won

Notice that these items are not necessarily expressed in complete sentences. Some of them might not even make sense to anyone but you, the writer. There's nothing wrong with this apparent disorder. The list is for your own benefit; if you understand its meaning, that's all that's necessary.

Look closely and you will see how some thoughts have led to others during the brainstorming. For example, item number one, consistently keeping the ball in play, leads naturally to the next item, avoiding foolish shots. Item three, placing the ball so the opponent runs, leads to item four, staying in good condition yourself, which in turn leads to items five, six, and seven—and so forth.

As you organize and write your paper, you will probably combine, modify, and omit some of the items on your list. Chances are that you will think of others to add as well. For now, though, you have a good start on the supporting material.

One final note is in order: if you have trouble preparing your brainstorming list, perhaps your topic isn't as interesting or as promising as you originally thought. Sometimes all you need is to take a break and then try again. But if you continue to have trouble, don't hesitate to modify or even completely change your thesis statement and start a new list of details to support this statement. Now—not later—is the time to redirect your efforts.

Organizing Your Information

The next step is to organize your details and ideas in some meaningful pattern. This pattern will guide your writing, and later it will help your reader to understand your ideas.

If you have ever listened to a disorganized speaker spill out ideas in no particular order, you probably recall that it was hard to keep your attention focused on the speech, let alone make sense of it. The ideas may have been valuable; but, if you couldn't follow them, how would you really know? The same holds true for writing. A garbled listing of ideas serves no one; an orderly presentation is essential for communication.

For large projects—for example, a library research paper or a technical manual—order is achieved by following a formal outlining procedure. In a formal outline, the main divisions are indicated by Roman numerals, and the various subdivisions are indicated (in decreasing order of importance) by capital letters, Arabic numbers, small letters, and so forth. (The formal outline is discussed and illustrated in detail on pages 278–282). However, a simpler, less formal written plan is usually sufficient to guide you in writing a relatively short paper. The important thing is to draw up a written plan; don't try to carry it only in your head. Ideas have a way of becoming hazy or slipping away entirely. The plan provides the pattern for your paper—the way you'll group your ideas and the order in which you'll present them—and putting it in writing ensures that you won't overlook any part of it.

When you draw up your plan, first determine the main points you want to make. If you chose the specific form of thesis statement, you already know them. If you chose the general form, however, you must determine them now. In any case, write each point at the top of a separate sheet of paper. For the tennis paper, the three points—or headings—would be:

1. conditioning
2. concentration
3. consistency

Under each heading list those items from your brainstorming list that will develop and support the point. When completed, your three sheets should look something like this:

Conditioning

stay in good condition yourself
running
jogging
skipping rope
keeps you on your toes
two-on-one drill
lob ball over their heads
return a down-the-line passing shot

Concentration

keep your mind only on the game
personal distractions
courtside distractions
temper distractions

Consistency

always keep ball in play
don't try foolish shots
place the ball so opponent runs
don't continually drive ball with power
don't try spectacular overhead
chance for opponent to make mistake
game of percentages
most games are lost, not won

At this stage you should reconsider how you will arrange your three main headings. Which one will come first? Second? Third? Your decision depends on your topic and your audience and may, of course, necessitate rephrasing your thesis statement. Chronological order—arranging the events in the order in which they happen in time—is one possibility. However, since conditioning, concentration, and consistency are ongoing activities for a tennis player, for that topic a better choice would be order of climax—presenting the ideas in a progression from the least important to the most important.

Following order of climax, you might write down the following sequence:

1. conditioning (important)
2. concentration (more important)
3. consistency (most important)

Once you have decided on this sequence, prepare a more detailed plan showing what you hope to discuss in each paragraph of your paper. Such a plan is illustrated below. As you examine it, notice that the plan is not definite. Your outline should always remain flexible and subject to change. For example, at this stage you can't know with certainty whether one or two paragraphs will be needed to develop each of the three main headings. A quick glance at the number of items under each heading suggests two paragraphs for conditioning, one for concentration, and two for consistency, but until you are actually writing you won't know for sure. Here is the plan:

FIRST PARAGRAPH: introduction (this will be discussed in the section entitled "Polishing Your Writing")

SECOND PARAGRAPH: discuss conditioning

THIRD PARAGRAPH: continue to discuss conditioning *or* start to discuss concentration

FOURTH PARAGRAPH: discuss concentration

FIFTH PARAGRAPH: continue to discuss concentration *or* start to discuss consistency

SIXTH PARAGRAPH: discuss consistency

SEVENTH PARAGRAPH: discuss consistency

EIGHTH PARAGRAPH: conclusion (this will also be discussed in "Polishing Your Writing")

Now for a word of encouragement. Strange as it may seem, the greater part of your work is now behind you. Writing is a process in which most of the steps are taken before you actually start writing. So don't feel discouraged because you have little to show for much planning. The finished product—a well-organized paper—will amply repay your efforts.

Writing the First Draft

Writing the first draft should be relatively easy. After all, you have a topic you are qualified to write about, a thesis statement that indicates your purpose and tells your reader what to expect, enough supporting details to develop the statement, and a written plan to follow.

Sometimes, however, you still may find it hard to get started. When you sit down to write, the words won't come, and all you can do is doodle or stare at the blank page. Perhaps the delay is caused by trying to write the introduction—the opening paragraph. For many writers, this is the hardest part of a theme to write. They want to get off to a good start but simply cannot figure out how to begin. If this happens to you, skip the introduction for the time being. Once you have your main points on paper, an effective opening will come more easily.

Begin with your thesis statement and written plan in front of you. They will start you thinking. To get actual words on paper, you might rewrite your thesis statement at the top of the page.

Now turn to the first main heading of your plan. For the tennis theme, it is *conditioning*. After you look over the items under this heading, prepare a suitable topic sentence for what will be your second paragraph. (The first, of course, will be your introduction.) Such a sentence might take this form: *Since you will be running continually, conditioning is necessary.*

Next, think back again to the different patterns of paragraph development discussed in chapter 1. Would it be best to organize this discussion of conditioning according to the general-to-specific pattern? Time sequence? Order of climax?

Perhaps the best choice will be time sequence. You decide that preliminary conditioning exercises off the court should come first, followed later by specific tennis exercises on the court. In fact, you now decide that your explanation is likely to call for two paragraphs, one for off-court exercises and one for on-court exercises. That's all right; as we said, the plan is supposed to be flexible.

At this point you are ready to develop the paragraphs with the specific details listed in your plan under conditioning. Write the first draft quickly, capturing the drift of your thoughts. Concentrate on content and organization. Get your main points and supporting details on paper in the right sequence. *Don't*, however, spend a lot of time trying to write smooth sentences. *Don't* pause to polish each sentence after you write it. These delays could cause you to lose your train of thought, and you might end up doodling or staring again. If your first draft contains fragments, loosely worded sentences, or other errors, you can correct them later. (For this reason, write on every other line and leave wide margins so that you will have room to add things later when you revise the draft.)

Sometimes a specific point can be adequately explained in a single sentence; at other times two or more sentences will be needed. Perhaps other related details, facts, or examples that are not on your list will occur to you. By all means, include them. If they later prove unnecessary, you can simply cross them out.

When your first draft of these two paragraphs on conditioning has been completed, it might look something like this. (At this point the sentences have not been polished.)

> Since you will be running continually, conditioning is necessary. This must start before one gets to center court. A lot of running in place or jogging 5 miles a day will help build up your endurance for a 3- or 5-set match. Remember, there's no one out there to help you, and there will be very little rest time. Jumping rope is also excellent. It teaches you to stay on your toes and not be flat-footed.
>
> That's not the whole story on conditioning. Later, when you're ready to take to the court, some tennis drills will help you. These include the two-on-one drill and the shadow drill. All these movements help prepare you for the actual conditions of a game. If you practice them now, they'll come naturally during a game.

Now that you have finished the first draft of the conditioning paragraphs, write the concentration and consistency paragraphs in the same manner. When you have completed these and start to write the conclusion, you may experience the same difficulty you had with the introduction. If you do, skip the conclusion, too, until later.

At this point you are finished (except, possibly, for your introduction and conclusion) with your first draft. That's enough work for now. Put the draft aside and take a break. This break is not merely a rest; it is an important part of the writing process.

Polishing Your Writing

Your last major step—polishing your writing—calls for a careful inspection of your first draft. This inspection involves examining what you have written word by word, sentence by sentence, paragraph by paragraph, and making whatever improvements are needed.

To do an effective job, you should wait at least a half day before you start. Unless you have put your writing aside for a while, you will not see it with a fresh eye and will overlook errors you would otherwise notice; that is, you will read what you *think* you have written rather than what you *actually have* written. An excellent way to catch many problems you might overlook is to read your paper out loud. You will be much more likely to notice errors such as word omissions, excessive repetition, clumsy sentences, and sentence fragments if you hear what you have written.

To polish thoroughly, read your paper several times, once for each of these reasons:

to check on the progression of ideas

to strengthen paragraph structure and development

to clarify sentences and words

to correct misuse of English

In addition, read your draft specifically for any problem or error that frequently recurs in your essays. Finally, if you haven't written your introduction and conclusion or come up with a title, you will want to fill these gaps now.

CHECKING ON THE PROGRESSION OF IDEAS

On your initial reading of your rough draft, make certain that you have said all that you meant to say. Fill in any gaps in thought or places where a reader might need more information. Make sure that your writing progresses logically and smoothly. The connections among ideas should be clear enough that a reader will have no difficulty moving from one point to the next. Trying to see your paper as your reader will see it nearly always improves your writing.

If you suspect that your paper is not as well organized as it might be, list each of its major and minor supporting points as you read it through. Then check this outline for logic and completeness. If necessary, add new points, rearrange existing parts, or rewrite weak sentences.

STRENGTHENING PARAGRAPH STRUCTURE AND DEVELOPMENT

Now examine your paragraphs one by one. Make sure that each is unified, organized, coherent, and adequately developed. Ask yourself these basic questions about each paragraph, and correct any shortcomings you find:

1. Does the paragraph have only one central idea?
2. Is there a topic sentence that states this central idea?
3. Does this topic sentence help to develop the thesis statement?
4. Does each sentence within the paragraph help to develop the topic sentence?
5. Does the paragraph follow an appropriate pattern of development?
6. Are the sentences within the paragraph connected by appropriate linking devices so each leads smoothly to the next?
7. Does the paragraph contain enough supporting detail?

CLARIFYING SENTENCES AND WORDS

Now examine all your words and sentences to make sure that your reader's job will be as easy as possible. As you check, consider these questions:

1. Are my sentences written in clear, simple language?
2. Am I sure of the meanings of the words I use?
3. Have I carelessly left out any words?
4. Have I become "windy," cluttering the theme with excess words?
5. Have I used punctuation properly to prevent confusion or misreading?
6. Have I explained the meanings of terms that my reader might not understand? (For example, to a card player "deuce" means two, but to a tennis player it means a tie at 40-40.)

CORRECTING MISUSE OF ENGLISH

Finally, check your writing for correctness. Since correctness defies brief explanation, the errors commonly found in student papers are discussed in a separate section at the end of this book. These writing errors include, in addition to improper punctuation, faulty pronoun reference, dangling modifiers, misplaced modifiers, non-parallelism, faulty comparisons, sentence fragments, comma splices, and run-on sentences—among others.

Spelling deserves special mention, since carelessness in spelling is likely to make your reader think you are careless in your thinking, too. A good way to check for spelling errors is to examine your theme backward, carefully, from the last word to the first. You can then concentrate only on the spelling of individual words, and content will not interfere. Whenever you are uncertain of how a word is spelled, check the dictionary. Keep a list of your own problem words so that you can be on the lookout for them.

THE INTRODUCTION

If you have delayed writing your introduction, do it now. Generally, the introduction to a short theme is a single paragraph with your thesis statement serving as its topic sentence, though writers of longer papers often use two or more introductory paragraphs. The introduction acquaints the reader with you and your topic. If your opening arouses interest and clearly indicates what will follow, you have a good chance of persuading the reader to continue reading and to accept what you say. On the other hand, all your other paragraphs may be wasted if you bore or confuse your reader with a poor opening.

You can attract the reader's attention in several ways. For example, you may make one or more arresting statements, cite a personal experience, present a case history, or note specific details related to the topic of the paper. The following opening from a student paper uses *arresting statements* to support the thesis statement:

> Today, as in the past, humans continue to infringe upon the basic right of nature's species to survive. Through ignorance, oversight, and technological changes, we are threatening the survival of some 130 species of animals. Until their natural environ-

ments are properly maintained, the last chance of survival for these species may depend upon captive breeding in the nation's zoos. But captive breeding is a complex undertaking fraught with many difficulties. Each species presents special psychological, social, and physical problems which must be solved if breeding is to succeed.

DeWayne Lubbers

Using *personal experience*, the writer of the following opening paragraph leads into his thesis statement:

In July 1979, I and 1,600 fellow employees of a large furniture company gathered for the company's annual picnic. Eating began about noon. By 2 P.M., several people started complaining of stomach distress, and by 5 P.M. over 800 had been stricken. All of us were victims of food poisoning, an illness that results from eating food that contains certain bacteria or their toxins.

Alan Helwig

Citing a *case history*, the writer of this opening paragraph similarly builds up to her thesis statement:

Jane and Dick Smith were proud, new parents of an eight-pound, ten-ounce baby girl named Jenny. One summer night, Jane put Jenny to bed at 8:00. Five hours later, Jane found Jenny dead. The baby had given no cry of pain, shown no sign of trouble. Even the doctor did not know why she had died, for she was healthy and strong. The autopsy report confirmed the doctor's suspicion—the infant was a victim of the "sudden infant death syndrome," also known as SIDS or "crib death." SIDS is the sudden and unexplainable death of an apparently healthy sleeping infant. It is the number one cause of death in infants after the first week of life and as a result has been the subject of numerous research studies.

Trudy Stelter

Following a general thesis statement, the writer of this opening paragraph catalogs *specific details* that may interest a particular audience:

Analyzing furnace-flue gas for carbon dioxide (CO_2) is a process that every furnace serviceman needs to know. When a furnace is operating normally, the CO_2 content of the flue gas will be 8 to 10 percent. A lower reading may denote an air leak in the furnace, the wrong type of fuel oil, a defective nozzle, an air shutter that is open too far, a flame with the wrong shape, or any of several other undesirable conditions.

Charles Finnie

Attention-getting devices are not always necessary, however. The introductions of technical papers often follow relatively rigid patterns in which such devices play no role. Later chapters discuss a number of those patterns. The type of introduction you choose depends upon who your reader will be, how much interest the reader has in the subject, and the kind of paper you are writing.

THE CONCLUSION

A conclusion rounds out your paper and signals that you have completed your discussion. Like the introduction, the conclusion is generally a single short paragraph, although longer papers may require two or more paragraphs. An adequate conclusion summarizes or supports the main idea that your theme has developed. Since it is your last chance to communicate with your reader, try to make it effective.

There are several common kinds of effective conclusions. You may, for example, summarize your discussion, offer a recommendation, present a challenge, or make a prediction. Whatever type you choose, your conclusion should in some way reinforce your thesis in terms that reflect the evidence or argument that you have presented. The following *summary* paragraph, concludes a theme describing the process of chicken grilling:

> Grilling chickens, then, is quite simple if you use quality meat, select a high-grade cooking oil, and baste and turn the meat regularly. Anyone who can follow directions can do a first-rate job.
>
> *Joe Fowler*

The concluding paragraph below offers a *recommendation:*

> TV advertisers rely mainly upon subtle exploitation of the viewers' egos and senses, and only in a small way upon facts.

Viewers should therefore become aware of what commercials are doing and critical of their messages.

Sherry Forrest

The writer of a theme about physical fitness concludes with a challenge:

And therein lies the challenge. You can't merely puff hard for a few days and then revert to your recliner. You must sweat and strain and puff regularly, week in and week out. They're your muscles, your lungs, your heart. The only caretaker they have is you.

Monica DuVall

The conclusion that follows makes a *prediction* based on observations developed in the body of the theme:

The factors that cause utopian communities to fail cannot be overcome. Any utopian settlement in the United States is ill-fated: our present society rests on ideals that are totally unlike utopian ideals. Utopia is a dream, a hope, an attempt to find peace and happiness, but in the end it will prove unattainable.

Jimmy Ray Belnap

Some specialized kinds of writing have specialized kinds of conclusions. These conclusions are discussed at the appropriate points in the text.

Several cautions are in order when you write a conclusion. First, don't veer off in an entirely new direction or introduce an entirely new topic. Imagine the effect if the writer of a carefully developed theme on playing tennis ended by saying, "Some of these suggestions can also help improve your handball game." Suddenly the reader is being asked to consider an entirely new topic, which is then left totally undeveloped.

Don't tack on a sentence or two in desperation when the hour is late and the paper is due the next day. Consider the following ineffective ending to the tennis theme: "Thus you can see the value of conditioning, concentration, and consistency." This ending is faulty because it is too weak to reinforce the significance of the theme. It, therefore, leaves the reader without any strong impression.

Don't apologize for your handling of the topic. Saying you could probably have discussed your points in more detail only calls your approach into question.

Some technical papers have no conclusion at all. Sets of instructions and descriptions of objects, for instance, may simply end when the last step has been presented or the last part described. The purpose and content lend a sense of completeness and make a conclusion unnecessary.

THE TITLE

Unless a title pops into your head as you are writing, it is usually best to finish your paper before choosing one. A good title is both specific and accurate. A specific title suggests the paper's exact focus rather than its general topic. For example, "The Three C's of Better Tennis Singles" is more effective than simply "Tennis." You aren't writing about the sport in general, but about ways of playing better singles. An accurate title is one that is not misleading. Your reader must see the connection between what the title promises and what the theme delivers. For example, "Tennis Singles: Moving to the Top" would be inaccurate; it suggests that you will explain how to become a champion (perhaps a professional) when in fact this aspect of the topic is never discussed.

The title of a nontechnical paper can be either common or catchy. A common title simply tells the reader what to expect, while a catchy one attempts to arouse the reader's curiosity. Here are some examples of possible titles for student themes.

COMMON: "Handling Your Hangover"
CATCHY: "The Mourning After"
COMMON: "Is a Hairpiece for You?"
CATCHY: "Toupee or Not Toupee?"
COMMON: "Buying Your Home with Other People's Money"
CATCHY: "Home Free"

Technical papers rarely have catchy titles. Instead, they rely on a title that gives a direct and straightforward indication of the paper's content. Such a title is in keeping with the purpose and audience of the writing.

The Finished Product

If you followed the steps discussed in this chapter, your tennis paper would look something like the following student theme. As you read it, pay careful attention to the marginal notes, which point out some of the key writing elements. (The thesis statement, topic sentences, and some of the linking devices are printed in italics.)

Title: specific accurate, catchy	*The Three C's of Better Tennis Singles*
Introduction: arresting statement	In the last few years tennis has enjoyed a rise in popularity unequaled by any other sport.
Linking device	*As a result,* many players are trying to improve
Thesis statement and statement of organization	their game. *Three keys to playing better tennis singles are conditioning, concentration, and consistency.*
Topic sentence, with links to preceding paragraph	*Since a singles match requires endurance, proper conditioning is necessary.* This condi-
Specific details: jogging, etc.	tioning should begin before you arrive at the court. Jogging three to five miles a day and running in place are both excellent exercises for
Linking device	increasing your stamina. *These* exercises help ensure that, in a deciding third set, you will not lose the match because of exhaustion. Jumping
Linking device	rope, *another good exercise,* conditions you to stay on your toes rather than play flat-footed. You'll have a much better chance of reaching and returning your opponent's shots if you start toward them from your toes.
Topic sentence, with links to preceding paragraph	*When you arrive at the court, a good conditioning exercise is the two-on-one drill.* Have two of your friends stand at the net and hit the
Specific details	ball to you in the opposite backcourt. Ideally
Linking device	*their* shots should be just out of your reach so that you are continually chasing the ball. On
Specific details: types of shots	your return shots, alternately try to lob the ball over their heads, drive it between them down the middle of the court, send a passing shot down the line, or drill the ball low and hard
Linking device	directly at the net players. With *this continual*

running and *these four returns,* you will be preparing for the actual conditions of your next match.

As you play that match, you should work on developing the ability to concentrate—the second key to improving your game. Concentration involves focusing your attention only on the game at hand and not allowing anything else to distract you. Courtside and personal distractions are the two most common among tennis players. Courtside distractions include

watching players in the next court, talking to a friend outside the court, and joking with your opponent between points. Personal distractions include such things as worrying about a test, mulling over a personal problem, and thinking about the refreshments after the game. *All of*

these distractions result in poorly hit balls and lost points. All good tennis players are able to discipline themselves to concentrate only on the game.

Probably the most important key to improving your game is consistency. Steady placement of your shots is much more effective than occasional brilliance. Many players make the

mistake of trying spectacular shots and using power strokes rather than playing a steady, consistent game. For example, don't try to blast a spectacular pro-style overhead or continually overpower your opponent with hard, driving shots. Such efforts will lose more points for you than they will win.

Tennis is a game of percentages. The *consistent* player keeps the ball *steadily* in play so the opponent is more apt to make a mistake. Hitting the ball away from your opponent with average speed is percentage tennis; drilling the ball with power is not. All experienced players realize that very often matches are not won, but lost.

Conclusion
(prediction)

> If you follow these suggestions, don't expect to successfully challenge Bjorn Borg or Chris Evert Lloyd. Do expect, however, to start beating some of the players who used to beat you.
>
> *Ferris Finnerty*

The marginal notes above point out only some of the elements that help make this paper effective; any attempt to indicate all of them would have made the notes confusing. The most important point to be made could not be noted in the margin, and it is the one with which this chapter opened: the paper is successful because the writer followed an orderly series of steps in arriving at an appropriate topic, establishing a specific focus, making a written plan, and writing and polishing the draft.

Suggestion for Writing

Select a broad subject that interests you and narrow it to a topic suitable for a two- or three-page paper. Determine your audience and focus, write a specific thesis statement, and compile a list of details that support the statement. Organize the details in an appropriate order and write, polish, and title the paper.

3

Comparison

Hardly a day goes by that you don't use comparison in some way. You may evaluate two different job offers, for example, or consider two health-insurance plans, or explain two methods of wallpapering a room. Whenever you examine two items and note their similarities and differences, you are comparing.

Comparison is also an effective method of presenting written material, one you will use often in the writing you do both for your classes and on the job. Your instructor may ask you to discuss, in an examination or report, the basic similarities or differences between two machines or principles—for example, the conventional gasoline engine and the Wankel engine, or preventive dental care and restorative dental care. Your employer may ask you to evaluate two different proposals for improving working conditions or to report on the performance characteristics of two X-ray machines, lathes, typewriters, or other pieces of equipment. These assignments, which involve explaining or evaluating two different items, call for papers of comparison.

Comparisons are not necessarily limited to only two items. You could, for instance, compare several investment possibilities, television sets, computers, or musical groups. You will have less difficulty, however, if you first master the techniques of comparing only two items. After all, it is always easier to focus your attention on two things than it is to deal with three or more.

Writing a paper of comparison involves five basic steps:

1. choosing your topic
2. establishing your focus
3. developing your thesis statement
4. selecting your details
5. selecting your method of organization

Each of these steps is discussed below.

Choosing Your Topic

If you are asked to choose the items to be compared, make sure there is some clearly evident basis for meaningful comparison between them. For example, you could compare two golfers on their driving ability off the tee, putting ability, and sand play, or two cars on their appearance, gas mileage, and manufacturer's warranty. But you could not very well compare a golfer with a car, since no basis for meaningful comparison is evident.

Be sure, too, that the items you select will provide an interesting comparison. This is rarely a problem for on-the-job comparisons. The work situation almost always determines the items you will discuss, and you can assume that your reader—your employer, a co-worker, or perhaps a customer or client—will be interested in the information. But for papers you write in class or for a general audience, you should try to choose items that will enable you to give your audience new information about them or, if the items are familiar to the audience, to provide your audience with a fresh way of thinking about them.

For example, it would be very hard to write an interesting paper comparing a pencil and a ball-point pen. There certainly is a basis for comparison—both are used for writing—and obviously there are similarities and differences that could be described at some length. The problem is that the similarities and differences *are* obvious; they would already be thoroughly familiar to anyone who might be likely to read such a comparison. It would be difficult to give the reader new information or a fresh way of thinking about the items.

On the other hand, it certainly is possible to write interestingly about commonplace objects, as long as the reader can learn something. For instance, you could write an interesting and useful comparison of two different types or brands of ball-point pen. Type A is a better buy than the more widely advertised Type B because, although Type A costs twice as much, it lasts three times as long. What's more, Type A can be refilled when it runs out, but Type B must be thrown away. Type A writes more sharply and is less likely to skip because it has a magnesium-alloy rather than a stainless-steel ball. Type B is inclined to leak; Type A does not—and so forth.

A comparison such as this meets all the requirements for choosing a topic. The items have enough in common to provide a basis for comparison, yet they are not so similar that the discussion of one merely echoes the discussion of the other. The similarities and differences are not too obvious to be uninteresting; on the contrary, they provide opportunities for a comparison that enables the reader to learn something or to see the items in a new way.

Establishing Your Focus

When you have two comparable items in mind, you are ready to start thinking about the particular points of comparison you will discuss—in other words, your focus. The focus you choose is determined by your *purpose in writing* and the desired *length* of your paper. The importance of these two considerations can be illustrated by the following example. Suppose you were in charge of the record and tape department of a local department store, with two excellent salespeople working for you. The manager of your store has told you of plans to open a branch store in a suburban shopping center and asked you to submit a brief written report—"just a page or two"— comparing the qualifications of your two salespeople for the job of managing the record department in the new branch store.

In this example, the items to be compared have already been chosen for you: the two salespeople. Your purpose in writing is also clear: to help the store manager decide which of the two salespeople should be offered the new position. Moreover, the manager has asked that the report be *brief;* and even if no restriction on length had been stated, you would have understood that the manager was very busy and not the sort of person to appreciate a report that was any longer than necessary.

Now, in order to see plainly how your purpose determines the proper focus for your comparison, consider how many possible points of comparison between the two salespeople you could think of if you did *not* have a clearly established purpose. Here is just a partial list:

1. clothes
2. religion
3. hobbies
4. sense of humor
5. eye color
6. mathematical ability
7. hair style
8. sales skills
9. use of tobacco
10. bowling ability
11. musical knowledge
12. social activities
13. attendance habits
14. interest in current affairs
15. cooperativeness
16. food preferences
17. smile
18. political views
19. knowledge of ordering and accounting procedures
20. ability to deal with customers

Obviously, many of the characteristics listed above have nothing at all to do with either person's suitability to manage a record department. When you think about your purpose, you can strike many items off the list—for instance, eye color, religion, and bowling ability. As you do this, you are establishing your focus.

But even after you have reduced the list to the characteristics that are somehow related to your purpose, you may have more points on the list than you can develop adequately in a *brief* report of "just a page or two." If you tried to cover all of them, you would have space for no more than one or two sentences about each. Questions would be raised but not answered, and your reader would probably fail to get a clear impression of the two individuals being compared. Since your report must be brief, you would do much better to limit the focus of your comparison to just the few points that are essential and then develop each of these points with specific details in a paragraph or more.

Here again your reason for writing can help you: since your purpose is to help your reader choose between the two salespeople, it will be most useful to focus mainly on differences rather than similarities. For instance, if *both* people are cooperative and have satisfactory attendance habits, you can eliminate these points. However, you may feel that sales skills are so important to the new job that, even though both salespeople are highly skilled, you should include that one important similarity in your comparison. The most significant differences between the two people as candidates to manage the record department, you decide, are in their musical knowledge and their knowledge of ordering and accounting procedures. Now you have established the focus for your comparison.

Notice an important feature of the three points of comparison just mentioned—sales skills, musical knowledge, and knowledge of ordering and accounting procedures. These are separate points; that is, they do not overlap. If, on the other hand, you had chosen sales skills and ability to deal with customers, essentially you would have been discussing one point of comparison instead of two, since ability to deal with customers is a sales skill. Whenever you choose points of comparison, make sure that they do not overlap.

Developing Your Thesis Statement

At this point you are ready to formulate your thesis statement. This statement tells your reader what is coming and helps you stick to your purpose as you write. If you were comparing the two salespeople mentioned above, your thesis statement might read as follows: *Although Pat and Lee are both excellent salespeople, I believe Pat would be the better choice for manager because of her wider knowledge of music and her greater familiarity with ordering and accounting procedures.* This statement does three things:

1. names the two items under discussion
2. states the specific points of comparison
3. shows whether the paper will point out similarities, differences, or both

The thesis statement for every comparison paper you write, regardless of the topic, should do these same three things.

Selecting Your Details

Merely stating that two items are similar or different is not enough; you must show your reader *how* they are similar or different. This is done with well-chosen specific details and examples.

Specific details give your reader a clear picture of what you are trying to convey. If you merely say that both Pat and Lee are excellent salespeople, you have no way of knowing that your reader will understand the statement in the same way you meant it. On the other hand, if you develop the statement in a paragraph with specific details—how both Pat and Lee are cheerful even with difficult customers, know what is in stock and where to find it, are careful to keep the stock in good order, consistently get extra sales by suggesting additional purchases related to their customers' interests, and so forth—you have given your reader a clear picture. Guesswork is eliminated, and communication succeeds.

Again, it is a good idea to jot down the specific details and examples that will help develop your thesis statement rather than trying to keep them in your head. You may find it useful to use the brainstorming technique described on pages 24–25. For each point of comparison, list all the supporting ideas that come to mind. And because you will be writing about two items, you should make a separate list for each. This procedure may seem cumbersome now, but later you'll be glad you followed it. With separate lists for each item, giving details for each point of comparison, you will be able to write your paper easily, no matter which method of organization you choose.

Selecting Your Method of Organization

At this point, the only major decision left to make is how to organize your paper. Basically there are two possibilities for a comparison paper: the *block method* and the *alternating method.*

In the block method, the basic organization is provided by the items being compared. In other words, the writer first presents—in one block—*all* of the information about one item and then—in another block—*all* of the information about the other item. Within each block the individual points usually are discussed in the same order. The paper comparing Pat and Lee, organized according to the block method, would follow a pattern such as this:

I. Introduction
II. Specific details about Pat
    A. Pat's sales skills
    B. Pat's musical knowledge
    C. Pat's familiarity with ordering and accounting procedures
III. Specific details about Lee
    A. Lee's sales skills
    B. Lee's musical knowledge
    C. Lee's familiarity with ordering and accounting procedures
IV. Conclusion

Note that the section on Lee includes the same points of comparison—sales skills, musical knowledge, and familiarity with ordering and accounting procedures—as does the section on Pat. Note too that the points follow the same order. Whenever you have a point of comparison for one item, include that same point for the other item, and use one order to present them.

You should use the block method only if your paper is short, that is, if it includes only a few points of comparison. With a short paper, your reader will be able to keep all the points in the first block clearly in mind while reading the second block. This would be difficult for the reader of a lengthy paper to do.

If your paper is long—that is, if it includes numerous points of comparison—it is better to use the alternating method. In the alternating method, the basic organization is provided by the points of comparison rather than by the items being compared. In other words, the writer brings up each point and compares the two items on that particular point before bringing up the next point. Usually, clarity is best achieved if you present the items in the same order each time. Organized according to the *alternating* method, a paper comparing Pat and Lee would follow a pattern such as this:

I. Introduction
II. Pat's and Lee's sales skills
    A. Pat's sales skills
    B. Lee's sales skills

III. Pat's and Lee's musical knowledge
    A. Pat's musical knowledge
    B. Lee's musical knowledge
IV. Pat's and Lee's familiarity with ordering and accounting procedures
    A. Pat's familiarity with ordering and accounting procedures
    B. Lee's familiarity with ordering and accounting procedures
  V. Conclusion

Generally, the alternating method is easier for your reader to understand. Because a specific comparison is completed at each point, the reader never has to pause in the middle of the paper and look back in order to grasp a similarity or difference.

Once you've decided upon your method of organization, you are ready to write your first draft. The first draft of a comparison paper is written and polished as is a draft for any other theme. Simply follow the procedure described in chapter 2.

EXAMPLES OF COMPARISON

Two Men at the Controls—One Airborne, One Grounded

(1) If you were to drive by the Kent County airport viewing area on almost any winter day, you would probably see several people watching the various aircraft departing and landing. But have you ever seen a crowd observing the operation of a modern snowplow? This is a snowplow that is equipped with both front and back plows, four-wheel drive, and two-way radio. Most people recognize the coordination and skill required of a pilot, but few realize that the snowplow operator has similar demands made upon his physical and mental powers.

(2) The pilot uses his hands and feet constantly. His hands are used to turn and adjust all the radio controls and flight instruments, to alter the angle of bank, and to change the aircraft's longitudinal axis with reference to the horizon. While he is airborne, the pilot's feet move in coordination with his hands to bank and turn the plane; on the ground, his feet actually steer the taxiing aircraft.

(3) Hand and foot movements are also critical for the snowplow operator. He uses his hands not only to steer but at the same time to raise, lower, and change the angle of the front plow. At certain points, the back plow must also be raised and lowered. Between the plow control movements, the operator's hands are busy shifting his transmission, using turn signals, flipping switches for radios and lights, and sometimes clearing fogged windshields. Meanwhile, his feet move so fast that they might appear blurry to a passenger. They are continually moving from the brakes to the clutch to the accelerator.

(4) Accompanying the high level of physical skill required of the airplane pilot and the snowplow operator is a considerable amount of mental strain. The pilot's duties include a great deal of preflight planning, during which he must consider the weather, the weight and balance of the plane, and the flight path. In the air, he must constantly sort out the picture presented by his radio and other instruments and think continually of the safest way to handle any problems that arise.

(5) The snowplow operator usually begins work in the early hours of the morning. He must allow for the limitations of the equipment while he works, considering, for example, extremely cold weather and brittle parts, both of which may impair efficiency. The operator must also work under time pressure, calculating every movement so that the work is accomplished in the least amount of time. He knows that in a few short hours traffic will increase and his efficiency will then decrease.

(6) At the end of a flight and after the route has been plowed, both individuals will be physically and mentally drained, but at the same time they will feel a sense of satisfaction from executing the duties of their occupations.

Jim Linscott

Discussion Questions

1. Identify the thesis statement and discuss its effectiveness.
2. Discuss the function of specific details in paragraphs 2 and 3.
3. Is this paper organized by the block method or the alternating method? Explain.

4. What is accomplished by the sentence in paragraph 1 that begins, "This is a snowplow that is equipped . . ."?

5. Point out why the title of this paper is appropriate.

Scissors and Razors: Tools of the Cosmetology Trade

(1) In order to serve patrons effectively, a cosmetologist must be able to perform many different services. Scissor cutting and razor cutting are two of the techniques used in creating a hairstyle. Both serve as a foundation for hairstyles, but they are employed on different types of hair, involve different techniques, and result in different effects.

(2) In deciding on the proper type of cut, the cosmetologist must take hair texture into account. Fine- and medium-textured hair suggest a scissors cut. Fine hair has strands of small diameter, and a blunt cut will keep the ends as full as possible. Coarse hair has strands of larger diameter and as a result is usually best suited for razor cutting. When coarse hair ends are tapered, they can be easily wrapped around rollers and will lie smoother in the finished hairstyle.

(3) When giving a haircut, the cosmetologist must often thin the hair. Thinning removes part of the hair without shortening that which is left, and thus it accentuates a particular style. It can be accomplished either with scissors or a razor, depending on the preference of the cosmetologist. If scissors are used, the method is called slithering. A small section of hair to be thinned is held straight out from the head. The open blades of the scissors are placed so that their junction is against the underside of this section and near the scalp. The open scissors are then repeatedly slid with light pressure toward the scalp and then out again in a back-and-forth movement, removing the hair from the underside of the section. The razor method of thinning is similar to the scissor method in that the hair is held straight out and the razor cuts from underneath. The movement is also back and forth, but the primary motion is toward the hair ends instead of toward the scalp. The two methods yield identical results.

(4) Unlike thinning, cutting shortens the hair uniformly. Scissors and razors are both used for cutting but create different effects. Scissors are most commonly used to create a blunt, full effect, which

is obtained by cutting the hair at right angles to the hair shaft. The diameter of each hair remains the same throughout its entire length.

(5) Razor cutting tapers hair. The technique involves laying the razor against the upper side of a hair section, then stroking downward and moving the razor with increasing pressure toward the hair ends. Hair diameter accordingly decreases gradually toward the ends.

(6) The technique used determines whether the hair is cut wet or dry. Scissor cutting can be done on either wet or dry hair, according to the preference of the cosmetologist. Shaping with a razor, however, must be done on damp hair; otherwise the razor will pull, causing the patron discomfort and dulling the razor.

(7) Whatever current fashion dictates, hair must be cut properly for best results. Mastering the use of scissor and razor techniques enables the cosmetologist to do just that.

Janet Love

Discussion Questions

1. What is the purpose of this essay? Where does the writer make this purpose clear?
2. Explain how the writer avoided points of comparison that overlap.
3. Cite several examples of specific information that help the reader understand the comparison.
4. Show where the writer discusses scissors and razors on each point of comparison.

Two Members of the Team: The Assistant and Hygienist

(1) Because of the spiraling demand for dental care, dentists must employ a dental health team in order to provide efficient service for their patients. The two team members who work directly with the patient are the dental assistant and the dental hygienist. Although they share some duties, there are marked differences in the schooling they receive and in most of the jobs they perform.

(2) Both the assistant and the hygienist perform such tasks as answering the telephones, scheduling and confirming appointments, accepting payments, and keeping books. In addition, both demonstrate basic oral care techniques—for example, the proper way of

brushing and flossing teeth and of utilizing a Water-Pik to care for crowns and bridgework. Furthermore, both team members expose and process dental radiographs, which the dentist uses to diagnose problems and plan treatment. This overlap in duties facilitiates patient care.

(3) The dental assistant pursues a two-year program which includes courses in dental materials, oral anatomy, bio-dental sciences, dental office management, clinical practice, and clinical procedures. Graduates are eligible to take a Certificate Examination, and, upon passing it, to work under the direct supervision of the dentist.

(4) The primary responsibilities of the assistant include preparing the patient, assisting the dentist at the chairside, and dismissing the patient. Preparation includes seating the patient comfortably in the dental chair, fastening the napkin in place, and adjusting the headrest. The assistant then sets up the instrument tray for the required procedure and, to help reassure the patient, may explain what the dentist is going to do. If the patient has been having problems with a certain tooth, the assistant may examine it in order to obtain information for the dentist. Chairside assisting includes passing instruments to the dentist, suctioning saliva and dental debris from the mouth, and keeping the working area clean and dry with the air and water syringe. In addition, the assistant retracts the tongue and pushes the cheek away from the jaw, holds the mirror near the tooth, and mixes the necessary medication and fillings. When the dentist has finished, the assistant records pertinent information on a chart and dismisses the patient after explaining any special care that the newly restored tooth needs.

(5) The two-year curriculum in dental hygiene prepares the student to work under the direction of the dentist but without direct supervision. Graduation requirements are more specialized than those for the dental assistant and include such courses as head and neck anatomy, histology and embryology, general and oral pathology, pharmacology, periodontia, dental health education, and clinical dental hygiene. In the clinic, the hygiene student works with patients on a one-to-one basis. Before starting to work, the new graduate must pass a set of licensing examinations. These exams help ensure that only highly skilled personnel will work in the patient's mouth, and they also allow the dentist to take out malpractice insurance on the hygienist.

(6) The hygienist provides clinical services that help prevent and control oral diseases such as inflammation of the soft tissue surrounding the teeth and destruction of the bone that anchors them. Among the most common services are scaling and cleaning the teeth and treating them with fluoride. The hygienist also compiles personal medical and dental history records that include information about past diseases, previous dental care, and present medication. Further, this team member casts plaster study models—impressions of the teeth and surrounding tissues—and charts patients' dental conditions.

(7) In summary, the dental assistant and the dental hygienist share some common tasks, but the different duties they perform enhance their value. The assistant works more closely with and under direction of the dentist. On the other hand, the hygienist, while still directed by the dentist, works more independently, performing a variety of specialized duties. Together, their contributions increase the efficiency of the dentist's work.

Lynn Schroder

Discussion Questions

1. Why is this topic appropriate for a comparison paper?
2. State the purpose that controls the direction of this paper.
3. Why do you think the writer devoted more space to the discussion of differences than similarities?
4. What type of organization does the writer use—the block or alternating method? Explain how the number of points compared influenced the choice.

Beta/VHS: What's the Difference?

(1) Beta and VHS (Video Home System) are the two video cassette formats currently available in the U.S. While they approach their task differently, they share a common recording principle— helical scanning.

(2) Broadcast television employs a quadraplex recording system in which four heads record at right angles to the path of a high-speed (15 ips) 2-inch tape. Fitting the wide bandwidth of video signals on a narrower tape (¼ inch) to be played at slower speeds for home use

requires a different approach. The helical system uses two heads on opposite sides of a tilted, rotating drum to lay down diagonal tracks.

(3) In the late 1960s and early 1970s when home VCRs existed mainly as ¼-inch open-reel or (Sony's) ½-inch U-Matic, a narrow guard band of blank tape was left after each recorded video track to reduce "crosstalk" between adjacent fields. Maximum recording time was 1 hour. A major breakthrough occurred in 1975, when Sony introduced its Betamax system, employing an *azimuth recording* technique. By slanting the gap 7 degrees in one direction on one head and the same amount in the opposite direction on the second head, Sony kept intertrack crosstalk to a minimum. This also eliminated the necessity for the guard bands and opened the door to longer recording times. About a year later the first VHS VCR appeared, using a slightly modified azimuth technique—the gap offset was 6 degrees.

(4) In both the original and azimuth recording methods, the head drum rotates at 30 revolutions per second. Extended playing speeds reduce the rate of tape travel past the rotating heads. To squeeze the same number of video tracks into a smaller space, VCRs with extended play modes must use smaller heads. While the number of tracks is constant, the quantity of video information that can fit in a particular field is reduced. Thus a standard-speed-only VCR has the potential for producing pictures of higher quality than those from a multispeed unit.

(5) **Tape path.** One of the primary differences between Beta and VHS is the tape path or "wrap." Beta machines use a U-shaped wrap. When you insert a cassette and close the compartment door, the plastic protective lid on the cassette and the tape reel locks are released. (A similar action occurs when you insert a cassette in a VHS machine.) For recording and playback, the tape is extracted from the cassette and drawn into a 2-foot-long path. Though somewhat complex, the path is such that you can rewind or fast-forward the tape without subjecting it to the stress of returning it to the cassette.

(6) VHS machines use an M-shaped path. When you place the deck in either PLAY or PLAY/RECORD, two guides and two tape-loading rollers extract the tape, moving it against the head drum. (A single guide is used in the Beta system.) While the tape path is simpler than Beta's, it is potentially more stressful. VHS machines must go through STOP before entering a fast-wind mode, since that involves returning the tape to the cassette, maintaining an exact cue point

tends to be more difficult on VHS than Beta. However, the time between pressing PLAY and the appearance of a picture on the screen is essentially the same for both formats.

(7) **Tape eject mechanism.** Another advantage the Beta approach offers is the process of ejecting a tape. When you push EJECT, the threaded portion of the tape winds back into the cassette and the compartment automatically rises to lift the cassette out of the machine. This design allows use of a cassette changer mechanism, such as Sony's BetaStack. Using BetaStack, which holds three cassettes, you can record up to 20 hours of programming automatically. The VHS design does not allow for a changer and, for the immediate future, must rely on longer playing times.

(8) **Tape length and speed.** In the standard speed mode, VHS tape travels at 3.335 centimeters per second and Beta at 2. To compensate for the slower speed, Beta machines use a larger head drum than do VHS models (74.5mm diameter compared to 62mm), resulting in a higher "writing speed." (The video heads rotate at a constant rate of 30 rps; the greater the diameter of the head drum, the greater the circumferential distance the heads must travel in 1/30 of a second, and thus the higher the linear speed with which they contact the tape.)

(9) As increasing emphasis has been placed on longer recording times, each format has added slower speed modes. Currently, you'll find VHS machines available with some combination of SP (standard play), LP (long play), and EP (extended play), which yield maximum recording times of 2, 4, and 6 hours, respectively. Beta machines have Beta II (standard speed) and Beta III (long play) with maximum recording times of 3 and 5 hours, respectively. Very few Beta decks still available will record the original Beta I (1 hour), although some Sony decks allow you to play back these tapes.

(10) The two formats code tape length differently. Beta uses an "L" prefix, followed by the length of the tape in feet. For example, an L-250 records for 1 hour at standard speed. VHS most often uses a "T" prefix, followed by the recording time in minutes. (A few brands employ their own, nonstandard designations for VHS tapes.) Thus a T-60 plays for 1 hour at standard speed. Those same tapes have a maximum recording time of 90 minutes (L-250, Beta II) and 180 minutes (T-60, extended play). And therein lies what many see as VHS's strongest advantage over Beta: maximum recording time for a

given length of tape. You can fit another 90 minutes of programming on the VHS cassette.

(11) AT-180, which would allow *9 hours* of recording, has yet to reach the U.S. market. The Beta camp recently introduced an L-830 tape with a maximum recording time of 5 hours. However, if you were to buy video tape tomorrow, the maximum lengths you'd find at most stores would be T-120 for VHS (365 minutes maximum) and L-750 for Beta (275 minutes maximum).

(12) One important point: The tape lengths and playing times are nominal. A tape manufacturer cannot realistically produce exactly the same length of tape for each cassette. Usually, reputable companies err on the high side, giving you a few extra feet in case your VCR runs slightly fast, as some do. Bargain brands are apt to try to hit the prescribed length exactly, and when played on a fast VCR, these tapes may yield *less* than the anticipated recording time.

(13) **Incompatibility.** The formats are basically incompatible. The Beta cassette is smaller than the VHS's, the tape wrap is different, the recording speed is different. There's simply no way you can play on one system a tape recorded on the other.

(14) But another form of incompatibility often exist *within* each format. This is caused primarily by the reduction in head size that comes with the longer play modes. In multispeed machines, the heads measure only about half the size of those in standard–speed–only models. Regardless of format, if you record a tape at standard speed on a multispeed machine and play it back on a standard–play–only deck, the picture will often be "noisy"; the wider head is picking up video information from the two adjacent tracks as well as from the narrow one it is tracking.

(15) Narrow tape heads also may affect the interchangeability of tapes among machines if the tapes were recorded in a long-playing mode. With the relative reduction in video information on these tapes, decks can have a difficult time locking on to an "alien" signal. Some decks come equipped with tracking and skew controls to overcome the flagging and jittery picture that can result, but the effectiveness varies from tape to tape.

(16) Although Beta was the first modern video cassette system, VHS has enjoyed a substantial margin of popularity almost from the time it became available. Estimates vary, but the consensus is that VHS decks constitute about 75% of home recorders and Beta about 25%. This makes little difference when it comes to buying blank

recording tape, since most tape companies offer a full line in both formats. With prerecorded cassettes, you'll find a slightly broader selection of VHS titles, especially if you use rental services.

(17) The issue of which format will ultimately dominate is hardly settled. If Agfa had a 400-ASA film but Kodak's fastest was 300 ASA, would Kodak give up? We don't expect Sony and the other Beta backers to either.

William Tynan, High Fidelity, *January 1981, pp. A6-A8.*

Discussion Questions

1. In terms of the essay as a whole, what does paragraph 2 accomplish?
2. Why do you think the writer uses headings in this article? What do they accomplish?
3. Which pattern of organization, alternating or block, does the writer use? Why do you think he used it?

Suggestions for Writing

Write a comparison paper on one of the topics listed below or, with your instructor's approval, select a topic of your own. Determine your purpose and focus, and formulate a suitable thesis statement. Select your details, arrange your points of comparison according to the block or alternating pattern, and then write the paper.

1. Two types of travel accommodations
2. Two types of music
3. Something natural and something artificial
4. Two auto mechanics (or substitute some other skilled occupation)
5. Single life and married life
6. Television detectives or policemen and real-life detectives or policemen
7. The physical or mental demands of two jobs
8. Two types of parents
9. Two methods of studying
10. Two advertisements
11. Two athletes
12. Two employers
13. Business, residential, or slum districts of two different cities
14. A favorite social spot during the day and during the evening

15. Two acquaintances who have different political views
16. Two types of leadership
17. Two sportscasters or news commentators
18. Two techniques for doing something in your own field
19. Two devices used in your field
20. The working conditions of two jobs
21. Two makes of computers
22. Two types of investments
23. Cassette and open-reel tapes

4

Classification

Classification is a useful way to explain a large, complex, or hard-to-grasp topic. A classification paper breaks a broad topic into separate categories according to some specific principle, and then discusses these categories one at a time. The explanation is thus simplified, for you deal with the topic in small, manageable parts.

You will use classification frequently in your written work, both for your classes and on the job. In the classroom, your instructor may assign a paper classifying carburetion systems, computer languages, drawing pens, furnaces, light-measuring instruments, oscilloscopes, respirators, or spectographs, to name only a few possibilities. If you are employed by a public health organization, you may be asked to classify the microorganisms in the water of a particular lake in order to determine the extent, type, and possible sources of contamination. Or as an agriculture extension agent, you may classify different types of soils of a particular county as part of a soil-mapping project. Whatever your career may be, you will use classification in a variety of ways.

Classification is a natural way for the mind to deal with many subjects. It is more difficult to grasp a large or complex topic when it is considered as a whole than it is to grasp that topic when it is grouped into separate categories. This is true not only for the writer but for the reader as well. Think how much more readily your reader could comprehend the broad topic of less-than-full-size cars if you classified these cars as subcompacts, compacts, and intermediates.

Specifically, classification makes the overall subject easier to grasp by allowing the reader to understand two things clearly:

1. the separate categories
2. the way these categories relate to one another

Thus, a paper that classifies cars as subcompacts, compacts, and intermediates might help the reader better understand:

1. the size, seating capacity, maneuverability, price, or other distinctive features of typical vehicles in each category
2. how these factors vary from category to category

Often the categories of a topic can be further broken down into subcategories, as shown in the following example:

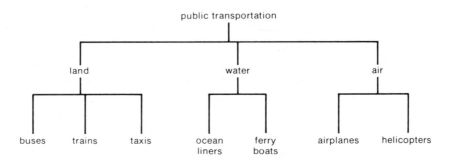

Like comparison, classification satisfies our instinctive desire to understand how things relate to one another. Comparison presents similarities and differences between items. Classification shows the relationships among different categories that make up a larger whole. Although they are both distinct methods of explaining a topic, both comparison and classification point out relationships that enable the reader to associate items or categories in a meaningful way.

Because classification is one of the most useful ways of presenting a subject, it is important for you to learn what is involved in writing a classification paper. Essentially, there are six steps:

1. choosing your topic
2. establishing your focus

3. avoiding overlapping categories
4. developing your thesis categories
5. selecting your details
6. organizing and writing your paper

These steps are discussed in the sections that follow.

Choosing Your Topic

When you write on the job, you will rarely need to choose a topic; the demands of your occupation will provide your writing assignments. For example, you might need to classify the different services your particular department performs. In the classroom, however, you may often be asked to choose a topic.

Choosing a topic should present no serious problems, for almost any subject that can be divided or grouped into categories is a possible topic. For example, you might classify light-measuring instruments into the categories of light-intensity meters, brightness meters, and visibility meters; secretarial positions into the categories of legal, medical, and executive; or drill presses into the categories of upright, radial, gang, and multiple. Your best bet is to choose a topic with which you are familiar, perhaps one related to your career.

Establishing Your Focus

Most topics can be classified in a number of ways. To write a successful paper, you must focus on and develop just one. The focus you select depends on your purpose in writing.

For example, if you were managing a produce market, you might wish to classify your customers in a number of ways. If you wanted to know whether to stock more exotic, expensive fruits, you might wish to classify the customers according to income—low, middle, and high—and select your stock to reflect this distribution. If you wished to advise new employees about the kinds of trouble they could expect from certain customers, you might group these customers by the types of undesirable behavior they exhibit. In neither case would you be preparing random lists of customers. Rather, you would be grouping customers into categories based on a single characteristic—income in the first case and undesirable behavior in the second. Notice that in the first case you are classifying all customers but that in the second you have already made one classification: you have selected those customers who behave badly from the larger group of all customers and have decided to classify them further by types of bad behavior. In both cases your focus is based on a specific purpose, and without a purpose, classification becomes a pointless exercise.

Once you have chosen a basis for your classification, you must decide whether your focus will include all categories or only selected categories—those that are most important, given your purpose in writing. For example, if your purpose is to give the reader a *comprehensive* view of undesirable produce market customers, some of the many types you could discuss include those customers who return apples to the orange bin, handle the produce excessively before they buy, continually complain, cheat the market, taste the fruit, and allow their children to run wild. On the other hand, if you want to describe those customers that annoy you the most, you might focus on just three types: those who handle the produce excessively before they buy, those who continually complain, and those who cheat the market. Frequently your writing assignments will require you to focus only on selected categories.

Avoiding Overlapping Categories

When you have a specific focus in mind, check to make sure that the categories you have chosen do not overlap. In other words, each category must be a separate grouping that does not extend into the "territory" of another grouping. Think back to the example of less–than-full-size cars at the beginning of this chapter. As we noted, these cars can be classified as

1. subcompact cars
2. compact cars
3. intermediate cars

This is a *proper* classification because none of the three categories overlaps into the "territory" of the others. Each is a separate grouping.

Now consider another classification of cars:

1. American small cars
2. European small cars
3. Japanese small cars
4. sports cars

This is an *improper* classification because some cars—the British Triumph, for example—are both European small cars *and* sports cars. Similarly, some Japanese and American small cars are sports cars, too. None of the categories is a separate grouping. This classification, therefore, would result in confusion—the very thing classification is supposed to clear up.

Developing Your Thesis Statement

At this point, prepare a specific thesis statement for your paper. This thesis statement should tell your reader three things:

1. the topic—what you are classifying
2. your focus—the categories you will discuss
3. the central idea—what you want your reader to grasp

For example, the paper classifying produce market customers might have the following thesis statement: *Undesirable produce market customers fall into three main categories—those who squeeze the fruit, those who complain constantly, and those who try to cheat the market—and when you meet them all in one day, you have one big headache.* The reader of this statement knows immediately that the paper will

1. discuss undesirable customers
2. focus on squeezers, complainers, and cheaters
3. point out the problems they cause

Selecting Your Details

Now choose specific details to develop your paper. These details will give your reader a clear picture of each category as well as the relationships among the categories. The choice of details will depend upon your topic, categories, and central idea.

List appropriate details for each category on a separate sheet of paper. For the essay on produce market customers, you might note that the squeezers poke their thumbs into the tops of cantaloupes, the complainers gripe at having to wait in line, and the cheaters add berries to boxes that are already full.

By using the appropriate details to explain every category, you will communicate effectively with your reader.

Organizing and Writing Your Paper

Once you have come this far, organizing your paper will not be difficult. All you have to do is decide on an effective order—which category to discuss first, which second, and so on. Perhaps you will select order of importance—least important, then more important, and finally most important. Or maybe the categories will suggest chronological order. The arrangement you choose depends on your purpose, your subject, and your categories.

In a paper classifying undesirable produce market customers, you might first discuss those who create small problems, then those who create worse problems, and finally those who create the worst problems of all. The number of paragraphs needed to describe each category will depend on how much you have to say.

The overall plan for a paper organized in the above way might look something like this:

FIRST PARAGRAPH: introduction

SECOND PARAGRAPH: discuss customers who handle produce excessively

THIRD PARAGRAPH: discuss customers who complain about the quality of the produce

FOURTH PARAGRAPH: discuss customers who complain about the service they receive from the employees

FIFTH PARAGRAPH: discuss customers who cheat the market

SIXTH PARAGRAPH: conclusion

Your paper could, of course, contain more than six paragraphs if you wished to discuss any of the categories more thoroughly.

EXAMPLES OF CLASSIFICATION

Undesirable Produce Market Customers

(1) You will find almost as large a variety of customers at a produce market as you will find fruits and vegetables. Undesirable produce market customers fall into three main categories—those who squeeze the fruit, those who complain constantly, and those who try to cheat the market—and when you meet them all in one day, you have one big headache. Perhaps you will recognize these people as I describe them.

(2) "Sammy Squeezer" is the least annoying of these undesirables. He wants to make sure that everything he buys is "just right." He pokes his thumbs into the top of a cantaloupe. If they penetrate very deeply, he won't buy this particular specimen, considering it to be overripe. He squeezes the peaches, plums, nectarines, and any other fruit he can get his hands on. After ten of these people squeeze one piece of fruit, it will surely be soft, even if it wasn't originally. Moving on to the corn, Sammy carefully peels back the husk to examine the kernels inside. If they don't suit him, he doesn't bother to fold the husk back to protect the kernels; he simply tosses the ear back into the basket. The problems he creates for the employees are primarily physical—removing the damaged items after he leaves.

(3) A more annoying customer is "Betty Bitcher." She is never satisfied with the quality of the produce: the bananas are too green, the lettuce has brown spots, the berries are too ripe, and the potatoes have green spots. Sometimes you wonder if Betty would have been satisfied with the fruit grown in the Garden of Eden.

(4) The produce has no monopoly on her complaints, however. Betty also finds fault with the service she receives from the employees. Talking to other customers or directly to the clerks, she can be heard saying such things as "Why is this the only place I ever have to wait in line? They must have trouble getting good help here." Even as she leaves the market, which is none too soon, she must make one last complaint: "You mean I have to carry my own potatoes to the car?" The problems she creates for the employees are primarily mental—she can make your nerves quite active.

(5) Perhaps the most annoying customer of all is "Charlie Cheater." You have to keep your eye on him constantly because he

knows all the tricks of cheating. He will add berries onto an already full basket. He will take 6/79¢ oranges and tell you they're the 6/59¢ ones. He will put expensive grapes in the bottom of a sack and add cheaper ones on top. Then he'll tell you that they are all the cheaper variety. Likewise, he will put expensive nectarines in a sack, place a few cheaper peaches on top, and try to pass them all off as peaches. If he is caught, he usually says, "I don't know how that happened. My little girl (or boy) must have put them in there." The child usually looks dumbfounded.

(6) The problem Charlie creates for the market is twofold: financial and legal. If you don't catch him, your profits suffer. If you do catch him, you almost have to prosecute, usually for amounts of only a dollar or two, or you'll have every Charlie in town at your door.

(7) Did you recognize any of these customers? If you didn't and would like to see some of them in action, stop in at Steve's Produce Market. That's where I work, and that's where I meet them.

Clarence DeLong

Discussion Questions

1. What is the student's purpose in writing this classification? Where is this purpose stated clearly?
2. How is this paper organized? Identify specific parts of the paper to support your answer.
3. Demonstrate that the writer has avoided overlapping categories.
4. If you were to classify customers at some business establishment that you have worked at or frequent, how would you categorize them?

Meeting a Special Challenge

(1) Having worked in hospitals as a nurse for several years, I have known nurses in many different specialties who are dedicated and well qualified. However, the four specialties that I consider the most demanding in the profession are surgical nursing, psychiatric nursing, emergency care, and terminal care.

(2) The surgical nurse is highly skilled in the postoperative care

of patients. She knows how to run complex equipment such as suction and ventilating machines. She knows how to respond to her patients so that they feel the operation was a success. For example, she helps the patient who has just undergone a radical mastectomy to see that the surgery was for her overall good. In response to obvious anxiety, the nurse reassures the patient that she is just as much a woman as before. The surgical nurse must have a special gift for winning the trust of her patients.

(3) The psychiatric nurse deserves a medal for courage. She deals with dangerous mental patients, pathological personalities who have no sense of right or wrong. For this reason, she must be on guard at all times; she must, in effect, have eyes at the back of her head. She must also have a great deal of self-control. When her patient displays anger and violence, she cannot respond in kind. On the contrary, she must be tolerant and understanding. Furthermore, she must be able to recognize attempts at deception. Sometimes a mentally ill person, just prior to suicide, will act in a completely normal way because he or she has made the decision to die. The nurse must understand this behavior and be alert for any possible attempt. Perhaps the most trying part of being a psychiatric nurse is never being able to relax. For this reason, these nurses often work a few years in a psychiatric hospital and then take a year off to work in a general hospital.

(4) The emergency room nurse must have analytical talents and must remain calm in the face of disaster. She has to assess the patient, determine how serious the situation is, and respond with the correct treatment. For example, she must know that a patient brought in short of breath and cyanotic in color probably has congestive heart failure. Immediately, she must establish an airway and administer oxygen, while appearing calm and serene to avoid the snowballing effect of panic. It's not an easy job to deal with the public when they or one of their loved ones is in a life-threatening situation. This nurse sees many horrible sights, such as the victims of motorcycle accidents. Sometimes the body is brought in first and then a part, such as a finger, is brought in later. Perhaps the most trying part of being an ER nurse is the sudden personal identification with a patient. If a seriously injured five-year-old boy is brought in and the nurse has a little boy at home, there is bound to be a bond of identification and pity. She must suppress this natural emotion because her alert actions quite possibly can keep the patient alive until the doctor arrives. Most nurses don't care for ER duty, but the ER nurse feels she can do the

most good there because someone's tomorrow may depend on her. It's a great feeling when she saves a life.

(5) Perhaps the nurse I admire most of all is the one who is able to care for the terminally ill patient. To be in constant contact with someone who is about to die takes a tremendous amount of courage, stamina, and tact. The basic foundation of all nursing is the care and welfare of the patient, but this nurse must face the fact that she can't ultimately help her patient. She can't bring out the element of hope as other nurses do. She must be honest and yet always tactful. She is often confronted with the horrible question, "Am I going to die?" She can respond by pointing out that everyone will die some day or by engaging the patient in a discussion. She can, for example, say, "Do you think you're going to die?" If the patient answers, "Yes," she can then ask why he thinks so. By this discussion she is helping the patient face the inevitable. She must be honest and not promise that he will recover, but she must also avoid saying bluntly that he will die. Even though this is the way the terminal care nurse "helps" her patient, her recognition of inevitability runs counter to the entire nursing philosophy.

(6) Nursing is never easy, and we should all be grateful to the people who choose this demanding profession. But the four types of nurses I have described deserve exceptional praise for meeting a special challenge.

Peg Feltman

Discussion Questions

1. What is the purpose of the following phrase in paragraph 1: "Having worked in hospitals as a nurse for several years"?
2. Does this writer focus on all categories of nurses or only selected categories? How do you know?
3. Point out effective details that give the reader a clear picture of the writer's categories.
4. If you were to classify the specialties in some profession, what would your categories be?

Direct Expansion Refrigeration Systems

(1) Anyone who intends to work as a refrigeration technician can expect to study the different types of direct expansion refrigera-

tion systems and how they operate. Of these types, the most important are the capillary tube system, the automatic expansion valve system, and the thermostatic expansion valve system.

(2) The capillary tube system consists of a compressor, a condenser, an evaporator, a temperature-sensing element (thermostat), and possibly a condenser fan motor. The special parts include a filter drier and a capillary tube flow control. The refrigerant is released from the compressor through the high side (or outlet) as a high-pressure gas. It flows through the condenser, where it is cooled to a high-pressure liquid. It then flows into the liquid line and from there to the filter drier, where all contaminants are removed. The refrigerant reaches the capillary tube flow control as a high-pressure liquid.

(3) This flow control is located in the middle of the system. Its job is to meter the refrigerant so as to maintain a pressure difference between the high side (inlet) and the low side (outlet). The metering is done while the compressor is operating. After the refrigerant is metered through the capillary tube and changed to a low-pressure vapor, it absorbs heat from the refrigerated space while moving through the suction line and back to the compressor. This cycle is repeated until the desired temperature is reached.

(4) The automatic expansion valve system (A.E.V.) consists of the same parts as the previous system with two exceptions. The A.E.V. uses a liquid receiver, and it has an automatic expansion valve instead of the capillary tube flow control. The refrigerant flows from the compressor as a high-pressure vapor to the condenser, where it is cooled. After being cooled it turns from a gas into a high-pressure liquid and goes to the liquid receiver. Here the refrigerant is stored until it is needed. At that time it flows through the filter drier and to the metering device, which in this case is the automatic expansion valve. This valve automatically determines whether refrigerant will flow through it to the evaporator. If the pressure is low enough in the evaporator coil, refrigerant is allowed through the valve. When the refrigerant reaches the outlet of the valve, it is sprayed into the evaporator coil and, because of the low pressure, boils rapidly, absorbing heat from the refrigerated space. The refrigerant flows back to the compressor to repeat the cycle until the desired temperature is reached.

(5) The thermostatic expansion valve system (T.E.V.) consists of the same parts as the A.E.V. system except for a different control valve. The refrigerant flows from the compressor through the con-

denser, liquid receiver, and filter drier, and finally to the thermostatic expansion valve. The operation of this valve is controlled by three forces: the pressure in the evaporator coil, the pressure of the control bulb, and the spring pressure in the valve. The control bulb is a thermal element that is mounted on the evaporator coil outlet and connected to the valve by a capillary tube. The pressure in the coil must be low, and the temperature of the bulb must be above the desired temperature before the valve will open. The warmer the evaporator, the wider the valve will open, and the faster refrigeration will take place. The valve will close once the desired temperature is reached.

(6) Because these are the three most common and important direct expansion systems, beginning students of refrigeration and air conditioning must be thoroughly familiar with all of them.

Charles Finnie

Discussion Questions

1. In paragraph 1 the writer mentions "the capillary tube system, the automatic expansion valve system, and the thermostatic expansion valve system." Why is the capillary tube system named and discussed first?
2. The writer discusses three categories of refrigeration systems. What pattern does each of these discussions follow?
3. Show that the writer has used specific details effectively. What functions do these details serve?

What Kind of Life Insurance Will Work Best for You?

(1) Allstate Life offers a wide variety of life insurance policies with features to help you meet your particular needs. Every policy is a variation or combination of one or more of three main types of life insurance . . . *whole life insurance, term insurance,* and *endowment insurance.*

(2) **What is Whole Life Insurance?** Whole life insurance, a form of **permanent life insurance,** provides a specific **protection amount** for as long as you live and for as long as your whole life policy remains in force. In the simplest form of whole life insurance, the premiums will be the same every year that the policy remains in

force. In addition, your policy will build a cash fund known as the cash value. Once the whole policy is issued, the company cannot terminate it, but the owner can terminate his policy at any time by not paying the premiums and taking the cash value, if any.

(3) **Why is the cash value important?** Generally, the cash value of a whole life policy begins to accumulate after the first or second year the policy has been in force. This cash value is yours and you may choose to use it in any of the following ways:

(After the policy has been surrendered, or "cashed in")

- for expenses during retirement years
- for paying off a mortgage early
- for any other purpose you desire

(Without surrendering the policy)

- for obtaining a low interest loan up to nearly the amount of the cash value accumulated
- for continuing a reduced amount of whole life insurance for as long as you live without paying any further premiums
- for continuing your insurance protection for a limited time, without paying any further premiums.

(4) **How do whole life policies differ?** Whole life policies are categorized either as *straight life insurance* or *limited payment life insurance*, depending upon the way in which premiums are paid. A straight life policy anticipates premiums will be paid as long as you live. A limited payment life policy is completely paid for after a specified number of years. This means you are covered for the original protection amount of your policy as long as you live, after your policy is paid for.

(5) Suppose you wanted to pay premiums only during the years of your highest income or to cease paying premiums at retirement age or at a child's age twenty-one, but did not wish to lose the policy's original amount of protection. Then, limited payment life insurance might be useful to you. However, remember that the premiums on any whole life policy may also be discontinued, and the cash value of the policy can be used to buy a *reduced amount* of paid-up whole life insurance.

(6) **What is Term Insurance?** Term insurance is designed to

provide temporary protection for a specified number of years. Term policies are either *level*, meaning the protection amount remains constant during the term period, or *decreasing*, meaning the protection amount decreases over the term period.

(7) Some term policies can be used to provide a level amount of protection for the life of the insured. This is made possible through the *renewable* and *convertible* features contained in such term policies.

- At the end of each term period, the policy can be renewed for an annual term period. The premium increases each time the policy is renewed because the insured is older. Such renewals can be continued to an age specified in the policy.
- At or before a specified maximum age, the term policy can be converted to a whole life policy and the protection can be continued in force as long as the premiums are paid when due. If the term policy is not converted to a whole life policy until the specified maximum age, it is quite possible that the premiums on a whole life policy may be more than you will be able to pay. Thus, conversion at an earlier age is often advisable.
- No proof of insurability is necessary at the time you wish to convert or renew either of these types of term policies.

(8) What are some advantages of term insurance?

- Term insurance is well suited to provide for your temporary needs.
- The premiums required for term policies are lower than the premiums for permanent life policies providing the same initial protection amount.
- Since all of Allstate Life's term policies are convertible, they may be exchanged for most permanent plans of insurance, regardless of your health at the time you convert.
- Level term insurance may be useful to you if you want a specific amount of insurance protection for a certain number of years (such as when children are young), but have a limited amount of money to spend on life insurance premiums.
- Decreasing term insurance is commonly used by people who want to cover a declining need. For example, many homeowners purchase a decreasing term policy to provide money to pay off their mortgage upon their death.

(9) **What are some disadvantages of term insurance?**

- Because the cost of life insurance rises with increasing age, term insurance will become more expensive each time you wish to renew or purchase a new term policy.
- When your term policy expires (after it is no longer convertible or renewable), you must be in good health in order to acquire a new policy.
- Your term policy will not cover a need that continues beyond the term period.
- Term policies generally do not provide any cash value.

(10) **What is Endowment Insurance?** Along with whole life insurance, endowment insurance is another form of permanent life insurance. Endowment policies emphasize your need to build a cash fund. These policies enable you to accumulate an *endowment amount*, or a sum of money, over a specified period of time—with the added guarantee that Allstate Life will complete the plan for you if you do not live to endowment amount.

(11) Should you die during those years, your *beneficiary* would receive a death benefit, which could equal or exceed the endowment amount.

(12) In order for you to accumulate an endowment amount, higher premiums are required than for other types of life insurance providing the same protection amount. So, if you can afford a comprehensive plan that provides for your life insurance needs until **maturity** and for a cash fund at that time, then endowment insurance may be for you.

> *From* Life Insurance, Some Basic
> Facts You Should Know,
> *Allstate Life Insurance Company*

Discussion Questions

1. Two of the three insurance categories are broken down into subcategories. What are these categories and subcategories?
2. What purpose do the headings in this excerpt serve?
3. Show how the writer successfully explains and distinguishes among the kinds of life insurance.

Suggestions for Writing

Prepare a plan for and then write a classification paper based on one of the subjects below or another approved by your instructor. Make sure that you establish a focus with a clear purpose in mind, that your categories do not overlap, that they are arranged in an effective order, and that each is developed by specific details.

1. Pocket calculators
2. Nursing degrees
3. Grasses
4. Computer languages
5. Auto mechanics
6. Police work
7. X-ray machines
8. Drawing pens
9. Carburetion systems
10. Sports announcers (or fans)
11. Water filtration systems
12. Advertising media
13. Financial statements
14. Retail stereo stores
15. Bonds
16. Hair dyes
17. People in line
18. Solar heating systems
19. Checking accounts
20. Bridges
21. Clouds
22. House designs
23. Sales clerks
24. Offset printing presses
25. Bacteria
26. Types of community government
27. Welding processes
28. Television comedies
29. Churchgoers
30. Assembly-line workers

5

Explanation of a Process

Process explanation is one of the most widely used types of written communication. A process explanation presents step-by-step directions for doing something or tells how a procedure was or is carried out.

Whatever your field of study, you will find that the ability to explain a process is essential. To mention just a few examples, you would use process explanation to tell how to test the brakes of an automobile, administer cardiopulmonary resuscitation, give an insulin injection, take fingerprints, program a computer, develop an X-ray film, measure air contaminants, charge a refrigeration unit, or analyze a chemical compound. Since you so often will find it necessary to explain a procedure to others, it is essential that you become skilled at this type of writing.

Seven basic steps are involved in writing a process explanation:

1. choosing your topic
2. developing your thesis statement
3. writing your introduction
4. discussing the theory
5. listing and ordering your steps
6. developing your steps
7. writing your conclusion

Choosing Your Topic

For the writing you do on the job, topic selection is seldom a problem since your topic is dictated by some particular work situation—the need to explain a procedure to your co-workers, for example, or perhaps to a customer, client, or even the boss. In the classroom, however, you may often be asked to choose a topic. As we have noted in earlier chapters, the topic you select should be one you are qualified to write about. Especially in the case of processes, the best qualification is personal experience. If, for example, you have never grilled hamburgers, you certainly should not try to explain the process to someone else. However, if you did the outdoor cooking for your family all last summer, grilling hamburgers might be an excellent topic. You would know very well the steps involved and be able to explain them clearly and completely.

Be careful not to choose a topic that is too simple or too complex. This is an especially important consideration when you are writing a paper of an assigned length. If you try to explain how to light a match, for example, you will soon run out of things to say. On the other hand, how to overhaul an automobile engine might be a fine topic if you have unlimited space, but it could not be explained adequately in a paper of only a few hundred words. In short, the topic you choose should be simple enough to be explained fully within the assigned length yet complex enough to provide material for an interesting paper.

Developing Your Thesis Statement

Once you have chosen your topic, you are ready to develop your thesis statement. The thesis statement, as you know, controls the direction of the entire paper. It indicates one specific focus, helps you decide what to include and exclude as you write, and tells your reader what to expect.

Consider the following example: *Grilling hamburgers on an outdoor charcoal grill is a simple process that almost anyone can master.* One specific focus is quite apparent here. When the writer says *grilling*, the reader knows the paper will not explain broiling or pan-frying. When the writer says *hamburgers*, the reader knows the paper will not discuss pork chops or hot dogs. When the writer says *outdoor charcoal grill*, the reader knows the paper will not deal with gas grills, electric grills, or open campfires.

Writing Your Introduction

You are now ready to write the rest of your introductory paragraph. This introduction should, if possible, include a list of all the items the reader will need to carry out the process. If the list would be too extensive, some or all of the items can be introduced at appropriate points later in the write-up. For a paper explaining how to grill hamburgers, the list might read as follows:

> You will need a clean grill, charcoal briquets, charcoal lighter fluid and matches, hamburger meat, a plate, a spatula, and some water to put out any flame caused by fat drippings.
>
> *E. M. Przybylo*

This list should include not only necessary items but also anything— such as water—that *might* be needed for the process. And if the purpose of some item—again, the water—is not immediately clear, you should indicate briefly what that purpose is.

In addition to the list of equipment and materials, the introduction often must include other information. If there is any question whether the reader will understand the value of the process, the introduction should tell the reader why the process is useful. Further, if a process requires special conditions, you must say what these conditions are. For example, the exterior of a building can be painted only if the temperature is above a certain point. Therefore, you would note this condition in your introduction. Similarly, if a person must have special training in order to carry out a process, this fact must be mentioned in the introduction. Thus, if a chemical procedure requires some special ability not every chemist has—for example, the ability to operate an X-ray spectrograph—then the introduction must specify this.

An introductory paragraph for the hamburger grilling paper might look something like this:

> Grilling hamburgers on an outdoor charcoal grill is a simple process that almost anyone can master. Before starting, you will need a clean grill, charcoal briquets, charcoal lighter fluid and

matches, hamburger meat, a plate, a spatula, and some water to put out any flame caused by fat drippings. The sizzling, tasty patties you will have when you finish are a treat that almost everyone will enjoy.

E. M. Przybylo

Discussing the Theory

With some technical papers, it may be helpful to state the theory on which the process is based before explaining the process itself. The theory, usually discussed briefly in a separate paragraph, should come immediately after the introduction.

Do not confuse the theory with the reason why a process is carried out. *Theory* means the basic principle or principles underlying a process. Suppose you are explaining the laboratory procedure for making oxygen from a mixture of potassium chlorate and manganese dioxide. You might state the theory somewhat as follows:

This process is based upon the fact that potassium chlorate decomposes to form oxygen when heated. The manganese dioxide does not supply oxygen but rather acts as a catalyst which promotes the decomposition of the potassium chlorate at a lower temperature.

Phyllis Jedele

The reason for carrying out the process—for example, to obtain oxygen for combustion experiments—would be mentioned elsewhere in the paper, probably in the introduction.

Unless some clear principle underlies the process, do not give a theory. Thus, an explanation of how to change a flat tire requires no theory. A scientific procedure, on the other hand, is often based on a theory, and you should acquaint your reader with it before you explain the procedure.

Listing and Ordering Your Steps

Once you have written your introduction and, if necessary, stated the theory, make a list of all the steps involved in carrying out the process. Although you are well acquainted with these steps, always assume that your reader is not. Only if you explain the procedure clearly and completely will your reader be able to understand and follow it successfully.

Perhaps the greatest danger in explaining a process is leaving out a step that is obvious to you but would not be to your reader. To avoid this danger, list on a separate sheet of paper all the steps you can think of. Above all, don't try to carry the steps in your head.

Your first list of the steps in grilling hamburgers might look something like this:

1. remove grill rack
2. prepare charcoal
3. light charcoal
4. make hamburger patties
5. replace grill rack
6. place patties on it
7. flip them over after they have cooked on one side
8. remove patties from grill when done to suit your taste

Now examine these steps to see whether anything is missing. You will soon find you have forgotten to tell your reader to wait about thirty to forty-five minutes after lighting the charcoal before putting the hamburgers on. By then the briquets will have turned an ash-white color—an indication that they are at their hottest. You know from experience to allow the briquets time to heat up. Your reader, however, may never have grilled hamburgers and, therefore, will not know that it is necessary to wait. Realizing your omission, simply insert the missing step in the proper place.

When you are satisfied with the steps you have listed, arrange them in a proper order. (Consider what would happen, for example, if you told your reader to place the patties on the grill before lighting the charcoal.) The steps in a process paper are arranged in one of two ways: fixed order or order of choice.

Fixed order means that there is basically only one correct way of arranging the steps: step one must be completed before step two is started, step two before step three, and so forth. Changing an automobile tire is an example of a fixed-order process. The car must be jacked up before the flat tire is removed, and the flat tire must be removed before the spare tire is put on.

Not all processes, however, must be performed in a fixed order. Sometimes there are several possible ways to arrange the steps. When you grill hamburgers, for example, it doesn't make much difference whether you light the charcoal before or after you gather the ingredients or whether you make the patties before or after you light the charcoal. But since some order is necessary for your explanation, present the steps in the order that has worked best for you. Arranging the steps in this way is known as *order of choice*.

If your paper is nontechnical, once you have arranged your steps you are ready to begin your explanation. In technical papers, however, it is usually desirable to list at least the major steps in a single sentence before taking them up in individual paragraphs. In such cases, this list is placed immediately after the discussion of theory. For two examples, see the second paragraph of "Hand Developing X-Ray Film" (page 87) and the second paragraph of "Compression Pressure Testing of an Automobile Engine" (page 88).

Developing Your Steps

Now you are ready to discuss your steps in detail. Because you want the reader to see them as separate actions, present the main steps in separate paragraphs or groups of paragraphs. Then develop the paragraph with enough specific details to make the process clear.

Whenever possible, try not to overburden your reader with numerous steps. If a process involves a considerable number of steps, see if you can combine related small steps into main steps that your reader can follow more easily. For example, of the items in the preliminary list for the paper on grilling hamburgers, you could combine the steps of removing the grill rack, preparing the charcoal, and lighting the charcoal. Similarly, you could combine replacing the grill rack, placing the patties on it, and flipping them over after they have cooked on one side. (Sometimes you may find that what you considered a step is actually a comment upon or an explanation of the step just before or after it. In this case, the comment or explanation belongs with the step that it refers to.) Your main concern, however, should always be clarity. If combining steps would result in confusion, use as many separate steps as are necessary to make the process clear to your reader.

The first main step in grilling hamburgers—removing the grill rack, preparing the charcoal, and lighting it—might be developed like this:

> The first step is to get the fire going. Remove the grill rack and stack about twenty charcoal briquets in a pyramid shape in the center of the grill. Stacking allows the briquets to burn off one another and thus produce a hotter fire. Next squirt charcoal lighter fluid over the briquets. Wait about five minutes so that the fluid has time to soak into the charcoal; then toss in a lighted match. The flame will burn for a few minutes before it goes out.
>
> When the flame goes out, allow the briquets to sit for another fifteen minutes so that the charcoal can start to burn. Once the burning starts, do not squirt on any more lighter fluid. A flame could quickly follow the stream back into the can, causing it to explode. As the briquets begin to turn from a pitch-black to an ash-white color, spread them out with a stick so that they barely touch one another. Air can then circulate and produce a hot, even fire—the type that makes grilling a success.
>
> *E. M. Przybylo*

Note that all of these directions are written in the active voice (see appendix) and take the form of commands. Instructions are almost always written in this form because it is the most straightforward and the easiest for readers to follow.

When you discuss the steps, be sure—unless the reason is obvious—to indicate the purpose of each action as well as how to perform the action. This was done at several points in the paragraphs just quoted. The reader who has this information will work more intelligently and efficiently and be less inclined to skip tasks that seem unnecessary.

If all or part of a step is especially hard to carry out, warn the reader and indicate how to overcome the difficulty. In addition, if there is a chance that an action might be performed improperly, caution the reader against varying the set procedure. This is especially important if an improper action can cause dangerous results. Thus, when explaining how to start the briquets, the writer of the paragraphs above warns his reader not to add lighter fluid once the briquets are burning.

Occasionally, two or more steps of a process must be performed simultaneously. In such a case, be sure to point out, before you describe the first of these steps, that the steps must be performed at the same time.

Writing Your Conclusion

When you finish the final step, make whatever concluding remarks are appropriate to prevent an overly abrupt ending. In a concluding paragraph, you could (1) summarize the process, (2) evaluate the results, or (3) discuss the importance of the process. Write whichever type of conclusion you think will be most appropriate for the paper and most helpful to your reader. The paper on grilling hamburgers might end in this way:

> Once the patties are cooked the way you like them, place them on buns. Now you are ready to enjoy a mouth-watering treat that you will long remember.

Not every process explanation requires a conclusion. For instance, many on-the-job explanations need no conclusion to round out the discussion; they simply end when the writer has presented the last step of the process.

Other Types of Process Papers

So far this chapter has explained how to write directions for someone to follow. Sometimes, though, you will be writing not to tell your reader how to perform a process but simply to explain how a process is carried out. And sometimes you may be reporting on how a particular process *was* performed. These latter types of explanations are written in the same way as a set of directions, with two differences:

1. The list of materials and equipment is sometimes omitted.
2. The steps are written in the passive voice (see appendix) rather than as commands.

The examples that follow show how the three methods of explaining a process differ. The first paragraph, like the hamburger process explanation, gives directions; the second simply explains how a process *is* performed; the third reports how a process *was* performed.

> To begin step one, slowly turn the intensity knob clockwise until a spot of light appears on the screen. Adjust the focus control to make the spot as small and sharp as possible. Next, turn up the horizontal gain control until there is a horizontal line about eight divisions long on the screen. Adjust the intensity so the line is just bright enough to be seen plainly, and readjust the focus for the finest possible line.
>
> *Glenn Jones*

> The tumbler is loaded with about 500 pounds of rollers. One scoop of abrasive grit is mixed with water until a thin gravylike mixture is obtained. Then the mixture is placed in the tumbler, which is set to rotate at about 40 revolutions per minute. During rotation, the rollers are worn down by the action of the abrasive mixture. Every twenty minutes, the tumbler is stopped and the diameter of a sample roller is checked. When the rollers are the right diameter, they are removed from the tumbler and rinsed free of grit in preparation for the next step.
>
> *Barry McGovern*

> The analyzer was adjusted so the scale read zero and connected to the short sampling tube which had previously been inserted into the smoke stack. The sample was taken by depressing the bulb the requisite number of times, and the results were then read and recorded. The procedure was repeated, this time using the long sampling tube and sampling through the fire door.
>
> *Charles Finnie*

EXAMPLES OF PROCESS EXPLANATION

The ABC's of CPR

(1) A heart attack, drowning, choking, or electrocution—any of these can stop an adult's breathing. The victim, however, need not always die. Many a life that would otherwise be lost could be saved

simply by applying the ABC's of CPR—Cardiopulmonary Resuscitation. Here's how you do so. When you are certain that the victim's breathing and pulse have stopped, begin CPR immediately. If breathing and circulation are not restored within five minutes, irreversible brain damage occurs. CPR requires no special equipment; presence of mind, however, is absolutely essential.

(2) *A* stands for opening the airway. The victim must be laid in a supine (face-up) position on a firm surface. Once the victim is correctly positioned, quickly tilt the head as far back as possible by placing one hand beneath the neck and gently lift upward. In an unconscious person, the tongue falls to the back of the throat and blocks the air passages. Hyperextending the head in this fashion pulls the tongue from that position, thus allowing air to pass. At the same time tilt the forehead back with the other hand until the chin points straight upward. The relaxed jaw muscles will then tighten, opening the air passage to the lungs. Remove your hand from the forehead and, using your first two fingers, check the mouth for food, dentures, vomitus, or a foreign object. Remove any obstruction with a sweeping motion. These measures may cause the patient to start breathing spontaneously. If they do not, mouth-to-mouth resuscitation must be started.

(3) *B* stands for breathing. While maintaining your grasp behind the neck, pinch the victim's nostrils shut with the index finger and thumb of your other hand. Open your mouth, and place it over the victim's mouth so that a tight seal is formed. Such contact allows air to reach and expand the lungs. If the seal is incomplete, you will hear your own breath escaping. Deliver four quick, full breaths without allowing the victim's lungs to deflate completely between breaths; the remove your mouth and allow him to exhale passively. At this point, check the carotid pulse to determine whether the heart is beating. To do so, place the tips of your index and middle fingers laterally into the groove between the trachea (windpipe) and the muscles at the side of the neck. If no pulse is evident, artificial circulation must be started.

(4) *C* means circulation. Locate the lower end of the sternum (breastbone), and move upward approximately the width of two fingers. At this point, firmly apply the heel of one hand, positioning the fingers at right angles to the length of the body and keeping them slanted upward. If the hand is positioned any higher or lower on the sternum, serious internal injuries in the abdomen or chest are possi-

ble. Now place the heel of your second hand on top of your first. The fingers may be interlaced or interlocked, but they must not touch the chest, or the force of your compressions may fracture ribs.

(5) Keeping your elbows straight and pushing down from the shoulders, apply firm, heavy pressure until the sternum is depressed approximately one and one-half to two inches. Rock forward and backward in a rhythmic fashion, exerting pressure with the weight of your body. This action squeezes the heart against the immobile spine with enough pressure to pump blood from the left ventricle of the heart into general circulation. Compress the chest, and then immediately release the pressure, fifteen times. Do not, at any point in the cycle, remove your hands from the chest wall. Counting the compressions aloud will help develop a systematic cycle, which is essential for success. When the fifteen have been completed, pinch the nose as described above, seal the victim's mouth with your own, and deliver a quick breath of air. As the victim exhales, inhale another breath and deliver it, and then compress the chest an additional fifteen times. Alternate respiration and compression steps, timing yourself so as to deliver approximately eighty compressions per minute.

(6) At various intervals, quickly check the effectiveness of your CPR techniques. Lift the eyelids and notice if the pupils are constricted—a key sign that the brain is receiving enough oxygen. In addition, if the bluish color of the victim is decreasing and spontaneous breathing and movement are increasing, the victim has responded favorably.

(7) To maximize the chances for survival, do not interrupt this technique for more than five or ten seconds. Continue the ABC's of CPR until competent medical help or life-support equipment arrives.

Kathy Petroski

Discussion Questions

1. How does the writer use the letters A, B, and C from the CPR technique in this paper?
2. How does the opening paragraph prepare the reader for the rest of the paper?
3. The writer cautions the reader twice about dangerous results that can occur from performing an action improperly. Locate these two cautions.
4. Has the writer used fixed order or order of choice to organize the paper?

The Mourning After

(1) How to handle a hangover is a problem many people share. Since the discovery of the grape, man has dedicated himself to the imbibing of alcoholic beverages. This imbibing often causes us to awaken to the rumbling of a thousand horses galloping across our foreheads and a volcano-like condition in our stomachs. But worry not—a remedy is as near as the kitchen.

(2) Once you are awake, chances are good you may want to die, but chances are even better that you'll survive. The first and most difficult task on the road to recovery is to pry your head off the pillow and plant both feet firmly on the floor. Don't despair if this seems impossible at first, since it sometimes takes four or five attempts. Now cautiously shuffle your feet toward the kitchen. Stay close to the wall and try not to jar the object on your shoulders that feels as though it's hosting the Stanley Cup Playoffs.

(3) The kitchen should bring a slight degree of relief as you sense that the soothing potion is near at hand. Locate a juice pitcher or any container that has a lid. Remove the lid and pour a third of a glass of concentrated lemon juice, the kind used for cooking, into your container. Add two-thirds of a glass of soda water, if available, or tap water. The next step requires the most finesse. Take a bottle of Tabasco sauce and ever so gently shake a dash into the cure. Add two Alka-Seltzer tablets and a half dozen cubes of ice. Your remedy is now ready to be mixed. Place the lid on the container and shake it vigorously for ten to fifteen seconds (this sometimes happens without your initiating the motion).

(4) The potion is now ready to be consumed. Pour it into a large drinking glass and place two buffered aspirin in your mouth. The moment of truth is at hand. Drink this exhilarating remedy in one sustained motion and feel the soothing coolness of your pipes as the wonder mix works its way to your stomach. As the aspirin sends relief to your banging head, the seltzer, lemon, and Tabasco will revitalize your stomach.

(5) As you sit and read the morning paper, you'll feel your senses being restored. Your head will stop throbbing, your pipes will cool, and your burning stomach will experience relief. The price you'll pay today for what you bought last night will be a bargain with this magic elixir. You can now ready yourself for the day and hope all matters of consequence can be avoided until noon.

Charles Case

Discussion Questions

1. Comment on the effectiveness of this paper's title.
2. In paragraph 3, what does the writer mean when he says "this sometimes happens without your initiating the motion"?
3. Are the steps arranged in fixed order or order of choice? Defend your answer by referring specifically to the paper.
4. Three types of conclusion were mentioned earlier in this chapter. Which does this writer use?

Hand Developing X-Ray Film

(1) X-ray film developing is a procedure whereby the invisible, latent image on exposed film is converted to a visible image by treating the film with a developer solution. The special equipment needed to perform this process includes an exposed X-ray film in its cassette, a film hanger, three solution tanks, and a dryer. The solutions needed are developer, fixer, and water, each in a separate tank at 68°F. The procedure is carried out in a darkroom.

(2) The process is based on the fact that an alkaline developer transforms exposed (ionized) silver bromide crystals on the film into clumps of black metallic silver that form an image. The unexposed (nonionized) silver bromide is not affected by this treatment. The complete development process consists of five steps: (1) developing, (2) rinsing, (3) fixing, (4) rerinsing, and (5) drying the film.

(3) The exposed film is first removed from the cassette and attached to the hanger. The film is then suspended in the developer solution for about five minutes. This solution softens and swells the gelatin on the outside of the film, then reacts with the ionized silver bromide crystals to reduce them to metallic silver.

(4) When the film is developed, it is placed in the rinse water tank, which contains running water, for thirty seconds. Running water ensures that the film is rinsed properly. It removes the alkaline part of the developer so it will not neutralize the acidic fixer.

(5) Next the film is placed in the fixer solution for ten minutes. This solution clears the film of nonionized silver bromide and hardens the gelatin emulsion, thus increasing its resistance to damage.

(6) The film is then returned to the rinse water tank. It is allowed to remain there for twenty-five minutes so that the fixing salts will be removed, since residual fixer would cause the image to discolor and fade.

(7) Finally, the film is removed from the rinse water tank and the excess water is allowed to run off. The film is then placed on the dryer, generally a type of rack. During the drying process, the film can be easily damaged. Since dirt from the air may become embedded in the film or the film may become scratched, extreme care is taken to protect the film at this stage.

(8) Drying takes approximately fifteen minutes. The dried film is a permanent, finished radiograph that helps diagnose a suspected condition.

Janet Brown

Discussion Questions

1. Has the writer chosen an appropriate process to explain? Discuss.
2. What is the purpose of the last sentence in paragraph 1?
3. Where is the theory discussed? Why is it desirable to include the theory for this process?
4. Why has the writer given the purpose for each step? In what way is this information helpful?
5. Earlier in this chapter we mentioned three types of process papers: those giving directions, those merely explaining how a process is performed, and those reporting on how a process was performed. Which type does this paper illustrate?

Compression Pressure Testing of an Automobile Engine

(1) Compression pressure testing is a process that indicates the compression ratio of an automobile engine. Here is a simple, accurate procedure for determining engine compression. The tools needed to carry out this process include a spark plug wrench, a large screwdriver, a remote-control starter switch, and a compression pressure gauge.

(2) The process is based on the fact that if the head gasket and piston rings are in good condition, the combustion chamber will be tightly sealed during the compression stroke. If a gauge is inserted in place of the spark plug, the amount of compression can be measured. A high gauge reading indicates a good seal, and a low reading indicates a poor seal. The three basic steps in the procedure are: (1) preparing the engine for testing, (2) pressure testing, which includes inserting the gauge into each cylinder and recording the readings,

and (3) comparing the pressure readings to one another and to the engine compression specifications.

(3) To prepare the engine, first remove the spark plug wire located at the top of each plug. Next, remove the plugs from the block with the spark plug wrench. Connect the remote-control starter switch to the starter solenoid terminals. To prevent the car from starting, disconnect and ground the ignition-coil tower wire located at the distributor. Finally, block open the carburetor throttle with the large screwdriver. This will prevent gas from overflowing.

(4) To pressure test the engine, force the end of the gauge into the number one spark plug hole. Make sure the rubber tip of the gauge completely seals the hole, or inaccurate readings will result. Depress the remote-control starter switch until the engine cranks seven complete compression strokes. Observe and record the compression reading, and the number of the cylinder tested. Remove the gauge and test each of the remaining cylinders in the same way.

(5) In order to interpret the results of the pressure tests, the readings must be compared with one another and with the engine compression specifications. First, compare the individual cylinder readings. They should be within 20 percent of one another. A greater variation indicates that excessive wear has caused an unbalanced engine, which cannot be corrected by mere tuning. The second comparison, between the average of the readings and the known engine compression specification, shows the amount of engine wear. If the average is within 20 percent of the specification, the engine is considered mechanically sound. If the average is more than 20 percent below the specification, the engine is excessively worn and should be rebuilt. If the average is more than 20 percent above the specification, the engine has heavy carbon deposits and needs to be decarbonized. Low pressure reading in two adjacent cylinders may indicate a faulty head gasket.

(6) Periodic compression tests will indicate the condition of an auto engine and alert the owner to any needed repairs or adjustments.

Frank Perry

Discussion Questions

1. Notice that paragraph 2 lists the three major steps involved in the procedure. How does this list help the reader?
2. At one point the writer warns the reader against performing a procedure improperly. Locate the warning.

3. Cite two places in paragraph 3 where the writer indicates the purpose of an action.
4. If you were asked to explain a technical procedure with which you are familiar, what procedure would you select? What would be the main steps in your explanation?

Let the Sunshine Do Your Cooking

(1) The backyard barbecue is a summertime ritual for millions of Americans. This year, why not give your picnic an energy-saving twist by cooking in a solar oven?

(2) The oven described here is adapted from plans developed by Volunteers in Technical Assistance, 3706 Rhode Island Ave., Mt. Rainier, Md. 20822.

(3) To build the oven, start with a box—an undamaged cardboard carton or, for a more durable oven, a box made of plywood or sheet metal. Whatever the material, the box should measure approximately 28 inches long, 18 inches wide and 14 inches tall. Other supplies include a sheet of rigid two-inch fiberglass insulation, a pane of thermal glass, duct tape and glue. (Cost to build using cardboard, about $5; with plywood or sheet metal, $7 to $10).

(4) Begin by cutting away the bottom and one end of the box. Now draw diagonals on two sides of the box, extending from a point one inch from the bottom corner of the open end to a point on the top of the box, 12 inches from the closed end. Trim on that line and cut off the flap from the top of the box. When the box is properly trimmed, it should resemble a scoop without a handle.

(5) Next, trace the sides of the box on the insulation. Use a linoleum knife to cut out slabs that fit precisely on the side and back walls of the oven. Glue them in with aluminum foil pressed against the box. Now cut slabs of fiberglass that match the front and top of the oven and extend one-half inch beyond the edge of the box. These pieces must fit snugly to minimize heat loss. After gluing the insulation to the top and back of the oven, paint the interior with flat black paint to absorb extra heat. When the paint is dry, fit a precut pane of thermal glass over the front of the oven. Trim the fiberglass that extends over the edge of the box at an angle so the glass panel will sit evenly on it. Then tape the glass securely over the opening with duct tape.

(6) Now, the oven needs a base. Start with a piece of plywood two inches wider and longer than the oven itself. Build a two-inch rim on all sides of the base and place a two-inch runner down the center for support. Fill the empty spaces with insulation and cover with a sheet of gypsum cut to size. Paint the gypsum board flat black. When the oven sits on the base, it should press into the gypsum so heat won't escape. If it does escape, add a rim of weather stripping.

(7) At this point, the oven could be used in the tropics. In North American latitudes, however, reflectors improve the oven's heating capacity. To make reflectors, cut out four pieces of cardboard the size of the glass panel plus two inches on one side. Crease the panels so the two-inch tab can be attached to the oven, and cover with aluminum foil, shiny side up. Glue the panels to the side of the oven and use straightened coat hangers to prop them at a 120-degree angle with the face of the oven.

(8) At last, it's time to start cooking. Choose a sunny day and try to cook shortly after noon when the sun's rays are most intense. (Depending on latitude and care in construction, the oven should reach between 200 and 300 degrees, so select a dish that does well with slow heat.) Recipes adapted for crock pots are good choices as well as traditional picnic fare, such as burgers, baked potatoes and franks and beans.

(9) Place the oven base on a table facing the sun. Put dinner in an ovenproof dish, set it on the base and cover it with the oven itself. Now stand back.

(10) To become better acquainted with the oven, place a thermometer inside. Adjust the reflectors to direct the sun's rays into the oven. As the sun moves, shift the oven to keep shadows out of the box. If you think heat is escaping, add insulation where the base meets the oven.

(11) Some cooks find they achieve higher temperatures by adding more reflectors or installing a second panel of glass. Experiment and have patience. Remember solar energy is still in the age of experimentation. With this oven, you can be one of the pioneers.

Carolyn Jabs, Family Weekly,
June 18, 1978

Discussion Questions

1. List the steps involved in this explanation.
2. The first seven paragraphs of this article actually explain two separate

processes. What are these processes and how do you account for the different amounts of detail included in each?
3. Why is the last sentence of paragraph 4 helpful?
4. Why is it desirable to write these directions in the form of commands?

Suggestions for Writing

Write a paper explaining one of the following processes or another approved by your instructor. Prepare a complete list of steps, select an appropriate order, and develop each step with sufficient details.

1. installing a manual throttle
2. preparing a blood smear for microscopic examination
3. balancing a cash register till
4. growing a specific type of fruit or vegetable in your home garden
5. using dental floss
6. monitoring the atmosphere for contaminants
7. drawing up an income statement
8. assembling or repairing some common household device
9. treating a bite from a poisonous snake
10. giving a sick patient a bed bath
11. making a blueprint
12. regripping a golf club
13. training a dog (or some other pet)
14. charging a refrigeration unit
15. conducting a Schilling test for pernicious anemia
16. taking an inventory
17. potting a plant
18. conducting a nitrate test for water potability
19. changing the oil in an automobile
20. sewing a zipper in an article of clothing
21. serving a tennis ball
22. making up a payroll
23. grinding a tool bit
24. repainting a car
25. cleaning and gapping spark plugs
26. cleaning teeth or treating them with fluoride
27. cutting internal threads on a workpiece
28. turning a taper on a lathe
29. installing, modifying, or overhauling a particular type of air conditioning or refrigeration unit
30. carrying out a process related to your field

6

Definition

As you write for your classes and on the job, you will often have to clarify the meaning of some term for your readers. The term may be unfamiliar, it may be used in an uncommon sense, or it may mean different things to different people. Whenever you clarify the meaning of a term, you are defining.

Defining is really a narrowing process that distinguishes a particular term from all others. *To define* comes from the Latin, *definire*, which means "to limit, to reduce, or to set boundaries." A *definite* time period, for instance, has boundaries that can be described precisely, and an *indefinite* period lacks fixed boundaries. Thus, when you define a term, you set a boundary around it so that, for your purposes, the term can stand for just so much and no more.

At times, a brief definition like those found in dictionaries will be satisfactory. Thus, in writing for a general audience about heating systems, it would probably be sufficient to define *furnace plenum* by explaining that it is "an air compartment maintained under pressure and connected to one or more ducts." Similarly, a paper for nonspecialists about treating wounds might briefly explain the special medical meaning of *proud* by a simple parenthetical phrase, as in this example: "the proud (excessively swollen and granulated) flesh surrounding the typical wound." The first of these examples defines an unfamiliar term; the second, a term used in an uncommon sense.

Both definitions, though brief, probably would provide all the information the reader needs.

Often, however, brief definitions are not enough. This is especially true when you are dealing with new terms. In recent years, social, political, and technological developments have spawned a whole host of new terms. Think, for instance, of examples such as *consumerism, supply-side economics, breeder reactor,* and *macroengineering.* When you use new and unfamiliar terms such as these in a piece of writing, it is often necessary to go beyond a single-sentence definition to explain them. Your reader may never have heard of the concept, and a dictionary definition, even if you could find one, might not provide enough information.

Terms that mean different things to different people likewise often require more than a brief definition. *Drug pusher* is one example. To many people, a drug pusher is anyone who illegally sells marijuana, hallucinogens, or any narcotic substance. Others limit the term to sellers of pure narcotics, such as heroin or opium. If you write a paper recommending stiff sentences for drug pushers, you must define clearly what you mean by the term. Otherwise, your reader might misunderstand your position.

Sometimes, an entire paper may be an extended definition. Your instructor may ask you to define a technical or social term such as *weather satellite* or *urban sprawl.* Your employer may ask you to define *corporate responsibility* or *cost-benefit analysis* for new employees.

Writing an extended definition involves more than merely comparing the item you are defining with something else or breaking it into categories or telling how it is made or carried out. For example, to convey the meaning of the term *fingerprint,* you must do more than explain how a fingerprint is made. Similarly, classifying printing into the categories of letterpress and offset is not defining the meaning of *printing.* To write an adequate definition, you must approach your subject from a number of perspectives.

Three basic steps are involved in writing an extended definition:

1. choosing your topic
2. establishing your formal definition
3. expanding your definition

Each step is discussed below.

Choosing Your Topic

When you are working, the duties of your job, not personal choice, will determine what definitions you write. In the classroom, however, your instructor may give you several topics and ask you to define one of them or may leave the choice entirely up to you. If you are given free choice, search for a term that really needs clarification. There would be little point, for instance, in defining the term *table*. Even if you could think of enough material to include, the final paper probably would not be very interesting.

Pick a topic that you already know about or can learn enough about in the time available to you. Your knowledge can be the result of personal experience, observation, reading, or any combination of these. Be certain, also, that the topic interests you. You will then be able to put your own personal stamp upon the topic by letting your reader know in detail what you think and feel about it.

Establishing Your Formal Definition

Your next step is to prepare a one-sentence formal definition, which functions as a thesis statement by naming what the paper will discuss. A formal definition does two things:

1. places the item being defined in a broad category
2. tells how the item differs from others in the same category

Constructing such a definition requires careful attention to detail. Consider, for example, the process of supplying a formal definition of *vacuum cleaner* for an encyclopedia article on the subject. Coming up with a broad category poses no serious problem: a vacuum cleaner is an appliance. A vacuum cleaner's chief purpose is to clean floors, carpets, and upholstery. But brooms and carpet sweepers also clean floors and carpets, and whisk brooms clean upholstery. To distinguish a vacuum cleaner from these other cleaning devices, you could indicate that it is operated by electricity and cleans by suction. When all these characteristics are combined, the result might be as follows:

A vacuum cleaner is an appliance that is powered by electricity and is used to clean floors, carpets, and upholstery by suction.

COMMON PITFALLS IN FORMAL DEFINITION

When you prepare a formal definition, you must avoid certain pitfalls.

Overly Broad Definition. A definition should not be too broad. If you define a skunk as "a four-legged animal that has black fur with white markings," you are committing this error. A cat or dog could also fit this definition. Instead, you might narrow the definition to "a skunk is a four-legged animal that has a bushy tail and black fur with white markings and that ejects a putrid-smelling secretion when threatened."

Overly Narrow Definition. The opposite extreme, an overly narrow definition, should also be avoided. "Motor oil is a liquid petroleum product used primarily to lubricate automobile engines" and "A kitchen blender is an electrical appliance used to mix foods" illustrate this error. After all, motor oil is used to lubricate other engines, and blenders do more than mixing. If the problem is caused by a limiting expression such as "automobile," drop the expression. Otherwise add the missing information. Correcting the above definitions by these methods gives us "Motor oil is a liquid petroleum product used primarily to lubricate engines" and "A kitchen blender is an electrical appliance used to chop, mix, and liquefy foods."

Circular Definition. A definition should not include the term being defined or another form of the term. If it does, the definition is circular and clarifies nothing. Saying that a psychiatrist is "a physician who practices psychiatry" will not help someone who does not know what psychiatry means. You must define the term with words that will be meaningful to your reader—for example, "A psychiatrist is a physician who diagnoses and treats mental disorders."

Omission of Category. Avoid using *is where* or *is when* instead of naming the category to which the term belongs. "A carwash is where automobiles are washed and polished" and "Procrastination is when a person habitually delays taking necessary action" illustrate this error. Both of these definitions are faulty because neither one explicitly names a category to which the item being defined belongs. Notice the improvement when each word's category is specified: "A carwash

is an establishment in which automobiles are washed and polished";
"Procrastination is the habitual delaying of necessary action."

Unfamiliar Terms. For obvious reasons, a definition should use terms familiar to a reader. When Dr. Samuel Johnson defined *network* as "anything reticulated or decussated, at equal distances, with interstices between the intersections," he violated this principle. The complexity of his definition contrasts with the clarity of "A network is an arrangement of cords, wires, or rods that cross at regular intervals and are fastened together at the points where they intersect."

This principle does not mean that you must avoid all technical terms when you write a formal definition. For example, a definition of *crustacean* for advanced biology students might appropriately state that this creature has a "chitinous or calcareous exoskeleton." It would be better, however, to tell a general reader that a crustacean has "a hard outer shell." Your guideline should always be your readers—speak to them in terms they will best understand.

Expanding Your Definition

You are now ready to expand your formal definition. This expansion can be accomplished by the use of any appropriate combination of the writing methods discussed below. The combination you choose will depend on your topic, purpose, and audience. Very few extended definitions are developed by only one of these techniques. As in all good writing, a generous supply of specific details is essential in a definition paper.

COMPARISON

Comparison is often helpful in defining a new or unfamiliar object, device, concept, or process. A comparison points out resemblances and/or differences between the new item and one your reader is familiar with. Several approaches are possible. You may, for example, focus on physical properties, construction, mode of operation, size, power, or efficiency. In the paragraphs below, the writer compares the means by which cooling is accomplished in a liquid-cooled engine and in the less familiar air-cooled engine.

In conventional liquid-cooled engines, the heat from the burning air-fuel mixture passes through the walls of the cylinder and into a coolant in a jacket surrounding the cylinders. The heated coolant is pumped through a radiator, where it is cooled by an air stream blowing past the thin-walled tubes or cells through which it passes. It is then returned to the jacket to absorb more heat.

In air-cooled engines, heat is absorbed directly by a stream of air passing over the outside of the engine. The outside cylinder walls have metal fins to increase the amount of surface from which engine heat is lost, and the cylinders may also have spaces between them for better air circulation. To provide the great volume of air needed for proper cooling, a fan or blower may be utilized. Special cowlings and baffles may also be placed around the engine near the cylinders to increase the flow of air.

Edward Daley

CLASSIFICATION

Classification is also useful for developing a definition since you will often wish to break a topic into separate categories and then discuss the categories one at a time. The following excerpt from a paper on air contamination uses classification to expand the definition of *respirators*.

Three major types of respirators—air-supplied devices, self-contained breathing devices, and air-purifying devices—are utilized for protection against air contaminants. Air-supplied devices consist essentially of a mask, hood, or suit connected by a hose to a stationary tank of air. With self-contained breathing devices, air is supplied from a tank carried by the user, or oxygen is generated in a chemical canister. Air-purifying devices are equipped with filters or chemical canisters which remove contaminants from incoming air before the wearer breathes it.

Alice Ludo

PROCESS EXPLANATION

Process explanation is an especially versatile method of developing a definition. You may use it, for example, to explain what a device does or how it is used, how a product is made, how a procedure is carried out, or how a natural event takes place. The paragraph below, part of a student paper defining the term *fingerprint*, tells how the process of fingerprinting is carried out.

> Fingerprinting is carried out by rolling the ball of each finger over a glass or metal inking plate coated with a thin film of special ink. The ink on the finger is then transferred by rolling to the appropriate box on a fingerprint card. Each print consists of a set of clearly defined gray ridges.
>
> *Jimmy Carvel*

ILLUSTRATION, CAUSATION, AND NEGATION

Illustration—that is, use of specific incidents, events, or examples—is especially effective for defining an abstract term or for tracing the changes in the meaning of a term. In the excerpt below, the student utilizes illustration (in this case a personal experience) to help develop a paper defining *fear.*

> Once I started school, I developed a great fear of tests, term papers, and speaking in front of the class. Formal speeches were especially hard for me. Heart pounding, cold sweat beading my forehead, I would suffer acute mental agonies as I stammered my way through my talk. This "academic fear syndrome" lasted until my junior year in college.
>
> *Diane Trathen*

Causation, which probes the causes behind events, conditions, problems, and attitudes, is often used to define. The following paragraph from a student paper defining *glaucoma* shows the use of causation.

> Glaucoma results when fluid inside the eye fails to drain properly. Pressure builds within the eyeball, damaging or killing the optic nerve, which connects the eye to the brain. Damage can range from impairment of vision to total blindness. The disease is responsible for one out of every eight cases of total blindness.
>
> *Rance Hafner*

Negation shows what a term does *not* mean. It is especially useful for defining events and occurrences and for correcting popular misconceptions. Notice how the student uses negation in the excerpt below.

Researchers do not know what crib death is, but they do know what it is *not*. They know it cannot be predicted; it strikes like a "thief in the night." Crib deaths occur in seconds, with no sound of pain, and they always happen when the child is sleeping. Suffocation is *not* the cause, nor is aspiration or regurgitation. Researchers have found no correlation between the incidence of crib death and the mother's use of birth control pills or tobacco or the presence of fluoride in water.

Trudy Stelter

These methods of writing represent some of the available options for expanding a definition. The challenge in writing a definition essay is to choose the combination of approaches that will explain the term most precisely.

EXAMPLES OF DEFINITION

The Food Chain

(1) Everyone knows that we must eat to stay alive and that all the plants and animals upon which we dine must do the same. How many of us, though, ever stop to consider whether or not any pattern underlies all the cross-dining that goes on? There is a pattern, and to understand it we must first familiarize ourselves with the concept of a food chain. Such a chain can be defined as a hierarchy of organisms in a biological community, or ecosystem, with each member of the chain feeding on the one below it and in turn being fed upon by the one above it. To put the matter more simply, a food chain starts with a great quantity of plant stuffs which are eaten by a large number of very hungry diners. These are then eaten by a lesser number of other animals, which in turn fall prey to an even smaller number of creatures. With the passage of time, the uneaten organisms die and become part of the soil for the plant to grow in.

(2) To illustrate, let's look for a moment at one particular biological community, a marshy ecosystem, and a few events that might take place there. First, there are the marsh grasses, with millions of grasshoppers busily feeding upon them. When one grasshopper isn't

looking, a shrew sneaks up and eats it. This process is repeated many times as the day wears on. Later, toward sunset, as the stuffed and inattentive shrew is crossing an open stretch of ground, a hawk swoops out of the sky and eats the rodent. The food chain is completed when the marsh hawk dies and fertilizes the marsh grasses.

(3) This illustration is not meant to suggest that hawks eat only shrews or shrews eat only grasshoppers; the circle is much more complicated than that, involving what biologists call trophic levels—the different feeding groups in an ecosystem (for example, some creatures eat green plants and some eat meat.) There are five major trophic levels. The beginning point for any food chain is green plants, known as producers, which absorb sunlight and through the process of photosynthesis turn carbon dioxide, water, and soil nutrients into food, especially carbohydrates, that animals can assimilate.

(4) All of the other life forms subsist either directly or indirectly on the producers. Animals that feed directly on green plants are the herbivores, called primary consumers. This group includes, among other creatures, most insects, most rodents, and hooved animals. The secondary consumers are the carnivores and omnivores. The term "carnivore," meaning an animal that eats only flesh, is more familiar than the term "omnivore," which designates an animal that eats both green plants and flesh. Carnivores include such animals as lions, leopards, eagles, and hawks, whereas omnivores are represented by foxes, bears, humans, and so on.

(5) The last feeding group in the food chain consists of the decomposers: bacteria and fungi. These microorganisms recycle the waste products of living animals and the remains of all dead things—plants, herbivores, omnivores, and carnivores alike—into fertilizers that plants, the producers, can use.

(6) Obviously each trophic level must produce more energy than it transfers to the next higher level. With animals, a considerable part of this energy is lost through body heat. The muscles that pump the lungs, continually pushing air out of the body and sucking it back in, consume energy. The muscles in the arms and legs sweat out energy. All of the life-supporting systems of the organism use energy to keep it going. Everything from worms to people lives in accordance with this law of energy loss. As long as life's fires burn, energy is lost, never to be regained.

(7) Throughout history we humans have tried to manipulate the food chain so as to provide ever-greater outputs of energy. On the

one hand, we have tried, by whatever means we could employ, to rid our fields of harmful birds, insects, and rodents, and our animals of diseases and parasites. On the other, we have constantly striven to produce healthier and more productive strains of plants and animals. Often, these attempts have been spectacularly successful. Sometimes, though, the results have proved disastrous, as with the insecticide DDT.

(8) Farmers first began using DDT on a large scale in 1946, right after it had proved its effectiveness in tropical military operations in World War II. As expected, the product proved equally effective as an agricultural pesticide, but there were some unexpected and disastrous side effects. The difficulties were caused by excessive DDT washing off crops, entering irrigation canals, and from there flowing to streams, rivers and lakes. All living creatures in the path of the chemical were contaminated—worms, fish, ducks, indeed all forms of aquatic life. Contaminated worms poisoned songbirds, causing massive dieoffs of birds and many humans developed serious health problems from eating contaminated aquatic animals. Although Congress has severely restricted the use of DDT in the country, the whole episode stands as a warning of what can happen when humans attempt to manipulate the food chain.

(9) As time continues and the population grows, efforts will be made to further increase the food supply. Let us hope in doing so we won't act in haste and create catastrophes of even greater magnitude.

Michael Galayda

Discussion Questions

1. Identify the formal definition in this essay. Explain how it does what a formal definition should do.
2. What method does the writer use to develop the definition in paragraph 2?
3. How is the definition developed in paragraphs 3–5?
4. Locate three places in the essay where the writer uses brief definitions.

Voiceprints

(1) A voiceprint is a graphic record of an individual's voice characteristics. The graph consists of a complicated pattern of wavy lines. As is true of fingerprints, no two voiceprints are alike.

(2) A voiceprint is made by using a sound spectrograph, an instrument that records the energy patterns of the spoken word. Voice readings are affected by such physiological characteristics as the configuration of the lower respiratory tract and the contours of the vocal cavities, as well as by the movements of the vocal cords, lips, and tongue. These factors, taken together, make each voiceprint unique. To obtain a voiceprint, the subject speaks into a microphone, and the voice is recorded on a magnetic tape. This tape runs around a cylindrical drum, where an electronic scanning device picks up the information. A pen then records the information on paper as a graph.

(3) The medical profession has utilized voiceprints in a number of studies. One study, reported in the March 1974 issue of *Scientific American*, investigated the cries of infants. The findings showed that a distress cry is louder, longer, and noisier than a hunger cry and tends to be irregular, with more interruptions and gagging. This same study also showed that abnormal cry characteristics appear to be associated with certain physical defects. In one instance the research-ers discovered that an apparently normal infant with an especially shrill cry had no cerebral cortex. Generally, abnormal infants had higher-pitched cries than those with no physical impairment. These findings suggest that voiceprints may have value as a diagnostic tool.

(4) Diagnosing infant problems is not the only medical use of voiceprints. Psychiatrists have used them to determine emotional stress in patients, and they have aided surgeons in repairing cleft palates.

(5) Law enforcement agencies rely heavily on voiceprints to identify bomb hoaxers, individuals making obscene phone calls, and other persons using telephones for illegal purposes. A voiceprint is taken during the phone call, held until a suspect has been appre-hended, and then compared with the suspect's voiceprint. This tech-nique has helepd the police obtain numerous convictions.

(6) The use of voiceprints in criminal proceedings has not been without controversy and setbacks, however. In a number of in-stances, appeals courts have reversed convictions obtained through use of voiceprints, holding that prints were unreliable. Also, some early studies showed that the percentage of voiceprints mistakenly identified could range as high as 63 percent, thus raising serious doubts about the validity of voiceprints as evidence. More recently, though, (see the January 10, 1972, issue of *Time* magazine) a massive study comparing 34,000 voiceprints has led to the conclusion that they do constitute a reliable means of identification.

(7) With this type of comprehensive evidence, the use of voice-prints in medicine and the courts seems assured for some time to come.

Terri Chapman

Discussion Questions

1. Identify the formal definition in paragraph 1.
2. What is the primary method of development in paragraph 2?
3. What method of development does the writer use in paragraphs 3–5?
4. What does paragraph 6 contribute to the definition?

What Is Cancer Chemotherapy?

(1) Chemotherapy means treatment of a disease by the use of drugs. In this case, the disease is cancer. Chemotherapy has been used in one form or another in the treatment of cancer for the past twenty-five years. In the last twenty years great strides have been made in discovering new drugs and new combinations of old drugs to control or produce a halt in the progression of the disease.

(2) The first type to be controlled, not cured, was leukemia; the knowledge gained there has been applied to many other forms of cancer.

(3) When a new chemotherapy drug is discovered, it is first used in experiments on animals to discover possible harmful effects. It is then subjected to a rigid series of tests in highly controlled situations to discover the most effective doses and schedules of administration that will work best for the destruction of cancer cells without harming normal tissue. The new drug is then approved by the Federal Drug Administration for general use. From the time a new drug is discovered until it is in general use may be from one to four years.

(4) These controls are necessary so that no one will suffer from improper use of a drug. The drug or drugs the doctor prescribes have gone through all these steps and have been used before with good results. A doctor would not give them unless he or she felt there was a good chance of that particular cancer responding to treatment. A doctor is the best judge of what drug, if any, is best to use in a particular situation, for only he or she is thoroughly familiar with the patient and his state of health.

(5) **Use of Chemotherapy.** As you are probably aware, chemotherapy is only one method of treating cancer. It may be used alone, or in conjunction with surgery or radiation. Formerly chemotherapy was used only after all else had failed. This is not true today. In some cases, chemotherapy is the treatment of choice and is considered curative in a few less common cancers. In others, chemotherapy may keep the cancer under control for months or even years. Some may not be benefited at all by chemotherapy. Again, only the doctor can decide how best to treat the cancer patient.

(6) **Effects of Chemotherapy.** Many different drugs may be used in chemotherapy. These drugs work by several different methods, but in general they prevent the cells from reproducing. Sometimes a cancer cell may become resistant to one drug, much as a germ can become resistant to penicillin. If this happens, the doctor can switch to a different medication or to a combination of drugs.

(7) Though the drugs are of different composition and may be given differently, they have some possible side effects in common. Some that may occur are loss of appetite, tiredness, nausea, vomiting, diarrhea, temporary loss of hair, and suppression of bone marrow function. The bone marrow produces blood cells. Periodic blood tests are given persons receiving chemotherapy to be sure that their blood is being produced in adequate amounts. Occasionally, sores may develop in the mouth or on the lips.

(8) Chemotherapy drugs affect rapidly dividing cells, and the cells of the hair follicles, mouth, skin, stomach, intestines and bone marow are rapidly dividing cells, so they are also affected. This is why side effects may appear. Nausea and vomiting may be controlled by other drugs. If any symptom becomes too severe, the chemotherapy drugs may be stopped and resumed later, or another drug might be substituted. These symptoms are only temporary and will clear up when the medicine is stopped. Many fortunate patients go through a complete course of treatment with no side effects at all. This does not mean that the drug is not working. The appearance or intensity of side effects has no bearing on how effective the drug will be in treating the cancer. It seems to be a matter of individual tolerance and tumor response.

(9) **How Is Chemotherapy Given?** Chemotherapy drugs can be given in several ways. They may be applied as an ointment or lotion as in skin cancer, taken by mouth, or given as an injection into the muscle or vein. They are usually given for several days in succession,

followed by a period of rest, then given again. This is one way that has been found to be effective against cancer without damaging the normal cells.

(10) Medication is usually given either in the hospital, the doctor's office, or at the outpatient clinic of a hospital. A doctor or a specially trained nurse will administer the medication.

(11) **Precautions.** Resistance to infections may be lowered during chemotherapy treatment. Therefore, patients should avoid people with colds or other infections. Unless the treatment is accompanied by severe side effects, patients can usually continue their normal activities, including sexual relations. Unless the doctor states otherwise, there are no special foods that should be eaten, nor are there any to avoid. No medications, including vitamins, aspirins, and birth control pills should be taken unless approved or prescribed by the doctor.

(12) Chemotherapy is something about which the patient will ask many questions: Will it work? Will I get sick? How will this affect my mate and/or my family? Should I practice birth control? What kind of contraception should I use? Patients should discuss these questions frankly and thoroughly with their doctors.

American Cancer Society

Discussion Questions

1. What reason can you give for the use of headings in this section?
2. By what writing method is paragraph 3 developed? Explain your answer.
3. Point out evidence that the writeup is addressed to a general audience.

The Bureaucrat

(1) Bureaucracy is a state of mind. True, every bureaucrat needs an organization, a milieu—to choose another useful word from the French—but it is the bureaucrat who makes the milieu, not the other way around.

(2) Most of us associate bureaucracy and all its attendant evils with large organizations, especially governments, and we are not surprised to see it getting worse. As the earth's population grows and computers multiply along with the people, burgeoning bureaucracy appears a natural consequence. What Thomas Carlyle, a hundred

years ago, could dismiss contemptuously as "the Continental nuisance called 'Bureaucracy'" is now to become the fate of all humanity simply because there are so many of us.

(3) Before resigning ourselves to the inevitable, however, we might pause to consider that one of the most pervasive bureaucracies the world has ever known was oppressing the population of the Nile Valley 5,000 years ago, when there were fewer people in the entire world than now live in North America. Add to this the thought that the same number of people can be organized into (a) an army, (b) a crowd or (c) a mob, and it is clear that something more must be involved than time and numbers.

(4) What distinguishes each of the aforementioned groups is not how many people it contains, nor where they happen to congregate, but their purpose for being there. And so it is with the bureaucrat.

(5) The true bureaucrat is any individual who has lost sight of the underlying purpose of the job at hand, whether in government, industry—or a bank. The purpose of a library, for example, is to facilitate the reading of books. Yet to a certain type of librarian, perfection consists of a well-stocked library with a place for every book—and every book in its place. The reader who insists on taking books home, leaving empty spaces on shelves, is this librarian's natural enemy.

(6) It is a cast of mind invulnerable even to the vicissitudes of war. We see it in James Jones's novel *From Here to Eternity* when American soldiers under surprise attack by Japanese planes at the outbreak of World War II rush to the arsenal for weapons, only to find the door barred by a comrade-in-arms loudly proclaiming that he cannot pass out live ammunition without a written request signed by a commissioned officer.

(7) One of these custodians forgot the purpose of a library, the other, the purpose of an army. Both illustrate how, in institutionalized endeavors, means have a way of displacing the ends they are originally designed to serve. In fact, it is one of the bureaucrat's distinguishing features that, for him or for her, the means *become* the ends.

(8) The struggle to prevent this subtle subversion is—or should be—a continual challenge to every policy maker in any organization, public or private. Bureaucrats love any policy and can be counted on to enforce it faithfully, as in, "I'm sorry, but that's the policy here." Unfortunately, they don't understand what a policy is.

(9) A policy is a standard solution to a constantly recurring problem, not an inviolable law. As a weapon in the hands of a literal-minded people, however, a "firm policy" can be as deadly as a repeating rifle. When matters finally become intolerable, the harassed administrator will usually "change the policy." Of course, this never helps because the problem was not the policy in the first place, but the manner of its application.

(10) Every college student seeking entry into a course for which he lacks the exact prerequisite, every shopper trying to return a gift without receipt of purchase, every bank customer seeking to correct an error in an account is in danger of discovering that the rules imagined by Joseph Heller are in service wherever rote is more revered than reason.

(11) The application of binary logic to human affairs through electronic computers has done nothing to retard the spread of *Catch 22* into the wider world. And thus the thought occurs that modern bureaucracy does, after all, present some problems new to history. Nothing lends itself so readily to "a standard solution to a constantly recurring problem" as a computer.

(12) In the best of all possible worlds we might look forward to the day when computers handle all standard solutions, freeing human brains to concentrate on the singular and the exceptional. In the real world, it does not always work out that way—as anyone knows who has ever become trapped in a two-way correspondence with a computer and appealed in vain for human intervention.

(13) A favorite student protest sign of the sixties read, "I am a Human Being. Do not fold, spindle or mutilate." What they objected to is real, only the fault is not in our computers, but in ourselves. It lies in our human propensity to let means become ends, and all too often to resemble Santayana's description of a fanatic: one who, having forgotten his purpose, redoubles his efforts.

(14) We can denounce the bureaucrats and condemn their works, but they will not go away. They have been with us since the dawn of history, and if they seem to be getting worse, it is because *we* are getting worse. For, in the words of the comic strip *Pogo:* "We has met the enemy, and they is us."

(15) Bureaucracy is a state of mind, and the best way to fight it—whether you work for government, industry, a private foundation or a bank—is not to be a bureaucrat. Or at least try not to.

Citicorp Publications

Discussion Questions

1. In what paragraph does the formal definition of bureaucrat appear? How does the definition relate to the opening statements in paragraphs 1 and 15? Locate the formal definition of *policy.*
2. What method of writing is used to develop paragraph 3? Paragraphs 5 and 6?
3. What seems to be the purpose of this piece of writing? Use references to the text to explain your answer.
4. To whom do you think the essay is addressed? Cite examples from the text to defend your answer.

Suggestions for Writing

Write an extended definition, using one of the suggestions here or a term approved by your instructor. You might select and define a word that has a special meaning for you. Expand your definition by any combination of the methods discussed in this chapter. Make sure that your essay includes a formal definition.

1. Salesmanship	19. Fashion design
2. Worker alienation	20. Retailing
3. Radiation	21. Isometric exercises
4. The "grease monkey"	22. Central processing unit
5. Evidence	23. Drag race
6. The secretary	24. Preventive dentistry
7. The boss	25. Restorative dentistry
8. The client or customer	26. Microcomputer
	27. The nerd
9. Routine	28. Courage
10. Stress	29. Auditing
11. Water table	30. Success
12. Erosion	31. Leader pricing
13. Viscosity	32. Vocational education
14. Handgun	33. The nurse
15. The police officer	34. Pitch
16. Hospitality	35. Some term from your field of study or occupation
17. Nutrition	
18. Refrigeration	

7

Description

There are two basic forms of description: impressionistic and objective. Impressionistic description appeals to the emotions by creating a vivid word picture of a person, scene, event, object, or situation. It can convey sensory impressions—impressions received through the five basic senses of sight, hearing, touch, taste, and smell. It can also re-create a mood—a particular state of mind or feeling that emerges through observation of the subject.

Objective description, the type with which this chapter deals, conveys factual information as clearly as possible. Its purpose is to present a factual image to the reader, and it focuses on details that can be measured and verified, rather than on impressions or emotional responses.

As a student, as well as on the job, you may often find it necessary to write an objective description. An instructor might ask you to describe a T-square, a surveyor's range pole, or something that you have examined under the microscope—a fly's wing, a white blood cell, or a section of leaf tissue. Your employer might call on you to describe a newly developed device for the shop or factory; a floor plan, a heating system, or a new report form. All such descriptions should follow a similar pattern of development.

To write successful descriptions, you must be thoroughly familiar with whatever you are describing. If it is a device that can be taken apart and put together, do so—preferably several times. Learn and use the proper names for the different parts. Finally, have the device on hand so you can check it while you are writing.

A typical objective description has three parts:

1. introduction
2. description of major components or functional parts
3. conclusion

These parts are discussed in the sections that follow.

Introduction

The introduction, generally one paragraph long, does three things:

1. defines whatever is being described
2. provides an overall description
3. lists the major components or functional parts

DEFINITION

The heart of the introduction is a one-sentence formal definition, which serves as the thesis statement. As we noted on page 95, a formal definition names whatever is being defined, places it in a larger category, and tells how it differs from other things in that category. A zipper, for example, might be defined in this manner:

> A zipper is a fastener made up of two rows of metal or plastic teeth that are meshed and separated by a slide.

This sentence shows that the zipper falls into the larger category of fasteners but differs from other fasteners—snaps, hooks, or buttons—in appearance and method of operation.

If the definition doesn't make the function clear, add a sentence or two of explanation. The function of a zipper might be explained as follows:

> It is used to fasten or unfasten adjacent pieces of fabric, as in garments and tents.

Follow the guidelines on pages 93–100 when you prepare your definition.

OVERALL DESCRIPTION

In writing this part of the introduction, be sure to consider every important feature of the item, such as its dimensions, shape, color, weight, texture or materials of construction. The features that are important will, of course, vary depending upon what you are describing. If you are describing a diode, for example, weight will probably not be important. However, weight is an important feature of a portable humidifier and should not be ignored.

Some descriptions are *general* (garden trowels, wire cutters) while others are *specific* (the Acme Model 41 garden trowel, the Snipwell Model R–2 wire cutter). When you describe a *specific* model of a device and include dimensions and weight, you must give them exactly. Thus, if you describe the Snipwell Model R–2 wire cutter, you must give the exact overall length of that model. If, on the other hand, your topic is wire cutters in general, a range of lengths is all you need provide.

You can often make a description clearer by comparing the shape of the object to that of something familiar. For example, an overall description of a new building might note that it has an H-shaped floor plan. Similarly, a light bulb might be likened in shape and size to a pear.

LIST OF COMPONENTS OR PARTS

List the components or functional parts in a sentence or two, and number them if there are more than three. Various logical arrangements are possible, depending upon what you are describing. If, for example, it is a TV broadcasting tower, you might start from the top and work down or vice versa. If you are describing some type of report, such as the annual reports that companies issue to stockholders, you might start with the first part and end with the last. For a device with several parts that operate one after the other, you might list them according to their order of operation. If the actual function is performed by just one part, you might list that part first. If some parts are concealed from view, you might first list the external parts and then the internal parts. The introduction below follows the typical pattern.

A dental mouth mirror is an instrument used by dentists, dental hygienists, and dental assistants to look inside the mouth and view the patient's teeth. The mirror makes it possible to see tooth surfaces in areas of the mouth that are beyond the range of direct vision. In addition to providing a view, it serves as a useful retractor of the patient's cheeks and tongue. The glass and metal instrument consists of two major parts, the mirror and the handle, and resembles a coin (the mirror) with a rod (the handle) welded at an oblique angle to the edge.

Description of Major Components or Functional Parts

When you write this section of the description, discuss the parts in the same order that you listed them in the introductory paragraph. Unless the information is obvious, explain the purpose of each part and then note whatever features will be important or interesting to your reader. The amount of detail needed will depend upon your audience and purpose. For instance, a description written to guide draftsmen in preparing drawings or diemakers in constructing dies would require detailed discussions of shapes, dimensions, wall thicknesses, and the sizes and locations of openings. A description intended to familiarize readers only with components, but not their functions, would require less detail.

Besides describing the components or functional parts, you must clarify their positions or locations. Often, you will also need to describe exactly how the parts are joined together. For instance, if you are preparing an engineering description of a T-square, it is not enough to note that the blade is centered on the head at right angles to it. You must also indicate the amount of overlap, whether or not the blade is set into the head, and—if it is—the depth of the inset.

Here is a description of the handle of a dental mouth mirror. Notice how carefully the writer has analyzed and described major features, omitting only the handle's purpose, which is obvious.

The handle is connected to the mirror by a small screw which extends ½ inch from the edge of the metal rim around the mirror and is set at an angle to the plane of the mirror. This screw threads into a socket in the end of the handle. The thick part of the handle is called the shank. It is approximately 2¼ inches in length, with a diameter of ¼ inch. The thinner portion is 2 $^{11}/_{16}$ inches long and has a diameter of ⅛ inch. The handle is made of brushed aluminum or steel.

In most cases, each part is discussed in a single, separate paragraph. However, for a complicated part that consists of more than one element, you may need two or more paragraphs. Similarly, if two parts are relatively simple, you may discuss them both in just one paragraph.

Illustrations

A drawing or photograph of the object or one or more of its parts often accompanies the description. An illustration allows you to write a shorter description and at the same time to convey a more precise impression of the device to your reader. Consider, for instance, how difficult it would be to create an accurate word-picture of a scissors or the head of a claw hammer. With a drawing or photo, conveying this image would not be a problem. Illustrations do not, however, adequately indicate the materials of construction, finish, or use of the device. These you must make clear in your written description.

Whenever you use an illustration, refer to it at the appropriate point in your description. (Illustrations are discussed in detail in Chapter 15.)

Conclusion

The conclusion of your paper, usually one paragraph long, can present several kinds of information. One common way to end is to tell the reader how to use the device. For example, a description of a dental mouth mirror might conclude with an explanation of the mirror's use.

Held with a modified pen grasp and inserted into the mouth, the dental mouth mirror is used to detect cavities and obtain a general idea of the patient's dental needs. It provides immeasurable assistance in detecting stains and deposits on the teeth as well as in locating spots of decay.

Lisa Hines

Another kind of conclusion explains how a device operates. This is especially appropriate for a mechanism in which some or all of the functional parts are concealed from view. The following conclusion tells how a tip-up for ice fishing operates.

> When a fish strikes the bait, line pulls off the spool, rotating the flag trip mechanism. This rotation releases the flag trip, allowing the flag to spring into the air. The person fishing sees the flag and knows that he or she has a strike.
>
> *Marty Jastrzembowski*

Still another effective conclusion—one suitable both for descriptions of devices and other kinds of items—emphasizes a particular advantage or feature of whatever is being described. For instance, if you are describing a new model of some machine, your conclusion may note that it is more powerful, efficient, or economical than earlier models. Or if you are describing a new kind of recordkeeping form, the conclusion might discuss the added efficiency it provides.

EXAMPLES OF DESCRIPTION

Imhoff Cone

(1) The Imhoff cone is a measuring device which determines the total amount of settleable solids in one liter of sewage. The sewage sample is placed in the cone and then left undisturbed for one hour, during which time the settleable solids fall to the bottom and can be measured. The device has an overall height of 23 inches, is made of cast iron and Pyrex, and weighs about 5 pounds. It consists of two functional parts: the metal support stand and the cone itself. The accompanying figure illustrates the assembled device.

(2) The support stand has a rectangular cast iron base 10 inches long, 6 inches wide, and 1 inch thick. Inserted into the base, equidistant from each side and 2 inches from the end, is a ½-inch solid steel rod which extends 22 inches vertically. Two inches below the top of this rod and extending over the base is a horizontal steel rod 2 inches in length which terminates in a circular steel loop with an inner diameter of 4½ inches. The support stand weighs 4 pounds.

IMHOFF CONE AND SUPPORT STAND
Scale — 1¼″ = 1″

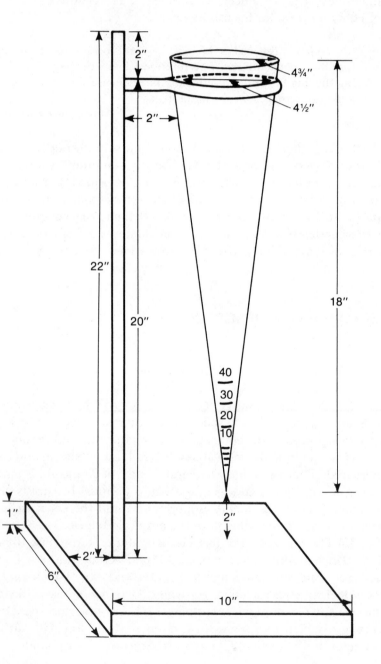

(3) The cone weighs 14 ounces, is 18 inches in height, and is made of clear Pyrex. It resembles an empty ice-cream cone. The opening at the top is 4¾ inches in diameter, and 1 inch below this opening a horizontal line has been etched into the glass. When the cone is filled to this mark, it contains one liter of sewage sample. At the pointed end is a graduated scale made up of forty units, with every tenth unit indicated by a numeral. This scale indicates, in milliliters, the volume of the solids that have settled.

(4) When the cone is filled with one liter of sewage, the settleable solids will sink to the pointed end. The total amount of settleable solids per liter of sewage can be determined by reading the scale. This information allows the sewage treatment operator to determine how effectively the plant is removing solids from sewage.

Philip Boesenecker

Discussion Questions

1. Identify the definition sentence in paragraph 1 and indicate what it accomplishes.
2. Indicate the purpose of this sentence in paragraph 3: "It resembles an empty ice-cream cone."
3. What purpose does the final sentence of the paper serve?

Sun Portable Vacuum-Pressure Tester

(1) The Sun Vacuum-Pressure Tester, Model VPT-212, is a testing device for checking the manifold vacuum and the fuel pump pressure of automobiles. The tester weighs 2.5 pounds, stands 9 inches tall, is 5 inches wide, and is made primarily from stamped steel. Its main parts, besides the case, include (1) an indicator dial, (2) a rubber-hose connection, (3) a damper valve, and (4) a sensing unit. Figure 1 shows a cutaway view of the tester.

(2) The 3¾-inch dial indicator occupies the upper center part of the front. This dial has two scales. The upper, or vacuum, scale, which is graduated from 0 to 22 inches, records the inches of vacuum. The lower, or pressure, scale, graduated from 0 to 7 inches, records inches of pressure. The dial and its needle are protected by a glass face held securely by a metal rim.

Figure 1.   SUN VACUUM-PRESSURE TESTER

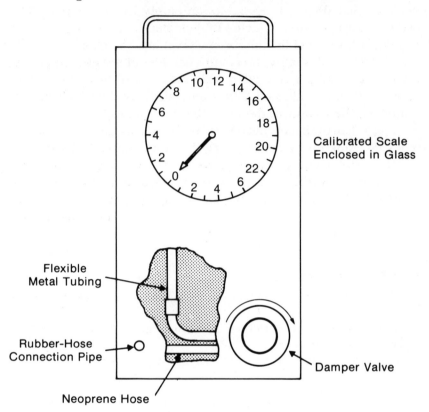

Figure 2.   ARRANGEMENT OF VACUUM-PRESSURE TUBE AND PIVOT DEVICE

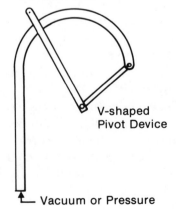

(3) The cylindrical rubber-hose connection is mounted in the lower left-hand corner of the front. This connection, ⅜ inch in diameter and protruding ½ inch, is used to connect the tester to the engine's intake manifold. The 1½-inch damper valve knob extends from the lower right-hand corner and is used to slow the back-and-forth swings of the indicator needle when a pressure reading is taken.

(4) The sensing unit, located inside the case, consists of a vacuum-pressure tube, a pivot device, and a hose. The vacuum-pressure tube is made from thin, flexible metal tubing and resembles the crooked end of a walking cane. One end of the V-shaped pivot device is connected to the top of the vacuum tube and the other to the base of the indicator needle. Figure 2 illustrates this arrangement. Attached to the lower end of the vacuum tube is a neoprene hose, which is fastened at its other end to the interior opening of the cylindrical hose connection. This hose passes through a clamp arrangement at the rear of the damper valve knob. Turning the knob pinches the hose and slows the swings of the needle.

(5) Connecting the tester with a rubber hose to the intake manifold of a running engine creates a partial vacuum in the hose and vacuum-pressing tube. This causes the tube to bend in a clockwise direction, activating the pivot device and allowing the amount of vacuum to be read on the upper scale. When the tester is connected to the fuel line, the tube bends counterclockwise, and pressure is shown on the lower scale.

(6) The amount of vacuum or pressure and the behavior of the needle can be used to diagnose a number of engine conditions. For example, at idling speeds a 15- to 22-inch vacuum and steady needle indicate that the engine is in good operating condition. If, however, the needle occasionally flicks rapidly down and back 4 inches, the engine has one or more sticky valves. A low, steady reading indicates a vacuum leak, and a slightly low, steady reading indicates a retarded ignition. An excessively low pressure reading (for most models of cars 2–4 pounds is normal) indicates a worn fuel pump, whereas an excessively high pressure reading indicates that the pump diaphragm is too tight.

Peter Cataldo

Discussion Questions

1. In what ways does the introduction to this paper meet the requirements discussed at the beginning of this chapter?

2. Paragraph 2 tells where the dial indicator is located, and paragraph 3 notes the location of the hose connection. However, neither tells how these parts are fastened to the case. How do you account for this omission?
3. Indicate the purpose of these phrases in paragraph 4: "resembles the crooked end of a walking cane" and "the V-shaped pivot device."

Clutch Pencil

(1) The clutch pencil is a draftsman's tool that holds drawing lead. It is designed to feed the lead when a release button is pressed. In overall appearance, the pencil resembles an ordinary ballpoint pen. It is constructed of plastic, brass, and steel. The components of the clutch pencil are (1) the barrel, (2) the plunger, (3) the tip, (4) the chunk, (5) the spring, and (6) the release button. The accompanying exploded-view drawing shows these components.

(2) The barrel, or main housing, is a hexagonal, pressure-molded plastic tube, which is $4\frac{3}{8}$ inches long and $\frac{11}{32}$ inch wide between opposite surfaces. One end is rounded and externally threaded for a distance of $\frac{7}{16}$ inch. The barrel is bored from the unthreaded end to a diameter of $\frac{9}{32}$ inch and to a depth of $3\frac{1}{4}$ inches. The remainder of the barrel, which constitutes the round section, is bored through to a diameter of $\frac{5}{32}$ inch.

(3) The plunger is a brass tube $4\frac{1}{2}$ inches long with a .145-inch outside diameter and a .100-inch inside diameter. One end is threaded internally to a depth of $\frac{1}{4}$ inch. Two ferrules of $\frac{1}{4}$–inch diameter and .040–inch thickness are swaged to the outside of the tube. One is $1\frac{1}{4}$ inches from the threaded end and the other is $\frac{1}{2}$ inch from the unthreaded end.

(4) The tip is a tapered brass tube $1\frac{1}{4}$ inches long and $\frac{11}{32}$ inch in diameter at the big end. The outside tapers down to $\frac{5}{16}$ inch over a distance of $\frac{7}{8}$ inch and then tapers to $\frac{1}{4}$ inch at the small end. The $\frac{7}{8}$-inch portion is knurled to provide a grip. The big end of the tip is threaded internally to a depth of $\frac{7}{16}$ inch. There is an internal taper at the small end, which has a large diameter of $\frac{7}{32}$ inch and a depth of $\frac{3}{16}$ inch. The remainder of the tip is drilled through to a $\frac{5}{32}$-inch diameter.

(5) The chuck is a steel tube of $\frac{7}{8}$ inch long which is split into three fingers along $\frac{5}{8}$-inch diameter and increasing to a $\frac{7}{32}$-inch

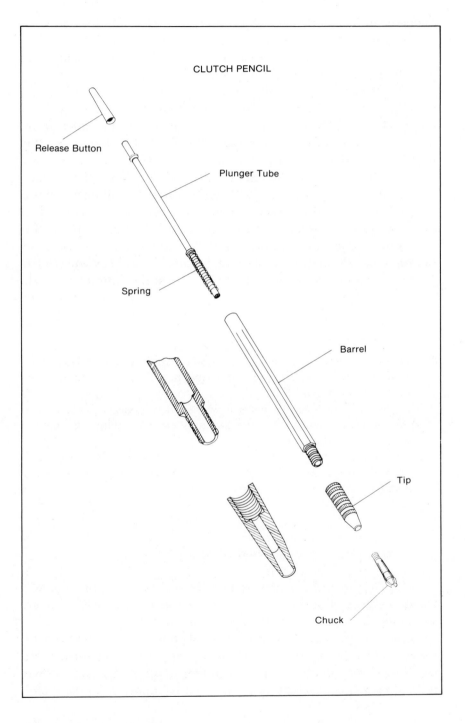

CLUTCH PENCIL

Release Button

Plunger Tube

Spring

Barrel

Tip

Chuck

diameter in $^5/_{32}$ inch of its length and then returning to a $^1/_8$-inch diameter in another $^5/_{32}$ inch of length. The remainder of the chuck is $^1/_8$ inch in diameter and is threaded for $^3/_{16}$ inch on the unsplit end. The chuck is bored through to a .080-inch diameter.

(6) The spring is #8-gauge music wire, has an outside diameter of $^1/_4$ inch, 13 coils and a free length of 1 inch. The release button is made of brass and is chrome plated. It is $^7/_8$ inch long and tapers from a $^1/_4$-inch diameter to a $^3/_{16}$-inch diameter. The button is bored on the large end to a diameter of .145 inch and a depth of $^5/_8$ inch.

(7) The clutch pencil is assembled as follows. Screw the tip onto the barrel, fit the spring over the threaded end of the plunger and the button over the unthreaded end until they rest against the ferrules, insert the plunger and spring into the top of the barrel, insert the small threaded end of the chuck into the tip, and while depressing the button, screw the chuck into the plunger tube. The chuck will release to grip a piece of drafting lead inserted into it as the button is pressed.

Alice Ludo

Discussion Questions

1. The writer gives the overall description of this device in a single sentence but uses five paragraphs to describe the individual parts. Explain this difference in length.
2. Paragraph 6 discusses two parts of the pencil whereas in paragraphs 2 through 5, each paragraph discusses only one part. How do you account for this difference?
3. Paragraph 7 details with assembling the pencil, a topic not ordinarily part of the description of an object. Why is assembly discussed in this paper?

Human Skin

(1) The skin is the largest organ of the body. It has approximately 20 square feet of surface area for potential contact with foreign substances in nature and in the industrial environment. It is a multi-functioning organ whose anatomical and physiologic properties subserve protection by regulating body heat, receiving sensations, secreting sweat, manufacturing pigment, and replenishing its own cellular elements. Each of these functions is important in the main-

tenance of a healthy skin, and any deviation from normal can alter the health of the skin and sometimes that of the entire body.

(2) The structure or anatomical design of the skin is protective because of its thickness, resiliency, and the capacity of certain of its layers to inhibit the entrance of water and water-soluble chemicals. Its thickness and elasticity protect the underlying muscles, nerves and blood vessels. Additionally, the thickness and color of the skin afford protection against the effects of sunlight and other sources of physical energy.

(3) Structurally, skin is composed of two layers—the epidermis and the dermis. Epidermis has two essential levels—an outermost stratified layer of horn [keratin] cells called the "stratum corneum" and the inner living cells from which the horn cells arise. Stratum corneum cells are shed, yet replenished continually because the inner living epidermal layer keeps reproducing cells which eventually become stratum corneum cells. In short, the epidermis has its own self-support system. The stratum corneum layer is essential for protection, being thickest on the palms and soles. Chemically, it is a complex protein structure which is relatively resistant to mild acids, to water and water-soluble chemicals; but vulnerable to alkaline agents, strong detergents, desiccant chemicals, and solvents (Figure 1).

(4) In the lowermost region of the epidermal layer are the basal cells from which all of the epidermal cells arise. Nestled within the basal cell layer are melanocytes or pigment-producing cells which furnish protection against ultraviolet radiation. This comes about through a complex enzyme reaction leading to the production of pigment or melanin granules which are engulfed by the epithelial cells which, in turn, migrate to the upper level of the skin and eventually are shed. Melanin serves as a protective screen against sunlight because the granules absorb photons of light. This mechanism occurs naturally throughout the lifetime of an individual. Sunlight and certain chemicals stimulate pigment formation and, at times, its activity can be inhibited.

(5) Dermis is thicker than epidermis and is composed of elastic and collagen tissue which provide the skin with its resiliency. Invested also in the dermis are sweat glands and ducts which deliver sweat to the surface of the skin; hair follicles in which hairs are encased; sebaceous or oil glands which excrete their products through the hair follicle openings on the skin; blood vessels; and nerves.

Figure 1.   DIAGRAM OF THE SKIN'S PROTECTIVE LAYERS

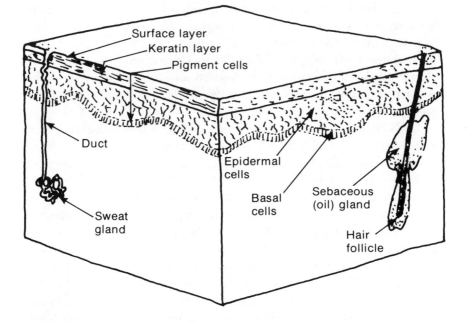

Source: Dermatology Department, Wayne State University, Detroit, Michigan.

(6) Body temperature is regulated by the excretion of sweat, circulation of the blood, and the central nervous system. Blood is maintained at a relatively constant temperature even though the body can be exposed to wide ranges of temperature variations. Sweat facilitates greatly the cooling of the overheated skin surface by evaporation. At the same time, dilation of the blood vessels within the skin also permits heat loss. Conversely, when the body is exposed to severe cold, blood vessels will contract to conserve heat. Nerve endings and fibers present in the skin participate in the receptor and conduction system which allows the individual to differentiate between heat, cold, pain and sense perception. This latter quality allows one to discriminate between dryness or wetness, thickness or thinness, roughness or smoothness, hardness or softness.

(7) Secretory elements within the skin are the sweat glands and the sebaceous glands. Perspiration or sweat contains products from

the body's metabolic function, but 99% of sweat is water. . . . Sebaceous or oil glands . . . manufacture an oily substance called "sebum," whose precise physiologic function is not well-understood. Present in normal amounts, it appears to offer some surface protection to the skin. Over-function of these glands is associated with acne.

(8) Coating the outer surface of the keratin layer is a waxy type of mixture composed of sebum, breakdown products of keratin, and sweat. It is believed that the emulsion-like mixture impedes somewhat the entrance of water and water-soluble chemicals, but its actual protective quality is minimal. It does assist in maintaining the surface pH of the skin, which is normally in the range of 4.5 to 6. Its protective capability is minimized because it is easily removed by soaps, solvents and alkalis. Nonetheless, it is continually replenished under normal conditions and does constitute an extra layer of protection which must be removed before keratin cells can be attacked.

(9) Absorption of materials through the skin occurs when the continuity of the skin is disrupted by an abrasion or a laceration or a puncture. Absorption of fat-soluble chemicals, fats and oils can occur via the hair follicle which contains the hair bulb and a portion of the hair shaft. Some substances as organophosphates are absorbed directly through the intact skin; further, skin permits the ready exchange of gases, except for carbon monoxide. Sweat ducts offer little, if any, avenue for penetration. From the above it is evident that the skin has its own built-in defense mechanism. . . .

> Donald J. Birmingham, "Occupational Dermatoses: Their Recognition, Control and Prevention," in The Industrial Environment—Its Evaluation and Control, U.S. Department of Health, Education, and Welfare (Washington, D.C. 1973), pp. 503–505.

Discussion Questions

1. Paragraphs 1 and 2, the introduction of the description, clearly establish its purpose. What is that purpose?
2. Paragraphs 3 through 8 discuss the two major components of the skin and the subcomponents of each. What are these components and subcomponents? How does the discussion support the purpose of the description?
3. Identify the organizational pattern of this description, and indicate why the writer used this particular pattern.

Suggestions for Writing

Write an objective description of one of the following items or one that your instructor approves. Begin with a definition sentence and an introduction to the item. Then discuss each of its components or functional parts.

1. Auditorium or concert hall
2. Ballpoint pen
3. Baster
4. Bite-wing X-ray film unit
5. Burette
6. Business form (some possibilities include life insurance application form and job application form)
7. Carpenter's level
8. Crescent wrench
9. Disposable safety razor
10. Draftsman's compass
11. Hydrometer
12. Hypodermic syringe
13. Light bulb
14. Overhead projector
15. Phone book
16. Pizza cutter
17. Pressure cooker
18. Putty knife
19. Ripe cantaloupe
20. Screwdriver
21. Sparkplug
22. Sparkplug gapper
23. Surveyor's plumb bob
24. Tire pressure gauge
25. Toaster
26. Tire pump
27. T-square
28. X-ray film cassette

8

Letters and Memorandums

Letters and memorandums are by far the most common types of written communication in almost every career field. They are used for countless purposes but especially to ask questions, provide answers, sell products or services, place orders, register or respond to complaints, and give instructions. Good business correspondence is easily understood, persuasive, and free from language that might cause readers to react unfavorably. Because of these features, letters and memorandums play an important role in creating goodwill and enhancing both your own image and that of your organization.

In this chapter we will discuss the basics of business correspondence and show you how to write the most common types of letters and memorandums.

Basics of Business Letters

LETTER FORMATS

There are three common formats for business letters: modified block (sometimes called balanced block), full block, and AMS (Administrative Management Society) simplified format.

Heading 209 Foster Hall
Case Western Reserve University
Cleveland, OH 44106
November 15, 1981

Mr. Francis C. Rhyte
Assistant Advertising Manager
Mine Safety Appliances Company **Inside Address**
400 Penn Center Boulevard
Pittsburgh, PA 15235

Dear Mr. Rhyte: **Salutation**

Thank you for XXXX XXXXXXXXXXXXXXXX XXX XX XXXXX XXXXXXXXXXXXX
XXXX XX XXXXXXXX XXXXXXXXXX X XXXXXXXX XXX XXXXXXX XXXXXX XXX
XXXXXXXX XXXXXXXXXXXXX XXXXX XXXXXXXX XXXX XXXXXX X XX XXXXXX
XXXXXXXXXXX XXX XXX XXXXXXXXX

I have reviewed XXX XXXX XXXXXXXX XXXX XXXXXX XXXXXXXX XXXX XXXXX
XXXXXX XX XXXXXXXX XX XXXX XX XXXXXXXX XXXXXXXXXXXXX XX XXXXX
XXXX XX XXXXXXXXXXXXX XXXX XXXXXXXXX XX XXXXXXX XXXXXX XXX XXX X **Body**
XXXXXXX XX XXXXXXXXXXX XXXXXXX X XXXX XXXXXXXXXX XX XXXXXXXXXX
XXXXXXXXXX XXXX XX XXXXXXX X XXXXXXX XX XXXXXXXXX XXX XXXXXXXXX
XXXX XXXXXXXXXX XXXX XXXXXX XX XX XXXXXXX XXXXXXXXXXXXXX XXXXXXXX
XXX XXXXXXXX XXXXXXXX XXXX XXXXXXXXXXXXXXXX

When I have XXXXXXXX X XXXX XXXXXX XXXXX XXXXXXXX XX X XXXXXX
XXXX XXXXXX XXXX XXXXXXXXXX XXX XXXXXXXXXX XX XXXX XXX XXXXXXX
XXX XXXXXXXX XX XXXXXXXXX X XXXX XXXXXX XX XXXX XX XXX XXXXXXXX
XXX XXXXX XX XXXXXXXXXX XXXXX XXXXXXX XXXX XXXXXX XXXXX XXXXX
XXXX XXXXXXX XX XXXXX XX X XXXXXXXXXXXXX XX XXXX XXXXX

Your assistance will XXXXXXXXXXX XXXXXX XX XXXXXX XX XX XXXXXXXXX
XXX XXXXXXXXXXXXXXX XX XXX XXXX XXX XXXXXXXXXXXXXXXXXX XXXXX
XXXXXXXX

   Sincerely yours, **Complimentary Close**

   Paul M. Leonelli **Signature**

   Paul M. Leonelli

MODIFIED BLOCK FORMAT

209 Foster Hall
Case Western Reserve University   **Heading**
Cleveland, OH 44106
November 15, 1981

Mr. Francis C. Rhyte
Assistant Advertising Manager
Mine Safety Appliances Company   **Inside Address**
400 Penn Center Boulevard
Pittsburgh, PA 15235

Dear Mr. Rhyte: **Salutation**

Thank you for XXXX XXXXXXXXXXXXX XXX XX XXXXX XXXXXXXXXXXXX XXX
XXXX XX XXXXXXXX XXXXXXXXXX X XXXXXXX XXX XXXXXXXX XXXXXX XXX
XXXXXXXX XXXXXXXXXXXXX XXXXXXX XXXXXXXX XXXX XXXXXX X XX XXXXXX
XXXXXXXXXXX XXX XXX XXXXXXXXX

I have reviewed XXX XXXX XXXXXXXX XXXX XXXXX XXXXXXXX XXXX XXXXX
XXXXXX XX XXXXXXXXXXXXX XXXX XXXXXXXXXX XX XXXXXXXXXXXXXX XX XXXX
XXXX XX XXXXXXXXXXXXX XXXX XXXXXXXXX XX XXXXXXX XXXXXX XXX XXX X
XXXXXX XX XXXXXXXXX XXXXXXX X XXXX XXXXXXXXXX XX XXXXXXXXX
XXXXXXXXX XXXX XX XXXXXX X XXXXXXX XX XXXXXXXXXX XXX XXXXXXXXXX   **Body**
XXXX XXXXXXXXXX XXXX XXXXXX XX XX XXXXXXX XXXXXXXXXXXXXX XXXXXXXX
XXX XXXXXXX XXXXXXX XXXX XXXXXXXXXX

When I have XXXXXXXX X XXXX XXXXXX XXXXX XXXXXXXX XX X XXXXXX
XXXX XXXXXX XXXX XXXXXXXXXXXX XXX XXXXXXXXXX XX XXXX XXX XXXXXXX
XXX XXXXXXXX XX XXXXXXXXX X XXXX XXXXXX XX XXXX XX XXX XXXXXXXX
XXX XXXXX XX XXXXXXXXXXX XXXXX XXXXXXXX XXXX XXXXXX XXXXXX XXXXXX
XXXX XXXXXXX XX XXXXX XX X XXXXXXXXXXXXXX XX XXXX XXXXX

Your assistance will XXXXXXXXXX XXXXXX XX XXXXXX XX XX XXXXXXXXXX
XXX XXXXXXXXXXXXXXX XX XXX XXXX XXX XXXXXXXXXXXXXXXX XXXXX
XXXXXXX

Sincerely yours,   **Complimentary Close**

Paul M. Leonelli **Signature**

Paul M. Leonelli Signature

FULL BLOCK FORMAT

```
209 Foster Hall
Case Western Reserve University        Heading
Cleveland, OH  44106
November 15, 1981


Mr. Francis C. Rhyte
Assistant Advertising Manager
Mine Safety Appliances Company         Inside Address
400 Penn Center Boulevard
Pittsburgh, PA  15235


REVIEW OF DATA ON NEW RESPIRATOR       Salutation


Thank you, Mr. Rhyte, for XXXX XXXXXXXXXXXXX XXX XX XXXXX XXXXXXX
XXXX XX XXXXXXXX XXXXXXXXXX X XXXXXXXX XXX XXXXXXXX XXXXXX XXX
XXXXXXXX XXXXXXXXXXXXXX XXXXXXX XXXXXXXX XXXX XXXXX X XX XXXXXX
XXXXXXXXXX XXX XXX XXXXXXXXX

I have reviewed XXX XXXX XXXXXXXX XXXX XXXXXX XXXXXXXX XXXX XXXXX
XXXXXX XX XXXXXXXX XX XXXX XX XXXXXXXX XXXXXXXXXXXXXX XX XXXXX
XXXX XX XXXXXXXXXXXXXX XXXX XXXXXXXXXX XX XXXXXXX XXXXXX XXX XXX X
XXXXXX XX XXXXXXXXXX XXXXXXX X XXXX XXXXXXXXXX XX XXXXXXXXXX
XXXXXXXXX XXXX XX XXXXX XXXXXX XX XXXXXXXXX XXX XXXXXXXXXXXX   Body
XXXX XXXXXXXXX XXXX XXXXX XX XX XXXXXXX XXXXXXXXXXXXX XXXXXXXXX
XXX XXXXXXX XXXXXXX XXXX XXXXXXXXXXXX

When I have XXXXXXXX X XXXX XXXXXX XXXXX XXXXXXXX XX X XXXXXX
XXXX XXXXXX XXXX XXXXXXXXXXXX XXX XXXXXXXXX XX XXXX XXX XXXXXXX
XXX XXXXXXXX XX XXXXXXXXX X XXXX XXXXXX XX XXXX XX XXX XXXXXXXX
XXX XXXXX XX XXXXXXXXXX XXXXX XXXXXXXX XXXX XXXXXXX XXXXXX XXXXXX
XXXX XXXXXXX XX XXXXX XX X XXXXXXXX XXXX XX XXXX XXXXX

Your assistance will XXXXXXXXXX XXXXX XX XXXXXX XX XX XXXXXXXXXX
XXX XXXXXXXXXXXXXXX XX XXX XXXX XX XXXXXXXXXXXXXXXXX XXXXX
XXXXXXXX


Paul M. Leonelli   Signature
```

AMS SIMPLIFIED FORMAT

In the *modified block format*, the heading, the complimentary close, and the signature start at the center of the page. All other elements, including first lines of paragraphs, begin at the left-hand margin. With the *full block format*, every line begins at the left-hand margin. This format can be typed more quickly than the others, but, unless balanced by a properly designed letterhead, the letters sometimes appear lopsided. The *AMS simplified format* follows the full block format but omits the salutation and complimentary close. To add a personal appeal to the letters, the recipient's name is included in the first paragraph. In place of the salutation, there is a subject line typed in capital letters without the word *Subject* and positioned three spaces below the inside address. The typed signature is also all capital letters. It is positioned four spaces below the last line of the body. The pattern letters on pages 128–130 show these three formats.

PARTS OF THE LETTER

The business letter has six basic parts:

1. heading
2. inside address
3. salutation
4. body
5. complimentary close
6. signature

In addition, a letter may include one or more of the following: attention line, subject line, stenographic reference, enclosure notation, and concurrent copy notation. If a letter is longer than a single page, a special heading is required for each additional page (see page 138).

Heading. If you are typing a letter on plain white stationery, the heading consists of your address—street, city, state, and zip code— and the date. Use the two-letter U.S. Postal Service abbreviation for the state (see page 140) but spell out every other word in the heading including the name of the month. Here is a typical typed heading:

325 South Bond Street
Los Angeles, CA 90020
October 6, 1981

The position of the heading depends on the format you are following: in the modified block format, it begins at the center of the page; in the full block and AMS simplified format, it begins at the left-hand margin.

Business letters often are not written on plain white stationery, however, but on company letterheads. Letterhead stationery is printed with the organization's name and address. Letterheads are arranged in a great variety of ways and may include decorative type, illustrations, or the like. When you use letterhead stationery, the only part of the heading that you have to type is the date. This is positioned, depending on the format you are using, at the left-hand margin or indented to begin at the center of the page, two or three lines below the preprinted address.

Inside Address. The inside address gives the name and address of the organization or person to whom you are writing. The position of the inside address is the same for all three formats. It begins at the left-hand margin, two line spaces below the date in long letters and three to eight line spaces in shorter ones. The shorter the letter, the more space you use.

When writing to an individual, give his or her personal title and full name in the first line.

Mr. Harold L. Calloway
Professor Morris Berger
Miss Jane Fontaine
Mrs. Myra R. McPhail
Ms. Noreen Wyman

"Ms." is an accepted title of address for both married and single women. Unless you know that a woman uses "Miss" or "Mrs." as a personal title, you should address her as "Ms." For abbreviations of personal titles, see "Abbreviations" in the appendix.

The individual's job title, if there is one, should follow the name. It may appear on the same line as the name or one line below it.

Ms. Noreen Wyman, Comptroller

Mr. Harold L. Calloway
Personnel Manager

If you know the job title but not the name of the person you wish to reach, begin the inside address with the title.

Vice-President for Research
Chairman, Board of Directors

In this situation, you can also omit the title from the inside address and include it instead in an attention line (see page 136).

When both name and title are unknown, begin with the organization's name.

Rockland Manufacturing Company

A complete inside address should look like this:

Mr. Mark Thornton
Director of Sales
White-Inland, Inc.
1100 Front Street
Baltimore, MD 21202

Except for the personal title and state name, avoid abbreviations in the inside address unless the organization to which you are writing uses an abbreviation such as "Inc.," "Corp.," or "Co." in its official title.

Salutation. The salutation, a formal greeting, begins at the left-hand margin. It is positioned two lines below the inside address. When you write to an individual, the salutation takes this form:

Dear Mrs. Nowicki:
Dear Ms. McCarthy:
Dear Dr. Corelli:

Letters addressed to departments within an organization should use the salutation "Dear Sir/Madam" or the job title itself.

Sales Department
Calmath Chemical Company
239 Dorman Drive
Birmingham, AL 35207

Dear Sir/Madam:

Sales Department
Calmath Chemical Company
239 Dorman Drive
Birmingham, AL 35207

Dear Sales Manager:

Letters addressed to organizations may use the salutation "Gentle-men/Ladies" or omit the salutation entirely and follow the AMS simplified format.

Able Tool and Die Corporation
188 South Cedar Lane
Topeka, KS 72163

Gentlemen/Ladies:

Able Tool and Die Corporation
188 South Cedar Lane
Topeka, KS 72163

YOUR ORDER NO. 72–839

Sales letters use a variety of salutations, such as "Dear Homeowner," "Dear Booklover," and "Dear Friend of the Environment."

Body. The body of the letter contains the message. It begins two lines below the salutation, unless a subject line intervenes (see page 136). Ordinarily, the body of a letter is single-spaced, with an extra line space between paragraphs. If the letter contains only one brief paragraph, it may be double-spaced. For an attractive appearance and easy readability, try to use short beginning and ending paragraphs. Vary the length of the middle paragraphs, and aim for an average sentence length of sixteen to twenty words. However, don't hesitate to use shorter or longer sentences if they are needed for emphasis or smoothness.

Complimentary Close. The complimentary close, a formal goodbye, is placed two lines below the last line of the body. In the modified block format, it begins at the page's center, and in the full block format, at the left-hand margin. The most common forms are:

Yours truly,
Sincerely yours,
Sincerely,

Other complimentary closes include "Cordially yours," appropriate when you are writing to someone you know well, and "Respectfully yours," used to show special esteem.

Note that in each case only the first word is capitalized. The second word, always lower-cased, is followed by a comma.

Signature. Your typewritten signature appears four lines directly below the complimentary close. If you are writing a letter on behalf of your company, your name should be followed by your title or your title and department. This will enable the person to whom you are writing to reply directly to you.

James W. Terry
Manager, Finance Department

A woman may choose to include her personal title in the type-written signature. This should be enclosed in parentheses.

(Mrs.) Mary Beeman
(Miss) Nancy Parker

In the four-line space above the typed signature, sign your name in longhand.

Your company may specify that its legal name should appear with your signature. This name is then typed in capital letters one line below the complimentary close and four lines above the typewritten signature.

Sincerely yours,
THE MORTON CORPORATION

James W. Terry

James W. Terry
Manager, Finance Department

Attention Line. The attention line—only occasionally employed—is useful (1) when you know only the job title of the person you are writing or (2) when you know the name of the person whose department you are writing but not the person's title or the name of the department. It is positioned between the inside address and the salutation, with an extra space above and below. It may begin at the left-hand margin or be centered on the page. Whenever you include an attention line, omit the recipient's name and title from the inside address and begin with the name of the organization. Since the salutation is determined by the first line of the inside address, the appropriate salutation is "Gentlemen/Ladies."

White-Inland, Inc.
1100 Front Street
Baltimore, MD 21202

Attention: Mr. John Thornton

Gentlemen/Ladies:

Subject Line. The subject line tells what the letter is about. It is used to refer to a specific policy number, file number, invoice number, or the like.

Subject: Your invoice LR-237
Subject: Account number 78-375-162

The subject line is positioned between the salutation and the body, with one space above and below. It may begin at the left-hand margin or be centered on the page.

Stenographic Reference. The stenographic reference is used when someone other than the writer types the letter. It includes two sets of initials—the writer's, in capital letters, and the typist's, in lower-case letters.

The two sets may be separated by a colon or slash mark, as shown below.

DLS:crt
DLS/crt

The reference appears two lines below the last line of the signature and starts at the left-hand margin.

Enclosure Notation. Whenever a brochure, drawing, check, money order, or other document accompanies a letter, an enclosure notation should be typed on the line following the stenographic reference. This can be the word "Enclosure" or the abbreviation "Enc." If more than one document accompanies a letter, it is a good idea to indicate the number of items enclosed.

DLS:crt
Enclosure
DLS/crt
Enc. 2

Documents of special importance are often named.

DLS/crt
Enclosure: Contract

Concurrent Copy Notation. A concurrent copy notation is used whenever two or more copies of a letter are sent. This notation is made up of the lower-case letters "cc" followed by a colon and the name of the person receiving the copy. If more than one person will receive copies, type the additional names directly below the first name.

cc: Dr. N. R. Prince
cc: Ms. S. L. Johnson
Mr. N. A. Ames

This notation is positioned on the line following the stenographic or enclosure notation.

Headings for Additional Pages. Although most business letters are a single page in length, additional pages are occasionally required. These pages are always typed on plain white stationery, with the same left and right margins as on the first page.

Each additional page must have a heading, which includes the reader's name, the date, and the page designation. Leave six lines of space at the top of the sheet above the heading. For the heading itself, any of the three styles shown below is acceptable:

Ms. Jennifer Arnett   2   July 23, 1981

Ms. Jennifer Arnett, July 23, 1981, page 2

Ms. Jennifer Arnett
July 23, 1981
Page 2

Below the heading, leave two lines of space before starting the continuation of the letter.

PUNCTUATION

Almost all business letters now use mixed punctuation. This style omits all end-of-line punctuation in the heading, inside address, typewritten signature, and any special part, such as the subject line or enclosure notation. Only when a line ends with an abbreviation is a period used. A colon follows the salutation, and a comma follows the complimentary close. The sample letters in this chapter illustrate mixed punctuation.

MARGINS

Proper margins enhance your letter's attractiveness and thus the chances that your message will be well received.

The size of the margins will depend on your letter's length. The longer the letter, the narrower the margins should be. For a full-page letter (roughly two to three hundred words), use 1-inch side margins and type the first line of the inside address 2½ inches below the top of the sheet. For a shorter letter (one to two hundred words), use 1½-inch side margins and begin the inside address 3 inches below the top of the sheet. For a very brief letter (fifty to a hundred words), use 2-inch side margins and begin the inside address 3½ inches from the top of the sheet. (The layout of certain letterheads may require you to vary the size of the top margin somewhat.) Bottom and top margins should be roughly the same size. In overall appearance, the letter should resemble a matted picture.

PREPARATION FOR MAILING

In typing the envelope of your letter, use the block form for both addresses and single-space between lines. To make sure that the post office's optical character readers can read your envelope, position the recipient's address so that all of it is between one-half inch and three inches from the bottom of the envelope. Leave at least a one-inch left-hand margin. The post office recommends that the recipient's address be typed entirely in capital letters and without punctuation. The example envelope below follows this format.

```
209 Foster Hall
Case Western Reserve University
Cleveland, OH  44106




                         MR. FRANCIS C RHYTE
                         ASSISTANT ADVERTISING MANAGER
                         MINE SAFETY APPLIANCE COMPANY
                         400 PENN CENTER BOULEVARD
                         PITTSBURGH  PA  15235
```

State names should be abbreviated as the U.S. Postal Service recommends.

Alabama	AL	Montana	MT
Alaska	AK	Nebraska	NE
Arizona	AZ	Nevada	NV
Arkansas	AR	New Hampshire	NH
California	CA	New Jersey	NJ
Colorado	CO	New Mexico	NM
Connecticut	CT	New York	NY
Delaware	DE	North Carolina	NC
District of Columbia	DC	North Dakota	ND
Florida	FL	Ohio	OH
Georgia	GA	Oklahoma	OK
Hawaii	HI	Oregon	OR
Idaho	ID	Pennsylvania	PA
Illinois	IL	Rhode Island	RI
Indiana	IN	South Carolina	SC
Iowa	IA	South Dakota	SD
Kansas	KS	Tennessee	TN
Kentucky	KY	Texas	TX
Louisiana	LA	Utah	UT
Maine	ME	Vermont	VT
Maryland	MD	Virginia	VA
Massachusetts	MA	Washington	WA
Michigan	MI	West Virginia	WV
Minnesota	MN	Wisconsin	WI
Mississippi	MS	Wyoming	WY
Missouri	MO		

Proofread your letter carefully, sign it, and then fold it neatly in thirds so that it will fit into a number 10 size business envelope.

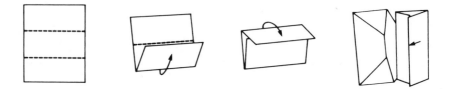

LANGUAGE AND TONE

Tone is the attitude conveyed by a writer or speaker. Whether or not you intend it, everything you write will have a tone—desirable or otherwise. When writing a business letter, you should strive for a tone that suits your audience and purpose and that arouses the right emotional reaction. Failure to do so can cause your reader to reject your message, create ill will, and damage your organization's business. You can achieve the right tone by avoiding wordiness, using the proper degree of formality, and being courteous at all times.

Wordiness. Wordiness results in dull, hard-to-read messages and stamps its writers as bores—even when they are not. Wordiness can take two forms. Business jargon, once the standard language for business correspondence, uses inflated and often elaborately polite expressions. Deadwood results when a writer says the same thing twice or uses several words where one or two would do. Here are some examples of wordiness and corrections for them.

Expression	Correction
at the present time	now
basic fundamentals	fundamentals
cognizant of	know
completely eliminate	eliminate
enclosed please find	we are enclosing
exactly identical	identical
I am in receipt of	I have
in view of the fact that	because
pursuant to your request that	as you requested
will you be kind enough to	please
we wish to acknowledge receipt of	we have, or thank you for

All of the corrected versions are more relaxed and natural than the originals.

Degree of Formality. Many of the letters you write will go to people outside your field of expertise and call for informal language. This kind of language is casual and relaxed, resembling the intelligent conversation of educated people. In writing it, strive to use relatively simple words and sentence structures and don't be afraid to use such personal pronouns as *I, me, we, you,* and *yours.* At the same time, though, avoid slang and overly casual expressions, which may cause your reader to doubt your seriousness. Be sure that your wording is precise, your sentences flow smoothly, and your thoughts unfold in an orderly way.

At times you will need to write someone else in your field. In such cases, you may need to use technical, rather than informal, language. Technical language employs specialized words that a general reader would find difficult or impossible to understand. Its sentences tend to be rather long and complex, and its tone is objective and authoritative, but without pomposity. Here is a segment of a letter that uses technical language.

> This new hypertensive agent is a synthetic prostaglandin of PGE1. It is a beta blocker which is selective for the beta receptors of the heart and, by sparing the beta receptors of the lungs, avoids many of the common side effects of this class of substances. Extensive clinical testing revealed that it significantly reduced blood pressure in 95 percent of the test subjects with renal hypertension and 82 percent of those with malignant hypertension.

Courtesy. Courtesy is as important in business letters as it is in face-to-face dealings with others. You can write courteous letters by following a few simple pointers. First, and most obvious, never use insults and sarcasm. These only create ill will. Be sure, too, to avoid expressions that may arouse your reader's resentment. When you say, "We have your letter *claiming* that the oscilloscopes we sold you were defective," you call the reader's honesty into question. When you say, *"It is our position that* our offer is very attractive," you imply that the reader is a quarrelsome person likely to take issue with you. It is a simple matter to rephrase these expressions to convey a friendly, courteous tone.

> We are sorry to learn that the oscilloscopes we sold you were defective.

> We think you will find our offer very attractive.

Cold impersonality is as destructive to courtesy as are sarcasm and insults. Consider the following letter.

Dear Mr. Furman:

Reference is made to the March 17, 1981, agreement between you and us in which you contracted to provide cafeteria catering services for our employees.

In accordance with paragraph 5(b) of the said agreement, we have elected to discontinue your services. Accordingly, the said agreement is hereby terminated in accordance with its terms without any further obligation or liabilities between the parties.

Sincerely yours,

This letter handles the cancellation in an abrupt, unfeeling manner. The caterer has undoubtedly expended considerable effort in coordinating and developing his services. Common courtesy demands both an expression of regret and an explanation for the action.

Whenever you present information that will be disagreeable to the reader, try to do so in a positive manner. The following example shows the improved tone that results when a negative statement is rephrased as a positive one.

Dear Mr. Furman:

I am very sorry to inform you that we must cancel your contract to provide cafeteria catering services. As you know, paragraph 5(b) provides for this cancellation.

Fifteen months ago, when we signed our agreement, we had approximately one hundred more employees in our plant than we have today. Our recent commitment to automated production makes further employee transfers likely in the near future. Therefore, cafeteria sales would not be high enough to justify any further expense on our part or on yours.

Thank you for the excellent service you have provided. We share your disappointment and wish you every success with your catering services.

Sincerely yours,

By adopting a natural, courteous, and positive tone, you will write letters that reflect favorably on both your organization and yourself.

Letters of Inquiry and Replies

LETTERS OF INQUIRY

A letter of inquiry asks for information. There are numerous situations in which you would write such a letter. You may, for example, wish any of the following:

1. more detailed performance data or specifications on a piece of equipment your company might buy
2. a fuller explanation of one aspect of a research project described in a magazine article
3. additional details about a safety program or an employee-rating system developed by another organization
4. statistical data for a term paper
5. clarification of an inadequate or ambiguous set of directions

Do not, however, ask for information that is readily available in handbooks, articles, and other sources. Your reader is not likely to appreciate, or honor, requests for data that you could obtain by doing a little digging in your library.

There are two basic types of inquiry letter. The first type is used to request information needed to complete a task or project or to make some decision. The second type is used to ask that directions be supplied or clarified.

First Type. In writing the first section of the letter, identify yourself, indicate the general subject, and state clearly that you are seeking information. Be sure to explain why you need or how you plan to use it, for many organizations are understandably reluctant to supply information for unknown purposes. Furthermore, by knowing your needs, your correspondents may better be able to help you. Unless it seems inappropriate, mention why you are writing to that particular individual or organization. This explanation gives your reader a greater sense of your purposefulness and also affords you an opportunity to make some favorable comment that will increase your chances of getting the desired information.

I have read with great interest your article in the November 1981 issue of *Health* magazine, in which you mention your survey of smoking regulations in Michigan hospitals.

I am a college student on a trainee assignment, and I would like to conduct a similar survey of hospitals in our state. Would you be kind enough to help me by answering the following questions?

Once you've explained the reason for the inquiry, list the actual questions or points you wish answered. This section should be planned so as to inconvenience the reader as little as possible. Keep questions to a minimum, make them brief, and whenever possible word them so they can be answered in a few short sentences. If you ask three or more questions, set them up in a numbered list. Numbering the questions will make it less likely that the reader will accidentally fail to answer one. Finally, indicate that you'll welcome any additional comments the reader can provide.

1. How were the hospitals contacted—by phone or letter?
2. Were all hospitals in the state contacted, or just a representative sample?
3. What did you accomplish by this survey?

I would also appreciate any additional information or material that you feel might help me.

To increase your chances of a favorable response, give careful thought to possible ways you can repay your reader for the help provided. If, for instance, you want information for use in a survey, you might offer a copy of the survey when it is completed. Sometimes, of course, it will not be possible for you to repay the reader.

Close the letter with an expression of appreciation. A simple "Thank you for any help you can give me" or "Any information you can provide will be appreciated" would be an appropriate closing. Never use the phrase "Thank you in advance for your help," which sounds pompous and suggests there's no chance you'll be turned down. Some readers may interpret this as a pressure tactic and therefore refuse your request.

When I have completed my survey, I will be happy to send you a copy of the results. Thank you for any help you can provide.

Second Type. When asking that directions be supplied or clarified, start by providing any necessary background information. Next, state the problem and the inconvenience it has caused, and then follow with your request for the directions. Be sure to provide enough details to convince your reader that the problem is serious enough to merit immediate attention. Conclude by asking that your reader respond as quickly as possible. Maintain a courteous tone throughout your letter; discourtesy will hurt your chances of getting a prompt reply.

REPLIES TO INQUIRY LETTERS

Replies to letters of inquiry can be favorable or unfavorable. In either case, answer as soon as possible, preferably within one day.

Favorable Replies. Begin favorable replies by referring politely to the original inquiry and indicating that you are supplying the required information or will do so soon. Your opening might look something like this:

> Thank you for your letter of February 20, 1982, requesting information about the survey we conducted to determine smoking regulations in Michigan hospitals.

> We hope the following answers to your questions will be helpful:

Such a beginning will leave the reader with a favorable impression of your organization. If you must refer an inquiry to another individual or department for an answer, tell your reader you have done so and, if possible, name the individual or department and a date by which the answer can be expected.

After this beginning, take up each question in the order asked, answering it as thoroughly as is necessary. If the questions are written in paragraph form, you may have to restate each briefly before answering. If they are presented as a numbered list, number your answers correspondingly. Whenever possible, make your job easier by including brochures, reports, or other materials that contain the desired information, perhaps with the pertinent parts underlined for the reader's convenience. There is no reason to compose lengthy answers yourself when printed materials are available. If you cannot supply an answer, either because you don't know or because the information is confidential, say so and give the reason. Never bypass a question without comment. If you have additional material that the reader may find useful, send it or offer to provide it. Similarly, if you can provide the name of someone who might furnish more information, do so. End the letter by offering to provide any further help the writer might need and making whatever other pleasant comment seems appropriate.

1. Hospitals were contacted by letter, addressed personally to the administrator. Each letter included a questionnaire and return envelope. (A sample of each is enclosed.) If we did not receive a reply within ten days, we mailed a follow-up letter or contacted the hospital personally.

2. All hospitals in the state were contacted in order to obtain a complete analysis.

3. Hospitals became more aware of the hazards of permitting smoking around people who were already ill; consequently, many changed their regulations to permit smoking only in specified areas.

Under separate cover we are sending you a complete copy of our survey results and also samples of our smoking literature.

We are pleased that you are planning a similar survey in your state and will be happy to receive a copy of your results. If we can assist you further, please let us know.

Letters that respond to customers' requests for directions differ slightly from letters supplying other types of information. Since the reader may have suffered serious inconvenience due to the lack of directions, begin by apologizing for any difficulties that might have been caused. For example:

I am sorry that the RIV-230 catalytic heater you purchased from us arrived without operating instructions. Because we are temporarily out of printed copies, we are including the instructions in this letter.

In most cases the customer does not send a list of questions but simply asks for clarification of all or part of the directions supplied with a product. In responding, include as many points as are needed for clarification. Set these up as a numbered list, so that the reader can clearly see the separate steps. As in the longer paper explaining a process (see chapter 5), present these steps in the form of commands and arrange them in the sequence in which they are to be carried out. If two steps must be performed simultaneously, warn the reader at the start of the first step. If there is a chance that the reader will not understand the reason for a step, explain it. If there is a danger that the reader will perform a step improperly, provide a warning.

1. Remove the filter cap from the tank and fill the tank with fuel. Use only Cata-Heet stove and lantern fuel; other fuels may contain additives that will clog the heater.
2. Replace the filter cap and tighten it firmly.
3. Turn the heater upside down until a small spot of fuel appears on the head of the heating element.
4. Set the regulating lever on the "start" position.
5. Light the fuel on the head with a match or lighter.
6. The heater will flare for two or three minutes. After the flaring has subsided, regulate the amount of heat by adjusting the control lever.
7. To extinguish the flame, move the regulating lever to the "low" position and place the snuffer cover firmly over the head of the heating element.

End the letter as you would any favorable reply to an inquiry—express the hope or belief that the information will prove helpful and offer to provide further help if it is needed. If you wish, you may repeat your apology so as to emphasize your regret that the problem occurred.

> This information should enable you to start your heater without any difficulty. If any further questions arise, we would be happy to answer them.

Unfavorable Replies. Writing a good refusal letter is not easy. Unless you exercise the utmost tact, you are likely to offend your reader. Whatever the reason for your refusal, try to be courteous and helpful throughout your letter.

Begin your letter with an opening that establishes a friendly tone; then state your refusal and tell why you cannot comply. Be specific here. For example, were you asked for information that you could not disclose, you might note that because of the newness of a project, the data are not available. Or perhaps the information was obtained under an agreement that does not permit any findings to be divulged to third parties. In the latter case, you could suggest that the other company might be willing to release the information and then provide an address. Avoid any suggestion that the reader might misuse the information if you supplied it. This would only cause animosity.

Whenever you can, soften your refusal by offering other information or helpful suggestions. Perhaps you can supply articles, bulletins, or reports that will prove useful. Or maybe you can suggest another source the reader can turn to. Take some time to consider the possibilities; the goodwill generated will amply repay your efforts.

The ending of the letter should be as courteous and helpful as the opening. Wish the reader success in the venture that prompted the inquiry and offer to provide assistance in other matters.

Here is an example of a refusal.

Thank you for your letter requesting information on our new comprehensive safety program. Although we would like to answer your questions, we are unable to do so. Because our program is relatively new, we have not yet compiled any statistical data on its effects.

Although we cannot help you, the Grigsby Tractor Company may be able to provide comparable data since their program is very similar to ours and has been in operation for several years. In fact, we modeled our program after Grigsby's because of their success. Address your letter to

> Mr. John Aldo
> Grigsby Tractor Company
> 149 Maplewood Street
> Line, NJ 08043

Mr. Aldo is the coordinator of the Grigsby program. We hope that any information he might provide will help you to establish a successful program in your organization. Please write whenever you need assistance on other matters. We're always ready to help whenever we can.

EXAMPLES OF LETTERS OF INQUIRY AND REPLIES

Elmhurst Bakery

11 Cicero Street
Elmhurst, IL 60126

February 8, 1981

Plant Manager
Kellogg Bakeries
129 Blanck Street
Hazelwood, MO 63131

Dear Sir/Madam:

Two weeks ago, while attending the American Bakers' convention, I met Mr. Orville Wales, your plant superintendent, who mentioned the participative management program you are using at your company.

As plant manager for Elmhurst Bakery, I am now looking into the possibility of introducing participative management into our plant. You can help me by providing me with information about your program. I would primarily like to know

1. What part does the character of the work force play in the success of such a plan?

2. How much resistance do employees show toward s   up changes?

3. How willing are employees to help in departments other than their own?

4. Is your program working as well as you had hoped? If not, in what way has it proved disappointing?

Thank you for any help you can give me.

Sincerely,

David L. Cobb

David L. Cobb
Plant Superintendent

DC/ma

Kellogg Bakeries

129 Blanck Street • Hazelwood, MO 63131

February 18, 1980

Mr. David L. Cobb
Plant Superintendent
Elmhurst Bakery
11 Cicero Street
Elmhurst, IL 60126

Dear Mr. Cobb:

We are gratified to learn of your interest in our participative
management program and happy to provide the following answers to
your questions:

1. The character of our work force has had much to do with
   the success of our program. Hazelwood is a solid work-
   ethic community, a fact that has had an important bearing
   on worker reaction.

2. On the whole, employees do not show any appreciable
   resistance to set-up changes. Being directly involved in
   management, they know in advance about any changes and
   the reasons behind them.

3. Similarly, employees are willing to help out in departments other than their own because they can see how such
   a contribution helps the entire plant.

4. Yes, this program has worked every bit as well as we had
   hoped. The whole work climate is much healthier and more
   dynamic--so much so that production has increased 15
   percent.

The person chiefly responsible for setting up our program is
Mr. Robert Melin of Melin Management, Inc., 1819 Jones Street SE,
Grand Rapids, Michigan 49504. If you write him, I am sure he
will be able to give you detailed information about the participative management concept.

I hope that, if you adopt this type of program, it will work as
well for you as it has for us.

Sincerely yours,

Charles Taylor

Charles Taylor
Plant Manager

CT/sr

Discussion Questions

1. What formats do these letters follow? How can you tell?
2. Explain how these letters conform to the requirements for inquiry
   letters and favorable responses.
3. Explain these notations in the two letters:
   DC/ma
   CT/sr
4. Why does David Cobb's letter begin with the salutation "Dear Sir/
   Madam"?

410 Main Street
Boise, ID 83424
November 26, 1981

Aquarium Filters, Inc.
162 South Main Street
Alhambra, MI 48702

Gentlemen/Ladies:

In October, I ordered your Model R-200 Aquari-Rite under-gravel
filter for my home aquarium.

About two weeks ago, the filter stopped bubbling and since that
time has not worked properly. To prevent the water from
becoming dirty and the fish from dying, I have had to change
the water every few days.

Because the literature you supplied with the filter does not
tell how to correct this problem, please supply me with
directions for doing so.

I would appreciate a reply as quickly as possible, as the
problem has resulted in serious inconvenience.

Sincerely yours,

John Beebe

Aquarium Filters, Inc.
162 SOUTH MAIN STREET
ALHAMBRA, MICHIGAN 48702

December 3, 1981

Mr. John Beebe
410 Main Street
Boise, ID 83424

Dear Mr. Beebe:

We are sorry to hear that the Aquari-Rite under-gravel filter
you purchased from us is not bubbling. Please don't be alarmed.
Occasionally bacterial growth will plug the air hose leading to
the filter. Here are several simple steps to clear the clog
without removing the filter from your aquarium.

    1.   Separate the air hose from the air pump.

    2.   Suck on the hose until the water in the tank has risen
        halfway up the hose. You may or may not see the clog
        at this point.

    3.   Now blow forcefully into the air hose until you see
        bubbles coming from the filter. Repeat steps two and
        three if you can't see any.

    4.   If this procedure does not work, the small stem on the
        filter is probably clogged, and you can open it by
        running a wire through it.

I hope this will solve your difficulty. If you have any further
problems, please call us collect at (717) 635-1424 between
8 A.M. and 5 P.M. Again, we are sorry for the inconveniece you
have suffered.

                Yours truly,

                Thomas Waun

                Thomas Waun
                Customer Relations Department

TW:net

Discussion Questions

1. Explain how these letters conform to the requirements for inquiry
   letters requesting directions and the replies to such letters?
2. Why does John Beebe use the salutation "Gentlemen/Ladies" in his
   letter?
3. Why do you think Thomas Waun ended as well as began his letter with
   an apology?

239 Denton Drive
Waterford, WI 53474
October 18, 1980

Ms. Della McCarthy
Propagation Manager
Princeton Nurseries, Inc.
Box 501
Princeton, NJ 20113

Dear Ms. McCarthy:

I am enrolled in the ornamental horticulture program at Brett
Junior College, and for one of my courses I must prepare a report
on plant propagation methods.

While reading the July 1980 issue of Nursery Management, I noted
in the "Research Briefs" section that you have developed a new
water-immersion system of propagation. Can you help me by
providing me with information about it for my report? I am
especially interested in obtaining answers to these questions:

    1. How do the misting nozzles differ from those used
       with other misting systems?

    2. Can any water source be used, and if not how must the
       water be treated?

    3. How often is the foliage misted and what misting
       pattern is used?

    4. What rooting hormones proved most effective?

    5. Must the greenhouse be heated or is an unheated
       house satisfactory?

I would greatly appreciate your assistance and will be happy to
provide you with a copy of my report as soon as it is completed.

Yours truly,

Dennis L. Scanlon

Dennis L. Scanlon

PRINCETON NURSERIES, INC.
BOX 501 • PRINCETON, NJ 20113 • 609-924-1789

February 8, 1981

Dennis L. Scanlon
239 Denton Drive
Waterford, WI 53474

Dear Mr. Scanlon:

We have your letter of October 18 in which you ask about our
new propagation system. Much as we would like to supply the
information you wish, we cannot do so. Just two weeks ago, our
company signed a contract with Norton Greenhouse Company, which
plans to further develop and then market the water immersion
system. The lawyers involved have instructed both companies
not to discuss the system until a patent application has been
filed.

To help you with your project, however, I am sending you two
reports that you might find useful. The first is by Dr. Robert
Blakely, the head of our research department; it deals with
root grafting compatibilities. The other is by Ms. Irma
Hardesty and describes our winter cutting operations.

Good luck with your paper, and please don't hesitate to write
again if you have questions about either report.

Sincerely yours,
PRINCETON NURSERIES, INC.

Della McCarthy

(Mrs.) Della McCarthy
Propagation Manager

DM/ro
Enc. 2

Discussion Questions

1. Explain why the notation PRINCETON NURSERIES, INC. appears beneath the complimentary close of the Della McCarthy letter.
2. Why does the notation "Mrs." appear in parentheses before Della McCarthy's typed signature?
3. Show how the Della McCarthy letter conforms to the requirements for unfavorable responses.
4. Explain this notation in the Della McCarthy letter: Enc. 2.

Sales Letters

A sales letter offers a product or service to a selected group of individuals or organizations. If you work for a small company or are self-employed, writing sales letters may well be part of your duties. Because of their importance as a marketing tool, they must be prepared with great care.

A successful sales letter must address the right audience persuasively. Mailing lists of potential customers can be bought from companies that specialize in grouping people according to characteristics that suggest likely buying habits. Or you can develop your own lists by drawing upon the names of past and present customers, membership rosters of local organizations, news items, and the like. For example, if you are operating a photography studio, you might assemble a list of yearbook advisers at nearby high schools or note the engagement announcements in your local paper.

A persuasively written sales letter does four things:

1. attracts attention
2. sparks interest in the product
3. convinces that the product is the best available
4. prompts action

Before starting to write, ask yourself what features of your product or service are most likely to appeal to your reader. Depending upon the product and the reader, these may be convenience, economy, durability, performance, appearance, safety, healthfulness, or status, among others. Whatever you decide, be sure the message you plan is plausible and accurate. Wildly exaggerated claims will turn many readers off and could result in legal liability.

ATTRACTING ATTENTION

Because of the great volume of sales letters that floods today's mail, many readers pay little attention to those they receive. Unless you can spark their interest by an attention-getting opening, all of your efforts will go for nothing.

Several techniques can be used to gain attention. The *intriguing question*, one of the most common, prompts the reader to continue in order to find the answer. Here are some examples.

Ever get the feeling you're spending money fuelishly?

> *Start of letter advertising a*
> *portable home kerosene heater*

Is there a thief in your car's engine?

> *Start of letter advertising an air filter*

A second technique, the *"If . . . then . . ."* *opening,* also works well—provided the "if" part actually applies to the reader.

If you own or expect to own a home, securities, savings bonds, or other assets with your wife or someone else, you should know the drawbacks of joint ownership.

> *Start of letter by the Research Institute of America, Inc.,*
> *advertising its weekly bulletin* Recommendations

Beginning with a *quotation* is a third popular option for opening sales letters. If you use this opening, be sure the quotation relates clearly to the subject of your letter.

There's an old adage that says, "Where there's smoke, there's fire." What better reason for buying our First Alert smoke detector?

> *Start of a letter by a home products*
> *supplier to local homeowners*

Yet another effective way of starting a sales letter is by *offering the reader a gift or by offering a product or service at a savings.*

We at Michigan Bankard are pleased to present at no cost for the next six months—that's correct—*ABSOLUTELY FREE*—a vital credit card protection service from the Hot-Line Credit Card Bureau of America.

> *Start of letter to Visa/MasterCard cardholders*

Now you can own the latest edition of one of the finest dictionaries in print—and at the same time save $40. This giant reference work, over 2,300 pages long and more than 4 inches thick, was originally published at $59.95. But Barnes & Noble—the world's largest bookstore—is offering it to you for the incredibly low price of only $19.95. That's less than 1/3 the original publisher's price.

> *Start of a letter to Barnes & Noble customers*

Salutations likewise play a rule in attention-getting, as evidenced by the great variety found in sales letters. Thus, a letter to a prospective book-club member might begin "Dear Booklover," while one offering new seat covers might being "Dear New Car Owner." For more intimacy, the salutation often ends with a comma rather than a colon.

Whatever devices you select, keep your opening short. A lengthy beginning is uninviting to your readers and will decrease your chances of making a sale.

SPARKING INTEREST

The next step is to interest your reader in making a purchase. You can do so by describing the product, noting its benefits, or both. In presenting your material you can appeal deliberately to your reader's feelings (emotions or senses), or you can adopt a purely factual approach. Here is a section of a sales letter that describes the product and appeals primarily to the reader's sense of taste.

> There are a variety of ways to enjoy Goodbee pecans . . . fresh, whole, and in the shell . . . Fancy mammoth whole halves . . . Pecan halves, slightly salted and roasted in pure, natural peanut oil . . . The divinity bar, rich and creamy candy smothered in fresh peanuts . . .
>
> *Goodbee Pecan Plantations*

The excerpt below focuses on specific reader benefits and uses a factual approach.

> LIFE PLAN 55 PLUS is an uncomplicated whole life insurance policy that requires no medical exam or health questionnaire of any kind. If you're age 55 to 87 you cannot be turned down during this Guaranteed Acceptance Period . . . and your policy cannot be cancelled for any reason as long as you continue to pay your premiums.
>
> Furthermore, your premiums will never increase, and your benefits will never decrease. And cash values continue building after the first or second year, depending upon your age when you become insured.
>
> *Colonial Penn Insurance Company*

Sometimes, of course, product features and reader benefits are combined in the same appeal, and sometimes an appeal blends both logic and emotion.

CONVINCING

To convince readers of the worth of your product or service, you may present facts, offer guarantees, or provide testimonials. The example below illustrates the use of facts. Taken together, these facts constitute a powerful buying inducement.

> Webster's Unabridged Dictionary has been a standard reference for more than 40 years. *The New Unabridged Twentieth Century Dictionary* continues that fine tradition and is one of the most complete and up-to-date dictionaries available today. Just look at what it contains:
> - clear and accurate definitions for 320,000 words and phrases used in American English, including new additions to the language from physics, chemistry, biology, and other specialized fields;
> - more than 3,000 black-and-white drawings;
> - 32 beautiful pages of full-color illustrations;
> - a complete collection of maps of the world;
> - thumb-indexing for easy reference.
> *Barnes & Noble Bookstores, Inc.*

Guarantees frequently help sell a product, assuring readers that they have nothing to lose by ordering.

> Mother Nature blessed our small area of Georgia with ideal growing conditions for pecans. And because this is so, we can boldly and flatly guarantee all of our pecan products. If they are in any way unsatisfactory, you have our inviolate promise of either your money being refunded or a replacement order. Your option.
> *Goodbee Pecan Plantations*

Testimonials—statements vouching for the merits of a product—are a powerful persuasive device provided they are accurate and credible. Large organizations often make use of testimonials by movie stars, athletes, and other celebrities to sell their products. However, the most credible, and therefore the best, testimonials are the ones offered by individuals qualified to make them—for example, people who have used or tested a product.

> "I really enjoy using *Yes*. The lightweight plastic bottle is easy to carry, and I love the springtime-fresh scent of my clean clothes!" says a letter we received just last month from Wilkes-Barre, Pennsylvania.
>
> *Texize Chemicals Company*

MOTIVATING ACTION

The conclusion of your sales letter should ask your readers to take some action. In most cases, your aim will be to have the readers purchase your product or service, but sometimes you will want them to request further information or samples, complete a questionnaire, or the like. To make responding easy, you can enclose an order form, provide an option to call collect in order to speed delivery, provide a money-back guarantee, offer to charge the order to a major credit card, delay the billing for a specified time, offer to provide a demonstration in the reader's home or workplace, or offer similar inducements. Include a postage-paid addressed envelope whenever you wish your readers to respond by mail. If your aim is to have them visit your place of business, you might supply directions for getting there. Here are several effective conclusions.

> To get your copy of *Webster's Unabridged Twentieth Century Dictionary,* simply fill in the enclosed order form and return it in the postage-paid envelope we've provided. If you are not absolutely convinced it's the finest dictionary you have ever used, you may return it for a full and prompt refund. So why not order a copy for your home or office today?
>
> *Barnes & Noble Bookstores, Inc.*

> For your convenience, we have enclosed an addressed, postage-paid card. Just indicate which evening would be most convenient for our representative to visit your home and give you our free landscaping analysis and cost estimate. And please accept the enclosed packet of geranium seeds with our compliments.
>
> *local landscaping service*

Visit our local office supply store and see for yourself how the Apple minicomputer can help you to run your home more efficiently. Our trained, professional staff will be happy to answer all your questions and show you our fully equipped service center. With our special payment schedule, we can help you sink your teeth into an Apple.

local office supply company

Writing a good sales letter is not easy, but when the job is well done, the resulting increase in sales will amply repay your efforts.

EXAMPLES OF SALES LETTERS

CITIBANK

Citibank Visa
P.O. Box 5256, F.D.R. Station
New York, New York 10022

VISA

Dear Cardmember:

If you know someone who's been hospitalized recently, you're probably aware that even the best medical plans don't cover *all* the costs of being hospitalized—costs that are rising every day.

In addition to hospital expenses for special treatments and medication, or for TV and telephone, there are always bills at home that must be paid. Rent, grocery, and child-care expenses continue when *any* family member is hospitalized.

To help meet this need for additional protection, a Supplemental Hospital Indemnity Insurance Plan is now being made available to Citibank Visa cardmembers. Underwritten by National Benefit Life Insurance Company, this Plan will pay a daily in-hospital benefit of $75.00 or $50.00 to help you meet expenses your present hospital insurance may not cover—at low group rates.

As the cost of living continues to rise, it's becoming impossible to plan for medical expenses (*and* daily living expenses) with any certainty. Supplemental Hospital Indemnity coverage can help you anticipate future needs—in the hospital or at home—without straining your present budget.

Please take a moment to read through the enclosed materials and take note that under this Plan:

- **You have a choice of benefit levels to coordinate your needs and your budget.**
  You can receive $75.00 a day under Plan A or $50.00 a day under Plan B.

- **Your rate will not increase as you grow older,** regardless of how much you collect in benefits.

- **Your benefit will double** for up to 30 days when you are confined in an Intensive Care unit.

Acceptance in this Plan is guaranteed for Citibank Visa cardmembers in good standing and their immediate families. And because this is a group plan, you'll pay economical group premium rates. Compared with similar plans, these are among the most economical rates now available for Supplemental Hospital Indemnity coverage.

We at Citibank are committed to providing our cardmembers and their families with services that will improve their financial security and meet their long-term needs. We feel that this Supplemental Hospital Indemnity Plan for Citibank Visa cardmembers is one of the best values in supplemental health care protection available today.

Because this is a group plan with group processing procedures, National Benefit requests that all Enrollment Forms be returned by May 8, 1981.

I urge you to seriously consider providing your family with the important supplement hospital protection this valuable plan offers. It's always reassuring to know you have planned ahead—not just financially, but for greater peace of mind.

Sincerely,

Joseph Altschuler

Joseph Altschuler
Senior Marketing Officer

P.S. Why not see for yourself the many benefits this plan offers by enrolling today. You have 15 days to examine your coverage at home, without obligation. If you aren't completely satisfied, just cancel your protection by returning your Certificate to National Benefit Life Insurance Company. Your Citibank Visa account will be credited in full, and the 15-day examination period will cost you nothing.

DENBY OFFICE SUPPLY COMPANY

129 SOUTH MICHIGAN AVENUE
GARY, INDIANA 46401

Dear Gary Office Manager,

Would you like to double the output of your stenographers and typists? Have your official letters and documents filed electronically, replacing bulky filing cabinets with small disk storage boxes? An MTR 8000 word processor can do these things for you, and it's available right here in Gary at the Denby Office Supply Company.

The MTR 8000 offers a totally different, totally superior approach to typing. Instead of reaching for typing paper and inserting it the way you would in a typewriter, you begin typing immediately. What you type appears on an easy-to-read screen that actually looks like a sheet of paper: full-size, with black characters on a white background. (The black-on-white screen is a major feature of the MTR 8000. Some competitive word processors have only a partial-page display on a green-on-green, computer-like background.) Because nothing is on paper yet, you can type at full rough-draft speed without worrying about typos and other errors. Mistakes are corrected easily right on the MTR screen. Words or paragraphs can be changed, added, or deleted, while the entire text is adjusted electronically. Only when the document is letter-perfect do you transfer it from the screen to paper. Just touch a button and the MTR 8000 printer produces a crisp original at the amazing speed of up to 540 words a minute.

WHAT OTHER FEATURES MAKE THE MTR 8000 REMARKABLE?

Everything you type on the MTR 8000 can be captured on small magnetic memory disks. Each disk holds up to one hundred business letters. Individual documents can be recalled to the screen in seconds. So you can update documents any time--as easily as you made corrections on the originals. With MTR's electronic filing system, you can replace <u>rows</u> of bulky filing cabinets with small disk storage boxes.

A new feature, found only on the MTR 8000 and other advanced word processors, is called "software programming." Preprogrammed disks allow you to prepare payrolls, keep ledgers, and handle bookkeeping and more. It's so simple that no special computer language or knowledge is necessary.

(continued)

- 2 -

EXECUTIVES AND SECRETARIES PRAISE THE MTR 8000

Although a comparative newcomer to the word-processing scene, the MTR 8000 has already won the warm acceptance of executives in hundreds of business offices. Here's what James Madigan of Adams Industries in Chicago writes: "I'm impressed. We got our MTR's just six months ago. Since then, they've almost doubled the output of our office workers and in so doing more than paid for themselves."

Secretaries are also strong advocates of the MTR 8000. They like it because it is easy to use, eliminates the drudgery of retyping to make simple revisions, and produces cleaner, crisper copy than any typewriter can.

Why not let us show you and your office staff just what an MTR 8000 can do for you? Just call 823-8100 and we'll be happy to arrange for a demonstration in your own office at any time that is convenient to you. Or if you prefer, you can stop by our store any weekday between 9:30 a.m. and 5:30 p.m. We're located just one block south of the new Mid-Gary Shopping Mall.

We look forward to meeting with you either at your place of business or ours and showing you why so many business people are turning to MTR 8000 word processor.

Sincerely yours,

Patricia Van Dyke

Patricia Van Dyke
Manager, Marketing Group

PVD/ol

Discussion Questions

1. What type of opening does each of these sales letters use?
2. Identify the attention-getting devices of each letter.
3. Which paragraphs in each letter seek to spark the readers' interest? Do they focus primarily on describing the product/service or upon noting its benefits? What type of appeal does each make?
4. Which paragraphs seek to convince readers of the work of the product/service? What devices does each employ to accomplish its purpose?
5. Identify the devices each letter uses to motivate action.

Order Letters

Letters are often used to order tools, equipment, or other supplies. Such letters must be carefully drafted to ensure that the supplier ships the right goods at the right time and in the right manner.

Order letters must be brief and to the point. Begin by saying, "Please send . . .," "Please ship . . .," or something similar. Then identify the goods by name, model or catalog number, size, weight, color finish, or whatever else is needed to prevent mix-ups. If you are ordering a single item, the letter may be written in paragraph form. Otherwise, list the items you are ordering. Note how many items of each sort you need, the cost of a single item, and the total cost of the order. To avoid misunderstanding and possible delay in processing your order, don't fail to mention any discounts to which you are entitled.

> Please ship the following items as listed in your March 1980 sale catalog:
>
> 2 Model B-110k Blender-avocado, 4 quart, 9
>   speeds. Unit price: $34.50 $ 69.00
>
> 1 Model Cp-283k Electric Coffee Maker-black, 20
>   cups, immersible. Unit price: $26.90 $ 26.90
>
> 1 Model M-306k Portable Mixer-yellow, 3 bowls,
>   12 speeds. Unit price: $30.15 $ 30.15
>
> 3 Model T-174k Toaster-6 slice. Unit price: $19.99 $ 59.97
>
> | | |
> |---:|---:|
> | Total | $186.02 |
> | 15% Disc. | 27.90 |
> | Adjusted Total | $158.12 |

If important, specify the means of shipment (truck, rail freight, railway express, air express, parcel post), the route to follow, and when you would like to receive the order. Provide any special instruction necessary to insure proper delivery. Also, tell when you wish to pay and how—by check, money order, or credit card. If payment is enclosed, say so in the letter, and be sure to include an enclosure notation in the lower left-hand corner.

> Send the order by parcel post to the above address by the end of this month. Deliver to door 9-B at the north end of the shopping plaza. Enclosed is a check for the total amount.

EXAMPLES OF ORDER LETTERS

ACME AUTO DIAGNOSTIC SERVICE
18 Ninth Street
Lowden, Iowa 52255

November 3, 1981

Nekoma Automotive Supply Company
239 Eisenhower Street
Seabrook, Kansas 66604

Gentlemen/Ladies:

Please supply the following merchandise as listed in your current
catalog:

1	Model KL-20 30-Ampere Charger for 6- and 12-volt batteries. Unit price: $99.95	$99.95
2	Model FJ-3 Floor Jack. Unit price: $259.95	519.90
1	Model SA-9 Sequential Analyzer. Unit price: $117.99	117.99
1	Model EM HC-CO Emission Meter. Unit price: $299.99	299.99
	TOTAL	$1,037.83

Ship the order collect by truck freight to the above address on or
before November 20, 1981. Deliver to door 3 at the south end of
the building. Payment will be by check.

Sincerely yours,

Jaques Wilson

Jacques Wilson
Service Manager

JW/nm

NONE-BETTER METAL FABRICATION

273 Bell Street • Rudyard. Montana 59540

July 15, 1981

Machine Tool Industries, Inc.
14 First Avenue
Stahlman, Tennessee 37201

Gentlemen/Ladies:

Please ship me one Model 241 three-speed metal-cutting
band saw with enclosed capacitor motor and floor stand.
This unit is listed in your April 1981 advertising
circular at a special discount price of $359.95,
including shipping.

I am enclosing a money order for this amount.

                Sincerely yours,

                Albert C. Nowicki

                Albert C. Nowicki
                Shop Manager

ACN/rl
Enc. Money order

Discussion Questions

1. Show how these letters conform to the requirements for order letters.
2. Why does Albert Nowicki mention that the price he is quoting is a special discount price? Why hasn't he included delivery instructions in his letter?
3. Why does "money order" follow the enclosure notation in Nowicki's letter?

Claim Letters and Replies

CLAIM LETTERS

Writing claim (complaint) letters is an unpleasant but necessary task in any organization. Claims arise in many ways. Orders may be improperly filled, packed, or shipped. Merchandise may be damaged or substandard. Disputes may arise over terms of payment or pricing. The purpose of the claim letter is to point out the error and have it corrected.

Courtesy—important in any business correspondence—may require a special effort when you prepare a claim letter. Faced with a costly, time-consuming mistake, you may well feel anger and resentment, but you must not let these feelings show. Remember your aim—to obtain a satisfactory settlement of your problem. With a tactful letter you are more likely to gain your ends and also keep the reader's goodwill.

Begin your letter by discussing the problem as fully as is necessary. Tell exactly what happened and when, citing sizes, colors, model numbers, finish, or whatever else the reader must know to investigate and make an adjustment. If you have suffered inconvenience, mentioning it may help to generate a sympathetic response.

Having presented the problem, state clearly the adjustment you wish. Back your position with whatever supporting arguments are likely to sway the reader. Possible adjustments may include replacement of all or part of the merchandise, a partial or total refund, a discount, or new terms of payment. You may also wish to set a date for the settlement. To help expedite action, you may enclose, or offer to supply, copies of orders, canceled checks, or other supporting documents.

End courteously, perhaps by expressing hope for a quick settlement, offering to supply any additional information that might be needed, or—if you have had previous business dealings with the organization—commenting pleasantly upon them. Here is a typical claim letter.

On July 26, I sent a check for $124.74 to your company, along with an order form for a 35 mm Perma-Pix camera, Model CY 741. Copies of the order and my canceled check are enclosed.

Yesterday, I received a package from your company, but when I opened it I was disappointed to find that you had sent the wrong camera. Instead of Model CY 741, I received Model SF 613, a Perma-Pix camera listed in your catalog at $94.86.

On August 15, I am leaving for a two-week Colorado vacation and hope to make a picture record of the trip. Therefore, I would appreciate your sending me the correct camera in time for me to receive it before I leave. As soon as I get it, I will return the incorrect order.

If you are writing a large company and don't know the name of the department that handles claims, address your letter to "Customer Adjustments Department" or "Customer Relations Department." If the organization is relatively small, address it to the sales manager. Any of these choices should ensure that it will quickly reach someone who can handle your problem.

REPLIES TO CLAIM LETTERS

Replies to claim letters, like those to inquiry letters, may be favorable or unfavorable. In either case, answer the letter quickly, within one day if possible, so that your reader knows the problem indeed concerns you. Your reply must have a pleasant tone. Never express anger, and try to avoid terms like "complaint" and "claim." These suggest that the reader is being a nuisance or the request is unjustified.

Favorable Replies. Begin the letter by apologizing for the trouble and indicating that you are taking steps to clear up the problem. Next, briefly discuss its causes if appropriate to do so. You obviously don't want to say that the mix-up was caused by an irresponsible stock clerk, but if there is a valid reason—the company is in the process of switching to a computerized order-filling or invoicing system, for example—by all means explain. This information will help reassure the reader that the problem won't occur again. The goal of your letter is to preserve or reestablish a friendly relationship with the reader, so it is important to end on a positive note. For example, you might tell the reader how highly you value your business relationship, express a willingness to deal with any future problems that might arise, repeat your apology, or comment pleasantly on something that your reader has said. The following letter meets these requirements.

> Please accept our sincere apology for our mix-up in filling your July 26 order. We are sending you the correct camera via special delivery, and it should arrive within a day or two. When it does, just give the carrier the incorrect order to return at our expense.
>
> To accommodate our growing business, we have recently moved our inventory to a new and larger warehouse. During the process of moving and reshelving, some of our merchandise was mixed up. Since receiving your letter, we have corrected this situation, so there should be no more mishaps such as the one you experienced.
>
> Your trip to Colorado should be very enjoyable this time of the year. I hope you will be happy with the pictures you take with your new Perma-Pix camera and that you won't hesitate to order from International Photography Equipment in the future.

Unfavorable Replies. Gracefully refusing a claim presents a greater challenge than perhaps any other writing task. Your reader naturally hopes for good news, but the news that you must convey is just the opposite. You must draft your letter carefully to retain the reader's good will. A carelessly written response will almost certainly create resentment.

Try to strike a harmonious note in your opening sentences. For example, you may thank the person for writing, express regret that there's been a problem, or agree with some statement in the original letter. Be careful, however, not to give the impression that you will grant the adjustment.

Next, turn to the situation that prompted the claim and discuss, in whatever detail and manner are appropriate, why it is necessary for you to refuse. It is important that you justify your position. For example, many claims involve supposedly faulty merchandise that investigation shows was improperly used or cared for. In such cases, note the findings and tell the reader how to prevent the trouble from recurring. To avoid suggestions of blame, which will only antagonize the reader, steer clear of expressions ike "faulty care," "misused," and "improperly maintained." Unwarranted claims for discounts, special credit terms, or refunds can be countered by reminding the reader that granting them would involve extra expense and be unfair to other customers.

Conclude the letter as you began—pleasantly and, if possible, helpfully. Sometimes you will be able to grant a partial adjustment or provide some special service, thus softening the blow. Offers of future help are also effective. If you follow these suggestions, your letter may disappoint the reader, but it will go a long way toward eliminating resentment.

The following letter exemplifies these points. It responds to a letter from a garage owner who had been forced to repeat repairs on several auto bodies when the filler failed and who wants the filler manufacturer to stand the cost.

> We agree that our P.Z.11 epoxy auto body filler should last much longer than a polyester body filler. For that reason we took immediate steps to determine why your problem occurred.
>
> As soon as we received your sample of failed epoxy filler, I inspected it visually but could find nothing wrong, so I sent it to our New Jersey laboratories to be checked. There, our technicians found that an excessive amount of catalyst had been added when it was used. The ratio of catalyst to filler is very important. If excess catalyst is used, the filler is weakened, a condition leading to blistering and loss of adhesion. For this reason, we cannot reimburse you for the failure that you experienced.
>
> To help you avoid further difficulties of this sort, we are enclosing a booklet that lists the recommended catalyst-filler ratio for every filler we manufacture. And because we want you to continue using our products, we are also enclosing a certificate that will entitle you to a 30 percent discount on your next order with us.
>
> If you have any questions about any of our products, please feel free to call us collect at (906) 466-2207 between 8 A.M. and 5 P.M.

This writer has made a convincing case for the refusal, a case that any fair-minded reader would find difficult to reject.

EXAMPLES OF CLAIM LETTERS AND REPLIES

Saint Lawrence Hospital
410 Saginaw Street
Lansing, Michigan 48914

April 20, 1981

William B. Jenkins, M.D.
Butterfield Clinic
809 South Hodges
Grand Rapids, MI 49503

Dear Dr. Jenkins:

On March 5, I sent you my completed registration form and check in the amount of $15 to cover registration fee and meal expenses at the Annual Fall Respiratory Disease Seminar held at the Hospitality Motor Inn, Grand Rapids, on April 10, 1981.

After talking with several participants, I now understand that since I was involved as a discussion leader I should not have paid any fee at all. Therefore, I am requesting that the amount of $15 be reimbursed. If you need any information in order to expedite this matter, such as my cancelled check, please let me know.

I would like to add that I thought the seminar was very well conducted, and I thoroughly enjoyed participating as a discussion leader.

Sincerely,

John W. Potter, RRT
Chief Respiratory Therapist

JWP/paf

BUTTERFIELD CLINIC
809 South Hodges
Grand Rapids, Michigan 49503

April 22, 1981

John W. Potter, RRT
Chief Respiratory Therapist
Saint Lawrence Hospital
410 Saginaw Street
Lansing, MI 48914

Dear Mr. Potter:

I have your letter of April 20 requesting reimbursement of
registration fee and meal expense.

I apologize for any misunderstanding you may have regarding the
fees paid by participants in the seminar. However, as has
always been the case at our lectures and seminars, the main
speakers are the only persons who are not charged registration
fees or meal expenses.

As you know, our seminars are not money-making ventures but
educational services to both lay and professional people. We
would prefer to charge no fee, but it is nevertheless necessary
to charge something to defray actual costs.

We certainly appreciated your help in making the Annual Fall
Respiratory Disease Seminar a success, and I hope that the
misunderstanding about the fees will not cause you to refuse
should we need your services in the future.

If I can be of any further assistance to you, please contact
me.

                            Sincerely,

                            William B. Jenkins, MD

                            William B. Jenkins, M.D.
                            Committee Chairman

WBJ/tfk

Discussion Questions

1. What information has Potter provided to help Jenkins evaluate his claim?
2. Cite several examples of the ways Potter achieves a courteous tone in his letter.
3. Explain how the reply by Dr. Jenkins conforms to the requirements for letters refusing claims.

Johnston
Sales
and
Service | 2359 South Street · Los Angeles, CA 90046 · (213) 439-6519

February 3, 1981

Customer Adjustments Department
Diesel Recon
145 Wayne Road
Austin, TX 78731

Dear Sir/Madam:

On January 24, we ordered twenty-four reconditioned barrels and
plungers (part number AA-40065) for PTD injectors. Today, the
order arrived, and we immediately used twelve of the units to
rebuild two sets of injectors for one of our customers.
Following our normal procedure, our technician installed the
reconditioned barrels and plungers and air-checked the injectors
on the ST34465 injector leakage tester. The manufacturer's
specifications call for a maximum leakage of 8 cc, but three of
the twelve failed at 10.0 cc, 10.5 cc, and 13.2 cc. We replaced
these with three others and completed the job.

Our schedule calls for us to use the other barrels and plungers
to repair another customer's injectors next Tuesday, February 10.
However, unless we get replacements for the defective items by
then, we cannot do so. To prevent us from having to delay the
job, and thus perhaps lose the customer's goodwill, please rush
three good AA-40065 barrels and plungers as fast as possible.
We are enclosing a copy of the invoice for our order and
returning the defective items under separate cover. We hope for
a speedy delivery of these items.

Sincerely,

David Johnston

David Johnston
Manager

DJ/co
Enclosure

DIESEL RECON
145 WAYNE ROAD • AUSTIN, TX 78731

February 5, 1981

Mr. David Johnston
Johnston Sales and Service
2359 South Street
Los Angeles, CA 90046

Dear Mr. Johnston:

We are very sorry to learn that three of the AR-40065 barrels
and plungers in your recent order proved defective. As soon
as your letter arrived, we checked, packed, and sent replacements to you via Emery Air Freight. They should arrive about
the same time that you receive this letter.

The problem occurred because we have recently started using a
new process of chroming worn plungers and then honing the
enlarged plunger to the exact size of the barrel. Some of the
worn plungers, including your three, were not properly cleaned,
so the chrome plating flaked off. Our workers are now
thoroughly familiar with the cleaning procedure, and I assure
you that the three we are sending you are within specifications.

We at Diesel Recon greatly value your business, and we hope
this mistake will not stop you from ordering from us in the
future.

Sincerely,

Elaine Rogers

(Mrs.) Elaine Rogers
Customer Service Department

ER/nt

Discussion Questions

1. David Johnston has addressed his letter to Diesel Recon's Customer Adjustments Department, but the signature on the answering letter indicates that Elaine Rogers is in the Customer Service Department. Explain the discrepancy.
2. What information has Johnston provided to expedite the settlement of the claim?
3. Explain how the reply by Elaine Rogers conforms to the requirements for letters granting claims.

Memorandums

Memorandums, or memos, are essentially short letters used within organizations to present data, announce meetings or their results, announce or suggest policy changes, request action, ask for recommendations, explain procedures, give directions, and the like. Many common types of reports—for example, proposals, accident reports, investigation reports, progress reports, and travel reports—may, when relatively brief, be written as memos.

Memos are the primary means by which members of a company or other organization keep one another informed. Because both your co-workers and your superiors will judge your professional ability partially by the memos you write, it is vital to your career that you learn to prepare them properly.

Although memos usually stay within the writer's organization, occasionally they may pass between two or more organizations that are involved in a joint enterprise. For example, when an advertising campaign is being developed, memos often circulate between the client company and the advertising agency.

Memos range from highly formal to very informal, depending upon their purpose and the relationship between the writer and reader. When you write a memo, follow the rules that apply to any business letter. Be courteous and natural. Keep your message brief and make it as readable as you can. Use short sentences, avoid overly long paragraphs, and use technical terms only when your readers will understand them and they will reduce the length of your message.

Most memos deal with matters requiring immediate action. Generally, the topic is quite narrow. For example, memos would be used to announce meetings held during the course of a research project, but probably not to present the research results.

VALUE OF MEMOS

Memos provide a flow of information among persons and departments of like rank (horizontal communication) as well as those occupying different positions in the organizational chain of command (vertical communication). The design engineer who asks the testing laboratory for tensile strength data on a new copper-alloy wire is communicating horizontally. The company president who announces a more liberal vacation policy is communicating vertically, as is the superintendent who informs the president that a new filing system has been adopted for company offices.

Besides conveying information horizontally and vertically, memos provide a permanent record of actions and decisions. Thus, they greatly reduce the number of oversights and misunderstandings that can occur in day-to-day business operations. The employee who must carry out a procedure involving several steps is much less likely to make an error if the instructions are presented by memo rather than orally. Similarly, transmitting complex, highly detailed information by memo rather than orally greatly reduces the chances that the recipient will misinterpret it. Memos also offer a convenient means of disseminating information to groups of people—for instance, the members of a department. Often, work schedules or the amount of worktime that would be lost prevents holding a meeting. However, by sending a memo to each person or posting it on the appropriate bulletin board(s), the writer can reach everyone easily and economically.

MEMO FORMS

Because memos are so widely used, most large and medium-sized organizations provide printed memo forms. A common size is 5 by 8½ inches, although many other sizes are also used. A memorandum consists of two main parts: the heading and the body. Ordinarily, the heading includes spaces for the names of the sender and receiver, the date, and the subject, as shown below:

To: _____

From: _____

Date: _____

Subject: _____

Some forms also have spaces for the department or building of the sender and receiver, the sender's phone number, and the names of persons receiving copies. In addition, some forms are imprinted with letterheads.

Unlike the usual business letter, a memorandum omits the complimentary close and typed signature. Some writers, however, place their initials after the typed signature in the heading or sign typed memos at the end.

When a memo runs to two or three pages, as occasionally happens, the headings for the additional pages are identical to those used for any business letter (see page 138).

WRITING THE MEMO

To write an effective memo, you must consider several matters. First, make certain that your subject line reflects accurately whatever you are writing about. Otherwise this line may mislead your reader temporarily or even cause the message to go unread.

In addition, decide whether your memo needs an introduction. Often your reader will have enough knowledge of the subject so that the subject line provides all the necessary background. If this is not the case, prepare a brief introduction to set the stage for what follows.

When you write the body of a memo, determine just what your reader will need or want to know and then supply that information. To illustrate, here are several kinds of memos and the basic information you might provide:

ANNOUNCEMENT OF AN APPOINTMENT: name of appointee and position; appointee's background and qualifications; duties of job if unfamiliar to reader

TRIP REPORT: name, purpose, and location of conference, convention, or meeting; name, title, and affiliation of each speaker or discussion leader; subject of discussion; conclusions, evaluations, or recommendations offered; significant exhibits, printed materials, and conversations with others in attendance

REPORT OF SAFETY VIOLATIONS: location and nature of each violation; unless the information is obvious, why it is dangerous and how to correct it

ANNOUNCEMENT OF NEW PRODUCT: properties; features; advantages; different forms

REPORT OF MINOR MISHAP: when, where, and why mishap occurred; results of the mishap

SETS OF DIRECTIONS: numbered list of steps, written as commands that include the articles *a*, *an*, and *the*, and presented in the order they are to be performed; mention of simultaneous steps; reasons step is necessary and warning against improper performance whenever reader may question the need for a step or perform it incorrectly

Finally, decide whether you need a conclusion. Memos can conclude in numerous ways. Among the most common endings are those that offer to provide more information, that make recommendations, and that set starting dates for procedures and policies. Don't provide a conclusion unless one is clearly needed.

Some types of memos, including those mentioned above, are very simple and require almost no writing guidelines. Others require detailed instructions. Chapters 9, 10, and 11 discuss proposals, progress reports, and investigation reports, three complex types that are often written as memos.

EXAMPLES OF MEMORANDUMS

To: Elmira Postiff, Owner, Postiff Surveying Company
From: Jonathan Kobylarz, Supervisor, Crew Chiefs
Date: February 6, 1981

Subject: Attendance at State Convention, American Congress on
          Surveying and Mapping

As you suggested, I spent January 28 at the state convention of
the American Congress on Surveying and Mapping, where I attended
the three sessions that your preview of the program indicated
might provide us with useful information. Here are my comments.

9:00 A.M. - 10:30 A.M. Session

This session featured two speakers, William Ballenger of the
state Department of Licensing and Regulation, and Frank O'Meara,
a state representative, who discussed two legislative proposals
for revamping the licensing and regulation of surveyors and
surveying companies. Following their presentations, several
people in the audience offered comments, sometimes acrimonious,
from the floor. Accompanying this memo are copies of the two
proposed bills. When you have read them, you may perhaps wish
to write our state senator and representative regarding them.

10:30 A.M. - 11:30 A.M. Session

T. R. Tucker, Lands Division, State Department of Natural
Resources, described the survey of state lands that was conducted
during the 1840s. Tucker advised that the field notes from that
survey still exist and he handed out sheets that told how to
obtain them. These notes would serve us in good stead for perhaps half of this year's upcoming projects.

2:00 P.M. - 3:30 P.M. Session

At this meeting, Gary D. Lester, a registered land surveyor who
is with the Gillis County Surveyor's Office, reported on his
county's efforts to remonument all of the section corners in the
county. His report, which was very detailed, covered the cost of
monumenting, the special procedures that were employed, the
number of individuals involved and their titles, and the time
required to complete the project. Copies of Lester's talk will
be available in about one week, and I have asked him to send me
one. As soon as I get it, I will pass it along to you. The
information in it should enable us to remonument the eastern
half of Winnebago County more easily and inexpensively than we
otherwise could.

3:45 P.M. - 5:00 P.M.

Following the Lester talk, I visited the exhibit area and talked
with the representatives of several companies that had exhibits
there. Of all the surveying instruments on display, the Wild

Elmira Postiff   2   February 6, 1981

D13S Distomat interested me the most. This instrument, the most
versatile surveying unit on the market today, can measure
distances of over a mile and, at the push of a button, will also
measure vertical angles. Angles and distances are read from a
digital source. Best of all, perhaps, the Distomat is competitive in price with other measuring units. I have brought back
with me a copy of the owner's manual for the unit and would like
to review it with you. I think you'll agree that we should
seriously consider replacing all of our older surveying units
with the Distomat.

I strongly recommend that you preview the ACSM's convention
program next year and have someone attend any sessions that
appear promising.

Jonathan Kobylarz

Discussion Questions

1. Discuss the adequacy of this memorandum's heading.
2. Show that the writer has done an adequate job of reporting on the
   convention.

To: Bernard Smith, Radar Maintenance Section Supervisor
From: Douglas Apsey, Safety Engineer *DA.*
Date: October 1, 1981

Subject: Safety Violations in Radar Maintenance Section

During my September 28, 1981, safety inspection of your section,
I observed a number of violations that require immediate corrective action. Noncompliance with safety regulations endangers the
lives of the workers and may result in the destruction of equipment. Therefore, in order for your section to continue operating,
these violations must be corrected within 30 days.

The most serious violation, and the one requiring the most urgent
attention, is the improper grounding of the AFP-960 radar trans-
mitter test console. The cable now being used is too light in
gauge and is connected to the cable tray, which does not provide
adequate grounding. This condition creates a serious electrical
shock hazard for technicians using the console and could result
in serious damage to the console. This condition can be
corrected by running a 6-gauge copper cable from terminal 8 on
the main power panel of the console to the common ground of the
section's electrical system. The exact grounding procedure is
described in the <u>AFP-960</u> <u>Radar</u> <u>Transmitter</u> <u>Test</u> <u>Console</u> <u>Instal-
lation</u> <u>and</u> <u>Maintenance</u> <u>Manual</u>, which you can obtain from the
shop's technical data file.

Another serious violation is the lack of rubber safety mats
around all of the test consoles. Under regulation 6-12-73A, each
piece of electrical equipment must be surrounded for a distance
of three feet by an approved electrical safety mat. I recommend
the mat manufactured by the Midwest Rubber Company, stock
number 3269-71-9356.

Finally, I noticed a number of personal violations by technicians in your section. These violations included the wearing of
watches and jewelry around energized equipment, failure to wear
ear plugs in high-noise areas, and failure to consult technical
manuals when equipment was being repaired. Each of these violations likewise represents a threat to employee well-being or
safety.

As section supervisor, you are responsible for insuring that
your personnel comply with company safety regulations at all
times. I suggest that you monitor your section more closely and
stress the importance of complying with these regulations. On
October 30, I will reinspect your section. Please correct these
violations by then so that I will not have to suspend the
operation of your section.

Discussion Questions

1. Cite several ways in which Apsey achieves a courteous tone in this
   memorandum.
2. Explain why the 30 days provided to correct the safety violations is or is
   not an unreasonably close deadline.

To: All Pruning Crew Foremen
From: Tom Foster, Superintendent
Date: April 30, 1981

Subject: Directions for Assembling New Bullhorse Chain Saws

As you will recall, the Parks and Recreation Department decided
last fall to replace our old chain saws with the new Model X-15
Bullhorse chain saws. Yesterday, the new saws arrived, but only
one set of assembling instructions was included. To permit you
to start assembling the saws right away, I am reproducing the
instructions here. If you follow them step-by-step, no problem
should arise.

1.   Remove the cover from the right-hand side of the saw by
     loosening the hex bolt with the Allen wrench included with
     the saw.

2.   Place the blade arm with the two slotted holes over the
     stationary and moveable posts, which are located under the
     cover.

3.   Next, unwrap the chain and slip one end around the clutch,
     making sure to seat the chain in the groove. The clutch is
     the small wheel-like part located just behind the stationary
     and moveable posts.

4.   Place the other end of the chain around the entire blade arm,
     making sure to seat the chain in the groove.

5.   When the chain is in place, put the cover back on the saw,
     making sure that the hex bolt is <u>not</u> tightened. Turn the
     bolt just far enough to hold the cover in place.

6.   Lift the blade arm up and turn the adjusting screw clock-
     wise with a flat-bladed screwdriver. (The adjusting screw
     is located on the front of the saw just below the blade
     arm.) Continue to turn the screw until you can lift the
     chain easily and can see a one-quarter inch gap between the
     chain and the blade arm. You must lift the arm while
     adjusting if you are to achieve the proper tension on the
     chain.

7.   Once the proper tension has been achieved, tighten the saw
     cover securely with the Allen wrench.

If you have any difficulty in assembling your saw, don't
hesitate to get in touch with me right away.

Discussion Questions

1. Explain why the subject line of this memorandum is appropriate.
2. Cite evidence that shows that this memorandum is intended for a technical audience.

To: All Technical Personnel

From: Arnold G. Forbes, Vice-President for Research

Date: April 3, 1981

Subject: New Antibiotic

On March 25, 1981, our company introduced commercially a new oral
broad-spectrum antibiotic called Larocin (anoxicillin). Larocin,
an analog of ampicillin, is a semisynthetic drug. Chemically, it
is a 2-amino-p-hydroxybenzyl penicillin trihydrate.

Larocin is similar to ampicillin in its action against susceptible
bacteria during the active multiplication stage. The product
acts against many strains of Gram-negative and Gram-positive
organisms. Susceptible Gram-negative organisms include
Hemophilius influenzae, Escherichia coli, Proteus mirabolis, and
Neisseria gonorrhoeae. Among the susceptible Gram-positive
organisms are Streptococcus faecalis, Diplococcus pneumoniae,
and nonpenicillinase-producing staphlococci.

The new product is stable in the presence of gastric acid and
may be given without regard to meals. It diffuses readily into
most body tissues and fluids. Most of the Larocin is excreted
unchanged in the urine, and the product is not protein-bound.

Larocin is available in capsules containing 250 mg and 500 mg
apiece, in oral suspensions containing 125 mg or 250 mg per 5
milliliters, and in a pediatric formulation containing 20 mg per
milliliter.

I know all our employees will share my feeling of pride in this
new and important addition to our line of human health products.

Discussion Questions

1. Does this memorandum represent a horizontal or vertical flow of information?
2. Two paragraphs are devoted to presenting background information and one short paragraph to presenting the writer's recommendation. Explain why.

To: Nora Johnson, Plant Superintendent

From: Robert Burtch, Safety Engineer

Date: December 21, 1981

Subject: Use of Defective Vehicles

On December 13, 1981, while making a delivery in Westville,
Michigan, one of our drivers passed through the Michigan State
Police Vehicle Inspection Point. The police found that the
brake lights on the truck were defective and issued a citation.
A memorandum reporting the defective lights was then relayed to
you and to John Anderson, head of Vehicle Maintenance. However,
due to the unavailability of parts and our shortage of trucks,
the vehicle was kept in service.

On December 20, 1981, this vehicle was involved in an accident at
the east end of the intersection of Oak and Maple in Westville.
While the vehicle was traveling east on Oak, a car pulled out of
a parking place and into its path. To avoid an accident, our
driver slammed on the brakes and stopped. Because the brake
lights did not work, the driver behind did not react soon enough
and collided with our truck. The damage to the truck was
estimated at $500, and the car was totally wrecked. We are
fortunate indeed that no one was injured.

To prevent similar occurrences, I suggest you issue a directive
informing all drivers that operating a defective company vehicle
is forbidden. If our own maintenance personnel are unable to
repair the vehicles, then we should contract with an outside
automotive repair shop. By taking these steps, we can prevent
accidents of the sort described above.

Discussion Questions

1. Why has the writer of this memorandum provided an introduction?
2. Discuss the adequacy of the directions presented in this memo.

Suggestions for Writing

1. Write a letter of inquiry requesting:

    a. More detailed information concerning the procedures used in a project reported in a magazine or newspaper article.

    b. Additional details concerning a safety program, employee-rating program, inspection system, time-study system, or traffic-routing system developed by another organization.

    c. Performance data or specifications on a piece of equipment your organization might buy.

    d. Clarification of an inadequate or ambiguous set of directions.

    e. Detailed information concerning the pricing, credit, and discount policies of a company with which your organization might do business.

    f. Information and data for a student research project or term paper.

2. Write a reply to your own letter of inquiry, either supplying the information or refusing the request.

3. Write a sales letter offering to supply some product or service. Use whatever devices are appropriate to attract the reader's attention, spark interest in the product or service, convince the reader of its worth, and motivate action.

4. Write a letter ordering:

    a. One or more pieces of furniture, household appliances, items of clothing, garden implements, or automobile accessories.

    b. One or more tools, machines, pieces of office or shop equipment, or laboratory devices.

5. Write a claim letter calling attention to one of the following and requesting an adjustment:

    a. An order that was improperly or incompletely filled.

    b. An order that was delivered late.

    c. Merchandise shipped by the wrong carrier or route.

    d. Merchandise damaged in transit because of improper packing.

    e. Improper billing for a recent order.

6. Write a reply to your own claim letter, either granting or refusing the adjustment.

7. Write a memorandum dealing with one of the following:

   a. Announcement of a meeting to discuss a new research project, advertising program, building project, or similar activity that will soon get under way. Outline several points that the meeting will cover and ask those attending to come prepared to talk about them.

   b. Recommendation that employee lunch hours be staggered to prevent congestion in the cafeteria. Point out some of the problems congestion has caused.

   c. Summary of the results of a meeting to discuss ways of coping with high employee absenteeism. Ask for employee comments.

   d. Report that a procedure is being carried out incorrectly by employees. Point out the error and explain how the procedure should be performed.

   e. Announcement of a change in the procedure for testing a particular material or product. Explain the new procedure and tell why the changes were made.

   f. Request that the recipient inventory the laboratory stockroom, note any items that are out of stock, and order them. Ask the recipient to report by memo the results of the inventory.

   g. Summary of safety violations in some organization or department and suggestions of ways of correcting them.

   h. Announcement of a meeting to discuss some production, inspection, or shipping problem that has arisen. Explain why the problem is serious, give several possible solutions, and ask those attending the meeting to come prepared to discuss them.

   i. Recommendation that your organization change a policy. List specific changes and tell why you think each is desirable.

   j. Summary of several additional duties that an employee will be expected to perform. List the various tasks and explain how each is to be carried out.

   k. Announcement that the development of a new device or product will be delayed at least two months. Give three reasons for the delay and indicate how you have tried to compensate for it.

   l. Explanation of how to connect a tape deck to a stereo set, collect a potable water sample, turn an angle in surveying, test the resistance of some electronic device, trigger an oscilloscope, package some delicate device, charge a sale with a credit card, make some kind of report, or perform some other task in your field of study.

   m. Report of your attendance at a convention, conference, or meeting.

9

Proposals

A proposal may be written for one of two reasons: (1) to provide a product or service or (2) to suggest that one's own organization do something for itself.

Proposals of the first sort, called *external proposals*, are sent to actual or potential customers. Generally they are prepared in response to a written or oral request by the customer. Sometimes, though, an organization will offer a proposal because information from other sources indicates that the receiver might be interested. Depending upon your organization's business, your proposal may offer to construct an office building, paint a water tower, overhaul a heating system, survey viewers' tastes in TV programs, conduct a time-motion study, prepare a service manual, analyze the workflow pattern in a manufacturing facility, carry out a market survey, or perform any one of an almost endless variety of other tasks.

Proposals of the second sort, called *internal proposals*, show similar versatility. You may, for example, suggest that your company purchase a new piece of office equipment, liberalize its vacation policies, establish a comprehensive safety program, reroute traffic within the plant, undertake a particular piece of research, or change a work procedure.

Proposals vary greatly in length and format. The more complicated the project, the longer the proposal is likely to be. A proposal to decorate an apartment could probably be written in a few pages. At the opposite extreme, a proposal to construct a large apartment complex or to completely reorganize a large company's marketing operation could require dozens, or even hundreds, of pages.

Because external and internal proposals serve different purposes and follow different formats, we will discuss them separately.

External Proposals

External proposals differ widely in content and arrangement. Many private companies and government agencies issue elaborate guidelines that specify in great detail what must be included in any proposal they receive and how the contents must be arranged. However, for most short proposals—the sort you are most likely to write—the format discussed in this section will prove entirely satisfactory. It can include all or most of the parts listed below.

1. heading
2. introduction
3. lists of materials, equipment, and supplies
4. cost breakdown
5. job schedule
6. list of supplementary materials
7. conclusion
8. appendix

Less frequently, an external proposal may also discuss personnel requirements and methods for carrying out the project. This discussion usually follows the job schedule section.

HEADING

The heading consists of the names and positions of the receiver and the sender, the date, and the subject. The subject line should be brief, yet describe the proposal clearly. Here is an example.

To: Marie Benedict, Owner, Benedict Manufacturing Company
By: Mark Adler, for Swazey Electric Company
Date: November 15, 1981
Subject: Proposal to Install New Lighting System in Shop Area

INTRODUCTION

The first sentence of the introduction should state what is being proposed and the total cost of carrying it out, unless the cost isn't known. To continue with the preceding example:

> Swazey Electric Company proposes to install 120 six-foot fluorescent lighting fixtures in the shop area of the Benedict Manufacturing Company for the total price of $12,530.00.

Do not neglect to point out any noteworthy features or details of the product or service you are offering. These will vary depending upon the specific situation. In proposing that the drafting department of a college install drafting tables made by your company, you might point out their rugged, lightweight construction and smooth, durable drawing surfaces. In proposing to install a subsurface sewage disposal system for a mobile home park, you might indicate the type and capacity of the septic tank, the size of the drainage field, and the configuration of the piping. In still other cases, you might emphasize low installation costs, ease or economy of operation, increased productivity, or high capacity.

Be sure, also, to present any pertinent facts concerning the project, including when it can be started, how long it will take to complete, and any limitations. For example, if you are proposing to construct a home but do not intend to finish the woodwork, be sure the proposal points this fact out clearly. Noting limitations is very important, for unless the reader knows just what the proposal will and will not include, misunderstandings and hard feelings are likely to result.

A good way to end the introduction is with a brief statement designed to create a favorable impression. You may mention your firm's excellent reputation, note your employee's exceptional skills, or the like. The following is an example of a complete introduction.

> Rainbird, Inc., proposes to install a Mist-a-Matic plant misting system in Ruby's Nursery's new greenhouses for the total cost of $8,234.00. This system features automatic control of misting and variable time intervals between misting periods. It includes our patented Rain Control Center, 265 Mist Stick spray heads, a 40-gallon-per-minute Hauson self-priming pump with holding tank, and all necessary piping complete with securing accessories. The

price also includes a cement foundation for the pump and control center, a steel bar frame to house them, and full insulation for the system, but does not include electrical hook-up, the cost of drilling a well, or the enclosure for the steel bar frame. Installation can begin within twenty days after we reach an agreement. The installation will take our four-person crew four working days to complete, barring unforeseen circumstances.

The Mist Stick system has a proven track record. In actual use it has given up to 48 percent better results than the old hanging drip head systems. Our firm has installed twenty-three such systems within the last year and has received several letters from greenhouse owners praising the quality of workmanship and the performance of the units. I am sure that you will be completely satisfied too.

Dennis L. Scanlon

LISTING OF MATERIALS, EQUIPMENT, AND SUPPLIES

The listing often contains brief descriptions of some or all of the items required for the project. Do not include too much detail in the listing. If your reader requires further information—as is often the case—you can supply pamphlets, specifications, and the like. When the list includes a very large number of items, it should be presented in an appendix rather than as part of the report proper. The listing of items required for the construction of a house, for example, should be handled in this way. When the listing is presented separately, tell your reader in the body of the proposal to refer to the appendix.

Here is a listing for a proposal to install special equipment in a town's police cruisers.

Equipment

Spotlights	Unity, model 1640 7-inch lens, 50,000 candle-power, interior controls.
Protection Cage	Kingston, model EKR, 120-gauge welded stainless steel wire construction.

Warning Lamps	Unity, model 2250-B, twin rotating strobe units enclosed in a 48-inch housing of high-impact ABS plastic, with an aluminum base.
Siren	Borg Warner, model 4621-042, underhood mounting.
Door Lock	Billings, model 24 12-vac, single-switch control, two-door units.

Michael Guisfredi

COST BREAKDOWN

The cost breakdown must include every expense that will be incurred in carrying out the proposed work. Depending upon the particular proposal, this breakdown would state the cost of such items as materials, equipment, supplies, labor, transportation, fees and permits, inspections, and room and board. Be sure not to overlook any anticipated cost. To do so is to invite hard feelings and possibly even legal trouble later. If the breakdown includes a large number of costs, provide a cost summary in the body of the proposal and a detailed breakdown in the appendix.

Following is the cost breakdown section of a proposal to decorate the reception area of a small lending institution.

Costs

1 Reception desk	$ 275.00
1 Desk chair	115.00
1 Sling-back gold couch	650.00
2 Sling-back green chairs ($165.00 each)	330.00
3 Chrome and glass end tables ($125.00 each)	375.00
1 Chrome and glass coffee table	175.00
3 Ceramic table lamps ($75.00 each)	225.00
1 Coat rack	50.00

3 Wicker plant stands ($45.00 each)	135.00
3 Plants for the plant stands ($25.00 each)	75.00
3 24" × 36" oil still-life paintings ($150.00 each)	450.00
1 12' × 15' green and gold shag carpet	300.00
3 Gallons beige paint ($12.00/gallon)	36.00
Labor (16 man-hours at $9.00/hour)	144.00
Delivery charges	50.00
Interior Beauty commission	500.00
Total Costs	$3,885.00

Martha Kelly

JOB SCHEDULE

The schedule should state exactly when each phase of the work will be carried out. This information allows your customers to plan around your activities and minimizes disruptions and slowdowns. The schedule for a proposal to install room air conditioners in a hotel might read as follows:

Daily Schedule

(6 units installed per day for 5 days)

7:00 A.M.–12:00 P.M.	Cut walls, connect wiring, and refinish
12:30 P.M.–2:00 P.M.	Install frames and units
2:00 P.M.–3:00 P.M.	Complete installation
3:00 P.M.–3:30 P.M.	Clean up

Craig S. Sherwood

This schedule tells the hotel manager that on each day of the installation period six rooms will be unavailable to guests until late afternoon.

Especially for short jobs, the schedule is sometimes omitted from the proposal. However, if the work is likely to interrupt the customer's operation in any way, be certain that the proposal includes a schedule.

LIST OF SUPPLEMENTARY MATERIALS

This section informs the reader of the printed or other separate materials accompanying the proposal. These may include blueprints, pamphlets, specification sheets, price lists, and the like. If, because of its length, the list of materials, equipment, and supplies is being attached to the proposal as a separate item, be sure to mention it in this section. You may also want to provide the reader with evidence of your firm's capabilities. Such evidence—reports describing similar projects successfully completed or testimonials from satisfied customers—would be part of the supplementary material. If reports and testimonials are unavailable, then names and addresses of customers can be supplied instead. The following example is from a proposal to construct a house.

> Accompanying this proposal you will find a detailed floor plan of the house, complete sets of specifications for both the house and the appliances to be installed, a listing of quantities and types of materials needed for construction, an artist's rendering of the finished house, and several testimonial letters from former customers.
>
> *Mark Jensen*

CONCLUSION

When the proposal states a price for the work, the conclusion should mention exactly how long the price will remain in effect. This information will prevent future misunderstandings, and—if costs are to rise soon—it may speed the proposal's acceptance. The conclusion may also briefly review the importance of the project, the advantages of your proposal, or your organization's qualifications for carrying out the project. If it seems desirable, you may offer to discuss the proposal personally. End by expressing your assurance that the work will prove satisfactory, offering to provide any further information, and perhaps thanking the reader for considering the proposal. Here is an example of a conclusion.

> The prices in this proposal will remain in effect until October 31, 1982, at which time they will increase to $12,560.00. Our schedule is filled until June 8, but after that date we can begin work at your convenience. If you need any further information,

please call me at 822-8179, and I will be glad to set a time for meeting with you.

I am confident that you and your customers will be well satisfied with the dependable Electra air conditioner and also with the work of Thomas Heating and Cooling, for we have been servicing the Minneapolis-St. Paul area for fifty years.

Craig S. Sherwood

APPENDIX

The appendix contains material that supplements the information in the report proper and that is mentioned in the "Supplementary Materials" section of the report.

OTHER PARTS

Occasionally, a proposal to supply equipment will need a section discussing the resulting personnel requirements. With some nonroutine projects, it may be necessary to discuss the methods that will be used or to offer reassurance of feasibility. Personnel requirements, methods, and reassurances of feasibility are discussed on page 204. Generally, such discussion follows the job schedule section.

EXAMPLES OF EXTERNAL PROPOSALS

Submitted to: Louise Montague, Producer, Acme Theatrical
                Productions, Inc.
By: Kathleen Van Meer, City Wide Costumes
Date: February 6, 1980
Subject: Proposal to build chorus costumes for "A Cole Porter
          Revue"

Introduction

(1) City Wide Costumes proposes to build twelve female chorus outfits for a production of "A Cole Porter Revue" at a total cost of $902.00. The costumes, from a stock design, will be white, sleeveless,

full-length gowns with removable chiffon overlays. Three overlays will be horizon blue, three peach, two red, two aqua, and two mint. Each overlay will have 100 rhinestone studs and be trimmed in coordinating marabou silk. Shoes will not be provided. The costumes will be ready for wear in fifteen days after a 15 percent deposit is made. This time includes initial and final fittings as well as construction of the gowns.

(2) City Wide Costumes has enjoyed building outfits for many of your productions in the past. We are certain that these costumes will greatly enhance the attractiveness and the mood of your production.

Costs

Material Costs Per Dress

3½ yards polyester ($2.39/yard)	$ 8.37
2½ yards chiffon ($1.29/yard)	3.23
100 rhinestones ($1.89/100)	1.89
3 yards marabou ($3.47/yard)	10.41
Total cost per dress	$ 23.90

Total Material Costs

(12 × $23.90)	$286.80

Labor Costs

Cutter and Seamstress (60 hours at $6.25/hour)	$375.00
Fitter (3 hours at $6.60/hour)	19.80
Supervisor (8 hours at $8.80/hour)	70.40
Total Labor Costs	$465.20

Delivery Charge $30.00

Profit $120.00

Total Cost of Costumes

Material	$286.80
Labor	465.20
Delivery	30.00
Profit	120.00
	$902.00

Supplementary Materials

(3) Accompanying this proposal you will find an artist's rendering of the gown in three views and samples of the material in all of the colors.

Conclusion

(4) We can begin work on the gowns at any time. Fabric prices are not expected to increase in the next few months. If you have any questions or would like to suggest any changes, please contact me at 292-8634. Thank you for once again suggesting City Wide Costumes for your production's costuming.

Discussion Questions

1. Show that the heading of this proposal meets the requirements given in the chapter.
2. The supplementary materials section of this proposal does not indicate that the proposal is accompanied by evidence of the firm's capabilities. Why has City Wide Costumes not provided such evidence?

Submitted to: Richard Bartlow, Chairman, Technical Illustration
                    Department
By: Ann Lundborg, for Drafting Supplies, Inc.
Date: August 1, 1981
Subject: Proposal to Supply Drafting Tables for Technical Illustration Department, Adams Technical Institute

Introduction

(1) Drafting Supplies, Inc., proposes to install twenty new drafting tables in the Technical Illustration Laboratory of Adams Technical Institute for the total sum of $3,542.00. The tables have lightweight frames and extra-large drawing surfaces for large illustrations. Each table has its own individual light, which can be adjusted to suit the needs of the user. The tables will be assembled on the site and positioned according to your directions. Removing the old tables and replacing them with new ones will take one day and

can be carried out at your convenience. We feel our tables are of the highest quality, and our workers will do a skilled job of installation.

Construction of Table and Light

Table framework	Welded aluminum
Table drawing surface	Pressed wood with plastic-coated surface. Dimensions: 48 inches by 36 inches.
Light	Clamp-on steel base, double 20-inch flexible gooseneck, 24-inch fluorescent tube in 25-inch-by-4-inch rectangular holder.

Costs

20 Tables ($130.00)	$2,600.00
20 Lights ($35.00)	700.00
Labor (24 man-hours at $8.00/hour)	192.00
Delivery charge	50.00
TOTAL COST	$3,542.00

Supplementary Materials

(2) Attached you will find a number of diagrams of rooms with the same dimensions as yours, showing possible ways that the tables can be arranged. Also attached are photographs of the actual tables with the lights in place and specifications for both tables and lights.

Conclusion

(3) The prices stated in this proposal will be effective until September 30, 1981, at which time rising costs will necessitate an increase of $5.00 per table. Our schedule permits us to install your drafting tables any time during August. If you need further information, please call me at 823-2776, and I will be glad to see you at your convenience.

Discussion Questions

1. Why does this proposal include a supplementary materials section?
2. Why is the concluding paragraph effective?

Submitted to: Mr. and Mrs. Anthony J. Powers
By: Mark Jensen, Superintendent, J and J Construction Company
Date: February 14, 1981
Subject: Proposal to Construct Powers' House

Introduction

(1) The J and J Construction Company proposes to construct a home at 290 Loudon Street, Cleveland, for Mr. and Mrs. Anthony Powers at a total estimated cost of $52,220.00, not including the lot. The house will have three bedrooms, one and one-half baths, a living room, a dining L, and a full unfinished basement. The price includes all lighting and bathroom fixtures; a dishwasher, electric stove, and garbage disposal unit for the kitchen; and all interior painting except for the woodwork, which will be left unfinished. The house will be Cape Cod style, with a dormer in the back to enlarge the upper floor. It will be constructed in forty-five days, barring complications, and construction can start within ten days after formal agreement is reached.

(2) Our company has been in the home construction business for over a quarter century, and our original designs have won several regional awards. We are confident that you will be very pleased with our product.

Estimated Materials and Labor Cost Breakdown

Excavation	$ 1,120.00
Basement	3,520.00
Concrete walks and drive—	
materials and labor	1,260.00
Carpentry	13,400.00
Lumber	9,450.00
Roofing materials	455.00

Windows and doors	3,500.00
Kitchen appliances	
dishwasher	425.00
stove	450.00
garbage disposal unit	110.00
Plumbing—materials and labor	2,485.00
Heating—materials and labor	3,220.00
Wiring—materials and labor	1,415.00
Light fixtures—materials and labor	350.00
Dry wall	840.00
Painting and decorating interior	560.00
Siding—aluminum exterior	1,680.00
Floor coverings—materials and	
labor	2,240.00
Contractor's profit	4,900.00
Extras: sod	840.00
TOTAL COST	$52,220.00

Supplementary Materials

(3) Accompanying this proposal you will find a detailed floor plan of the house, complete sets of specifications for both the house and the appliances to be installed, a listing of quantities and types of materials needed for construction, an artist's rendering of the finished house, and several testimonial letters from former customers.

Conclusion

(4) The prices indicated will be effective through June 30, 1981. We have a major project scheduled in May, but construction of your house could easily be completed by April 30 if a decision is made within three weeks.

(5) If you have any questions concerning the proposal, please feel free to contact me at 796-7346, and we can meet at a time convenient to you. Thank you for considering J and J Construction.

Discussion Questions

1. What information has the writer included to create a favorable impression of his organization and thus increase the likelihood that his proposal will be accepted?

2. It is important that any proposal to carry out a project note clearly just what the project will and will not include. Why is it unlikely that any misunderstanding will occur concerning the scope of this project?
3. Note that the writer of this proposal has not included a detailed schedule for the completion of each phase of construction. Why can this omission be justified?

Internal Proposals

Internal proposals address specific problems, argue for the adoption of a policy for dealing with these problems, and list the benefits that will result from adoption. Depending upon circumstances, an internal proposal can include all or most of the following sections.

1. heading
2. introduction
3. statement of the problem
4. recommendations
5. discussion of methods
6. assurances of feasibility
7. list of personnel
8. list of supplementary materials
9. conclusion
10. appendix

In short internal proposals, the statement of the problem and the recommendations are treated as parts of the introduction. In longer reports, the three sections are separate.

HEADING

Internal proposals have the same four-part heading as external proposals.

Submitted to: Robert Lutz, Owner, Lutz Television
By: Wayne Green, Service Technician
Date: May 10, 1981
Subject: Proposal to purchase test equipment for radio and television service

INTRODUCTION

This introduction, like that of an external proposal, should state exactly what is being proposed. Often, you will not know the costs of carrying out your suggestions, but when you do, you should state the total in your introduction. The example following includes a statement of costs.

> I propose that our company purchase one Cromeco Z-2H hard disk computer system, one Cromeco SDI graphic interface, four Hazeltine 1500 video terminals, and the associated program software to implement the equipment listed above. The total cost of this equipment will be $18,500.00.
>
> *Stephen F. Hoult*

STATEMENT OF THE PROBLEM

Once you have stated your proposal and perhaps noted its cost, you must convince your reader that a problem exists and a solution is needed. To do so, define the problem and specify the resulting difficulties and disadvantages. Depending upon the situation, it may be helpful to trace the history of the problem. In discussing the problem, use whatever evidence will help buttress your case. This evidence may include statistics, opinions, and personal experience.

Statistics—data showing how much, how many, or how often— can lend powerful support to your proposal, providing they are adequate. Don't, as an employee of a city's street department, use the results of one day's traffic count to contend that the city should install a traffic light at a certain corner. Your reader might think that the results were atypical and reject the proposal. However, if you cite figures showing that traffic has caused problems at the intersection for a number of weeks, you have a strong case.

Opinions may represent the thinking of trained experts or of untrained persons with first-hand experience of the issue. Thus, in proposing that your company install dust-control equipment in a particular plant, you might cite statements by the plant physician who has treated workers for respiratory complaints as well as statements by the workers themselves.

Your own personal experience can also bolster a proposal. Suppose that two years ago you were badly injured by a tornado. Today you are proposing that your company establish a tornado-warning system at one of its plants. By describing your injury and the lengthy hospitalization that followed it, you might influence the company decision more than you could in any other way. To be effective, personal experience must be combined with other kinds of evidence. If it is used alone, the reader may reject it as unusual.

The following excerpt illustrates the use of statistics. It is from the problem section of a proposal suggesting that a county health department immunize school children against measles.

> A July survey by the State Public Health Department shows that only 39 percent of the children under eight years old in this county have been immunized against measles. This situation, unless corrected, makes a measles outbreak very possible when school resumes. Last year a measles outbreak in Ebb County resulted in more than 3,000 lost school days.
>
> *Michael Locke*

RECOMMENDATIONS

Having established that a problem exists, offer your specific suggestion for correcting it. Provide as much detail as individual circumstances warrant. To improve your proposal's chances, try to mention one or more advantages that would result from its adoption. Here again you may find it possible to use statistics, opinions, or personal experience. For example, if you are proposing that your company establish a comprehensive safety education program, you might cite figures showing the decrease in accidents that occurred when a nearby plant adopted a similar program. The recommendations section shown below is from a proposal to establish a fixed vacation time for a plant's employees.

> Specifically, I recommend that the plant cease operations for three weeks every August, beginning the first Monday of the month. The vacation period falls at a time when hot weather has its worst effects on worker productivity. Because the period does not overlap the start of school, employees would be able to take vacation trips.
>
> Shutting the plant down would eliminate the need to replace vacationing workers with unskilled temporary replacements and thus would substantially help product quality. In addition, all general maintenance, including painting and floor resurfacing,

could be done at this time rather than on weekends, as is now the case. The Brandt Company, our maintenance contractor, has informed me that if all the work was done at one time we could expect to save $5,250.00 in overtime costs.

Clint V. Scouten

DISCUSSION OF METHODS

Whenever the methods that will be used in the work are likely to be unfamiliar to the reader, discuss them. Generally such discussion is required only when you propose special research projects, time-motion studies, market surveys, and the like. In your discussion, consider each step in detail and explain why it is necessary. Discuss any testing or analytical procedures in the same fashion. If designs, blueprints, flow charts, and similar materials will be prepared, give details.

ASSURANCES OF FEASIBILITY

If there is a chance that the reader may doubt the feasibility of your proposal, offer reassurances. This is generally necessary only if the project is highly unusual. Reassurances may consist of laboratory findings, a brief discussion of a similar project that has proved successful, or any verified data that will convince the reader of your proposal's practicality.

LIST OF PERSONNEL

For most projects, no listing of personnel will be required. When one is, indicate both the number of employees that will be involved in the project and their departments. Frequently, you will need to mention key personnel by name. This information allows management to evaluate the effects of the personnel shift and to compensate for them. When newly installed equipment will require operators, their number and qualifications should also be given so that management knows in advance the need for added personnel.

LIST OF SUPPLEMENTARY MATERIALS

As in an external proposal, this section lists the printed or other supplementary material accompanying the proposal. Page 194 discusses the types of materials that such a listing may include.

CONCLUSION

The conclusion offers you a final chance to "sell" what you are proposing. You can accomplish this by doing such things as restating any benefits, noting the consequences of adoption or nonadoption, or calling attention to the ease with which the proposal can be carried out. If circumstances warrant, you can also offer to meet with the reader, to provide more information, or to help in whatever way you can if the proposal is adopted. The following conclusion incorporates several of these elements.

> Our department has long needed new flowmeters; and the efficiency, accuracy, and low cost of the Fluidyne Corporation's instrument make it an ideal replacement for our present instruments. If you have any questions, I will be happy to meet with you at your convenience.
>
> *Marc Conley*

APPENDIX

The appendix contains material that supplements the information in the report proper and that is mentioned in the "Supplementary Materials" section of the report.

OTHER PARTS

Occasionally, an internal proposal must include a cost breakdown or work schedule. In these cases, follow the guidelines for external proposal cost breakdowns on page 192.

EXAMPLES OF INTERNAL PROPOSALS

Submitted to: Jack McNeeley, President, Livonia Civil Engineering
By: Robert Burtch, Surveying Party Chief
Date: February 14, 1981
Subject: Proposal to Purchase Two Theodolites and One Electronic Distance Measuring Device

Introduction

(1) I propose that our company purchase two Acumark Model A theodolites and one Acumark Model C electronic distance measuring device (EDM) before our work load increases this spring. The total cost of the combined purchases will be $14,000—$4,000 for each theodolite and $6,000 for the EDM.

(2) The field survey crews presently need two new instruments. The transits now being used are old and subject to built-in errors. Although we could replace these instruments with new transits, I strongly recommend that we purchase theodolites instead. An Acumark Model A theodolite costs several hundred dollars more than a transit, but this added cost is more than offset by features not present in transits.

(3) For example, each theodolite has an optical plummet that reduces the time needed to set the instrument over points on windy days. Even on calm days, theodolites can be set up much more quickly than transits. A theodolite is also much more accurate. Our present transits can read out only to the nearest 20 seconds, whereas a theodolite can read out to the nearest second. This feature would eliminate many man-hours in the field when closure of a traverse loop is important. The readout is likewise more convenient and faster, for each theodolite is equipped with an additional scope from which the angles are read. For the money, the theodolite is the best possible instrument for our needs. It combines accuracy with speed, allowing the surveyor to achieve better field results within a shorter period of time.

(4) The EDM would also reduce costly man-hours. Although it would not eliminate the tape, it would allow long distances to be measured more accurately and easily, for it eliminates the errors that are inherent in a tape (i.e., sag, plumbing, and expansion). Measurements that would take hours with more conventional methods of taping can be completed within minutes. The EDM is accurate to within 1 foot per 100,000 feet, whereas a tape is accurate to within 1 foot per 5,000.

Supplementary Materials

(5) Attachment #1 is a report by the American Congress on Surveying and Mapping, showing the savings in man-hours that can

be realized by using precision instruments. Attachment #2 compares the cost of the Acumark Model A theodolite with the costs of several available transits.

Conclusion

(6) The purchase of these instruments is long overdue. The time and money they will save and the accuracy they will provide more than justify their use by our firm. Therefore, I strongly urge you to study this proposal before considering the purchase of any other new instruments.

Discussion Questions

1. Why has the writer not included separate problem and recommendation sections in this proposal?
2. The writer notes that replacing his organization's old transits with different devices will be more expensive than purchasing new transits. How does he justify the added cost?
3. Discuss how, primarily, the writer achieves clarity in this proposal.

Submitted to: Wilbur R. Budd, Executive Vice-President
By: Wendell Moore, Personnel Director
Date: May 1, 1981
Subject: Proposal to Create Van Pool for Employees

Introduction

(1) I propose that our company purchase five three-quarter ton passenger vans in order to form an employees' van pool. The total cost of purchase will be between $43,500 and $44,625. The exact amount will depend on the make of vehicle chosen.

Problem

(2) As you know, our present parking facilities are woefully inadequate, and we have no room for expanding them. Many employees must therefore leave their vehicles in commercial parking

garages or lots and walk long distances to work. This situation has given rise to considerable employee discontent, and has helped create a serious tardiness and absentee problem which has at times led to a disruption of our operations.

Recommendations

(3) As noted above, five vehicles will be needed. The vehicles I propose will have power steering, power brakes, a seating capacity of ten exclusive of the driver, and the ability to get not less than 27 miles per gallon.

(4) Within the last two years, the West Bend Corporation and the Sun Company have successfully established similar pools. In each case, absenteeism and tardiness have been reduced by nearly two-thirds. Assuming we achieved the same reductions, our annual savings would be about $10,000 per year.

(5) The idea of a van pool has been well received by all the employees with whom I have discussed it, and putting my proposal into effect will undoubtedly improve management-employee relations.

Costs

(6) The estimated cost per vehicle and total cost of all vehicles are given in Supplement A. These costs, less the estimated discount and including taxes, total $43,500 for the least costly vehicle and $44,625 for the most costly. These figures are only estimates, and bidding should lower them.

(7) Supplement B indicates the weekly gasoline expenses for each vehicle, assuming the proposed pickup routes are adopted, while Supplement B-1 shows total weekly gasoline expenses. Since the routes differ in length, the gasoline costs likewise differ. Total gasoline cost for the vehicles is $21.48 per week.

(8) Supplements C and C-1 show the estimated weekly income from the vehicles, after gasoline expenses are deducted. The income after gasoline expenses amounts to $398.52. Supplement C-2 calculates the final yearly income after all expenses have been deducted. This final income comes to $19,513.04.

Method

(9) The county will be divided into five areas, each serviced by a different van. Each area will have a central pickup point with an ample parking lot for employee cars. These lots will be checked hourly by the Sheriff's Patrol, so parked cars will be safe from vandalism. The vehicles will be placed in charge of our regular motor-pool personnel, who will maintain a log book containing a record of miles driven, gasoline and oil costs, and other maintenance expenses. Vehicles will be operated by present personnel from our driver pool. Each driver will spend about three hours per day busing employees.

(10) This proposal not only offers the advantages mentioned earlier but will establish our company as a leader in fighting city air pollution and in conserving gasoline.

Supplementary Materials

(11) Accompanying this proposal are detailed cost and income estimates for this project.

Conclusion

(12) The estimated costs for vehicles apply to this year's models only. Late this summer, when the 1982 models come out, costs will undoubtedly rise. I therefore urge quick approval of the proposal. I realize the proposal may generate questions, and I am ready to provide any additional information you may wish. Call me anytime at ext. 275, or if you like I will be happy to meet with you in your office at your convenience.

Appendix

Supplement A: Vehicle Cost Estimate

Vehicle type	Chevrolet	Dodge	Ford
Standard cost, including tax	$ 9,300	$ 9,100	$ 9,400
Less estimated discount	450	400	475
Total estimated cost	8,850	8,700	8,925
Number of vehicles purchased	× 5	× 5	× 5
Estimated total cost (tax & license inc.)	$44,250	$43,500	$44,625

Supplement B: Maintenance and Expense Estimate

Vehicle number	1	2	3	4	5
Miles traveled per day	9	14	17	21	24
Days per week used	× 5	× 5	× 5	× 5	× 5
Total miles per week	45	70	85	105	120
Divided by average mpg	27	27	27	27	27
Total gallons per vehicle per week	1.7	2.6	3.2	3.9	4.5
Average price per gallon	$1.35	$1.35	$1.35	$1.35	$1.35
Gasoline cost per week per vehicle	$2.30	$3.51	$4.32	$5.27	$6.08

Supplement B-1: Total Weekly Gasoline Cost

Vehicle Number 1	$ 2.30
Vehicle Number 2	3.51
Vehicle Number 3	4.32
Vehicle Number 4	5.27
Vehicle Number 5	6.08
	$21.48

Supplement C: Estimated Income Provision

Vehicle number	1	2	3	4	5
Number of passengers	7	8	9	9	9
Cost per week to passenger ($0.40 per day × 5)	$10.00	$10.00	$10.00	$10.00	$10.00
Gross income per vehicle	$70.00	$80.00	$90.00	$90.00	$90.00
Less gasoline per week	2.30	3.51	4.32	5.27	6.08
Income per vehicle after gas	$67.70	$76.49	$85.68	$84.73	$83.92

Supplement C-1: Total Net Weekly Income

Vehicle Number 1	$ 67.70
Vehicle Number 2	76.49
Vehicle Number 3	85.68
Vehicle Number 4	84.73
Vehicle Number 5	83.92
	$398.52

Supplement C-2: Total Net Yearly Income

Weekly income after gasoline expense	$	398.52
Times 52 weeks per year		52
Total		$20,723.04
Less estimated expenses		
(oil, antifreeze, maintenance, etc.)		1,200.00
Final income after deducting all		
expenses		$19,523.04

Discussion Questions

1. What kinds of evidence does the writer use to support his proposal and where in the proposal is each kind found?
2. This proposal is quite long, yet it is clear and the reader can follow it easily. Point out the ways in which clarity has been achieved.
3. Why is the conclusion of this proposal effective?

Suggestions for Writing

1. Write an external proposal offering to
   a. Design an interdisciplinary course, an advanced placement test, or an independent study course for a college or technical institute
   b. Paint a house or some other structure
   c. Study the traffic-flow pattern of a campus or industrial plant and suggest improvements
   d. Redecorate an office or a room in a private residence
   e. Buy a generator, furnace, or some other piece of equipment
   f. Install a sewage or water system for a single-family dwelling

g. Compare the cost and performance characteristics of two furnaces, drying ovens, refrigeration systems, or other devices or systems

h. Run comparative tests on two or more adhesives, coatings, fibers, casting, or other materials or products

i. Provide outside secretarial or stenographic services to some business firm

j. Design a system to control dust, chemical vapors, noise, or radiation in a laboratory or other facility

k. Investigate the effects of water pollution on a lake or stream

l. Conduct a survey to determine public attitude toward a local political candidate or an existing or proposed ordinance

m. Develop and carry out a sales campaign for a local department store

2. Write an internal proposal requesting that

a. Your company stagger its work hours or change its vacation policy

b. Your town switch to a different type of traffic light, rezone a particular section of town, or spray for mosquitoes

c. Your school extend the library hours, change its grading system, or make some other needed improvement

d. Your company improve its lighting, reduce the noise level, install vending machines, provide an employee lounge, or develop a new traffic-flow pattern

10

Progress Reports

Progress reports are used to trace the development of a particular project or, at times, the activities of an individual or organization. The project may occur within an organization, or it may be carried out for a customer.

Depending upon the nature and scope of the project, progress reports may be issued weekly, monthly, quarterly, annually, at some other set interval, or irregularly—when major steps in the project are completed. With a few exceptions, such as sales reports, production reports, and annual reports put out by corporations, progress reports are prepared for projects that will be finished at some future time. Projects that take only a week or two to finish seldom require progress reports.

Progress reports vary greatly in length and complexity. If the project is simple, they may be issued as letters or memorandums. If the project is more complex, they may extend to many pages, especially if they are issued infrequently. In rare cases, the reports may even be issued as bound volumes. Like the examples in this book, however, most progress reports are likely to be rather brief.

Progress reports are written in every field, for projects of every sort. For example, you may be asked to write reports that summarize:

1. the progress in a laboratory or research project
2. the progress in the construction of a building, dam, bridge, or highway

3. the course of an advertising or public-relations campaign
4. the stages in the remodeling of a building or other facility or in the installation of new machinery or equipment
5. the activities of your organization over a six-month or one-year period

Value of Progress Reports

Progress reports are valuable for several reasons. To begin with, they enable project directors to schedule equipment and supplies—so that they are on hand when needed—and to start separate phases of a project as soon as preparatory work is completed. Thus, progress reports help keep projects running smoothly and on or ahead of schedule.

Progress reports also allow management to check on the direction and emphasis of a project and change them if necessary. Assume, for example, that a company has discovered an inexpensive way to make a compound that formerly was very costly. Produced at low cost, this compound may now have utility as both a dry-cleaning solvent and a metal-degreasing solvent. The company sets up a six-month research project and budgets $50,000 to investigate each use. Progress reports are issued every two months. The first phase of the dry-cleaning investigation shows that the compound causes some dyes to fade. On the other hand, preliminary evidence indicates that the compound is an even better metal-cleaning solvent that originally thought. Armed with this information, management can stop work on the dry-cleaning application and use the remaining funds to expand work on the metal-cleaning application.

Management may use progress reports to evaluate the work already done on a project in light of what remains to be done and to drop the project if this action seems called for. For example, a large bottling company may budget $5,000—but no more—to determine whether a new adhesive for bottle labels is better than the one presently used. If progress reports show that more than the allotted sum will be needed to obtain the information, the project can be canceled and the unspent money saved.

Moreover, progress reports can prevent a last-minute crisis that might otherwise develop if a project is delayed. Suppose a college has planned to begin using a new dormitory by the beginning of the fall semester, but a shortage of structural steel has caused a six-month construction lag. By reading progress reports, school officials will become aware of the situation in time to make alternate plans.

Progress reports have value for the writer as well as the receiver. Unless you write periodic reports, there's some danger that you'll waste time on unimportant aspects of the project or perhaps even forget a primary aim. As a result, the project may be delayed, or you may need to repeat part of the work. If you prepare progress reports, however, these problems are less likely to occur, for you must reconsider the aims of the project every time you write a new report.

Parts of Progress Reports

A typical progress report consists of two parts: the heading and the body. The initial report on a particular project also includes an introduction. These parts are discussed below.

HEADING

The heading of a progress report includes the writer's and recipient's names and titles, the name and the number (if any) of the project, and the time period covered by the report. Do *not* give the dates for the entire project. A typical heading might be:

To: John Ashton, General Contractor

From: John Burtch, Site Foreman

Progress Report: Job No. 579-103-074, Construction of "Knoll on the Lake" Apartment Complex

Time Covered by Report: December 1981 through January 1982

INTRODUCTION

Ordinarily, only the first progress report in a series includes an introduction. The introduction presents the background and goals of the project, indicates when the work is scheduled to be finished, and points out any special requirements that must be met. If, for example, the project involves designing a device that meets certain specifications, then these specifications should be pointed out. Similarly, the introduction should note any special materials or test methods to be employed, as well as any special limitations on the scope of the investigation. If the project involves only a small number of people, the introduction customarily includes their names. As personnel join or leave the project, the changes are noted at the appropriate point in the body of the report. Here are two example introductions.

> This is the first progress report on our company's project to prepare and print the 1983 owner's manual for the Model HK 192 Home Aid Power Saw. The manual will include sections on operation, maintenance, storage, winterization, and safety and be illustrated with seven photographs and two exploded-view diagrams. The design specifies an 8½-by-11-inch, 16-page publication that will be offset-printed in two colors and have a three-color cover. Our schedule calls for completing the project by September 20, 1982.
>
> *Karyn McNabb*

> On January 17, Martin Smith and I received an assignment to construct a binary-to-hexadecimal decoder that conforms to the specifications supplied by Professor Adelaide Winkelmann. The decoder must incorporate 7400 Series integrated subcircuits employing Nand logic. The total circuit must include no more than fourteen integrated subcircuits. It must use less than 250 milliwatts under full load and handle at least 3500 binary inputs per second without any false outputs due to noise. For experimental testing, the output must be displayed on an eight-segment numerical light-emitting diode display. The deadline for completing the project is February 28.
>
> *Craig Richter*

BODY

Although practice varies, the body of most progress reports is organized in three sections.

1. Work completed—what has been done since the last report
2. Present status—where the project stands now
3. Work remaining—what will be done during the next reporting period and those following it.

The complexity of the report will determine whether or not formal captions—titles identifying each section—will be needed and how many should be included. Very brief reports that discuss current status in one or two sentences may omit captions entirely. If captions will improve the clarity of the report, then they should be included.

Overview of Last Reporting Period. Sometimes—for instance, when there are long intervals between progress reports—it is useful to review briefly the activities of the last reporting period or summarize the state of the project at the time of the last report. In such cases, the work completed section of the report may begin with a preliminary paragraph that presents this information. Here is an example.

> During the last reporting period, all remaining drainage structures were installed, the interior concrete floors were poured, and the underground electrical connections were completed. In addition, the housing for catch basin C-B 14 was rebuilt after its accidental destruction by a caterpillar operator, and two defective sections of the water main were replaced.
>
> *Donald R. Burgin*

Information to Include in Body. In most progress reports, it is enough simply to mention the specific procedures that have been carried out in connection with the project. If, however, a procedure is likely to be unfamiliar to your readers, you may wish to include some details or refer readers to a separate process explanation. And if there have been unexpected difficulties or the project has fallen behind schedule, tell your reader what happened and what has been or will be done to correct the situation.

> Earthwork has fallen five days behind schedule because of excessive down-time of heavy equipment and unseasonably heavy rains. These rains have made the soil unstable and delayed the paving of entrance roads by four days. Because our paving contractor, Rieth Riley Construction Company, suspends operations for the winter on November 17, we must correct the soil situation so that paving can be completed by the shutdown date. Unless it is, existing soil conditions will not allow heavy truck traffic in early winter or spring, thus seriously jeopardizing the projected date for finishing the project. To ensure that paving will be carried out, we have requested that all available earth-moving and compaction equipment be transferred to this site as soon as possible.
>
> *Donald R. Burgin*

If it seems desirable to change the direction of a project or even to abandon it, do not hesitate to say so. Be sure, though, that you have enough evidence on hand to justify such a recommendation, for preliminary findings are often contradicted by later work. If additional materials, equipment, or personnel will be needed, ask for them. Finally, do not hesitate to make cautious predictions concerning findings, ability to meet the project schedule, and the like, but at the same time avoid hasty promises. Position whatever information you provide at the appropriate place in the body of the report. For example, if you carried out an unfamiliar procedure, discuss it in the work completed section; predictions should come in the work remaining section.

Depending upon the project, you may need to include tables and graphs in your report. Don't, however, break up the report with so many of them that they interfere with the discussion. Instead, place them in a separate section at the end, and discuss the data in the body of your report.

Here is the body of a progress report on a program to immunize a county's elementary school children against an expected outbreak of measles.

Work Completed

On August 13, we established three immunization clinics, one in each of the county's three school districts, and began distributing informational flyers door to door throughout the county. Later that week we distributed posters to be displayed in stores and houses of worship. These flyers and posters warned of the possible complications of measles and listed the locations of the clinics and times they are open. On August 20, we sent publicity releases containing the same information to radio station WNRT and the *Spring City Clarion*. The next day, the radio station began broadcasting our information three times each day, and on the following day the paper incorporated the information in an editorial urging that every child be immunized.

Present Status

The overall effect of our campaign has been fair. A just-completed survey of the clinics, doctors, and hospitals in the county indicates that above 60 percent of all grade school children have been immunized. Unfortunately, these children are unevenly distributed throughout the county. While 90 percent of the children in the Yorkshire and Richardson school districts have been immunized, only 40 percent of those in the Rivercity district are now protected. This situation is due in large measure to the fact that the Rivercity Board of Education has refused to make immunization a requirement for enrollment in school. To make matters worse, Rivercity is a low-income area, and its children would probably suffer more complications than the children of other districts in case of a measles outbreak.

Work Remaining

To correct this situation, on August 25 we will close the Yorkshire and Richardson clinics and stop the door-to-door distribution of flyers in these districts. Most of the personnel now assigned there will be shifted to the Rivercity district and used to increase awareness of the measles threat, mainly through personal contacts with community organizations. At the same time, efforts will be made to have the Rivercity Board of Education reconsider its immunization stand. If these efforts fail, and we have not immunized at least 60 percent of the children in the district by September 7, we will end the program on that date. Otherwise, we will continue it for two more weeks.

Michael Locke

Organization by Topics

The three-part chronological organization works well when the project is a simple one. But some projects involve a number of tasks being carried out simultaneously, sometimes at different locations. When a project is this complex, it is easier to both write and understand the progress report if it is organized according to the various tasks. Thus, a report describing the progress in the construction of a large apartment complex would include such main captions as plumbing, wiring, heating and ventilation, and the like. Within each major section, however, the discussion should be organized in the past-present-future pattern that is used for reports on simple projects.

Format Uniformity

When a project is finished, the separate progress reports are sometimes gathered together and issued as a single unit. Sometimes, too, an overall report is written from the information contained in the separate reports. Because of these possibilities, it is important that all the progress reports on a particular project follow the same pattern.

EXAMPLES OF PROGRESS REPORTS

To: Kimberley Gillette, Professor of Engineering

From: Ronald Jones, Student

Progress Report: Design of Pump No. P10400

Time Covered by Report: January 30, 1981, through February 28, 1981

(1) On January 30, you supplied Christopher Lichty, Kurt Myers, and me with specifications for a small pump and asked us to design a pump that would meet them. The pump is to be constructed as an integral unit that is driven by a belt and pulley powered by a small air-cooled engine. Its height must not exceed 10 inches and its weight must be less than 10 pounds. It must be capable of delivering 10 gallons per minute at 550 revolutions per minute, and its parts must withstand a maximum pressure of 400 pounds per square inch. The pump is to be designed and drawn by April 30.

(2) On February 1, the group decided in a brainstorming session that a positive displacement pump would be adequate to meet the required specifications. Cast 1013 aluminum was selected as the material of construction for most parts because of its low cost and ability to withstand vibration. Two pistons, each with a diameter of 1¾ inches and a 1-inch stroke, will provide an even displacement. The cylinder walls will be ⅛ inch thick—a thickness easily capable of withstanding the 400 psi load specified. Rough sketches of the internal assembly have now been drawn.

(3) Two major parts of the pump must still be designed. I will design the type and size of valves needed to produce the correct

volume of flow, while Myers will determine the size of the shaft and its material. Finally, Lichty will design the other parts required. These determinations will be completed by March 5 and further analysis of the design within three weeks thereafter. Final assembly and detail drawings will then be started, and they will be finished by the April 30 deadline date if everything goes as planned.

Discussion Questions

1. Why does this report include a discussion of the project's background?
2. Which sentence deals with the present status of the project? Why is the present status not discussed more fully?
3. Why have captions been omitted from this report?

To: John R. Miller, Chief Technologist
From: Glenn Jones, Engineer
Progress Report: Project No. 900, The Impact of Integrated Circuits
      on the Electronics Industry
Time Covered by Report: April 1, 1976, through May 31, 1976

(1) On April 2, a preliminary meeting of the investigation committee was held. At the meeting, it was decided to consider the following three aspects of the impact of integrated circuits: (1) extent of possible use, (2) costs, and (3) problems of utilizing the circuits in electronic equipment.

(2) On April 8, detailed discussions were held with several major manufacturers of integrated circuits during the National Instrument Technologists' Convention in New York City. These discussions revealed that about 70 percent of all existing electronic circuits could be produced in integrated form.

(3) Following the New York meeting, the chief engineers of several major semiconductor manufacturers were contacted and asked to comment on the relative costs of designing and manufacturing integrated circuits. These engineers agreed that design costs were quite high, since any overall design program must include:

1. design of the functional circuit, often in breadboard form
2. design of each individual circuit element and the geometric layout, including the interconnection pattern
3. design of the photomasks required for the oxide-removal stages
4. development of suitable test programs
5. hand assembly of trial test units

Because of the great variety of integrated circuits required for the different types of electronic devices now manufactured, no general development-cost figure is possible.

(4) At present, a 150-item questionnaire concerning the problems of incorporating integrated circuits into electronic equipment and marketing the resultant products is being prepared. Since great care must be taken to phrase the questions properly, the questionnaire will not be completed until late July.

(5) Once the questionnaire is completed, it will be sent to some 200 manufacturers of electronic equipment with the request that it be filled out and returned by August 15. The findings will be analyzed and summarized in the final progress report at the end of September.

Discussion Questions

1. In the discussion at the beginning of this chapter, it was stated that progress reports prevent the writer from forgetting the primary aims of the project. What evidence is there that the writer of this report has kept the aims in mind?
2. What advantage has been gained by tabulating the individual elements of the design program in a formal list rather than presenting them in a regular sentence form?
3. In which paragraphs does the writer discuss work completed, present status, and work remaining? What techniques besides paragraphing are used to distinguish between these three segments of the report?

To: James Reich, York College Surveying Department

From: Randy Richards, Student

Progress Report: Triangulation Traverse of Area North of York College

Time Covered by Report: May 10, 1981, through May 26, 1981

Work Completed

(1) On May 10, we began the actual triangulation traverse. As noted in the first report, a reconnaissance survey revealed that the college campus had been triangulated under the Lambert Projection Coordinate System and monuments had been set at various points on campus. Thus, we tied our traverse into the traverse on campus.

(2) To begin, we established a traverse point over a manhole by turning angles to two known monuments, one at the Marymar Street entrance to the campus and the other at the Science Building. We then turned angles to points 87–4, 87–3, and traverse point No. 2, located at the front entrance of the Science Building. By traversing to the top of the hill at the intersection of Chestnut Street and Hill Avenues, we were able to turn angles to points 86–4, 86–3, and 86–2 from one traverse point, TP_3. From here, we traverse to the intersection of Locust Street and Hill Avenue, where we turned angles to TP_5, TP_6, and TP_7.

Present Status

(3) Currently, we are turning the remainder of the angles to all points up to point 84–1, which is located on a manhole cover by the Maple Street bridge. Because of unanticipated road repairs in the surveying area, we are two days behind schedule.

Work Remaining

(4) Once our present activities are completed, we will return to TP_1, measure the distance to all points with an electronic distance-measuring device, and calculate the vertical angles. Finally, we will traverse southward on Ives Street from point 84–2 and pick up any point missed in the northward traverse up Hill Avenue. When the project is finished, we will have established coordinates on all sixteen points from 84–1 through 87–4.

(5) We plan to complete the project on June 11, weather permitting. This will be two days later than anticipated. When we are finished, we will have a second-order-of-accuracy survey. The maximum angular closure per triangle will be 5 seconds. The average angular closure will be 3 seconds. Distances will be accurate to 1 foot in 10,000 feet.

Discussion Questions

1. Why are captions included in this report?
2. Why does the report omit an introduction?
3. The report notes that the project is two days behind schedule and that it will be completed at least two days later. What purpose does this information serve?

To: Jack Powers, Commissioner, Monroe County Health Department

From: Paul Lewis, Sanitarian, Monroe County Health Department

Progress Report: Improvement of Restaurant Inspection Scores in Monroe County

Time Covered by Report: January 1, 1980, through January 1, 1981

Introduction

(1) This is the first progress report on our department's program to improve the overall scores of restaurant inspections. A 1979 survey showed that Monroe County had the worst restaurant inspection scores of any county in New York State. The state average at that time was 30 points, and Monroe County's average was 42.

(2) To correct this situation, the present program was put into effect January 1, 1980. The program aims to lower the average inspection score for the county to 30 and to eliminate all scores over 40 by January 1, 1985. The program involves doing these things:

1. inspecting restaurants more frequently and enforcing the food code more stringently
2. establishing mandatory management certification programs for restaurant managers
3. establishing a cooperative board of sanitarians, restaurant owners and managers, and restaurant employees to coordinate the program and deal with any problems that arise

Work Completed

(3) This program has now been in effect for one year. During this period, restaurants were inspected every three months rather than

semiannually, as in the past. The average inspection score has been reduced 6 points below the 1979 figure. Much of the improvement is due to the increased strictness of the inspectors, who were instructed to suspend the license of any restaurant that scored over 40 points on two successive inspections. Once this fact became known, most restaurant owners quickly complied with the food-service code.

(4) The first mandatory management certification course got under way on June 2, and the first meeting of the cooperative board was held on July 1.

Present Status

(5) The management certification program is off to a good start; over 30 restaurant managers have completed the two-month course. This training has already resulted in the elimination of many food-code violations.

(6) Because of the rapid turnover of restaurant employees, the cooperative board has been without an employee representative for five of the six months it has been in existence. Without the employee voice, the board has become largely a management-health department group. As a result many employees feel that their opinions are not wanted and refuse to work with the board. A public-relations consultant has been called in to work on the problem.

Future Plans

(7) During 1981, we hope to reduce the average restaurant inspection score by another 3 points. To help achieve this goal, we plan to continue inspecting restaurants on a quarterly basis and to suspend licenses whenever more than 40 points are scored on two successive inspections. By the end of the year, some 90 restaurant managers—about one-half the total in the county—will have completed the management certification program.

Discussion Questions

1. Show that the writer has produced a proper introduction for his report.
2. In the discussion at the beginning of the chapter, it was stated that progress reports prevent the writer from forgetting the primary aims of the project. What evidence is there that the writer of this report has kept these aims in mind?

3. At one point, the writer discusses a problem that has arisen in connection with the project. Locate this discussion.

Suggestions for Writing

Write a progress report on:

1. A research, design, or construction project carried out as part of a course
2. The reorganization of the floor plan of some retail business establishment or small shop
3. The construction or remodeling of a store or house
4. The reorganization of a factory assembly line
5. The resurfacing of a section of roadway
6. A sales campaign for a local store or other business
7. A public immunization campaign
8. The remodeling of a laboratory or X-ray facility in a hospital
9. A local fund-raising drive
10. The installation of machinery in a shop
11. The installation of a furnace or air-conditioning system in a commercial building or private house
12. The activities of a professional or student organization
13. The reorganization of a town's traffic-flow pattern
14. A survey being conducted among the citizens of a community
15. Your progress in one of your courses
16. A program to improve the safety of a shop or laboratory
17. The landscaping of an office or a home
18. The installation of a sewage disposal system or electrical wiring system for a trailer park
19. A campaign to recruit new members for a campus organization
20. Your progress in writing a library research report

11

Investigation Reports

The investigation report describes and discusses the results of a test or other investigation carried out in the laboratory, the shop, or the field. Unlike a library research paper, which depends largely or entirely on published ideas and information, the investigation report uses data developed by the writer or some person or group closely associated with the writer.

You can expect to write investigation reports both for your courses and on the job. In your classes, an instructor may ask you to describe, for example, the results obtained when you checked a water sample for coliform organisms, determined the specific heat of a metal, analyzed a chemical compound for a particular impurity, determined the cylinder pressures in an automobile engine, or ran a soil percolation test. Such a report helps an instructor gauge your progress by showing how well you have mastered the apparatus, procedures, theory, and calculations involved in the work. It helps you by reinforcing what you have learned in the classroom and through your reading, and it familiarizes you with the format you will follow later when you write on-the-job reports.

On the job, investigation reports have a variety of uses. You may have to report and discuss the results of tests showing the properties of some adhesive, coating material, lubricant, or metal alloy; the condition of an air, water, or soil sample; or the best apparatus or procedure for manufacturing a product. The information these reports provide can be used to improve products or procedures, correct undesirable conditions, or take whatever other action is appropriate.

Full-scale reports are rarely required for work that is performed routinely. For such work, forms are usually provided, and the pertinent information is simply filled in. However, when work is nonroutine, a detailed report must be written. Such a report includes all or most of the following sections.

1. heading
2. purpose
3. theory
4. procedure
5. results
6. discussion of results
7. recommendations
8. appendix

These sections are discussed below.

Heading

The heading of an investigation report is similar to that of a proposal or progress report. It includes the name and title of the receiver and the sender, the title of the investigation, and the date of the report. A typical heading follows.

To: Jeffrey L. Sloan, Director, Parks and Recreation Department
From: Paige Lukens, Marine Biologist
Subject: Determination of Brandt River Lamprey Eel Population
Date: February 18, 1981

Purpose

In stating the purpose of your work, provide precise identification for whatever you have tested. If, for instance, you are reporting the results of a series of tensile strength tests you conducted on aluminum and brass wire, give the formal designation for each alloy—aluminum AZ 210, brass B12, and the like. Likewise, tell what prompted the investigation. This part of the report need not be long. Four or five sentences at most should be enough. A statement of purpose follows.

> The purpose of this investigation was to determine whether the Narco Mark–12 navigation unit, serial number 3055, taken from the wreckage of the Beech Bonanza plane, N 6804 W, that crashed in the Deadstream Swamp area the night of February 7 met FAA and Manufacturer's specifications. The airplane crashed 28 nautical miles south of its predetermined flight path and 107 nautical miles beyond its destination. It is believed that the pilot lost his bearings, possibly because the navigation unit was faulty, and flew until his fuel ran out.
>
> *Joel Johnston*

Theory

Following the statement of purpose, present the theory if one is needed. The theory is the underlying principle or principles that make the procedure possible. Generally, procedures in chemistry, physics, and other sciences are based on some clear principle. In contrast, other types of investigations—for example, to survey the deer population of a county or the buying habits of some group of people—are not. Any report on a scientific procedure should, therefore, include a theory unless the reader already knows it. Instructors in the sciences often require that students writing investigation reports include statements of theory to demonstrate their knowledge of the principles behind the work.

Here is the theory section from a student report on the determination of the specific heat of copper and aluminum.

> The principle of thermal equilibrium states that whenever materials are placed together in an insulated container they will eventually reach the same temperature because of a transfer of energy from the warmer material to the cooler. The heat lost by the one material must equal the heat gained by the other. Once the equilibrium temperature is determined, it is possible to solve for the specific heat.
>
> *Anne Bauer*

Procedure

This section of the report tells the reader how the investigation was carried out. In describing the procedure, be brief. Don't try to write an explanation that would enable the reader to carry out the process. Instead, say just enough to give the reader an intelligent idea of what was done. You can usually accomplish this in a few sentences. Here is how the procedure for analyzing furnace flue gas for carbon dioxide might be written:

> Before the test was begun, a one-fourth-inch hole was drilled in the smoke stack between the boiler breeching and the draft regulator. A second hole was drilled in the fire door. The short sampling tube was inserted in the smoke stack; then the analyzer was adjusted to read zero. The sample was taken by depressing the analyzer bulb eighteen times, and the results were read and recorded. This procedure was repeated using a long sampling tube and sampling through the fire door.
>
> *Charles Finnie*

Results

The results are the findings obtained during the investigation. Depending upon the particular investigation, the results may consist of the actual observations, measurements, or readings; they may also include figures derived from the measurements or readings by using a formula, chart, or graph. In a report of an investigation to determine the hourly cash intake of a candy concession operated by college students, the results are simply the individual cash counts.

Hourly Cash Intake (Dollars)

Week 1

Day	8:00 A.M.-9:00 A.M.	9:00 A.M.-10:00 A.M.	10:00 A.M.-11:00 A.M.	11:00 A.M.-12:00 M.	12:00 M.-1:00 P.M.
Monday	.75	2.50	5.00	4.50	1.30
Tuesday	.80	1.05	2.40	.20	.10
Wednesday	1.20	6.75	5.00	6.90	1.20
Thursday	1.10	4.50	5.75	4.50	.70
Friday	.30	.45	.60	.00	.20

Week 2

Day	8:00 A.M.- 9:00 A.M.	9:00 A.M.- 10:00 A.M.	10:00 A.M.- 11:00 A.M.	11:00 A.M.- 12:00 M.	12:00 M.- 1:00 P.M.
Monday	.80	3.25	4.00	4.90	1.25
Tuesday	.95	2.00	4.00	.30	.40
Wednesday	1.25	7.00	8.15	3.70	1.00
Thursday	1.15	5.00	5.25	4.80	.90
Friday	.20	.65	.60	.15	.00

Diane Wojcik

When the test findings are determined by use of a formula, the results section includes the measurements or readings, the formula, and the findings. A report on an investigation to determine atmospheric concentrations of suspended particulate matter might have the following results section:

	North Sampling Location	South Sampling Location
Initial weight of filter, grams	3.0969	3.0947
Final weight of filter, grams	3.1896	3.1692
Volume of air sampled, cubic meters	2,218	1,904

The mass concentration of particulate matter was then calculated by use of the following formula:

$$SP = \frac{(W_f - W_i) \times 10^6}{V}$$

where: W_f = final weight of filter, grams
W_i = inital weight of filter, grams
V = volume of air sampled, cubic meters
SP = suspended particulate matter, micrograms/cubic meter

The results of the calculations are shown below.

	North Sampling Location	South Sampling Location
SP	41.8	39.1

Sherry Durren

Similarly, when the test findings are determined by use of a chart, the results section would include the observations, the chart, and the findings.

Discussion of Results

This section of the report evaluates the test results and discusses their significance. The content will vary according to the investigation and its purpose. If the investigation involved checking a property of some material—say, the specific heat of copper—you would compare the experimental results with the expected value and try to account for any discrepancy. If you tested several materials for possible use in a particular application, you would discuss how well or poorly each meets the requirements. If the purpose of the investigation was to determine whether or not a particular condition exists, your discussion would answer the question or, if the results are inconclusive, point out the need for further work. Here's how two writers discuss their results. The first report assesses the noise levels at different locations in a factory. The second compares the suitability of solder and plastic filler for repairing auto panels.

The Occupational Safety and Health Administration (OSHA) has ruled that any noise level which exceeds 85 decibels for an eight-hour work period constitutes an occupational hazard. Our study shows that the drill press, grinding, fabricating, and stamping press areas exceed that level.

Steven Warner

These tests show that the panel repairs made with the plastic filler began to crack, bubble, and lose adhesion within three months. At the end of the six-month test period, all repairs had failed completely. In contrast, repairs made with solder showed no evidence of failure.

Shawn J. McFarlane

Sometimes the pattern of the results or the spread between the highest and lowest values obtained may be significant. If this is the case, not only the results but their pattern or spread should be discussed. For example, with automobile cylinder-pressure tests, the pattern of results is very important. If two consecutive cylinders have below-normal pressures, the problem is likely to be a bad head gasket, although it could also be worn rings. If, on the other hand, only one cylinder or several nonadjacent cylinders display low pressures, then a bad head gasket can be ruled out. Be sure to note any gaps or irregularities in your data, as well as any deficiencies in measurement, and to discuss their possible effects on the results.

Recommendations

Whenever the results will be used to decide some future course of action, the report must include a recommendations section. Student reports written for laboratory or shop courses are seldom used for this purpose, so they usually do not contain recommendations. For on-the-job reports, however, a recommendations section is almost always a requirement.

The specific recommendations will, of course, depend upon the purpose and scope of the test. You might, for example, recommend that another material, procedure, or device be adopted in place of one presently used; that a product be taken off the market; that a piece of equipment be overhauled or repaired; or that certain precautionary measures be taken. If the scope of the test work was limited, you may recommend that further work be carried out. In this case, be sure to tell your reader exactly what type of work is needed. Here are the recommendations accompanying the two discussions shown in the preceding section.

> To remedy the noise problem, we should conduct an in-depth study of the machines and operations involved, and use the information to institute adequate engineering controls at the source of exposure. Until these controls become a reality, all workers in areas with excessive noise levels should be required to wear polyurethane foam ear plugs.
>
> *Steven Warner*

> I recommend that our firm continue to solder all brazed metal repairs rather than switch to plastic filler.
>
> *Shawn J. McFarlane*

Frequently cost, as well as test results, determines the recommendation that is made. Assume that a company that manufactures wall paneling is testing several glues as possible replacements for the one it now uses. Test results show that none of the experimental glues provides bonding strengths equal to those now obtained. However, one experimental glue yields only slightly lower strengths and costs 35 percent less. Here, the recommendation might be to switch to the less expensive glue. It is quite common to include the discussion and the recommendations in a single section, especially when both are very brief.

Appendix

The appendix contains material that supplements the information in earlier sections of the report. If there is no supplementary material, the report will have no appendix. Supplementary material may include:

> test data too detailed to include in the body of the report
> mathematical calculations used in preparing the report
> brochures, bulletins, letters, and reports
> drawings, graphs, maps, photographs
> field, laboratory, and shop notes
> case histories
> equipment lists
> specifications

When more than one type of information is included in the appendix, group each type in a separate, clearly labeled section. Refer to pertinent information at the appropriate points in the body of the report so that the reader knows when to consult the appendix.

Ordinarily, test data are included in the appendix only when they are too voluminous to be presented in the results section in their entirety. When data consist of many individual measurements, the measurements can be grouped and averaged and the averages presented in the report proper. Thus, 100 readings or measurements might be divided into ten groups of ten, averaged, and the ten average values considered in the results section. All 100 readings, however, would be listed in the appendix.

EXAMPLES OF INVESTIGATION REPORTS

To: Marian McCollum, Professor, Environmental Health Department

From: Leonard Petroski, Student, EHS 215

Subject: MPN-Presumptive Test, Water Sample Furnished for Student Testing

Date: October 10, 1981

Purpose

(1) This experiment was conducted to determine the most probable number (MPN) of coliform organisms present in a water sample supplied by the instructor. It is one of ten experiments required in EHS 215, environmental health laboratory.

Theory

(2) The coliform group of bacteria are capable of fermenting lactose sugar to form gas. The presence of gas in an inoculated tube indicates that coliform organisms were present in the water sample; the number of tubes showing gas provides a measure of the degree of contamination.

Procedure

(3) Five lactose-broth tubes, each containing smaller inverted tubes, were aseptically inoculated with 10 ml. of the water sample. These tubes were then incubated at 35°C for 48 hours.

Results

(4) After this 48-hour incubation period, the tubes were examined for evidence of gas formation. The observations were as follows:

tube no. 1—gas
tube no. 2—no gas
tube no. 3—no gas
tube no. 4—gas
tube no. 5—gas

(5) The MPN Index was then calculated from the following chart:

Number of Tubes with Gas	MPN Index/100 Ml. Sample
none	less than 2.2
1	2.2
2	5.1
3	9.2
4	16.0
5	infinite

(6) Since three tubes showed the presence of gas, the most probable number of coliform organisms was 9.2/100 ml. of the water sample.

Discussion of Results

(7) Although the results show an MPN Index of 9.2 coliforms/ 100 ml., this presumptive test indicates only the presence or absence of gas production, not actual colony morphology. It is possible that the gas produced in the tubes was due to some other type of organism capable of fermenting lactose sugar to form gas. To obtain positive proof the gas was generated by coliform organisms, other and more precise tests would be required.

Discussion Questions

1. Why does this report include a statement of theory?
2. Which data in the results section are actually test results? What is the purpose of the other information?
3. Why does this report omit a recommendations section?

To: Robert Lewis, Civil Engineer, Michigan Department of State Highways

From: Steven Bowman, Civil Technician

Subject: Sieve Analysis of Sand and Gravel from Paris Cement Company

Date: November 12, 1981

Purpose

The purpose of this test was to determine the size composition of the sand and gravel stockpiled at the Paris Cement Company, Paris, Michigan. Both aggregates must meet the specifications of the Michigan Department of State Highways in order to be used for the construction of bridge number R–1439, which will be built across the Muskegon River near Big Rapids.

Procedure

A sand sample weighing approximately 400 grams and a gravel sample weighing about 900 grams were obtained by a department employee and brought to the testing laboratory, where each was weighed accurately. A set of sieves was stacked with the coarsest sieve on top and the finest on the bottom. The sample of aggregate was placed in the top sieve, the lid put on, and the sieves agitated for 10 minutes in a mechanical shaker. The weight of the material on each sieve was determined, and this information was used to calculate the precent of material retained on each sieve, the cumulative percent retained, and the percent passing each sieve.

Results

The following table compares the results of the sieve analysis with the state specifications for these aggregates.

Sand Analysis (original Weight 410 gms)

Sieve Size	Weight Retention (gms)	Percent Retention	Cumulative Percent Retention	Percent Passing	Michigan State Highway Specification #2NS
⅜"	0	0	0	100	100%-C
#4	19.1	4.6	4.6	95.4	95–100%
#8	53.7	13.0	17.6	82.4	65–95%
#16	53.5	12.9	30.5	69.5	35–75%
#30	69.2	16.7	47.2	52.8	20–55%
#50	161.6	40.2	87.4	12.6	10–30%
#100	45.8	11.0	98.4	1.6	0–10%
#200	5.9	1.4	99.8	0.2	0– 3%
PAN	1.1	0.2	100.0	——	——
TOTAL	409.9 gm	100.0			

Gravel Analysis (original weight 902 gms)

Sieve Size	Weight Retention (gms)	Percent Retention	Cumulative Percent Retention	Percent Passing	Michigan State Highway Specifications #64
1½"	0	0	0	100	100%
1"	34.0	3.8	3.8	96.2	95–100%
½"	424.5	47.1	50.9	49.1	30–60%
#4	442.0	49.0	99.9	0.1	0–8%
#10	1.0	0.1	100.0	0	——
#200	0.1	0.01	——	——	——
PAN	——	——	——	——	——
TOTAL	901.6 gm	100.01			

Discussion and Recommendations

Both the sand and the gravel met state specifications for use in the construction of a bridge. We therefore recommend that they be used for bridge number R-1439.

Discussion Questions

1. Discuss the adequacy of the heading.
2. Note that this report does not include a statement of theory. How can this omission be justified?.
3. Justify the use of a combined discussion and recommendations section.

To: Malcolm O'Reilly, Director of Research and Development
From: Thomas Gauthier, Test Engineer
Subject: Road Testing Radial Highway Tires Model XT–225
Date: April 9, 1981

Purpose

(1) This work was carried out to test the mileage capability of our newly developed Model XT-225 radial highway tire. This study is the first segment of a field-testing program designed to determine

whether or not our tire is equal or superior in wearability to the corresponding models made by our three competitors. Laboratory testing had previously shown the XT-225 to be slightly superior in wearability to the others.

Procedure

(2) The National Bus Company was contacted and agreed to participate in the tests. One set of our tires was installed on a bus, and one set each of Ace T-34, Mercury R-29, and All-Grip M-40 tires was placed on three other buses. Each of these buses operated on the same 350-mile run.

(3) The tires were inflated to the manufacturers' recommended pressures, the depth of the tread measured with a dial indicator, and the average depth calculated for each of the four models. After 7,000 miles, the depth of tread was again measured, and the number of miles required to produce each one-thousandth inch of wear was calculated (see Appendix).

Results

Tire	Miles per one-thousandth inch of wear
XT-225	79.9
Ace T-34	80.1
Mercury R-29	78.6
All-Grip M-40	79.5

Discussion and Recommendations

(4) Test results show our XT-225 tire to be slightly inferior in wearability to the Ace T-34 tire but slightly better than the Mercury R-29 and All-Grip M-40.

(5) It is recommended that the remaining phases of the field-testing program and the safety-testing program, outlined in report 23-597RHT, be carried out. Preliminary market research and pricing studies should also be initiated as soon as feasible.

Appendix

Tire Tread Wear Data

Make of Tire	Tire Number	Original Tread Depths, Thousandths Inch	Final Tread Depths, Thousandths Inch	Difference, Thousandths Inch	Average Difference, Thousandths Inch
	1	500	416	84	
	2	500	410	90	
	3	500	412	88	
XT-225	4	500	412	88	87.6
	5	500	414	86	
	6	500	415	85	
	7	500	411	89	
	8	500	409	91	
	1	501*	413	88	
	2	499	415	84	
Ace	3	500	416	84	
T-34	4	502	414	88	87.4
	5	503	411	92	
	6	500	413	87	
	7	505	420	85	
	8	501	410	91	
	1	504	415	89	
	2	501	415	86	
Mercury	3	504	411	93	
R-29	4	502	411	91	89.0
	5	497	409	88	
	6	496	404	92	
	7	503	416	87	
	8	501	415	86	
	1	498	413	85	
	2	498	410	88	
All-Grip	3	497	407	90	
M-40	4	502	411	91	88.1
	5	503	419	84	
	6	497	406	91	
	7	496	407	89	
	8	503	416	87	

*Variations probably occurred because tires were made in different molds.

Calculation, Miles per One-Thousandth Inch of Wear

XT-225 $\dfrac{7000}{87.6} = 79.9$

Ace T-34 $\dfrac{7000}{87.4} = 80.1$

Mercury R-29 $\dfrac{7000}{89.0} = 78.6$

All-Grip M-40 $\dfrac{7000}{88.1} = 79.5$

Discussion Questions

1. Discuss the adequacy of the procedure section of this report.
2. Why does this report include an appendix?
3. Do the average values presented in the results section accurately reflect the value of the individual measurements from which they were derived? Support your answers with specific evidence.

To: Andrea Nye, Director, State Department of Public Health
From: Joseph Hibberd, Sanitarian
Subject: Percolation Test Report, Lot #17 Victoria Hills Subdivision
Date: June 4, 1981

Purpose

(1) The purpose of this test was to determine whether the soil on lot #17, Victoria Hills subdivision, Highland Township, is suitable for the installation of an on-site sewage disposal system. This test was performed at the request of the Saginaw County Health Department.

Procedure

(2) Six holes were dug at the rear (south) portion of the lot, on the site of the proposed absorption field (see Appendix). Each hole was 6 to 8 inches in diameter and 40 to 42 inches deep. The holes were presoaked for 10 hours, causing the soil particles to swell and simulating conditions during the wettest part of the year.

(3) A nail was placed in the side of each hole six inches from the bottom, and water was poured into the hole up to the nail marker.

After 30 minutes the drop in water level was measured and recorded. The holes were refilled to the marker, and the procedure was repeated until eight readings were recorded (Table 1). The last reading taken in each hole was used to calculate the percolation rate (Table 2). The temperature during the test was 62°F.

Results

Table 1. Drop in Water Level

Test No.	Time	Drop in Inches, Hole No.					
		1	2	3	4	5	6
1	9:30 A.M.	6	6	6	6	6	6
2	10:00	6	6	5½	6	5	6
3	10:30	6	6	5	5¾	4½	5
4	11:00	6	5	5	5	4	5
5	11:30	5½	5	4½	4½	3¾	4½
6	12:00 M.	5½	4½	4	4¼	3½	4
7	12:30	5	4½	4	4¼	3	3¾
8	1:00	4¾	4	3½	4	3	3¼

Table 2. Calculation of Percolation Rate

Hole	Drop in Inches, Final Reading	Rate of Drop, Minutes/Inch
1	4¾	6
2	4	8
3	3½	9
4	4	8
5	3	10
6	3¼	9
	Total	50

Average percolation rate 50/6 = 8 minutes/inch

Discussion of Results

(4) This percolation rate meets the requirements of the State Department of Public Health for on-lot sewage disposal systems.

(5) The soil appears to be a loamy sand with approximately 80 percent sand, 10 percent silt, and 10 percent clay. No rock formations, fragipan, or mottled soil were observed; these items would

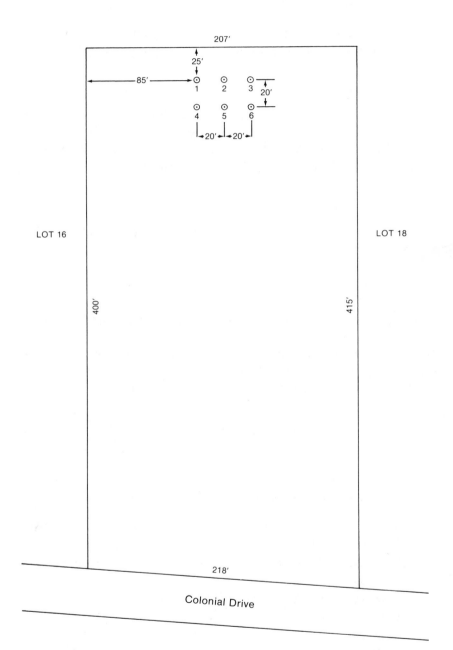

LOT 17, VICTORIA HILLS
HIGHLAND TOWNSHIP

impair the efficiency of the sewage disposal system. There were no surface drainage or slope limitations in the location tested.

Recommendations

(6) The rear of lot #17, Victoria Hills subdivision, is suitable for the installation of an on-lot sewage disposal system. It is recommended that a permit be issued by the Saginaw County Health Department to allow construction of the system.

Appendix: Location of Percolation Test

(7) The accompanying diagram shows lot #17, Victoria Hills subdivision, and the location of the percolation test holes.

Discussion Questions

1. Comment on the adequacy of the purpose section, supporting your evaluation with specific evidence.
2. What kinds of information does the discussion-of-results section include, and what purpose does this information serve?
3. Why does the writer include a diagram showing the location of the test holes?

Suggestions for Writing

Write an investigation report on work carried out to determine:

1. The stability of transistor bias circuits or the effect of a diode in a simple AC circuit
2. The validity of Ohm's Law, the transformer turns equation, or some other equation
3. The concentration of particulate matter in air
4. The specific heat of aluminum, brass, or some other metal
5. The most probable number of organisms in water or a standard plate count on milk
6. The normality of an acid or base, the identity of a chemical compound, or the aspirin content of aspirin tablets
7. The maximum density and optimum water content value for a soil

8. The acreage of a parcel of land
9. The moisture content of aggregate for concrete
10. The nitrate and detergent levels in sewage effluent
11. The cylinder pressures, oil pressure, or dwell angle for an automobile
12. The physical characteristics of two or more adhesives, coatings, fibers, castings, or other materials or products
13. The performance characteristics of two furnaces, drying ovens, refrigeration systems, or other devices or systems.
14. The traffic flow pattern on a campus or in a trailer park
15. The attitude of the voters in a town toward a particular candidate or proposal
16. The pricing practices of the merchants in a small town
17. A problem in the physical plant of your campus
18. The reaction of students at a college toward a proposed change in some campus regulation
19. The adequacy of the recreational facilities in a town

12

Abstracts

An abstract—sometimes called a summary, précis, or synopsis—is a brief notation or condensation of the essential points in a speech or in some piece of writing, such as a book, article, or report.

The ability to abstract is one of the most commonly employed and useful skills any student can acquire. Whenever you take lecture notes or underline the important points in a text, you are performing part of the procedure involved in abstracting. In preparing for an important examination, you may complete the abstracting process by combining lecture notes and underlined passages into a write-up containing the essence of several weeks of study. At times, too, an instructor may ask you to summarize the plot of a short story, novel, or play, or the contents of an article or textbook chapter.

When you become employed, your supervisor may ask you to summarize the contents of a report, article, or chapter in a book or to write the abstract for a long report prepared by you or someone else. And when you attend a talk or meeting, note taking will once again help you to capture the essence of what you hear.

Abstracts are vital to the functioning of any large modern enterprise. Without them, executives could not begin to cope adequately with the flood of reports that cross their desks. During a single week, these reports might number several dozen, many of them very lengthy and all requiring some sort of action. Abstracts reduce an otherwise impossible reading task to manageable proportions. The executive merely reads the abstracts and then routes the reports to the person best able to take the appropriate action, perhaps reserving a few reports to handle personally.

Without abstracts, professionals at all levels would find it impossible to keep up with new developments in their areas of interest. Thousands of technical and nontechnical professional magazines are now published in the United States and elsewhere. Each year they print several million articles, nearly 100,000 in engineering alone, for example. To impose order on this enormous mass of information, numerous abstracts journals now exist, each minutely subdividing a field such as chemistry, economics, or education. These abstract journals allow readers to locate the articles that interest them.

Types of Abstracts

Two types of abstracts are widely used—the *descriptive* and the *informative* abstract. A descriptive abstract names the subject of the original piece of writing and notes the main points that the original covers. It does not, however, reveal any findings and is seldom more than ten lines long. An informative abstract is a highly condensed version of the original. Besides naming the subject and noting its main parts, the informative abstract presents the most important findings of the original, including any decisions, recommendations, and conclusions. Its length may range from 15 percent of the original for short pieces of writing to less than 1 percent for long chapters or books. The following examples illustrate the difference between the two types.

Descriptive Abstract

This report analyzes the July operating statement of Granger Autos, Inc., Baltimore, Ohio. It compares net profit and various operating expenses to total sales volume, as well as the salesmen's compensation to the gross profits on vehicle sales. It notes that the parts and service department is operating at a loss and suggests several ways of correcting the situation.

Informative Abstract

Granger Autos, Inc., is a Baltimore, Ohio, dealership employing 22 persons and selling approximately 500 vehicles per year. The July operating statement showed the net profit to be 4.5 percent of the total sales volume. Advertising, rental costs, and fixed and semifixed expenses totaled 0.7, 1.3, and 7.8 percent, respectively, of the total sales volume, while salesmen's compensation totaled 18 percent of the gross profit from all sales of vehicles. The sales department sold 42 vehicles during the survey month, 18 more than necessary to break even, for a gross profit of $37,800. Because of decreasing business, the parts and service department showed a loss of $2,555. The report suggests that the company institute a customer follow-up program to correct the situation, offer more liberal credit to customers, boost its charges for labor, and decrease by one person the parts and services staff.

Joe Mayer

A descriptive abstract indicates whether or not the original piece of writing contains information that will interest you, and thus it helps you decide what to read and not to read. It cannot, however, be used as a substitute for the original.

Informative abstracts, on the other hand, can be and often are used in place of the original. In such cases, the user consults the original only when it is necessary to know what specific evidence supports a particular finding or recommendation.

Descriptive or informative abstracts often precede chapters in technical books and articles in professional journals. Abstracts are also used on dust jackets and in advertisements for some academic books and often accompany the titles on the table-of-contents pages of magazines. Abstracts produced in school and on the job are nearly always informative rather than descriptive. This chapter will, therefore, focus on writing the informative type.

Writing an Informative Abstract

When you abstract, following a systematic procedure is important. The steps presented here will enable you to produce informative abstracts with a minimum of trouble.

Begin by scanning the article, chapter, or report, paying particular attention to the title, headings (captions and subcaptions), and the opening and closing paragraphs. These parts will provide important clues to the central message. Then read the material carefully until you are thoroughly familiar with its content and organization. As you read, look for the thesis statement. Usually, it occurs in the first or second paragraph, although sometimes it is found in the conclusion. If the thesis statement is implied rather than presented directly, state it in a sentence or two of your own.

Now look for the main points that support the central idea. If you own the original, underline the points; otherwise, copy them as complete sentences in their original order on separate sheets of paper. Frequently the topic sentences of paragraphs will state the main points—ideas, opinions, findings, or events. Don't underline or record specific details; similes, metaphors, or other figurative language; illustrative examples; or repetitive statements. If part of an idea occurs in one sentence and the remainder in another, underline the appropriate parts or note them as a single sentence. When you finish, use these points to prepare a first draft of the abstract. Follow the original order of presentation unless it makes more sense to start with the conclusion from the original or a poorly written original makes rearrangement necessary. Use the original wording or a close approximation of it. Be sure you don't accidentally omit any important information. Don't worry if the abstract is too long or the writing is rough in spots; you can correct these matters later.

When you write the final draft, condense as necessary to achieve the proper length by substituting words for phrases and clauses and by rewriting sentences in a shorter form. Don't, however, omit the words *a*, *an*, and *the*, and don't abbreviate anything that isn't abbreviated in the original. At times you may need to summarize a number of individual points in a general statement. Make any changes in phrasing and add any linking devices needed to ensure a smooth flow of thought. Generally these devices will consist of words or phrases, although occasionally you may have to supply a short sentence. If the original has technical terms but the readers of the abstract will include nontechnical people, translate these terms into everyday language. As always, you must be aware of your reader.

When the draft is complete, check it against the original to make sure you have not omitted an important point or distorted the emphasis by overstating or understating a point. Polish the draft by checking for and correcting any misspellings, word omissions, and mistakes in grammar and punctuation.

When the abstract is finished, add the heading. For articles and chapters of books, follow the forms shown below.

Abstract of "Sodom and Gomorrah: A Volcanic Disaster," by Joel Block, *Journal of Geological Education*, (May 1975), p. 75.

Abstract of Chapter 3, "Air Contaminants," by R. W. Allen et al., *Industrial Hygiene*, Englewood Cliffs, N.J., Prentice-Hall, 1976.

If the abstract will accompany the original piece of writing, use only the word *abstract* for the title.

AN EXAMPLE OF ABSTRACTING

Below is an original piece of writing with the important points italicized and with marginal notes that serve as a guide to abstracting. Following the original are rough and final drafts of an abstract prepared for a general audience.

Omit generally known fact.

Everyone knows that a human being, like a chicken, comes from an egg. *At a very early stage, the human embryo forms a three-layered tube, the inside layer of which grows into the stomach and lungs, the middle layer into bones, muscles, joints, and blood vessels, and the outside layer into the skin and nervous system.*

Usually these three grow about equally, so that the average human being is a fair mixture of brains, muscles, and inward organs. *In some*

Omit figurative language.

eggs, however, one layer grows more than the others, and when the angels have finished putting *the child* together, he *may have more gut than brain, or more brain than muscle.* When this happens, the individual's activities will often be mostly with the overgrown layer.

Omit repetition.

We can thus say that while the average human being is a mixture, some people are mainly "digestion-minded," some "muscle-minded," and some "brain-minded," and correspondingly digestion-bodied, muscle-bodied, or brain-bodied. *The digestion-bodied people look thick; the muscle-bodied people look wide; and the brain-bodied people look long.* This does not mean the taller a man is the brainier he will be. It means that if a man, even a short man, looks long rather than wide or thick, he will often be more concerned about what goes on in his mind than about what he does or what he eats; but the key factor is slenderness and not height. On the other hand, a man who gives the impression of being thick rather than long or wide will usually be more interested in a good steak than in a good idea or a good long walk.

Omit secondary points.

Medical men use Greek words to describe these types of body-build. For the man whose body shape mostly depends on the inside layer of the egg, they use the word **endomorph.** If it depends mostly upon the middle layer, they call him a **mesomorph.** If it depends upon the outside layer, they call him an **ectomorph.** We can see the same roots in our English words "enter," "medium," and "exit," which might just as easily have been spelled "ender," "mesium," and "ectit."

Omit derivation of names and their connection with body types.

Since the inside skin of the human egg, or endoderm, forms the inner organs of the belly, the viscera, the endomorph is usually belly-minded; since the middle skin forms the body tissues, or soma, the mesomorph is usually muscle-minded; and since the outside skin forms the brain, or cerebrum, the ectomorph is usually brain-minded. Translating this into Greek, we have the viscerotonic endomorph, the somatotonic mesomorph, and the cerebrotonic ectomorph.

Words are beautiful things to a cerebrotonic, but a viscerotonic knows you cannot eat a menu no matter what language it is printed in, and a somatotonic knows you cannot increase your chest expansion by reading a dictionary. So it is advisable to leave these words and see what kinds of people they actually apply to, remembering again that most individuals are fairly equal mixtures and that what we have to say concerns only the extremes. Up to the present, these types have been thoroughly studied only in the male sex.

Include basic physical description.

Viscerotonic endomorph. *If a man is definitely a thick type* rather than a broad or long type, *he is likely to be round and soft, with a big chest but a bigger belly.* He would rather eat than breathe comfortably. *He is likely to have a wide face, short, thick neck, big thighs and upper arms, and small hands and feet. He*

Omit simile.

has overdeveloped breasts and looks as though he were blown up a little like a balloon. *His skin is soft and smooth, and when he gets bald,* as he does usually quite early, *he loses the hair in the middle of his head first.*

Omit specific example of type except for behavioral information that applies to all thick types.

The short, jolly, thickset, red-faced politician with a cigar in his mouth, who always looks as though he were about to have a stroke, is the best example of this type. The reason he often makes a good politician is that *he likes people, banquets, baths, and sleep; he is easygoing, soothing, and his feelings are easy to understand.*

Omit secondary point.

His abdomen is big because he has lots of intestines. He like to take in things. He likes to take in food, and affection and approval as well. Going to a banquet with people who like him is his idea of a fine time. It is important for a psychiatrist to understand the natures of such men when they come to him for advice.

Include basic physical description.

Somatotonic mesomorph. *If a man is definitely a broad type* rather than a thick or long type, *he is likely to be rugged and have lots of muscle. He is apt to have big forearms and legs, and his chest and belly are well formed and* *firm, with the chest bigger than the belly.* He would rather breathe than eat. *He has a bony head, big shoulders, and a square jaw. His skin is thick, coarse, and elastic, and tans easily. If he gets bald, it usually starts on the front of the head.*

Omit specific examples of type.

Dick Tracy, Li'l Abner, and other men of action belong to this type. Such people make good lifeguards and construction workers. They like to put out energy. They have lots of muscles and they like to use them. They go in for adventure, exercise, fighting, and getting the upper

Include behavioral information.

hand. *They are bold and unrestrained, and love to master the people and things around them.* If the psychiatrist knows the things which give such people satisfaction, he is able to under-

Omit secondary point.

stand why they may be unhappy in certain situations.

Include basic physical description.

Cerebrotonic ectomorph. *The man who is definitely a long type is likely to have thin bones and muscles. His shoulders are apt to sag and he has a flat belly with a dropped stomach, and long, weak legs. His neck and fingers are long, and his face* is shaped like a long egg. *His skin is thin, dry, and pale, and he rarely gets bald.* He

Omit simile.

looks like an absent-minded professor and often is one.

Include basic behavioral information.

Though *such people* are jumpy, they like to keep their energy and don't fancy moving around much. They *would rather sit quietly by themselves* and keep out of difficulties. *Trouble upsets them, and they run away from it.* Their friends don't understand them very well. They

Omit secondary point.

move jerkily and feel jerkily. The psychiatrist who understands how easily they become anxious is often able to help them get along better in the sociable and aggressive world of endomorphs and mesomorphs.

Omit repeated behavioral information.

In the special cases where people definitely belong to one type or another, then, one can tell a good deal about their personalities from their appearance. When the human mind is engaged in one of its struggles with itself or with the world outside, the individual's way of handling the struggle will be partly determined by his type. If he is a viscerotonic he will often want to go to a party where he can eat and drink and be in good company at a time when he might be better off attending to business; the somatotonic will want to go out and do something about it, master the situation, even if what he does is foolish and not properly figured out, while the cerebrotonic will go off by himself and think it over, when perhaps he would be better off doing something about it or seeking good company to try to forget it.

Include thesis.   Since these personality characteristics depend on the growth of the layers of the little egg from which the person developed, they are very difficult to change. Nevertheless, *it is important for the individual to know about these types, so that he can have at least an inkling of what to expect from those around him,* and can make allowances for the different kinds of human nature, *and so that he can become aware of and learn to control his own natural tendencies,* which may sometimes guide him into making the same mistakes over and over again in handling his difficulties.

Eric Berne, "Can People Be Judged by Their Appearance?"
from A Layman's Guide to Psychiatry and Psychoanalysis,
(New York: Grove Press, 1962), pp. 3-5.

Here is a rough draft made from the italicized portions of the original article.

At a very early stage, the human embryo forms a three-layered tube, the inside layer of which grows into the stomach and lungs, the middle layer into bones, muscles, joints, and blood vessels, and the outside layer into the skin and nervous system.

Usually, these three grow about equally. In some eggs, however, one grows more than the others, and thus some people are digestion-bodied, some muscle-bodied, and some brain-bodied. The digestion-bodied people look thick, the muscle-bodied people look wide, and the brain-bodied people look long. If a man is a thick type, he is likely to be round and soft, with a big chest but a bigger belly. He is likely to have a wide face, short, thick neck, big thighs and upper arms, and small hands and feet. He has overdeveloped breasts. His skin is soft and smooth, and when he gets bald, he loses the hair in the middle of his head first. He likes people, banquets, baths, and sleep; he is easygoing, soothing, and his feelings are easy to understand. If a man is a broad type, he is likely to be rugged and have lots of muscle. He is apt to have big forearms and legs, and his chest and belly are well formed and firm, with the chest bigger than the belly. He has a bony head, big shoulders, and a square jaw. His skin is thick, coarse, and elastic, and tans easily. If he is bald, it is usually on the front of the head. He is bold and unrestrained and loves to master the people and things around him. The man who is definitely a long type is likely to have thin bones and muscles. His shoulders are apt to sag, and he has a flat belly with a dropped stomach and long, weak legs. His neck and fingers are long, as is his face. His skin is thin, dry, and pale, and he rarely gets bald. Such people would rather sit quietly by themselves. Trouble upsets them, and they run away from it. It is important to know about these types, so that one can have an inkling of what to expect from those about him and so that he can become aware of and learn to control his own natural tendencies.

This first draft includes all the main points of the original article, but no attempt has been made to condense or tighten the write-up or to ensure a smooth flow of prose at all points. These shortcomings, however, have been corrected in the final version of the abstract, which appears below.

The human embryo very early forms a three-layered tube. The inside layer grows into the stomach and lungs, the middle layer into bones, muscles, joints, and blood vessels, and the outer layer into the skin and nervous system. Sometimes one layer grows more than the others, and thus some people are digestion-bodied, some muscle-bodied, and some brain-bodied. A digestion-bodied man has round, soft physical features, soft, smooth skin, and a belly that is larger than his chest. He is easygoing, soothing, and likes people. A muscle-bodied man has rugged, prominent physical features, thick, coarse, elastic skin, and a chest that is bigger than his belly. He likes to master the people and things around him. A brain-bodied man has thin, weak-looking physical features, thin, dry, pale skin, and a flat belly with a dropped stomach. He like quiet and solitude, and avoids trouble. Knowing about these types helps a person to anticipate the behavior of others as well as to recognize and control his own natural tendencies.

This final version is about 40 percent as long as the rough draft. Brevity has been gained by rewriting sentences in shorter form, summarizing individual points in general statements, and omitting some points that a rereading revealed were less important than the others. For example, the final sentence of the rough draft reads:

> It is important to know about these types, so that one can have an inkling of what to expect from those about him and so that he can become aware of and learn to control his own natural tendencies.

The same sentence in the final draft reads:

> Knowing about these types helps a person to anticipate the behavior of others as well as to recognize and control his own natural tendencies.

Thirty-nine words have become twenty-four. Most of the comments about specific physical characteristics have been replaced with general remarks that capture the essence of the more detailed statements. The following two passages, the first from the rough draft and the second from the final draft, illustrate this generalizing.

> If a man is a thick type, he is likely to be round and soft, with a big chest but a bigger belly. He is likely to have a wide face, short, thick neck, big thighs and upper arms, and small hands and feet. He has overdeveloped breasts. His skin is soft and smooth, and when he gets bald, he loses the hair in the middle of his head first.

> A digestion-bodied man has round, soft, physical features, soft, smooth skin, and a belly that is larger than his chest.

Baldness patterns have not been mentioned because of their relative unimportance.

Suggestions for Writing

1. Read the following article carefully, noting the central idea and main points. Prepare the first draft of an abstract of the article and convert the draft into a finished, informative abstract by condensing, revising and polishing.

Silencing Pneumatic Equipment

Pneumatic [compressed-air] components in equipment as diverse as packing machines and computer peripherals can produce noise exceeding daily exposure limits mandated by OSHA [The Occupational Safety and Health Act of 1970]. Besides being dangerous to hearing, such noise can interfere with communications, contribute to lowered productivity, and cause frequent errors and inattention. Also, the vibrations that produce the noise can damage machinery and pipes.

Fortunately, noise generated by air systems is comparatively easy to control and can be kept well below OSHA limits. Although the burden of noise control normally falls on the user, information on noise characteristics and noise control is readily available from manufacturers. The decision on how to control noise generally depends on a consideration of costs, operating environment, worker comfort, and legal requirements.

When is Noise a Problem?

The determination of whether noise is a problem depends on how people react to the sound emitted. Many factors about noise are relative and subjective, a fact that should be taken into account when planning a noise-attenuation [noise-reduction] program. For instance, a compressor operating in a metal-stamping plant might go unnoticed, but the same compressor in a dental office could be quite annoying.

To establish whether a problem exists at the objective level, the sound must be analyzed with a sound level meter or an octave-band analyzer. Such equipment is useful in determining potential hearing damage, annoyance, and speech interference.

Annoyance level and loudness may not be synonymous, although a loud noise is usually more annoying that the same sound that is somehow muted. Given the same sound pressure level, higher-frequency sounds (above 2,000 Hz [*hertz*—a unit of frequency equal to one cycle per second]) are usually more annoying than lower-frequency sounds.

The vibrations produced by air equipment range from the subaudible to the limit of human perception. A low-speed pump, for instance, can produce low-frequency vibrations (less than 15 Hz) that are felt rather than heard. As frequency rises, the vibrations are accompanied by noise, with the audible range beginning at about 30 Hz. In this range, noise control usually becomes an important consideration.

Two Ways to Reduce Noise

Generally, noise is reduced at two locations: the source or the listener's ear (by changing the sound path). The first correction involves installing equipment at the intake or discharge end of a compressor, vacuum pump, or air motor. Or the equipment can be placed in a specially built enclosure.

Noise reduction at the listener's ear can involve simply moving either people or equipment to another location. . . .

The sound path also can be changed by modifying the acoustical environment or placing appropriate barriers between the source and listener. Sound follows a line-of-sight path; obstructing the path reduces noise. The intent of these methods is not necessarily to silence the equipment, but to reduce noise to levels that are physically and psychologically tolerable and to reduce vibrations to levels that pose no danger to the equipment itself.

There are many types of noise attenuation devices for air equipment. Dampeners and mufflers covering the range of pulsations from 1 to 20,000 Hz are available. Some are based on the phase-shift principle, which is analogous to cancelling out or stabilizing three-phase alternating current. Also, absorptive and dissipating mufflers, in which the compressed air passes over perforations that lead to sound-absorbing materials, can be used.

One of the most economical and most effective devices to attenuate noise over a wide spectrum is the low-pass filter. This filter, which can be as simple as a glass or plastic jar, allows only lower-frequency sound waves to pass through. In more sophisticated versions, a succession of tubes with different cross-sectional areas and lengths act as a low-pass filter for sound waves passing through them. The ratios of the cross-sectional areas to each other and to the tube lengths determine the frequency range of the sounds that are attenuated and passed. A tube with equally spaced side orifices acts as a high-pass filter.

The effect of a low-pass filter is the same as that produced by passing the sound waves through alternating layers of different media, each transmitting only certain frequencies. The power transmission ratio—the ratio of average power emerging from the medium to that entering it—can be calculated to determine the influence of the layer. This ratio depends on medium thickness and specific acoustic resistance for a plane wave. (For instance, water has a specific acoustic resistance 3,800 times that of air.) Various types of media thus could be used to build an acoustic filter that either blocks or selectively transmits waves of certain frequencies.

Compressors and vacuum pumps also can be modified by inserting a plastic-foam liner directly into the units. This can reduce pump and compressor noise by up to 14dBA [decibel—a unit of sound intensity], depending on the amount of pressure or vacuum being generated. Modification of a unit with a readily available kit is easy; the end plate is removed and the liner simply slipped between the shroud and body of the pump or compressor.

Acoustically insulated cabinets are also available to reduce air-equipment noise to office levels (about 50 dBA). One version of such an enclosure quiets—by as much as 17 dBA—the equipment by holding it on a vibration isolator inside a foam-lined, baffled cabinet.

Compressors and vacuum pumps engineered to run quietly are, of course, the best choices for applications that require noise levels even lower than those mandated by any "official" standard—in dental and medical offices, for example. One such unit reduces noise output by as much as 15 dBA because its motor is suspended on brackets within a plastic-foam-insulated canister. The unit also is fitted with rubber mounting feet. (The standard unit, by contrast, is rigidly mounted directly to the motor.) The quiet model also can be fitted with a double-length cartridge muffler to reduce noise even further.

Noise Trade-offs

The technology and data required to reduce noise in air equipment are readily available. The major criterion for selecting a method is to buy only as much quietness as is required. Indeed, it may be more difficult to define required noise attenuation—regulatory, comfort, and aesthetic considerations could have significant impact—than it is to select a muffling technique.

The least expensive cure is to simply increase the distance between the noise source and the listener. However, this may not be possible if space is already at a premium.

Applying the various sound-deadening techniques costs

somewhat more than merely moving equipment around. Minor modifications such as quiet boxes or kits are the least expensive, add-ons such as larger mufflers are moderately expensive, and specially engineered units are the most expensive.

Robert Moffatt, "Beating OSHA to the Punch by Silencing Pneumatic Equipment," Machine Design, 52, No. 6 *(March 20, 1980), 74-77.*

2. Abstract a journal article dealing with a subject that interests you. Follow the guidelines presented in suggestion 1.

13

The Library Research Paper

Library research involves gathering ideas and information on a particular topic from books, magazines, newspapers, government publications, and other library sources. This material is then properly focused, clearly organized, and formally presented in a written report that documents your sources. Writing a research paper familiarizes you with the resources and services of the modern library, promotes careful reading and note-taking, and provides essential experience in assimilating and evaluating printed material. Once you have mastered the research paper process, you will be able to apply it to any field, not only in school but also on the job.

Producing a library research paper requires five distinct steps:

1. choosing your topic
2. using your library's reference tools to assemble sources
3. taking your notes
4. preparing your outline
5. writing your paper

Each step is discussed fully in this chapter.

Choosing Your Topic

Instructors differ in their assignment of topics for library research papers. Some assign specific topics, others limit topics to a general subject area, and still others allow students a free choice. Even if you are limited to a general subject area, you will have some control over the direction your research takes. Let your interests guide your preliminary choices. For example, if you are an avid amateur astronomer and have been assigned a paper on some aspect of the United States' space program, "The Significance of Voyager II" would be a more appropriate topic than "The Politics of NASA Appropriations for Cape Kennedy Maintenance." Similarly, let personal interests guide you if you have a free choice of topic. Interests often develop suddenly and unexpectedly. An instructor's lecture might spark a desire to investigate an intriguing business trend, a medical milestone, a technological development, or a scientific discovery. A discussion with a friend might spur you to consider the economic feasibility of solar heating or the safety of nuclear power plants. A television documentary about the nineteenth-century naturalist Charles Darwin might suggest a paper on the current controversy between creationists and evolutionists.

When you choose an area to research, avoid overly broad topics such as "The Effects of Chemical Food Additives" or "Recent Medical Advances," which could not be discussed adequately in a paper or even, perhaps, in a book. More appropriate topics might be "The Effects of Sodium Nitrite as a Meat Preservative" or "Eye Surgery with Laser Beams." The extent to which you limit your topic will, of course, depend on the materials available in your library, the assigned length of the paper, the time you have to complete it, and your purpose and audience.

Also avoid topics that are fully explained in a single source and those based entirely on personal opinion. For example, process explanations and descriptions of geographical locations do not require you to evaluate and coordinate material from several sources. Although you may find a number of articles on such topics, they will, to a large extent, report the same information. Topics based on personal opinion or experience, such as "The Thrills I Have Enjoyed Waterskiing," are unsuitable because you can't support them with library research. Personal insights, judgments, and conclusions can, of course, be used to support or contradict material obtained through research. Furthermore, you may draw your own conclusions from a variety of documented sources. For the present, however, you are concerned only with selecting and narrowing your research topic.

Using Your Library's Reference Tools to Assemble Sources

When you have a good idea of what you are looking for, determine whether your library has what you will need to develop the topic satisfactorily. Several tools are available to you. The most useful are reference books (particularly encyclopedias), the card catalog, and periodical indexes.

ENCYCLOPEDIAS

Encyclopedias are collections of articles on an array of subjects or on subjects within isolated fields, such as education or physics. Encyclopedias are a useful starting point for research because their articles can provide an overview of the field into which your topic fits. Suppose you are investigating the impact of commercial television on its first audiences during the early 1950s. General encyclopedia articles about television would be good starting places because they would supply you with concise background information. Furthermore, the bibliographies that often follow encyclopedia articles might provide additional references for your research. On the other hand, if you have decided to focus on some technical aspect of television, such as the development of the color picture tube, you would consult one or more general encyclopedias as well as specialized encyclopedias such as *Harper's Encyclopedia of Science* and the *McGraw-Hill Encyclopedia of Science and Technology.* The following list includes many of the best known general and specialized encyclopedias.

General Encyclopedias

Encyclopaedia Britannica	*Collier's Encyclopedia*
Encyclopedia Americana	*New Columbia Encyclopedia*

Specialized Encyclopedias

Encyclopedia of Accounting Systems

Encyclopedia of Advertising

Encyclopedia of Banking and Finance

Encyclopedia of Biological Science

Encyclopedia of Chemical Technology

Encyclopedia of Chemistry

Encyclopedia of Computer Science

Encyclopedia of Ecology

Encyclopedia of Education

Encyclopedia of Educational Research

Encyclopedia of Electronics

Encyclopedia of Environmental Science

Encyclopedia of Higher Education

Encyclopedia of Human Behavior: Psychology, Psychiatry, and Mental Health

Encyclopedia of Management

Encyclopedia of Occupational Health and Safety

Encyclopedia of Physics

Encyclopedia of Social Work

International Encyclopedia of the Social Sciences

McGraw-Hill Encyclopedia of Science and Technology

Universal Encyclopedia of Mathematics

Van Nostrand's Scientific Encyclopedia

Encyclopedias, which are usually shelved alphabetically, are generally kept in the Reference Area of the library. As you read encyclopedia articles, note any points that you might work into your paper and any useful-looking references listed in article bibliographies. For any article that you consider using, jot down the following information:

title of article

author(s) of article (This information is not always available. Sometimes an author is identified only by initials at the end of an article. In such cases, check the list of contributors at the front of the first volume for the full name.)

name of encyclopedia

year of publication

THE CARD CATALOG

The card catalog, a file of three- by five-inch cards, indexes all the books in the library. In some libraries, the card catalog also lists magazines, newspapers, government documents, college catalogs, records, and tape recordings; in others, these materials are listed separately. Your librarian can explain the type of catalog your library uses.

The card catalog contains three types of cards for each non-fiction book the library owns—author, title, and subject cards (fiction, obviously, is not listed by subject but only by author and title). The cards are arranged alphabetically, and the three types may be filed together, separately, or in some other manner, such as title and author cards in a single file and subject cards elsewhere. As the example on page 266 illustrates, these cards provide you with helpful information.

Except for the top line, which shows whether the card identifies author, title, or subject, the cards for a book are identical. In addition to providing a call number for the book, each card offers other valuable information. The publication date, for example, may show whether a book is useful: if you are writing about the Wankel engine and find a card for an automotive text published in 1949, you can rule the book out because it is older than the engine. An index will help you to locate useful information, and a glance at the card will tell you whether the book you are considering includes one. Most important, the list of subjects under which a book is catalogued may lead you to investigate subject headings that you would otherwise overlook. Suppose you are writing a paper about the computer revolution's effect on small businesses. You would probably check the subject cards under *computer* as a matter of course, but without examining the subject listing on each card, you might overlook subject categories such as *artificial intelligence* and *calculating machines* and miss other useful books.

For every promising item in the card catalog, copy down the following information on a three- by five-inch card:

author(s)

title

editor(s) and translator(s), as well as author(s) of any supplementary material

CATALOG CARDS FOR ONE BOOK

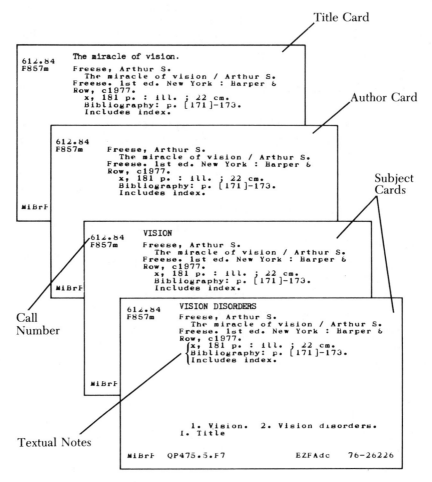

Title Card

Author Card

Subject Cards

Call Number

Textual Notes

612.84
F857m   The miracle of vision.

         Freese, Arthur S.
            The miracle of vision / Arthur S.
         Freese. 1st ed. New York : Harper &
         Row, c1977.
            x, 181 p. : ill. ; 22 cm.
         Bibliography: p. [171]-173.
         Includes index.

612.84
F857m   Freese, Arthur S.
            The miracle of vision / Arthur S.
         Freese. 1st ed. New York : Harper &
         Row, c1977.
            x, 181 p. : ill. ; 22 cm.
         Bibliography: p. [171]-173.
         Includes index.

MiBrF

612.84   VISION
F857m
         Freese, Arthur S.
            The miracle of vision / Arthur S.
         Freese. 1st ed. New York : Harper &
         Row, c1977.
            x, 181 p. : ill. ; 22 cm.
         Bibliography: p. [171]-173.
         Includes index.

MiBrF

612.84   VISION DISORDERS
F857m
         Freese, Arthur S.
            The miracle of vision / Arthur S.
         Freese. 1st ed. New York : Harper &
         Row, c1977.
            x, 181 p. : ill. ; 22 cm.
         Bibliography: p. [171]-173.
         Includes index.

MiBrF

            1. Vision. 2. Vision disorders.
            I. Title

MiBrF QP475.5.F7   EZFAdc 76-26226

   total number of volumes (if there is more than one) and the
      number of the specific volume that you wish to use
   city of publication
   name of publisher
   date of publication

Although some of these items might at first seem irrelevant to your
search for sources, you will need all of this information when you
prepare your bibliography (your information cards are, in fact, your
working bibliography).

There is one final item from the card catalog that you must copy down—the *call number* located in the upper left-hand corner of every catalog card. Writing this number (often a combination of letters and numbers) on the reverse of the card will allow you to arrange the cards by call number when you are ready to look for the books themselves.

The call number indicates where the library shelves a particular book. Each book has its own number, which appears on the spine of the book. Most libraries store books in *stacks*, which may be open for browsing or closed to most library users. If the stacks are closed, give a librarian a list of your call numbers and ask to see the books. If you have direct access to the stacks, locate the general area where your book is shelved. Most libraries post charts to guide you; if yours does not, consult a librarian. Once you have found the number range that includes your call number, follow the figures on the book spines numerically and alphabetically until you find your book. By all means browse in the general vicinity of each book: you may find other useful sources that you overlooked in the card catalog.

Examine each book that you consider using by skimming the preface, table of contents, and other introductory matter to determine the volume's scope and approach. Also check the index for discussions that relate to your topic and note their page numbers. Then skim these discussions and any chapters that look promising. If you find that you cannot use the book, throw away the bibliography card for it.

PERIODICAL INDEXES

Periodical indexes catalog articles appearing in magazines and newspapers. The entries are generally listed by subject and author, and sometimes also by title. Periodical indexes are issued frequently—many are biweekly or monthly. These indexes are later collated in volumes covering several months or years. Because they appear frequently, periodical indexes provide access to recent information that might not be published in books for several years—if at all.

Of all the periodical indexes that your library is likely to have, the *Readers' Guide to Periodical Literature* (1900–date) is the most useful for a subject that has been discussed in popular magazines. The *Readers' Guide* lists nonfiction articles by subject and author and creative works by title and author. The first pages of the *Guide* identify the abbreviations used for the 100 magazines that are indexed. The example illustrates the arrangement of the index and the "see also" cross-references that direct you to related subject headings:

> MINES and mineral resources
> > *see also*
> > Ore deposits
> > Quarries and quarrying
> Mineral crisis. M. Sheils and J. Buckley. il
> > Newsweek 96:98 N 10 '80
> More than just oil in short supply here. il
> > U.S. News 89:38 N 24 '80
> Resource wars. M. T. Klare. Harpers
> > 262:20 + Ja '81

The *Readers' Guide* lists article titles, authors, whether an article is illustrated (il), periodical titles, volume numbers (before the colon), page numbers (after the colon), month, and year.

Several recently compiled periodical indexes are available only on microfilm or similar microforms. Microfilms are filmstrips on which printed material is photographically reduced page by page. The filmstrips are read through an enlarging viewer that your librarian can explain how to use. Don't let yourself be intimidated by microfilms and other microforms: they are easy to use and, for some material, they are the only available sources.

Among microfilmed indexes, *The Magazine Index* is particularly useful. Indexing 375 popular publications by subject, author, and title, each monthly issue covers the past five years and includes material that may be no more than two weeks old. The film is read on a screen attached to a device that, like traditional microfilm viewers, allows both fast, motorized film movement for skipping through the index and slow, manual movement for browsing. In addition, the index publishes a list of recent articles on twenty to thirty topics of current interest.

The *National Newspaper Index* covers three national papers—the *Christian Science Monitor,* the *Wall Street Journal,* and the *New York Times.* Each monthly microfilm issue includes three years of references and is read on a viewer identical to that of the magazine index.

Two newspaper indexes—the *New York Times Index* and *News-Bank*—are issued in printed form and refer readers to photographically reduced materials. The *New York Times Index* (1913–date) lists news articles, book reviews, commentaries, and features that have appeared in the *New York Times*. The index's preface explains how to read entries, which relate to the final "Late City Edition" of the daily paper—the edition that is on microfilm in most libraries. (Your library might subscribe to a regional edition of the paper, and actual copies of the *Times* might not correspond with the index.) *NewsBank* indexes stories of local, state, and regional interest from over 120 newspapers in all fifty states. *NewsBank* is issued monthly as a looseleaf notebook, and the articles indexed are reproduced on microfiche—small cards bearing a series of reproduced pages that can be read only on microfiche viewers.

Specialized periodical indexes are also available, and the following list is a survey of those that you may wish to consult.

Accountants' Index, 1921–date. (indexed by subject)

Agricultural Index, 1916–1964. (indexed by subject; titled *Biological and Agricultural Index* from 1964 on)

Applied Science and Technology Index, 1958–date. (indexed by subject)

Biological and Agricultural Index, 1964–date. (indexed by subject)

Business Index, 1979–date. (indexed by subject, author, corporation, and persons mentioned in articles; microfilmed)

Business Periodicals Index, 1958–date. (indexed by subject)

Consumer's Index, 1974–date. (indexed by subject and product)

Criminal Justice Periodicals Literature, 1975–date. (indexed by subject and author)

Cumulative Index to Nursing Literature, 1956–1976. (indexed by subject and author; titled *Cumulative Index to Nursing and Allied Health Literature* from 1977 on)

Cumulative Index to Nursing and Allied Health Literature, 1977–date. (indexed by subject and author)

Education Index, 1929–date. (indexed by subject and author)

Engineering Index, 1884–date. (indexed by subject and author)

Environment Index, 1971–date. (indexed by subject and author)

Index to Dental Literature, 1963–date. (indexed by subject and author)

Index to Legal Periodicals, 1909–date. (indexed by subject and title)

Industrial Arts Index, 1913–1958. (indexed by subject; divided,

1958, into *Business Periodicals Index* and *Applied Science and Technology Index*)

Legal Resources Index, 1979–date. (indexed by subject, author, statute, and case; microfilmed)

Public Affairs Information Service Bulletin, 1915–date.

Quarterly Cumulative Index Medicus, 1927–date. (indexed by subject and author)

Technical Book Review Index, 1935–date. (indexed by subject, author, and title)

Vision Index, 1975–date. (indexed by subject and author)

Wall Street Journal Index, 1958–date. (indexed by company and subject

Your topic will, of course, determine how you choose to use indexes, but a good idea is to begin with general indexes such as the *Readers' Guide* and then proceed to more specialized listings. As in your search through the card catalog, record bibliographic information for promising articles. Copy the following items for each potential source on a three- by five-inch note card, which will become part of your working bibliography.

author(s), if identified

title of article

name of periodical

volume or issue number (for professional and scholarly journals only)

date of periodical

pages on which article appears

Take these cards and any periodical references that you found in encyclopedia bibliographies to the card catalog or whatever catalog your library uses for periodicals. The catalog will indicate whether the library subscribes to the periodicals and, if so, where they are located. Current periodicals—often those issued during the past six months—are usually kept in a special part of the library such as a periodical room. Back issues are bound into convenient volumes, given a call number, and shelved with other books. As in your book search, copy the back issue call number on the reverse of your bibliography card, find the volume, and skim through the article in question to assess its value. Back issues of some magazines and scholarly journals and those of most newspapers are kept on microfilm.

ALMANACS, HANDBOOKS, AND DICTIONARIES

Almanacs, handbooks, and dictionaries are reference tools that you may wish to consult throughout the research and writing process. They are often the most efficient sources for clarifying a concept or verifying a fact.

Almanacs. General almanacs are annual books of up-to-date facts. If, for instance, you are writing about federal budget deficits, an encyclopedia is unlikely to provide you with a table showing the deficit for each fiscal year including the year just ended, but a current general almanac would offer just such a table. Among general almanacs, the *World Almanac and Book of Facts*, the *Information Please Almanac*, and the *Reader's Digest Almanac and Handbook* are particularly useful.

Handbooks. More specialized than almanacs, handbooks supply excellent background information in addition to facts. Further, handbooks describe practices, processes, and methods in particular professions and fields. A selection of noteworthy handbooks is listed below.

Handbook for Community Professionals
Handbook for Environmental Planning
Handbook for Managers
Handbook for Nurses
Handbook for the Technical and Science Secretary
Handbook of Air Conditioning, Heating, and Ventilating
Handbook of Chemistry and Physics
Handbook of Community Health
Handbook of Environmental Control
Handbook of Industrial Engineering and Management
Handbook of Highway Engineering
Handbook of Industrial Noise Control
Handbook of Industrial Research Management
Handbook of Industrial Waste Disposal
Handbook of Occupational Safety and Health
Handbook of Pharmacology
Handbook on Contemporary Education
Handbook on Urban Planning

Dictionaries. There are two types of dictionaries. The first, and more familiar, type defines words and shows their pronunciation, development, and use. The second type, like handbooks, provides concise information on specialized subjects. No matter what your topic is, you should always use the first type to find the meanings of new words encountered in your research and to check spellings and usage in your final draft. Any of the following standard dictionaries should be adequate for college and on-the-job use.

Large Dictionaries

Funk and Wagnall's New Standard Dictionary
Random House Dictionary of the English Language
Webster's Third New International Dictionary

"College" Dictionaries

The American Heritage Dictionary of the English Language
Funk and Wagnall's Standard College Dictionary
Webster's New Collegiate Dictionary
Webster's New World Dictionary of the American Language

Following is a sampling of respected specialized dictionaries.

Chambers' Technical Dictionary
Comprehensive Dictionary of Psychological and Psychoanalytical Terms
Dictionary of Business and Science
Dictionary of Criminal Justice
Dictionary of Economics and Business
Dictionary of Education
Dictionary of Genetics
Dictionary of Geology
Dictionary of Law
Dictionary of Personnel Management and Labor Relations
Dictionary of Psychology
Dictionary of Scientific and Technical Terms
Dictionary of Sociology
Dictionary of Sociology and Related Sciences
Dictionary of Visual Science
Dictionary of Water and Waste Engineering

Funk and Wagnall's Dictionary of Electronics
Stedman's Medical Dictionary
Thorpe's Dictionary of Applied Chemistry
UNESCO Dictionary of the Social Sciences
Webster's Geographical Dictionary

Once you are familiar with your sources and the reference books that you will have at your disposal, you may decide to modify the scope or emphasis of your topic. Insufficient library materials may require you to expand your topic and your working bibliography or, conversely, you may be so swamped with sources that you must narrow your topic and trim your working bibliography. Unfortunately, there is no firm rule for how many sources you need to produce a good research paper. The best advice is "Don't skimp, but don't go overboard either." At this point, you can probably judge what you need to do the job well.

Taking Your Notes

When you have assembled your sources, you are ready to start note-taking. At this point your encyclopedia reading and skimming of other sources may suggest a tentative plan for your paper. If, for instance, you are investigating the problem of medical malpractice suits, your initial research might suggest these main divisions.

1. causes of increasing numbers of malpractice suits
2. effects of malpractice problem
3. methods of coping with malpractice problem

Until you finish taking notes, you can't hope to develop a comprehensive outline. Nevertheless, knowing the general direction in which you are heading will focus your investigation.

Note-taking requires you to read all of your references carefully and to record any significant information. You will write your paper directly from these notes. Properly taken, notes will save you considerable time and also help ensure a good paper.

Copy each note onto a separate four- by six-inch (or larger) card so that you will not confuse the cards with your bibliography cards.

Record only one note on a card even when you take several notes from a single page, as you may use these notes at different points in your paper. Cards enable you to test different arrangements of notes and use the best one. Don't copy notes into a notebook; you will be unable to shuffle them into the proper order.

Before you take a note, copy its source at the bottom of the note card so that you can give the author proper credit when you write the paper. Failure to do so is plagiarism, a serious offense (see page 284). In most cases, the author's last name and the page number or numbers will be enough. Occasionally, though, you will need to add initials to distinguish between two authors with the same last name or add partial titles to distinguish between different works by the same author. *Do not forget to include the page number or numbers for each note.* If you do, you'll only spend time looking them up later when you prepare endnotes. Key each note card to a division in the tentative outline by penciling the appropriate heading in the upper right-hand corner. If you're not sure where the note will go, indicate its general subject. Once you have finished note-taking, your plan will be expanded into a complete outline and the subject headings on the cards altered, if necessary, to reflect the final outline.

A note may be a summary, a paraphrase, or a direct quotation.

SUMMARY

A summary is a condensation of the original material, written primarily in your own words. It must, however, retain the sense and spirit of the original and may include brief quotations provided they are enclosed within quotation marks. A properly written summary concisely states the core idea of the original. It presents points in their original order without distorting their emphasis or meaning, and it excludes specific examples, supporting details, and repetition. Summaries present your reader with "the heart of the matter" and permit you to produce a much shorter paper than you otherwise could. Here is a passage from a student's source, followed by a summary note card.

The burning of 180 grams of sugar in cellular respiration yields about 700,000 calories, as compared with the approximately 20,000 calories produced by fermentation of the same

quantity of sugar. This process of combustion extracts all the
energy that can possibly be derived from the molecules which it
consumes. With this process at its disposal, the cell can meet its
energy requirements with a minimum expenditure of substance. It
is a further advantage that the products of respiration—water and
carbon dioxide—are innocuous and easily disposed of in any environment.

It is difficult to overestimate the degree to which the inven-
tion of cellular respiration released the forces of living organisms.
No organism that relies wholly upon fermentation has ever
amounted to much. Even after the advent of photosynthesis,
organisms could have led only a marginal existence. They could
indeed produce their own organic materials, but only in quantities
sufficient to survive. Fermentation is so profligate a way of life that
photosynthesis could do little more than keep up with it. Respiration used the material of organisms with such enormously greater
efficiency as for the first time to leave something over. Coupled
with fermentation, photosynthesis made organisms self-sustain-
ing; coupled with respiration, it provided a surplus. To use an
economic analogy, photosynthesis brought organisms to the subsis-
tence level; respiration provided them with capital. It is mainly
this capital that they invested in the great enterprise of organic
evolution.

> *George Wald, "The Origin of Life,"*
> Scientific American, *191 (Aug. 1954), p. 53*

Impact of cellular respiration

Cellular respiration produces 28 times
more energy from a given amount of sugar
than does fermentation. Fermentation provided
a marginal existence for living organisms.
The advent of cellular respiration provided
a surplus of energy and made organic
evolution possible.

Wald, p. 53

PARAPHRASE

Like a summary, a paraphrase restates original material in your own words. Unlike a summary, however, it is usually about the same length as the original or slightly longer. A paraphrase makes technical or specialized material more understandable to your reader. Suppose a source says that "Toxicological testing of dioxan revealed that low dosage levels can cause chloracne responses, hyperplasia, and teratogenic effects." Such information would only puzzle or antagonize a general audience. In contrast, a paraphrase stating "Low levels of dioxan can cause skin eruptions, abnormal increases in body tissue cells, and malformed fetuses" would cause no communication problems. Besides helping communication, paraphrasing contributes to a consistent writing style.

QUOTATION

A quotation is a copy of original material. Because your paper should demonstrate your mastery of your sources, don't rely extensively on quotations. In addition, reproducing the words of others gives you no practice in expressing yourself.

Generally, you should use quotations only when the original is especially clear and forceful or you really need support from an authority. For example, the following passage, from Loren Eisley's book *The Unexpected Universe*, would be nowhere near as effective if presented in any other way.

> Man is himself, like the universe he inhabits, like the demoniacal stirrings of the ooze from which he sprang, a tale of desolation. He walks in his mind from birth to death the long resounding shores of endless disillusionment. Finally, the commitment to life departs or turns to bitterness. But out of such desolation emerges the awful freedom to choose beyond the narrowly circumscribed circle that delimits the rational being.
>
> *Loren Eisley,* The Unexpected Universe
> *(New York: Harcourt Brace Jovanovich, 1969), p. 88*

Special rules and conventions govern the use of quotations. If, for the sake of clarity, you need to alter the original by adding some explanation or substituting a proper name for a personal pronoun, enclose the addition in *brackets*.

> Our admiration for this splendid man [Johannes Kepler] is accompanied by another feeling of admiration and reverence, the object of which is no man but the mysterious harmony of nature into which we are born.
>
> *Albert Einstein*, Ideas and Opinions
> *(New York: Crown Publishers, 1954), p. 262*

Reproduce any grammatical and spelling errors exactly as they appear in the original. To let your reader know that the original author, not you, made the mistake, insert within brackets the Latin word *sic* (meaning "thus") immediately after the error.

> As Walsh notes, "The threat to our envioment [sic] comes from many directions."

If you exclude an irrelevant part of a quotation, indicate the omission by using ellipsis marks—three spaced periods. Indicate omissions within sentences in the following way.

> Gamow concludes his discussion of the problem by saying, "We can not demonstrate this proof, since it is fairly complicated . . . but the reader can find it in various books on topology and spend a pleasant evening (and perhaps a sleepless night) in contemplating it."
>
> *George Gamow*, One, Two, Three . . . Infinity
> *(New York: Viking Press, 1947), pp. 51–52*

When an omission comes at the end of a sentence and the quoted part can stand as a complete sentence, use an unspaced period followed by three spaced periods.

> As one analyst noted, "Williamson's campaign focused primarily on the issue of hazardous chemical wastes because he hoped to capitalize on the fears of voters in his district. . . . Nevertheless, he was unsuccessful in his attempt to unseat the incumbent."

Shortening a quotation by deleting irrelevant or superfluous material is perfectly acceptable, providing the omission does not change or distort the original meaning. The following example illustrates such distortion.

Original passage   VitaHelth vitamin products are advertised as being superior to other brands, but laboratory tests have shown them not to be significantly better than competitive vitamin supplements.

Quotation distorting   "VitaHelth vitamin products are . . . significantly
meaning   better than competitive vitamin supplements."

At times you may wish to summarize or paraphrase the original but retain a few words or phrases that indicate a precise shade of meaning or add vividness. In such cases, use quotation marks but omit ellipsis marks.

Because of the "passionate advocacy" of its supporters, the push to halt the use of strip mining gained considerable support across the state.

When you copy a quotation onto a note-card, put quotation marks at the beginning and end so that you will not mistake it for a paraphrase or summary when you write the paper.

As you read and take notes, don't expect to find useful material on every page. Sometimes a page will yield several notes, but at other times you will read several pages and find nothing. If you are uncertain about the value of a piece of information, make a note. Too many notes are always better than too few.

Preparing Your Outline

At this point, you are ready to prepare a formal outline. This blueprint details the divisions and subdivisions of your paper. The outline shows how you will arrange your ideas—which will come first, second, and so on—and clarifies the relationships among these ideas and the details that support them. The more complex your writing task, the greater the need for a formal outline. There are two types of outlines—the numeral-letter-number outline and the number-decimal outline.

THE NUMERAL-LETTER-NUMBER OUTLINE

In this type of outline, the major and minor ideas and the specific details are indicated by a system of numerals, letters, and numbers followed by periods:

I.
    A.
    B.
        1.
        2.
            a.
            b.
II.

Writing from such an outline, then, ensures proper subordination and coordination of your materials. You can see the significance of an item in the outline both by its numeral, letter, or number designation and by its distance from the left-hand margin: the farther it is indented, the less important it is. All items preceded by Roman numerals are major points of roughly equal significance. Similarly, each of the other designations includes approximately equivalent points.

When you construct your outline, phrase items of equal value in similar, or parallel, fashion. This format helps clarify the relationships among items. To illustrate:

I. Effects of malpractice problem
    A. On doctors
    B. On the public
    C. On insurance companies.

Clearly the writer intends to discuss how medical malpractice affects doctors, the public, and insurance companies.

To develop your outline, sort your note cards into stacks according to the subject headings you have penciled at the tops. Change or combine these headings where necessary. Next, review each stack carefully to determine further divisions and subdivisions. Finally, use these decisions to write a final outline.

There are two kinds of formal outlines—topic and sentence. The first presents entries as words, short phrases, or short clauses. The second presents the entries as complete sentences. Although neither form is necessarily better than the other, a sentence outline can include more details as well as your attitude toward each topic. Here are samples of both topic and sentence outlines for a paper on medical malpractice.

Topic Outline

   I. Introduction: Examples of how malpractice cases increase costs
  II. Causes of malpractice suits
     A. Less legal business with no-fault auto insurance
     B. Public expectations about medicine
     C. People's attitude toward doctors
     D. Incompetence of some doctors
 III. Effects of malpractice problem
     A. On doctors
        1. Early retirement
        2. Higher fees
     B. On the public
        1. Longer hospital stays
        2. More tests
     C. On insurance companies
        1. Lost money
        2. Coverage abandoned
 IV. Methods of coping with the problem
     A. Private arbitration agreements
     B. Hospital inspections
     C. Plans from professional organizations
        1. Specific compensation for specific injury
        2. No-fault legislation
     D. Arbitration legislation
     E. Detailed rules for proceedings
        1. California law
        2. Indiana law
  V. Conclusion: Combination plan

Sentence Outline

   I. Introduction: Examples illustrate how malpractice cases increase medical costs.
  II. At least four causes contribute to the increase in malpractice cases.

A. Lawyers are now more interested in such cases because they have lost business with no-fault auto insurance.

B. People expect medicine to cure everything and become resentful when it does not.

C. People have lost their awe of doctors.

D. Some doctors are incompetent and make mistakes.

III. Malpractice cases cause problems for doctors, the public, and insurance firms.

A. Doctors are forced to pay enormous increases in insurance premiums.

　1. Some doctors are retiring early to avoid lawsuits and insurance costs.

　2. Other doctors must charge higher fees to cover the added insurance costs.

B. The public is also hurt by the increase in malpractice cases.

　1. Doctors fear lawsuits and keep patients in hospitals longer than they used to.

　2. To guard against malpractice suits, doctors insist that patients have more tests and X-rays.

C. Insurance firms also suffer.

　1. Despite increased insurance premiums, the awards in malpractice cases have caused some insurance companies to lose money.

　2. Such losses have caused some companies to leave the malpractice business.

IV. Several attempts have been made to cope with the malpractice problem.

A. Some doctors require patients to accept private arbitration agreements.

B. Some hospitals are hiring experts to check their facilities for deficiencies that could trigger malpractice suits.

C. Several professional organizations have proposed plans for dealing with the problem.

　1. The American Medical Association and the American Hospital Association have recommended specific compensation for specific injury.

　2. The American Bar Association has suggested no-fault legislation.

D. Arbitration legislation is being considered and has already been passed in Michigan.

E. California and Indiana have established detailed rules for malpractice awards and proceedings.

V. A plan borrowing elements from several of these approaches seems best.

THE NUMBER-DECIMAL OUTLINE

A second type of formal outline uses combinations of numbers and decimals rather than numerals, letters, and numbers. The number-decimal system may be used with both topic and sentence outlines. Here is part of the previous topic outline, with decimal-number notations.

3.0 Effects of malpractice problem
    3.1 On doctors
        3.1.1 Earlier retirement
        3.1.2 Higher fees
    3.2 On the public
        3.2.1 Longer hospital stays
        3.2.2 More tests
    3.3 On insurance companies
        3.3.1 Lost money
        3.3.2 Coverage abandoned

Use whichever type of outline, numeral-letter-number or number-decimal, your instructor assigns. If your instructor indicates no preference, use the type that you feel best suits your project.

When your outline is finished, key your note-cards to it. Write at the top of each card the letters and numbers—such as II A or III B 2—for the appropriate outline category. Now arrange the cards into stacks according to the major headings: one stack for I, one stack for II, and so on. Next, arrange each stack internally, grouping together all cards with the same number and letter codes. Finally, start with the first card in category I and number all of the cards consecutively. Once numbered, if they fall off the table or slide out of place, you can then easily put them back in order again. A few note cards may be left over when you complete this keying. Some may go unused. Others you may be able to work into your paper as your write or revise it.

Writing Your Paper

You already know the general procedure for writing a paper that is entirely your own. Now, however, you must integrate other people's material into *your writing*. Many students erroneously believe that a research paper consists merely of quotations, paraphrases, and summaries, one after the other throughout the paper. To be sure, you use the material of others, but you select and organize it according to your own purpose, you develop insights, and you draw conclusions about your sources.

Prepare your thesis statement as for any other type of writing (see pages 22–24). Generally, you should present it in your introduction. Sometimes—for example, if you are analyzing a problem and offering a solution—you may wish to reserve your thesis for the conclusion. In such a paper state the problem clearly at the outset. Because a research paper is relatively long, your introduction should also specify your organizational plan—the main points you will discuss and the order in which you will present them. The following excerpt from the introduction to a paper shows its three-part organization.

> The beauty of sharks can be seen through their perfect construction, well-developed sense organs, and great power and grace.

To develop individual sections of the paper, use appropriate methods discussed in the early chapters of this book.

Write your first draft section by section, linking the material from your note cards with transitional elements and your detailed comments and assessments. Keep track of the sources for all information so that you can easily prepare your endnotes and bibliography. When your draft is done, review your introduction and conclusion to make certain that your thesis and purpose are clear. Allow this version to sit for a day or two. Then polish and revise where necessary, just as you would with a shorter essay.

Type your final draft on 8½- by 11-inch paper, leaving one-inch margins on all four sides. Double-space the text, including indented quotations and references. Number each page except the first in the upper right-hand corner. In this corner on the first page, type your name, the course number, and the date. Two lines below this, center the title, and then double-space twice before you type your first paragraph. If your instructor requires a title page instead of this heading, the page should include the title of the paper, typed in capitals and centered about two inches below the top of the sheet; your name, centered in the middle of the sheet; and the course designation and date, centered about two inches from the bottom of the page. Prepare your endnotes and bibliography as directed on pages 285–294.

DOCUMENTATION AND PLAGIARISM

When you write a library research paper, you must acknowledge the source of the material you borrow. Documentation directs readers to the original source so that they can verify your borrowing or read at greater length, should they desire to do so. It also lends authority to what you say. Sources are acknowledged through endnotes (see pages 285–290) and bibliographic references (see pages 290–294).

Plagiarism is the failure to document—that is, the use of another person's words or ideas without acknowledging their sources. Plagiarism is a serious offense because it is dishonest and robs the original writer of recognition. Students caught plagiarizing risk failing the course or perhaps being suspended from school. Material that must be documented includes summaries, paraphrases, and quotations. In short, any information obtained through your reading requires documentation unless it is a fact available from many sources, such as the year of Einstein's death or the size of the 1970 national budget deficit. Whenever you are unsure of the status of a piece of information, document it.

HANDLING QUOTATIONS

Quotations that are less than five lines long are set off by quotation marks and run into the text of the paper. For longer quotes, do not use quotation marks. Instead, indent the material ten spaces from the left margin. If more than one paragraph is quoted, indent the first line of each quoted paragraph an additional three spaces; if only one paragraph is quoted, no further indentation is necessary. Type the material double-spaced, with three spaces above and below it. Use single quotation marks for a quotation within a shorter quotation and double marks for a quotation within a longer, indented quotation. The first of the following examples illustrates the use of quotations within quotations. The second illustrates the extended quotation of a single paragraph.

The report further stated that "All great writing styles have their wellsprings in the personality of the writer. As Buffon said, 'The style is the man.' "[12]

In *Lives of a Cell*, Lewis Thomas draws an unflattering portrait of the likeness between humans and ants:

> Ants are so much like human beings as to be an embarrassment. They farm fungi, raise aphids as livestock, launch armies into wars, use chemical sprays to alarm and confuse enemies, capture slaves. The families of weaver ants engage in child labor, holding their larvae like shuttles to spin out the thread that sews the leaves together for their fungus gardens. They exchange information ceaselessly. They do everything but watch television.[8]

Whenever you quote, provide some context for the passage. At times, particularly when you first cite a work, you may name the author, the source, or both. For subsequent citations, an expression such as "this book" or "[author's name] points out" will usually be sufficient. Such a context makes for smoother writing; the quote is not abruptly sprung upon the reader. Also, the reader does not have to check the endnote to identify the source.

ENDNOTES AND FOOTNOTES

Endnotes and footnotes indicate the sources of the materials you have used. Endnotes and footnotes are identical in terms of the information they contain. Endnotes, commonly used in research papers, are double-spaced and listed following the text of the paper; footnotes, formerly standard, fall at the bottom of the page on which a reference to a particular source is made and are single-spaced with a space between each. This discussion deals with endnotes. If your instructor prefers traditional footnotes, proceed as for endnotes until you are ready to type your final draft. Then calculate the amount of space you will need for your notes at the bottom of each page. Allow four lines of space above the first note on each page.

There are two types of endnotes—primary and secondary. A *primary* endnote is used when a particular source is first cited in the paper. *Secondary* endnotes are used for any later citations of that source.

Each note is keyed by number to a citation in the text of the paper. Indicate each citation by inserting a number in the text at the end of the material used. Raise this number one-half space above the line (unless your instructor prefers you to place it on the line and enclose it in parentheses). Place the same number before the note itself. Number all the notes consecutively throughout your paper.

Your list of endnotes begins on a new page that follows the last page of your paper's text. Head this page *Notes*. Indent the first line of each note five spaces, type its number one-half space above the line, skip a space, and then begin the endnote. Double-space each line within an entry. The examples below illustrate other conventions of form, based on the *MLA Handbook*. For special situations not covered by these examples, consult that handbook or Kate L. Turabian's *A Manual for Writers of Term Papers, Theses, and Dissertations*, both of which are probably available in your college library and bookstore.

Primary Endnotes for Books. The basic endnote for a book includes:

> the name of the author, in normal order
> the title of the book, underlined
> the place of publication, the name of the publisher, and the date of publication, within parentheses
> the page or pages on which cited material appears

A *p.* precedes a citation from one page while *pp.* is used for a citation from two or more pages. Other facts of publication may be added to the basic form as necessary. Use the following examples as models for your own footnotes, paying close attention to punctuation as well as content.

A book with one author:

[1] Gail Sheehy, <u>Passages: Predictable Crises of Adult Life</u> (New York: Dutton, 1973), p. 89.

A book with two authors:

[2] A. B. Bolt and M. E. Wardle, <u>Communicating with a Computer</u> (Cambridge: Cambridge Univ. Press, 1970), pp. 97-98.

A book with three or more authors often uses the first author's name followed by "et al."—a Latin abbreviation meaning "and others":

3 Roger William Alder et al., Mechanisms in Organic Chemistry (New York: Interscience-Wiley, 1971), p. 159.

A book with corporate authorship and no author identified by name treats the corporation as author:

4 United Nations, Public Administration Division, Local Government Training (New York: United Nations, 1968), p. 57.

An edition other than the first:

5 Kate L. Turabian, A Manual for Writers of Term Papers, Theses, and Dissertations, 4th ed. (Chicago: Univ. of Chicago Press, 1973), p. 74.

A book with an editor rather than an author:

6 James Deetz, ed., Man's Imprint from the Past: Readings in the Methods of Archaeology (Boston: Little, Brown, 1971), p. 58.

A book with both an author and an editor:

7 Edward Chiera, They Wrote on Clay, ed. George C. Cameron (Chicago: Univ. of Chicago Press, 1938), p. 79.

A translation:

8 Jean Piaget, The Child and Reality, trans. Arnold Rosin (New York: Penguin Books, 1976), p. 41.

An essay or chapter in a collection of works by one author:

9 Loren Eiseley, "The Judgment of the Birds," in The Immense Journey (New York: Random House, 1956), p. 123.

An essay or chapter in a collection containing several authors' contributions compiled by an editor:

^{10} Richard Selzer, "The Art of Surgery," in The Sense of the 70s, ed. Paul J. Dolan and Edward Quinn (New York: Oxford Univ. Press, 1978), p. 377.

Primary Endnotes for Periodicals. The basic footnote for a periodical includes:

the name of the author, in normal order
the title of the article, within quotation marks
the name of the periodical, underlined
the volume number of the periodical
the date of publication, within parentheses
the page or pages from which cited material is taken

If a periodical is published weekly, monthly, or seasonally and each issue is paged separately, specify the full date of publication within parentheses. For popular periodicals—those sold on newsstands to the general public—omit the volume number and parentheses and include just the full date. Note these distinctions and others in the following sample notes.

An article in a journal consecutively paged through the entire volume (when a volume number is given, "p." or "pp." is not used):

^{11} Gerald L. Holden, "Nation's Income and Maintenance Policies," American Behavioral Scientist, 15 (1972), 673.

An article in a journal that pages each issue separately:

^{12} Joel W. Block, "Sodom and Gomorrah: A Volcanic Disaster," Journal of Geological Education, 23 (May 1975), 75.

An article in a popular magazine:

^{13} Nick Katz, "Hunger in America: Let Them Eat Words," Look, 2 Dec. 1969, p. 71.

A signed article in a daily newspaper (if sections are paginated separately, the section is also identified; the city is underlined if it is part of the newspaper's title):

14 Joyce Walker-Lynn, "The Marine Corps Now Is Building Women, Too," Chicago Tribune, 30 Oct. 1977, Sec. I, p. 5.

An unsigned article in a daily newspaper:

15 "Lawmakers Unite on Mileage Rules," Detroit Free Press, 21 Oct. 1975, Sec. B, p. 3.

Primary Endnotes for Encyclopedia Articles. The basic footnote for an encyclopedia article includes:

the author's name, in normal order
the title of the article, within quotation marks
the name of the encyclopedia, underlined
the year

16 Harold S. Davis, "Team Teaching," The Encyclopedia of Education, 1974.

If the article is unsigned, the citation begins with the title of the article.

17 "Hydrography," The American People's Encyclopedia, 1969.

Secondary Endnotes. Secondary endnotes are used for second and subsequent citations of a particular source. Indicating the source with a Latin abbreviation, such as *ibid.*, *loc. cit.*, and *op. cit.*, is no longer recommended. In the newer and most commonly used system, a secondary endnote ordinarily consists of the author's last name and the page or pages from which material has been taken. Part of a typical set of primary and secondary endnotes is shown at the top of the following page.

¹⁸ Roger A. MacGowan and Frederick A. Ordway, <u>Intelligence</u>
<u>in the</u> <u>Universe</u> (Englewood Cliffs, N.J.: Prentice-Hall, 1966),
pp. 25-26.

¹⁹ Harry L. Shipman, <u>The</u> <u>Restless</u> <u>Universe</u> (Boston:
Houghton Mifflin, 1978), p. 61.

²⁰ Shipman, pp. 89-90.

²¹ MacGowan and Ordway, p. 123.

²² MacGowan and Ordway, pp. 146-147.

If your endnotes include authors with the same last name, use
the initials of their first names to distinguish them. Suppose that your
sources include a book by Margaret Thornton and a magazine article
by William Thornton. Secondary endnotes for each would be:

²³ W. Thornton, p. 249.

²⁴ M. Thornton, pp. 47-48.

Similarly, if your endnotes include several works by the same
author, add shortened forms of the titles to secondary notes for that
author. Underline shortened book titles and use quotation marks
around article and essay titles.

THE BIBLIOGRAPHY

The bibliography, prepared from your bibliography cards, lists
all the sources you actually used in writing your paper. The bibliography begins on a new page, headed "Bibliography," and follows the
endnotes. List each entry alphabetically according to the author's last
name or, if no author is given, the first significant word in the title.
For a work with more than one author, alphabetize according to the
name that appears first. Begin the first line of each entry at the
margin; indent the next lines in each reference five spaces. Double-
space every line, within and between entries. Conventions for entries
are illustrated below, based on the *MLA Handbook*. Should you need
additional information, consult the handbook or Kate L. Turabian's
A Manual for Writers of Term Papers, Theses, and Dissertations.

Bibliographical References for Books. The basic bibliographic reference for a book includes the information you should already have on your bibliography cards:

the name of the author, last name first
the title of the book, underlined
the place of publication
the publisher
the date of publication

As with endnotes, other facts of publication may be added as necessary. Carefully examine the following sample bibliography entries, particularly noting how the punctuation differs from that in footnotes.

A book with one author:

Sheehy, Gail. <u>Passages</u>: <u>Predictable</u> <u>Crises</u> <u>of</u> <u>Adult</u> <u>Life</u>.
      New York: Dutton, 1973.

A book with two authors (the second author's name is not reversed because it is not used in alphabetizing the bibliography):

Bolt, A. B., and M. E. Wardle. <u>Communicating</u> <u>with</u> <u>a</u> <u>Computer</u>.
      Cambridge: Cambridge Univ. Press, 1970.

A book with three or more authors often uses the first author's name followed by "et al."—a Latin abbreviation meaning "and others":

Alder, Roger William, <u>et</u> <u>al</u>. <u>Mechanisms</u> <u>in</u> <u>Organic</u>
      <u>Chemistry</u>. New York: Interscience-Wiley, 1971.

A book with corporate authorship and no author identified by name treats the corporation as authors:

United Nations, Public Administration Division. <u>Local</u>
      <u>Government</u> <u>Training</u>. New York: United Nations, 1968.

An edition other than the first:

Turabian, Kate L. <u>A</u> <u>Manual</u> <u>for</u> <u>Writers</u> <u>of</u> <u>Term</u> <u>Papers</u>,
      <u>Theses</u>, <u>and</u> <u>Dissertations</u>. 4th ed. Chicago: Univ. of
      Chicago Press, 1973.

A book with an editor rather than an author:

Deetz, James ed. <u>Man's Imprint from the Past</u>: <u>Readings in</u>
    <u>the Methods of Archaeology</u>. Boston: Little, Brown,
    1971.

A book with both an author and an editor:

Chiera, Edward. <u>They Wrote On Clay</u>. Ed. George C. Cameron.
    Chicago: Univ. of Chicago Press, 1938.

A translation:

Piaget, Jean. <u>The Child and Reality</u>. Trans. Arnold Rosin.
    New York: Penguin Books, 1976.

An essay or chapter in a collection of works by one author:

Eiseley, Loren. "The Judgment of the Birds." In <u>The Immense</u>
    <u>Journey</u>. New York: Random House, 1956, pp. 174-75.

An essay or chapter in a collection containing several authors' contributions compiled by an editor:

Seltzer, Richard. "The Art of Surgery." In <u>The Sense of the</u>
    <u>70s</u>. Ed. Paul J. Dolan and Edward Quinn. New York:
    Oxford Univ. Press, 1978, pp. 375-80.

Bibliographical References for Periodicals. The basic bibliographical reference for a periodical includes the information you should already have on your bibliography cards:

>the name of the author, last name fist
>the title of the article, within quotation marks
>the name of the periodical, underlined
>the volume number of the periodical
>the year of publication, within parentheses
>the pages on which the article appears

As with endnotes, if the periodical is published weekly, monthly, or seasonally and each issue is paged separately, specify the full date of publication. For popular periodicals, omit the volume number and parentheses.

An article in a journal consecutively paged through the entire volume (when a volume number is given, "p." or "pp." is not used):

Holden, Gerald L.   "Nation's Income and Maintenance Policies."

    American Behavioral Scientist, 15 (1972), 673-95.

An article in a journal that pages each issue separately:

Block, Joel W.   "Sodom and Gomorrah: A Volcanic Disaster."

    Journal of Geological Education, 23 (May 1975), 74-77.

An article in a popular magazine:

Katz, Nick.   "Hunger in America: Let Them Eat Words."   Look,

    2 Dec. 1969, p. 71.

A signed article in a daily newspaper (if sections are paginated separately, the section is also identified; the city is underlined if it is part of the newspaper's title):

Walker-Lynn, Joyce.   "The Marine Corps Now Is Building Women,

    Too."   Chicago Tribune, 30 Oct. 1977, Sec. I, p. 5.

An unsigned article in a daily newspaper:

"Lawmakers Unite on Mileage Rules."   Detroit Free Press, 21

    Oct. 1975, Sec. B, p. 3.

Bibliographical References for Encyclopedia Articles. The basic bibliographical reference for an encyclopedia article includes the information you should already have on your bibliography cards:

    the author's name, in reverse order
    the title of the article, within quotation marks
    the name of the encyclopedia, underlined
    the year

Davis, Harold S.   "Team Teaching."   The Encyclopedia of

    Education.   1974.

If the article is unsigned, the reference begins with the title of the article.

"Hydrography." The American People's Encyclopedia. 1969.

SAMPLE LIBRARY RESEARCH PAPER

The marginal notes for the following library research paper point out some of the conventions discussed in this chapter; others you can identify on your own.

Trudy Stelter

English 113

November 1980

MALPRACTICE: THE PEOPLE'S NIGHTMARE

    Detroit, in the United States, and Windsor, in Canada, are
less than a mile from each other. Prices in these two cities
are pretty much the same--except for the price of medical
malpractice insurance. Charles Boyce of Detroit and Richard
Bourke of Windsor are both obstetricians, but in 1975 Dr. Boyce
was paying about $5,000 a year for medical malpractice insurance,
Dr. Bourke only $100.[1] Dr. Boyce's huge premium is a graphic
reflection of the great and growing number of medical malpractice cases now flooding our country's courts.

    Although American doctors have been carrying malpractice
insurance since the 1930s, malpractice litigation first became
a significant problem in the years immediately following World
War II.[2] By 1970, some 13,000 claims were filed; and by 1976,
the figure had jumped to 25,000. In a number of states, the
annual rate of increase totaled 15 to 25 percent. According to
a Health, Education, and Welfare Department report, the malpractice problem was adding 3 to 7 billion dollars to our medical
costs each year.[3] This problem, the result of legislative and
social changes, has had serious repercussions among many groups,
and strong efforts to cope with it are now under way.

    Precisely what has caused this tremendous increase in the
number of malpractice cases in the United States? Many doctors

Thesis
statement

Short quotation run into text
and enclosed by quotation marks

2

believe that the lawyers are tackling them because the adoption
of no-fault auto insurance in many states has deprived lawyers
of the large fees they once earned in auto liability cases.
Now, these doctors feel, lawyers find it financially attractive
to initiate malpractice suits. Under the fee system adopted by
the legal firms that handle such cases, lawyers receive 50
percent of a successful settlement.[4] In 1974, the average
settlement was about $12,000,[5] and much larger awards are far
from uncommon. During 1974, for example, over thirty claims
were settled for $300,000 or more. Nationally the same number
of million-dollar judgments were handed down between 1970 and
1975.[6] Obviously, half of such fees would hold great attraction
for a lawyer.

Dr. Frederick von Saal, a New York orthopedist, says,
"Easily nine out of ten cases are frivolous; they're just bids
to make money."[7] Supporting the doctors' views, lawyer Jake
Edelman contends that lawyers often "bring suit against doctors
without consulting the patient [for specific details concerning
the claim], simply listing all medical personnel remotely
connected with the case."[8]

Nevertheless, the malpractice problem does not stem
entirely from the greed of patients and lawyers; the attitude of
the public toward medicine and its practitioners has also played
a vital role in creating the present situation. Over the past
few decades, medical science, by developing new and improved
drugs, instruments, and diagnostic techniques, has taken on an

Context
provided
for quotation

Explanation
enclosed
in brackets

3

aura of omnipotence. Patients have come to assume that medicine should cure their every ill, and if it does not, disappointment may lead to litigation.[9]

Paradoxically, this worshipful attitude finds little reflection in the way present-day patients look upon the physicians themselves. Once regarded as a species of miracle worker, doctors are now seen as mere human beings, capable of making errors and just as accountable as anyone else for their mistakes. This harsher outlook stems in considerable measure from a breakdown in the traditional patient-doctor relationship brought about by a decline in the number of family practitioners and an increase in specialists.[10] This decline began around 1945 and has reached the point where we need twice the number of generalists we now have in order to provide adequately for our medical needs.[11] As a result, the traditional consultation and physical examination carried out by a doctor, who in many cases was also a personal friend, has largely given way to batteries of tests conducted in an impersonal way by a group of people, many of whom the patient may never even see.[12]

Some physicians alienate patients by displaying arrogance, egotism, condescension, and an inflated concern for the monetary rewards the profession brings. Louise Lander cites an unnamed doctor's attorney who describes such practitioners as follows:

> The typical physician who gets sued for malpractice is the surgeon who will read the Wall Street Journal while the jury is out. He's got the businessman's

Extended quotation, indented without quotation marks, double spaced

4

> personality, and it shows in the way he runs his
> practice. He's usually the one who has eight
> patients in six rooms, with half a dozen more in the
> waiting room, and with a flock of nurses checking
> Blue Shield cards.[13]

Clearly these dehumanizing influences have contributed to the
malpractice problem.

Furthermore, there is considerable evidence that incompe-
tence within the American medical establishment is far from
negligible. For example, estimates indicate that 16,000
doctors--about 5 percent of the total--are unfit to practice,
that faulty prescriptions claim 30,000 lives each year,[14] and
that an additional 10,000 people suffer fatal or near fatal
attacks from unnecessary doses of antibiotics.[15] In addition,
recent congressional testimony indicated that 3 million Americans
undergo unnecessary operations each year and about 15,000 of them
die.[16] To make matters worse, medical societies and regulatory
agencies have been noticeably reluctant to take any corrective
action.[17]

Obviously, the medical malpractice problem is many-faceted,
and blaming it exclusively on lawyers, patients, or doctors
would be a serious error.

As the example of Drs. Boyce and Bourke demonstrates, the
proliferating problem has led to enormous increases in the
malpractice premiums that American doctors are forced to pay.

Independent conclusion:
no footnote necessary

5

Premiums vary greatly among the different branches of medicine,
with the probability of lawsuits and the size of damage awards
associated with each specialty determining the rates. Thus,
rates for psychiatrists and dermatologists are much lower than
those for orthopedic surgeons and anesthesiologists.[18] By
1976, the annual premium for an orthopedic surgeon in Southern
California had reached $36,000.[19]

These larger premiums are a serious problem with widespread
effects. Older doctors contemplate retiring early to save their
hard-won prestige and reputation from a malpractice suit and to
beat the rising costs of obtaining coverage.[20] Dr. Kenneth
Lehman of Topeka, Indiana, was one of those who solved the
problem by quitting. He reasoned:

> I am getting out because I do not want to be in the
> untenable situation where a jury rules on my medical
> competence. A malpractice decision should be made
> by individuals who know medicine, and there should
> be some limits as to what damages belong with certain
> kinds of cases.[21]

Those who remain in the profession compensate for the added
cost of insurance by raising their charges for medical care.
Dr. Russel B. Roth, former head of the American Medical
Association, has said of the increased malpractice premiums,
"There's only one place a doctor can get this money, and it's
from his patients." He further suggested that the increases had

6

added \$1.50 to \$2.00 to the cost of each office visit.[22]

The public is also hurt through increased hospital costs. Fearful of lawsuits, doctors are practicing "defensive medicine" by keeping patients in hospitals longer than necessary and insisting on more laboratory tests and unneeded X-rays.[23] By 1975, these tactics were adding \$50 to the average hospital patient's bill.[24] Piled on top of already high medical costs, these additional fees undoubtedly deter many people from seeking needed treatment and adversely affect the nation's health.

Insurance firms suffer, too. Although premiums have sky-rocketed, so have numbers and sizes of awards, causing companies to lose money. As a result, some companies are leaving the malpractice business or starting to cover only "low risk" specialists.[25] Thus Pacific Indemnity Company of Los Angeles and the Star Insurance Company of Milwaukee dropped coverage of 2,000 Los Angeles doctors. Argonaut Insurance Company of California--which wrote four-fifths of the malpractice policies for New York doctors--pulled out of New York on July 1, 1975.[26] Dr. Malcolm Todd, former president of the American Medical Association, has stated, "If doctors can't get insurance, it's hard to expect them to practice medicine."[27]

Attempts to cope with the medical malpractice problem include private efforts by the medical profession as well as legislative approaches. In California, the contracts issued by one large group medical-practice organization require the subscriber-patient to submit any malpractice claims to

7

arbitration--the hearing and decision of a case by a panel chosen
by all parties in a particular dispute. This arrangement has
proved advantageous both to subscribers and doctors. In over
four decades, only twenty cases have gone to formal arbitration.
Subscribers with minor claims, who might have problems finding
lawyers to represent them in court, obtain quick, fair settlements following informal investigations. Finally, doctors in the
organization enjoy extraordinarily low malpractice insurance
costs--about 20 percent of what they would normally be.[28]

Spurred by this success, a number of California hospitals
are asking incoming patients to accept arbitration agreements.
Of some half million persons asked, only about 1,000 have
refused. One case has gone to arbitration, and a few minor
claims have been settled informally.[29]

Acting on the old adage "an ounce of prevention is worth a
pound of cure," some hospitals are hiring experts to go over
their facilities and point out deficiencies that could result in
malpractice actions. Commenting upon this kind of "risk
management," Henry C. Damn, the founder of a firm that provides
such service, notes that the great majority of the actions
result directly from the failure of hospitals to observe their
own fail-safe standards.[30]

The American Medical Association and the American Hospital
Association have devised a plan under which each injury would
call for a specific amount of compensation--much like workmen's
compensation. This plan would reduce the importance of

8

negligence as a factor in malpractice suits, reflecting the fact that many injuries stem not from negligence but rather from the fact that medicine is an inexact science.[31] The American Bar Association has advanced the concept of no-fault legislation—an arrangement that would pay victims of malpractice less than they might win from a jury but with no need to pin the damages on the shortcomings of a particular practitioner.[32]

Another solution that has been considered in many quarters is arbitration along the lines established by the California practitioners' group-insurance provider. A typical panel might include one arbitrator selected by the plaintiff, a second selected by the doctor or hospital, and a third chosen by these two members. Findings might or might not be binding.[33] On January 1, 1976, a new, noncompulsory arbitration law went into effect in Michigan. This legislation allows patients to seek arbitration instead of going to court to file damages for improper medical treatment. It does not set a limit on the amount of money they can collect. Under the law, a voluntary arbitrator is selected to examine the validity of a complaint. Observers predicted at the time of its passage that the bill would end "the spectacle of emotional trials before inexpert juries" and the awarding of huge settlements.[34]

A number of states have passed laws designed to control the costs of malpractice settlements. California law now calls for paying settlements of $50,000 or more over a period of time, rather than all at once, with the judge setting the amounts.

9

Payments end if the plaintiff dies before the end of the payment
period. Juries are informed of the benefits the plaintiff will
receive through Social Security, workmen's compensation, and
the like. No plaintiff can receive more than $250,000 for "pain
and suffering" and similar noneconomic complaints, and there is
a sliding scale of contingency fees for the plaintiff's
lawyer.[35]

Indiana requires that a claim be screened by a three-doctor
panel chaired by a nonvoting lawyer before it can go to court.[36]
The state limits the liability of the doctor or hospital to
$100,000 but has established a compensation fund, financed by 10
percent of the malpractice premiums paid by practitioners and
hospitals, from which the plaintiff can receive up to $400,000
more.[37] As is true in California, limitations are placed on the
contingency fees for lawyers.[38]

It would seem that the malpractice crisis can best be met
through a plan borrowing elements from several of these
approaches. Under such a plan, a claim would first have to be
screened by a panel of representatives from the medical and
legal professions and the public. Cases that cleared the first
hurdle would then go to a panel of professional arbitrators,
whose decision would be binding. Limitations would be placed on
the size of settlements, and a sliding scale set up for lawyers'
contingency fees. Thus, a lawyer might receive 40 percent of the
first $50,000 of a settlement, an intermediate percentage of the
next $200,000. Large settlements would be paid to the claimant

Independent conclusions
drawn from research;
no footnote needed

10

in installments.

Such a plan offers several advantages. For one thing, it would discourage unscrupulous patients and lawyers from filing meritless claims in order to collect from insurance companies. For another, it would eliminate what is perhaps the prime disadvantage of court trials--the excessive settlements granted by juries that have been unduly swayed by emotionalism. Note that this plan does not include the concept of no-fault, and thus avoids providing unwarranted protection to incompetent doctors.

Unless something is done to resolve the malpractice problem soon, the results could be disastrous--at best, sharp rises in the already high cost of health care; at worst, the crippling of the medical profession. In either event, the people who stand ultimately to lose the most are the patients themselves.

Government
document as source

Notes

¹ Murray Teigh Bloom, "Malpractice--the Mess That Must be Ended," Reader's Digest, Apr. 1975, p. 77.

² George A. Silver, "The Medical Insurance Disease," The Nation, 27 Mar. 1976, p. 367.

³ "Malpractice: What Are the Facts Behind the Crisis?" Better Homes and Gardens, Apr. 1976, p. 6.

⁴ David Makofsky, "Malpractice and Medicine," Society, 14 (Jan.-Feb. 1977), 28.

⁵ "Lawsuits: A Growing Nightmare for Doctors and Patients," U.S. News and World Report, 20 Jan. 1975, p. 53.

⁶ "Doctor's Dilemma," Scientific American, 232 (Mar. 1975), 48.

⁷ Matt Clark and Marina Gosnell, "Doctor's New Dilemma," Newsweek, 10 Feb. 1975, p. 41.

⁸ "Doctor's Counterattack," Time, 19 Apr. 1976, p. 89.

⁹ U.S. Cong., Hearings Before the Subcommittee on Health and the Environment of the Committee on Interstate and Foreign Commerce on the Medical Malpractice Insurance Issue and Its Effect on the Delivery of Health Care Services, 94th Cong., 2nd sess., Serial No. 94-130 (Washington, D.C.: GPO, 1975), p. 38.

¹⁰ U.S. Cong., p. 38.

¹¹ Makofsky, p. 26.

¹² Louise Lander, "Why Some People Seek Revenge Against Doctors," Psychology Today, July 1978, p. 91.

¹³ Lander, p. 94.

¹⁴ Makofsky, p. 25.

Secondary
footnotes

[15] Silver, p. 369.

[16] Silver, p. 369.

[17] U.S. Cong., p. 39.

[18] "Malpractice Nightmare," _Time_, 24 Mar. 1975, p. 62.

[19] "Malpractice: What Are the Facts," p. 6.

[20] "Malpractice Nightmare," p. 62.

[21] "Lawsuits," p. 53.

[22] "Lawsuits," p. 53.

[23] Ronald E. Gots, _The Truth About Medical Malpractice_ (New York: Stein and Day, 1975), pp. 178-79.

[24] "Malpractice Nightmare," p. 62.

[25] Silver, pp. 367-68.

[26] Clark and Gosnell, p. 41.

[27] "Malpractice Nightmare," p. 63.

[28] Murray Teigh Bloom, "We Can End the Malpractice Mess Now," _Reader's Digest_, May 1975, pp. 100-101.

[29] Bloom, "We Can End," p. 101.

[30] "Doctor Fail-Safe," _Time_, 26 July 1976, p. 79.

[31] "Malpractice Nightmare," p. 63.

[32] "A Way to Clean Up the Malpractice Mess," _Business Week_, 24 Feb. 1975, p. 32.

[33] "Malpractice: What Are the Facts," p. 17.

[34] Sylvia Porter, "New Law Puts Focus on Michigan," _Detroit Free Press_, 8 Dec. 1975, Sec. B, p. 12.

[35] David S. Rubsamen, "Medical Malpractice," _Scientific American_, 235 (Aug. 1976), 23.

Since author is cited twice, both author and title needed in secondary footnote

Book with
corporate authorship

[36] Duke Law Journal, <u>Medical Malpractice</u> (Cambridge, Mass.:
Ballinger, 1977), p. 281.

[37] Rubsamen, p. 23.

[38] Makofsky, p. 29.

Bibliography

Bloom, Murray Teigh. "Malpractice--the Mess That Must be Ended."
     Reader's Digest, Apr. 1975, pp. 77-80.
----------. "We Can End the Malpractice Mess Now." Reader's
     Digest, May 1975, pp. 99-102.
Clark, Matt, and Marina Gosnell. "Doctor's New Dilemma."
     Newsweek, 10 Feb. 1975, p. 41.
"Doctor Fail-Safe." Time, 26 July 1976, p. 79.
"Doctors' Counterattack." Time, 19 Apr. 1976, p. 89.
"Doctor's Dilemma." Scientific American, 232 (Mar. 1975),
     48-49.
Duke Law Journal. Medical Malpractice. Cambridge, Mass.:
     Ballinger, 1977.
Gots, Ronald E. The Truth About Medical Malpractice. New York:
     Stein and Day, 1975.
Lander, Louise. "Why Some People Seek Revenge Against Doctors."
     Psychology Today, July 1978, pp. 88-104.
"Lawsuits: A Growing Nightmare for Doctors and Patients."
     U.S. News and World Report, 20 Jan. 1975, pp. 53-54.
Makofsky, David. "Malpractice and Medicine." Society, 14
     (Jan.-Feb. 1977), 25-29.
"Malpractice Nightmare." Time, 24 Mar. 1975, pp. 62-63.
"Malpractice: What Are the Facts Behind the Crisis?" Better
     Homes and Gardens, Apr. 1976, pp. 6-17.
Porter, Sylvia. "New Law Puts Focus on Michigan." Detroit
     Free Press, 8 Dec. 1975, Sec. B, p. 12.

Rubsamen, David S.   "Medical Malpractice."   Scientific American,
      235 (Aug. 1976), 18-23.

Silver, George A.   "The Medical Insurance Disease."   The Nation,
      27 Mar. 1976, pp. 366-71.

U.S. Cong.   Hearings Before the Subcommittee on Health and the
      Environment of the Committee on Interstate and Foreign
      Commerce on the Medical Malpractice Insurance Issue and Its
      Effect on the Delivery of Health Care Services.   94th Cong.,
      2nd sess.   Serial No. 94-130.   Washington, D.C.: GPO, 1975.

"A Way to Clean Up the Malpractice Mess."   Business Week, 24
      Feb. 1975, pp. 30-32.

14

Oral Reports

When you have started working, there will probably be many occasions when you will be asked to make an oral presentation. For example, your supervisor may ask you to explain a new departmental policy, describe a new procedure for testing a product, show how to operate a device, report on the progress of a research project or sales campaign, or discuss the possible impact of some piece of regulatory legislation.

Some of your talks may be given after working hours. The vocational counselors of the local high school may ask you to take part in the school's Career Awareness Days program by telling students about your job. An environmental group may wish to know what procedures your company follows to prevent air and water pollution. The Jaycees or local merchants' association may ask you to discuss the economic impact of your company's expansion or retrenchment plans. Because of these demands, you need to develop the speaking skills that will enable you to make an interesting and effective presentation.

The speeches you are likely to make fall into either of two categories—informative or persuasive. An informative speech primarily explains or teaches; a persuasive speech seeks to change the attitude of its hearers or cause them to take some action. There are four steps in preparing and delivering an effective speech of either type:

1. understanding your audience
2. determining your purpose and thesis
3. developing your presentation
4. making your presentation

These steps are discussed below.

Understanding Your Audience

Understanding your audience is as important when you give a speech as when you write a paper. Unless you know your audience's interests and expectations, you are unlikely to communicate effectively, and there is a very real risk that you will irritate or antagonize your listeners. Few problems of this sort should arise when you speak to members of your own department—you already know them quite well. However, to communicate effectively with less familiar audiences, you must answer such questions as "Are they technical, professional, or blue-collar workers?" "What is their general level of education?" "How much do they know about the subject?" Explaining a new procedure to a group of employees from another department may require you to define one or more technical terms. And for an audience that lacks a technical background—for example, a group of high-school students or the members of a local club—you may need to omit all or nearly all technical terms.

You must also consider what aspects of your topic are likely to interest your audience the most. Suppose, for example, that you are a nutritionist in a school system and wish to persuade your audience that the federal school lunch program should not be cut but expanded to include many more children. For a group of farmers, you might focus on the added income they would receive from the program. For an audience of health care personnel, you might stress the improvement in health that would result, and for school officials, you might argue that improved classroom performance and higher grades would result. When you tailor your message to your audience, your listeners will be much more likely to accept what you have to say.

Finally, give some thought to the probable size of your audience. Small groups are ideal for informal presentations; often there is plenty of time for questions and answers afterwards. Larger groups lend themselves to more formal approaches, and you may need to limit the time for questions or omit the question-and-answer period entirely.

How do you obtain information about the audience for an off-the-job presentation? The best way is to question the person who has asked you to speak. If possible, talk also with one or two of the people who will be hearing you. Successful audience analysis and successful speaking go hand-in-hand, so don't overlook this phase of your presentation.

Determining Your Purpose and Thesis

To determine your purpose, you must first decide what you want your audience to know, to believe, or to do once you have made your presentation. On the job, the situation often determines your purpose for you. Suppose there have been several changes in your department's safety regulations. Your supervisor calls you into his office and asks you to explain to your coworkers, at the next safety meeting, the differences between the old and the new regulations and why the changes were made. Presumably you wish to present the changes as positive steps; in this case, your purpose has been provided for you.

Off-the-job speaking situations will probably require considerable thought. Let's suppose that you are a police captain in a town with a college that has just started offering a degree in criminal justice. A local business group, knowing that you have helped set the program up, asks you to talk about it at their monthly luncheon meeting. The group is considering endowing a scholarship fund, and your job is to persuade them that the program is worthwhile. Your first task is to decide what aspect of your topic is most likely to command your listeners' attention. Because they are probably not greatly interested in the actual details of establishing the program, you decide to focus on the benefits the program will provide for the community. After a little thought you jot down the following benefits:

1. The program will provide police officers who have been trained in every major aspect of law enforcement.
2. The program will provide police officers who have been trained in coping with various kinds of emergencies.

At this point, you are ready to draft your thesis statement, which may be something like this:

> The new criminal justice program at Carter College will benefit this community and others in two ways. First, the police officers it graduates will be well versed in every major aspect of law enforcement. Second, it will provide students with the training to cope with several kinds of personal and community emergencies.

Developing Your Presentation

Developing your presentation consists of expanding your thesis statement into an outline, fleshing out the outline with supporting details, preparing your introduction and conclusion, and choosing your mode of delivery.

PREPARING YOUR OUTLINE

The outline for a speech, like that for a paper, serves as a road map for your ideas, helping you to present them so that your reader can follow y ou without getting lost. Depending on the length of your talk, you may use a formal topic or sentence outline like those discussed on pages 278–282 or a less formal written plan. Here is a topic outline for the talk about the benefits of Carter College's criminal justice program.

How Carter College's Law Enforcement Program Will Benefit Our Community

Introduction (includes thesis statement)
I. Training in law enforcement
    A. Administration of police units
    B. Police laboratory techniques
    C. Collection of evidence
    D. Handling of convicted law violators
    E. Defense tactics
    F. Prevention and control of juvenile delinquency

II. Training for emergencies
    A. Required training
        1. Administering first aid
        2. Handling emergency childbirths
    B. Optional training
        1. Fighting fires
        2. Dealing with floods, tornados, and other natural disasters
Conclusion (reinforces thesis)

Speeches can follow any of the patterns used to develop pieces of writing. If you are telling a group of new employees how to perform a test, each major subdivision of your outline would undoubtedly represent a step in the procedure. When tracing the development of an advertising campaign, you would probably adopt a time sequence. For a discussion of the changes in a set of safety regulations, a comparison-and-contrast format might well prove best. If you are describing a new office building or other facility, you might use a spatial pattern, listing each different area of the facility in turn. The preceding outline reverses the order-of-climax pattern of development: first it takes up the training directly connected with law enforcement; then it moves to auxiliary training. In any case, your thesis statement should reflect the arrangement of your outline.

PROVIDING SUPPORTING DETAILS

Much of the information you use to develop your talk will be based directly on your own knowledge and observations. Sometimes, though, you will need to draw upon written materials or ask other people for help. If you are reporting on a particular research project, you might have to reread the proposal that helped create it or to check one or more of the progress reports tracing its history. Similarly, in preparing the talk about the criminal justice program, you might consult college brochures on the program or ask a fellow officer to clarify a point about which you are uncertain.

Once in a while you may need to obtain library information to support your talk. In this case, proceed in the same manner as when you obtain material for a paper (pages 263–278). Skim encyclopedia articles for background material. Check the appropriate subject headings in the card catalog and one or more periodical indexes for promising titles. Obtain the material, read it, and make a note card for each piece of information you select. Be sure to take down enough bibliographical information so that you can mention the source and lend weight to your presentation.

PREPARING YOUR INTRODUCTION AND CONCLUSION

Most speakers find that they have less trouble with their introductions and conclusions if they prepare them after they have determined an organizational pattern and developed a list of supporting details.

A good introduction catches the listener's attention and sets the stage for what will follow. To accomplish these aims, you may make an attention-getting statement, offer a quotation, tell a real or made-up story, ask a question, or use any of the other techniques that are suitable for beginning a paper. For example, if you are talking about some new and highly promising product your company has developed, you might lead off by saying something like, "Today, I'm going to tell you about a product that has more money-making potential than anything we have marketed up until now." If you are talking on recent advances in coping with childhood leukemia, you might tell about a child who developed the disease but was cured by a new type of chemical therapy. Whatever approach you take, the introduction must prepare your listeners for your ideas.

In contrast, a conclusion wraps up your ideas and leaves your listeners with the sense that you have fulfilled your purpose in talking. Any of the techniques for ending a paper can also end a speech. To conclude your talk on the benefits of the criminal justice program, you might restate the main points you have developed. To end your discussion of leukemia, you might predict that the time will soon come when this affliction will no longer menace our children. In other cases, offering an evaluation, quoting a recognized authority, or challenging your listeners to take some action will prove most effective.

CHOOSING YOUR MODE OF DELIVERY

You can use one of three basic approaches in the delivery of your speech:

1. memorizing your talk and repeating it word for word
2. writing it out and reading it from manuscript
3. talking from a set of note cards

Talking from memory presents a couple of problem. First, unless you have been trained in acting, your delivery is likely to be stilted and flat. In addition, if you temporarily forget a sentence or two, you may accidentally repeat part of your message or skip an important point when you start talking again. Reading from a manuscript eliminates the danger of forgetting but increases the chance that you will give a dull, mechanical performance. As you read, you may also neglect to maintain eye contact with your audience and thereby reduce or destroy the effectiveness of your presentation. Some situations, however, do require use of a manuscript. For example, your talk may include a number of direct quotations or statistical items that must be presented accurately. When your talk will be timed precisely, a manuscript will help ensure that you are not cut off before you can present your complete message. Unless circumstances dictate that you deliver your message verbatim, however, your best approach is to talk from note cards.

Note cards lessen your chances of giving a mechanical performance, losing contact with your audience, or accidentally skipping important points. When you make your notes, copy each of the items in your outline onto a four- by six-inch card. Then expand the set with cards that contain additional material. Since notes are intended only as guideposts to keep you on track, use short phrases or clauses rather than sentences, which take too long to read. Avoid making so many cards that you spend most of your time checking them. By leaving most of your message unwritten, you can make your talk sound spontaneous and natural.

Making Your Presentation

To give an effective presentation, you must consider what you wear, counter any nervousness you might feel, begin properly, and make the right use of your voice, body, hands, and eyes. In addition, you must use any visual aids effectively and know how to deal with questions after your talk.

CHOOSING APPROPRIATE CLOTHING

Before you utter a word, your audience will note your appearance and start to judge you, so dress appropriately for your speaking engagement. If you are addressing a group of fellow employees, wear your customary on-the-job clothing. At other times—for example, if you are talking to a group of supervisors—you may need to dress more formally than you usually do. Occasionally, it may be appropriate to wear on-the-job clothing when you talk to outside groups. Thus, the police officer who talks about crime prevention to a group of townsfolk might wear his uniform to lend authority to his remarks.

COPING WITH NERVOUSNESS

Despite adequate planning and preparation, you may experience nervousness as your time to speak approaches. If this happens, you can take several countermeasures. For one thing, thinking rationally about the sweating, trembling, or other bodily reactions you may be experiencing can often lessen their intensity. As you wait, try sitting in a relaxed position and taking deep breaths. To ease tense throat muscles, drop your chin slightly and move your head inconspicuously from side to side. Review one final time your opening remarks and the message you want your hearers to carry away. Once you are speaking, any remaining tension will very likely diminish or even disappear entirely.

BEGINNING YOUR TALK

When your time comes to speak, rise slowly, take your position at the speaker's stand, place your note cards in front of you and briefly scan your audience before you begin speaking. Experienced speakers often begin with a few preliminary comments before starting their actual presentation. If you adopt this approach, you might thank the master of ceremonies who introduced you or note that you appreciate the opportunity to speak. Another common approach is to comment on the importance of the occasion. Remember that you and your audience need a little time to adjust to each other, so a minute or two of pleasantries before launching into your presentation will help establish the contact that communication requires.

USING YOUR VOICE

As you talk, listen to yourself and correct any harshness, squeakiness, or similar voice faults. Without shouting, modulate the level of your voice so everyone can hear you. Be careful to speak clearly and smoothly, A series of "dontchas," "goin's," and other slurred words, punctuated with "ers" or "uhs," will create the impression that you are careless and lessen the acceptance of your remarks. To show enthusiasm and help keep your audience alert, vary the speed of your delivery. Thus, you might speak more rapidly to convey your excitement or slow down to emphasize a particular point. Rehearsals are invaluable for detecting and overcoming voice problems. The evening before your presentation, go through the whole talk while a knowledgeable friend listens or you make a tape recording. Then have your friend criticize your performance or play the tape back. Repeat the procedure until you are satisfied with the way you sound.

USING BODY MOVEMENTS AND HAND GESTURES

Body movements and hand gestures are two prime devices that help speakers communicate effectively. Start your talk with your feet about eight inches apart and one slightly ahead of the other. This position will allow you to turn from one side of the audience to the other without seeming awkward. Don't feel that you must remain rooted to one spot during your presentation. For example, to dramatize an important point you can lean forward or move from behind the podium and take a few steps toward your audience. To show disbelief, you can step back slightly. And if you use visual aids, you will undoubtedly have to move about to manipulate them.

Hand gestures serve a variety of speaking purposes providing you keep them natural. You may raise your index finger to call attention to a point or make a jabbing motion for added emphasis. You may turn your palms down to reject information or ideas, turn them up to signal acceptance, or extend them toward the audience to show caution or deliver a warning. You may clench your fists to show anger or strong resolve, or place your hands on your hips to show skepticism. Hands, then, can strengthen your presentation; but they can also weaken it if you use them to play with pencils or chalk, straighten your tie, smooth your hair, or otherwise fidget. Such actions betray nervousness and will distract your listeners from your message.

MAINTAINING EYE CONTACT WITH YOUR AUDIENCE

To create a bond with the members of your audience, look directly at them, not down at the floor or toward some remote spot beyond them. If the audience is small, look directly at one person for a few seconds, then shift your attention to someone nearby. Try to make eye contact with all or most of your listeners before you finish. If the audience is large, mentally divide the room into sections and follow the same procedure as for smaller audiences, shifting each time to someone in a different part of the room. Maintaining eye contact will allow you to gauge the response of your audience and take action to correct any undesirable developments. Thus when you notice people straining forward as if unable to hear, you can raise your voice. If people seem puzzled, you can slow down and provide more clarifying details.

USING VISUAL AIDS

Visual aids can add clarity, precision, and variety to your presentation. So while you are planning your speech, take time to think about spots where they might be helpful. Four visual aids—chalkboards, posters, flip charts, and overhead projectors—should prove particularly useful.

Chalkboards. A chalkboard will serve nicely when you need to present an occasional figure, formula, short list, brief outline, or the like during your talk. You can also use it to present more extensive information providing you put it on the board in advance so that you will not need to stop speaking in order to write. If you are using a small, portable chalkboard, keep pre-written material covered until the time comes to show it; then cover it again. Concealing such material until the proper time will prevent it from distracting your listeners.

Posters and Flip Charts. A poster is a card, usually two feet by three feet or larger, that is made of pasteboard or some similar material. A flip chart is a set of similarly large sheets that are hinged together at the top. Both are suitable for presenting a series of tables, graphs, drawings, and written matter. These two types of visual aids are prepared ahead of time, usually with colored felt-tip markers. Posters are arranged in a suitable sequence, placed on a viewing stand at appropriate points during the talk, and then removed again. A flip chart is fastened securely to an easel and each page flipped over and out of view as the speaker finishes discussing what is on it. Posters are somewhat clumsier to handle than are flip charts, but they can be arranged in any order—an important advantage if a speaker must give different versions of the same talk.

Overhead Projectors. An overhead projector is a machine for throwing an enlarged image from a transparency onto a wall or screen. The graphs, drawings, or other materials to be shown are first drawn on opaque sheets, usually about the size of business stationery, which are then run through a transparency maker. An overhead projector gives speakers the option of using overlays or masking. An overlay is a transparency that is placed over another one to add more information to whatever is being shown. For example, a speaker may superimpose a sales curve for the current year over the curve for the previous year. Masking consists of covering up part of a transparency and then removing the cover when the time has come to reveal the hidden information. During the presentation, the speaker can use a grease pencil to mark or write on the transparencies. Afterward, these markings can be removed for the next presentation.

Make sure that whatever visuals you use are not overcrowded or too complicated and that all of your listeners can clearly see what's on them. Unless they can be easily read and understood, visuals will confuse and irritate, rather than help, your audience. Don't just show a visual; take a few minutes to go over it to be sure your audience has grasped the material. Once you have finished with it, put it away so it won't be a distraction. If you use handouts at all, wait until after your talk to distribute them. Otherwise, some people may read them when they should be listening to you.

For information on preparing tables and graphs, see pages 322–333.

ANSWERING QUESTIONS AFTER THE TALK

Question-and-answer periods allow listeners to obtain fuller explanations of points they do not understand and to raise points that you have not covered. Make sure your audience understands each question you are asked before you answer it. If the question is ambiguous, you might say, "If I haven't misunderstood you, you would like to know . . ." If the questioner has spoken in an overly low voice, you may wish to repeat the question. Answer each question straightforwardly, taking as long as time allows or the question merits. In case you do not know an answer, admit that fact rather than trying to bluff. Sometimes a questioner may be hostile or sarcastic. In this case, do not respond in kind, but reply as courteously as you would if your questioner were friendly. A civil reply is another means of winning acceptance for your ideas.

Most question-and-answer periods have some definite time limit. When the time has about expired, tell your listeners that there will be time for just one or two more questions. If a number of listeners wish to continue, you may do so providing no other speaker is scheduled to follow you and the room will still be available. If you have prepared thoroughly for your presentation, the question-and-answer period should give no more trouble than the talk itself.

Suggestions for Speaking

Complete one of the following assignments or one approved by your instructor. Determine your audience and purpose, prepare a thesis statement and an outline, provide suitable supporting details, develop an introduction and a conclusion, and prepare a set of note cards.

1. Prepare a ten-minute talk for the graduating class of your high school, telling its members what to expect in college.
2. Convert one of the papers or reports you have written for the course into a ten-minute presentation that includes the use of at least one visual aid.
3. Prepare a ten-minute talk on the opportunities in your career field. Obtain pertinent background materials by checking your placement office, consulting one or more periodical indexes in your college library, and asking the librarian for pertinent government documents and other materials.
4. Prepare a ten-minute talk on some controversial issue in your community. For example, you might discuss a local bond issue, traffic congestion, industrial pollution, mosquito control, or a rezoning proposal. Check back issues of the newspaper for news stories, editorials, and letters on the issue.

15

Tables, Graphs, and Illustrations

Tables, graphs, and illustrations accompany much of the writing produced for the world of work and are often used to support oral presentations. Use of these aids allows writers and speakers to

add variety and interest to their presentations

focus attention on important parts of reports and speeches

reduce the length of explanations

present, in easily understandable form, ideas and information that would otherwise to difficult, perhaps even impossible, to convey

Because of their value, you should know how to prepare and use tables, graphs, and illustrations. This chapter will help you to do both.

Tables

A table systematically groups related facts or figures in parallel rows and columns for ready reference. Tables serve two important functions. First, they allow you to show slight differences in values.

For example, it is quite easy to see the difference between 589 and 596 when these figures appear in a table. However, if you tried to represent these same values with bars of different lengths, as in a bar graph showing values of 0 to 1,000, the difference would be too slight to detect. Second, tables can accommodate large quantities of data without confusing the reader. Suppose you wish to compare, month by month, your company's production of some item over an eight-year period marked by monthly fluctuations that follow a different pattern each year. This could be done quite easily with a table listing the monthly figures in eight columns, one for each year. In contrast, listing the information in the text would make monthly comparisons quite difficult.

When you prepare a table, follow these guidelines:

1. Give each table a title that briefly but accurately describes its contents. If a piece of writing includes more than two tables, number the tables consecutively. You may use either of the styles below to identify tables. Each style positions this designation above the table.

TABLE 1
PHYSICAL PROPERTIES OF TUNGSTEN

Table 1. Physical Properties of Tungsten

Note that the second style follows the table number with a period and observes the guidelines for capitalizing titles (see "Capitalization" in the appendix).

2. If the different columns have different kinds of information, provide each column with a heading that clearly identifies its subject matter. If several columns contain the same general type of information, center a single major heading over the columns; then provide each column with a subhead that shows the breakdown of the information. If, for example, you are showing the monthly hirings in a certain industry for 1977 through 1981, your heading and subheads might look like this:

Monthly Hirings in Electronics Industry

| 1977 | 1978 | 1979 | 1980 | 1981 |

Write major headings in capital letters or in capital and lower case letters. For subheads, use capitals and lower case letters, unless numerals are needed.

3. If the information is expressed in units, note the units in the heading. Use standard abbreviations and symbols (*in., kg., %,* and the like) whenever necessary to save space.

4. Align columns of whole numbers on the right-hand digit, columns of decimals on the decimal point.

25	3.5
3,284	.81
8	14.051

5. If you need to include an explanatory footnote, position it at the bottom of the table. Identify the item being explained with a lower case letter or a printer's symbol (for example, *, †, ‡,) that is positioned directly after the item and raised one-half space. Place this same letter or symbol before the note itself. Do *not* use numbers for footnote identification, as your reader may confuse them with data.

6. If you have taken the table from another source, document the source at the bottom of the table. If you must obtain permission to reproduce the table, use whatever credit line the source specifies. Otherwise, use standard footnote format to present the pertinent information. Pages 285–290 will show you how to document material from books, magazines, newspapers, and encyclopedias.

7. Try to hold each table to a single page. Sometimes you can do this by placing the table the long way on the page. In this case, the title should be to the left when the page is held in the regular reading position. If you must use more than one page, write *continued* or *cont.* at the bottom of the first page, immediately below the table. Repeat the title of the table and the column headings at the top of the next page, with *continued* or *cont.* following the title.

8. Mention the table in the text at whatever point is most appropriate. Provide whatever discussion the reader will need to understand the table.

9. As a general rule, position the table on the same page that you refer to it or as close to that page as you can. However, if the

data supplements your presentation rather than forming a part of it, put the table in an appendix.

The following table shows the sizes of anchors to use with different-length boats.

Table 1. Hi-Tensile Anchor Selection Guide

Anchor Size	HORIZONTAL HOLDING POWER IN LBS*		Recommended Boat Length (feet)	Recommended Rope Size (Open Laid Nylon Only)
	Soft Mud	Hard Sand		
5-H	400	2,700	17-24	$5/16$
12-H	900	6,000	25-38	$3/8$
20-H	1,250	8,750	39-44	$7/16$
35-H	1,600	11,000	45-54	$1/2$
60-H	2,400	17,000	55-70	$5/8$
90-H	2,900	20,000	71-90	$3/4$
150-H	3,100	21,000	over 90	$7/8$
190-H	3,500	23,000	over 90	1

*Refers to the pulling force on the anchor, not the weight of the boat.

Source: Reprinted by permission of Danforth Division, the Eastern Company.

Graphs

A graph is a pictorial presentation of numerical data. Three types of graphs—line graphs, bar graphs, and circle graphs—are especially common. A line graph has a vertical axis, a horizontal axis, and one or more curved or jagged lines that chart the relationship between two or more sets of values. A bar graph also has a horizontal and vertical axis but tells its story with a set of vertical or horizontal bars. A circle graph looks like a pie that has been sliced into a number of different-size segments.

Graphing makes data visually accessible so that they make their point much more clearly and readily than they would in table form. Presenting the monthly fluctuations in a store's sales by means of a line graph rather than a table would make it much easier to gauge the magnitude of the jumps and dips and to spot any trends. On the other hand, such a graph could not be used to present exact monthly sales figures—these would require a table. Because tables and graphs complement each other so nicely, the two are often used in tandem.

Footnotes and source lines for graphs are handled exactly as they are for tables; see the guidelines on pages 285–290. Each graph should also be referred to at the appropriate point in the text of the report and positioned as close as possible to that reference, preferably on the same page. Identify a series of graphs by writing "Figure 1" (or "Fig. 1"), "Figure 2," and so on above or in front of the titles. Titles can be positioned above or below graphs.

LINE GRAPHS

In its simplest form, a line graph shows the relation between two sets of numbers or other items, one set being measured by a horizontal scale and the other by a vertical scale. The horizontal scale, usually at the bottom of the graph, measures time or some other regular progression. This progression is called the independent variable. The vertical scale measures quantity or some other quality that fluctuates with changes in the horizontal scale. The item measured on the vertical scale is called the dependent variable.

Suppose, for example, that you wish to graph a hospital's monthly admissions over a one-year period. You would plot the twelve months of the year along the horizontal scale. The vertical scale would represent the number of admissions during each month. A line graph such as this one would not be limited to two sets of items: you might expand it to compare the monthly admissions to three hospitals. Whenever a graph includes two or more sets of dependent variables, they must be the same kind of items.

The hospital admissions example points up one of the most common uses for line graphs—to chart fluctuations (or trends) over periods of time. However, line graphs also serve many other purposes. Thus, you might graph the freezing points of a series of ethyl alcohol–water mixtures or plot the changes in the fuel consumption of an automobile over a range of speeds.

Here is the procedure for preparing a line graph.

1. Start by drawing a vertical line and a horizontal line that intersect at right angles at the base of the vertical line. In a graph, these lines are called *axes*. Unless special circumstances dictate otherwise, position the vertical axis at the left end of the horizontal axis so that the axes resemble an "L."

2. Plot the items that show a regular progression, such as time, along the horizontal axis and the items that fluctuate, such as amounts, along the vertical axis. If you wish to show the number of tourists visiting a state park each day for a particular seven-day period, note days along the horizontal axis and numbers of tourists along the vertical axis. For the horizontal axis, follow a left-to-right arrangement, starting with the earliest point in time or the smallest quantity. For the vertical axis, work from the bottom up.

3. Plot your axes so that the resulting graph makes its point clearly. Choosing an inappropriate range of values can result in an undesirable exaggeration of differences or it can minimize differences to the point where they hardly show.

4. Pinpoint the fluctuating values by placing a series of points at the appropriate heights above the segment markers along the horizontal axis. If, for example, the state park had a total of 145 visitors on Sunday, you would place a point directly above the marker for Sunday on the horizontal axis, at the same height as 145 on the vertical axis. You would plot the number of visitors for the other days of the week in the same manner and connect the seven points with a line.

5. If the vertical axis has a short caption, position it at the top of the axis. Position longer captions vertically along the axis so that they read up.

6. If a graph includes two or more sets of fluctuating values, use a different kind of line for each set. For example, if there are three such sets you might use a solid line for one, long dashes for the second, and short dashes for the third. Label each line carefully or, if space is a problem, supply a key that identifies them. If you have so many lines that they would clutter a single graph, make two.

Figure 1 shows the decline in the number of American farms between 1950 and 1978.

Figure 1.   NUMBER OF FARMS IN THE UNITED STATES

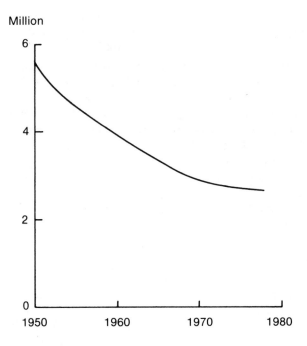

Source: Lyle P. Schertz, *Another Revolution in U.S. Farming?* Bulletin 441 (Washington, D.C., Economics, Statistics, and Cooperatives Service, U.S. Department of Agriculture, 1979), p. 15.

BAR GRAPHS

Bar graphs show relative sizes and quantities with rectangular blocks or bars. One common use for bar graphs is comparing quantities of the same item at different times—for example, a company's annual profits for each of four successive years. This kind of comparison can be extended to include several items, as when a graph compares the tonnage of wheat that Argentina, Australia, Canada, and the United States sold to Russia in 1979 and in 1980. Conversely, bar graphs offer a way of comparing different items at the same time—for example, a ranking of the welfare budgets of the fifty states for a single year.

Bar graphs need not involve a particular span of time. A bar graph might show levels of illumination in different parts of a building. Another might show the percentages of different soil types in a county. Graphs of the latter sort, often called "column graphs," show the percentage of components in some whole thing and customarily consist of a single bar, representing 100 percent of the whole, divided into appropriately sized segments. These segments may be distinguished from one another by labeling, shading, or a combination of the two. Several such bars can be included in a single graph (see Figure 2).

Although vertical bars seem more common than horizontal bars, ordinarily it does not matter in which direction they are drawn. However, there are exceptions. If you are comparing heights, it is logical to use vertical bars. On the other hand, comparisons of mileages logically call for horizontal bars.

Prepare bar graphs according to the following steps.

1. Begin by drawing intersecting horizontal and vertical axes, as for a line graph. For vertical bars, plot the scale of measurement on the vertical axis and label each bar on the horizontal axis. For horizontal bars, reverse the functions of the axes.

2. Select a bar width that is appropriate for the range of heights or lengths; the bars should not look too thick or too narrow. All bars in a graph should be the same width.

3. As a general rule, separate the bars so that the graph can be read easily. However, if you are comparing groups of several items, do not separate the items of each group. The following example illustrates the pattern for two groups of four items each.

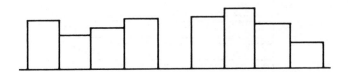

Keep the spaces between bars or between groups of bars the same width.

4. Unless you are showing how something varies with time, arrange the bars in order of increasing or decreasing length. A

Figure 2.   WATER-QUALITY-RELATED R&D FUNDING AT EPA—1972-81 *

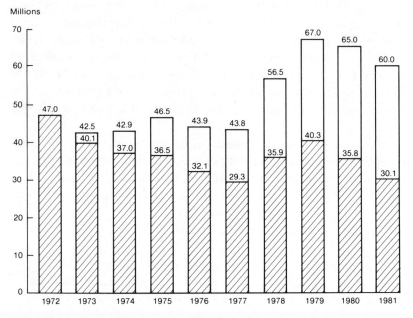

*Shaded areas represent equivalent 1972 dollars.

Source: D. V. Feliciano, "R & D at E.P.A.: Uphill Responsibilities and Downhill Funding," *Journal of the Water Pollution Control Federation*, 52 (March 1980), 444.

Figure 3.   BENEFITS PAID —1976-80 *

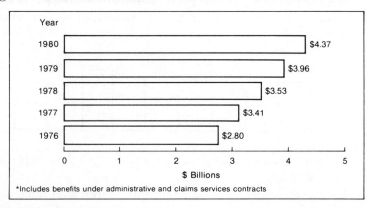

Source: Reprinted by permission of The Equitable Life Assurance Society of the United States.

graph showing the number of homicides in each of the fifty states for a certain year would be so arranged. A graph showing the annual homicides in a single city over several years would not be.

5. Position short captions for the vertical axis at the top of the axis. Position longer captions vertically along the axis, reading from bottom to top.

Figure 2 shows the funds allocated from 1972 through 1981 by the Environmental Protection Agency for research and development projects related to water quality. Figure 3 compares annual benefits paid by the Equitable Life Assurance Society of the United States from 1976 through 1980.

CIRCLE GRAPHS

Circle graphs, sometimes called "pie graphs," show how the parts of some whole thing compare in magnitude. A company might include in its annual report a circle graph that compares its outlays that year for wages and salaries, payments to stockholders, debt retirement, and so forth. A college might use a circle graph to show the percentages of its students who are in two-year, four-year, and graduate programs. A time-motion study might include a circle graph comparing the times spent by a worker performing different tasks during a seven-hour work shift.

To make a circle graph, carry out the following steps.

1. Draw a circle of suitable size with a compass. Ordinarily a four-inch diameter will be about right. Since a circle is 360° in diameter, each 3.6° segment of the diameter equals 1 percent of whatever whole thing is being graphed.

2. If the parts of the whole thing are not given as percentages, calculate the percentages. For example, if you are graphing the seven-hour workday of someone who spends forty-five minutes on task A, two hours and fifteen minutes on task B, three hours on task C, and one hour on task D, you must convert each of these times to a percentage of the total number of hours worked.

3. Draw a vertical line from the center of the circle to the twelve o'clock position. Using a protractor and proceeding clockwise,

Figure 4.   SALES OF U.S.-PRODUCED CHEMICALS BY
COMPANY TYPE °

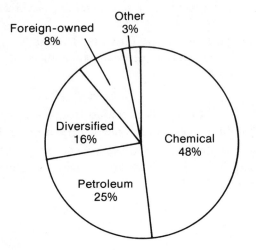

°Total 1980 U.S. chemical sales = $132 billion

Source: Reprinted with permission from *Chemical and Engineering News*, June 21, 1981,
p. 10. Copyright 1981, American Chemical Society.

Figure 5.   TYPICAL PROCESS FLOW, RECOMPRESSION
EVAPORATOR (SINGLE-STAGE)

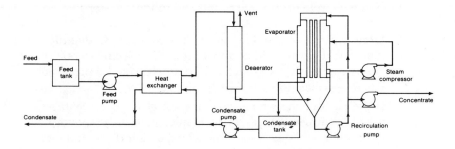

Source: Resources Conservation Co. reprinted from Frank N. Kemmer, "Optimizing
Water-Supply, Treatment and Recycle Practices," *Chemical Engineering*, 6 October
1980, p. 173.

measure off the largest segment. For the workday graph, this would be the segment denoting task C. Continue around the circle, measuring off successively smaller segments.

4. If the thing you are graphing has several very small parts, combine them in a single segment so that the graph will be uncluttered and easy to read. Label this segment "other" or "miscellaneous" and, if a breakdown is needed, provide a key that shows what the segment includes. This segment should follow all of the others.

5. Be sure the segments add up properly. For instance, the segments in the workday graph should total seven hours, not some smaller or larger number.

6. Provide each segment with a caption, lettered horizontally, and include any other appropriate information, such as percentages, hours, dollars, or the like. When a slice is too narrow to accommodate this information, position the information outside the circle and draw a line from it to the segment.

Figure 4 breaks down the total 1980 sales of U.S.-produced chemicals according to company type.

Illustrations

An illustration is a representation of an object, a scene, a process, or the like. The kinds of illustrations discussed here are flow diagrams, drawings, and photographs. Flow diagrams convey information through sets of shapes that bear relatively little physical resemblance to what is being shown. Photographs and drawings, on the other hand, show things as they actually look.

FLOW DIAGRAMS

A flow diagram traces the steps in a process, procedure, or natural occurrence. This kind of diagram is especially useful for clarifying discussions of complex refining, manufacturing, and operating procedures. To illustrate, a flow diagram might accompany an article telling about a new process for removing sulfur-containing contaminants from natural gas or a report recommending a new procedure for conducting marketing surveys and evaluating their results.

Before you begin to draw a flow diagram, list the steps you will be showing; otherwise, you may forget one and have to start over. Beginning at the left side of the page, draw a series of regularly spaced rectangles or circles, one for each step in the process, and connect them with arrows that show how and in what direction the process proceeds. If the process involves machinery or equipment, you may wish to use shapes that suggest what the items look like, rather than circles or rectangles, and to arrange them according to a plant floor plan. Such complexity is not, however, necessary, and a simple row of rectangles or circles is often the clearest representation of a process. If you need to show more steps than can be accommodated in a single row, start a second row, running from right to left, beneath the first one and connect the two rows with an arrow, as shown below.

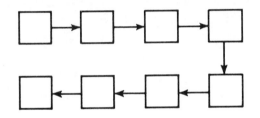

Label each box, circle, and shape, and provide a key to any symbols your reader might not understand. Handle titling and numbering, documentation, and positioning as you would for a graph, and be sure to mention the diagram at the appropriate place in your text.

Figure 5 is an elaborate flow diagram for a process to remove contaminants that build up in water used for industrial processing.

DRAWINGS

Drawings can provide interior as well as exterior views of objects. Internal details may be shown with either a cutaway or exploded-view drawing. A cutaway drawing omits part of the casing,

Figure 6.   FLOGUARD CHECK VALVE

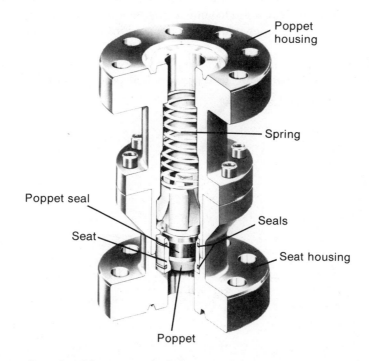

Poppet housing

Spring

Poppet seal

Seals

Seat

Seat housing

Poppet

Source: Reproduced by permission of Flocon Products, Inc.

allowing the viewer to see the internal parts and their arrangement. An exploded-view drawing shows the device disassembled, with the parts arranged in the same relative position they occupy when it is together. Cutaways are generally used for large devices and exploded views for small, complex ones. Exploded views are especially effective for showing how devices are assembled.

Following are guidelines for preparing drawings.

1. If the object has several parts, be sure to draw them in the proper proportions.
2. Label each part with its name, positioned either on or next to the part. If the object has so many parts that they cannot be

labeled, number each one and identify it in an accompanying key. Use connecting lines as necessary.

3. Position the title and figure number, if any, either above or below the drawing. Document, position, and mention drawings in accordance with the guidelines for tables (page 324).

Figure 6 is a cutaway drawing of a flow control valve, and Figure 7 an exploded-view drawing of a belt guard assembly.

Figure 7. BELT GUARD ASSEMBLY FOR ECONO-O-MITRE SAW

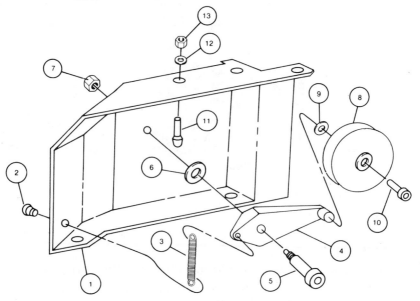

Part #	Part Name
1	Belt Guard R&L Hand
2	Idler Spring Anchor
3	Idler Spring
4	Idler Arm
5	Idler Axle
6	Idler Spacer
7	Idler Axle Lock Nut
8	Idler Pulley
9	Idler Pulley Spacer
10	Idler Pulley Axle
11	Idler Damper
12	Idler Damper Washer
13	Idler Damper Lock Nut

Drawing courtesy of LeTarte Company, Inc., Smith Creek, Michigan.

Figure 8.   HAND-HELD NOISE METER

Photo reprinted courtesy of the Bendix Corporation, Environmental & Process Instruments Division.

PHOTOGRAPHS

Photographs, like drawings, can be used to show external views of objects. Photographs provide true likenesses, however, and for this reason they are often used to show unfamiliar objects or to call attention to staining, damage, wear, or some similar condition. On the other hand, photographs make no distinction between important and unimportant details. If emphasis is important, the photograph must be retouched, cropped, or lighted to accent the desired features.

Follow these guidelines when you take and use pictures.

1. Position the object so that its salient features appear to best advantage. For example, if you wish to show the pitting on a rectangular object, try to angle it to show a side, an end, and the top or bottom.

2. Whenever possible, photograph the object against a neutral background so that its features stand out more clearly. If this cannot be done, have the photograph airbrushed to remove interfering items.

3. If the object is unfamiliar, consider photographing it with something familiar, such as a coin, or a ballpoint pen, so that the viewer can tell its size.

4. Use rubber cement to mount the picture to the page. If you use glue or paste, the page may wrinkle.

5. Position the title and the figure number, if any, either above or below the photograph. Document, position, and mention photographs in accordance with the guidelines for tables (pages 323–324).

Figure 8 is a photograph of a sound-level meter.

Suggestions for Making Tables, Graphs, and Illustrations

1. Make a table that compares the monthly housing starts in the city of Midville for 1980 and 1981. Use the following data:

   1980: January (155), February (140), March (165), April (178), May (186), June (205), July (215), August (220), September (190), October (165), November (150), December (130).

   1981: January (120), February (108), March (133), April (145), May (130), June (163), July (160), August (150), September (143), October (130), November (116), December (110).

2. Make a line graph that gives a month-by-month comparison of the housing starts in the city of Midville during 1980 and 1981. Use the data from item 1 above, and chart each year with its own line.

3. The summer production record for a certain company is as follows: June—575 lathes, 850 shapers, 600 drill presses; July—690 lathes, 950 shapers, and 800 drill presses; August—450 lathes, 700 shapers, and 675 drill presses. Prepare a bar graph comparing the production of these items for each of the three months.

4. Prepare a circle graph showing the percentage of different types of appliances sold by the kitchenwares department of a store during a one-

month period. The items and percentages are as follows: refrigerators, 43 percent; stoves, 31.5 percent, dishwashers, 13 percent; blenders, 6 percent; coffeemakers, 3.5 percent; toasters, 1.8 percent; electric can openers, 1.2 percent.

5. Prepare a flow diagram for a process in your field. Choose a process that includes at least six steps.

6. Prepare a cutaway or an exploded-view drawing of some relatively simple object or device used in your field of study.

16

Finding A Job

The key to successful job hunting is a well-organized campaign which begins with the search for openings. Unfortunately, many candidates overlook one or more of the sources of information about jobs. Others are not seriously considered for the openings they uncover because they do a poor job of presenting themselves as candidates. This chapter will show you how to locate job openings; write effective application letters, personal data sheets, and postinterview letters; and prepare for and handle job interviews.

Locating Job Openings

Most job openings are found through campus placement offices, word-of-mouth information, or advertisements. Sometimes, you may also wish to seek a job directly by writing to companies that may have openings in your field or by having a professional organization refer your name to prospective employers.

PLACEMENT OFFICES

Perhaps the best place to start looking for job openings is your campus placement office. Find out where it is located; then early in your final year of school pay it a visit and ask what services it performs. Tell a staff member about your job interests, and find out how forthcoming visits by company representatives are announced as well as how to sign up for interviews. Fill out a placement registration form and provide the office with appropriate materials—for example, certificates of commendation, instructor evaluations, letters of recommendation—so that it can set up a placement file for you. This material will be reviewed by company representatives before they talk with you, or sent to prospective employers. Check also to see whether your college has internship or cooperative education employment arrangements with organizations. Often, these are excellent stepping stones to permanent positions. Before leaving the placement office, take a look at the *College Placement Annual*. This publication lists the occupational requirements and locations of several hundred industrial, business, and governmental employers, whom you can contact directly.

WORD-OF-MOUTH INFORMATION

Word-of-mouth job information may come from instructors and from friends or acquaintances who are employed by or have knowledge of organizations for which you might wish to work. Start by making a list of all the people who might be able to help you. Phone or visit each person and ask whether he or she knows of any suitable openings. Be sure to explain exactly what type of position you are looking for. Ask whether you can use the person's name when you write to the organization.

ADVERTISEMENTS

Advertisements of job openings appear in the classified sections of newspapers and trade publications—that is, periodicals devoted to particular occupations or professions. Read every advertisement carefully, taking special note of the qualifications required for the position. Also note any information concerning the size and location of the organization, job duties, job benefits, and salary.

DIRECT INQUIRIES

Like the *College Placement Annual*, corporate directories can furnish you with names of organizations to write. Standard corporate

directories include *Dun and Bradstreet's Million Dollar Directory,*
Standard and Poor's Index, Moody's Industrials, and the *Thomas*
Register of American Manufacturers. For names of smaller companies not included in these publications, you can consult the manufacturing directories issued for the different states. To check these
directories, go to your college or city library and ask a librarian where
they are shelved. Before using any directory, check the front pages to
learn how it is organized.

The yellow page section of the telephone directory is another
good source of company names. Many libraries have statewide
phonebook collections as well as books for all major U.S. cities. If the
library doesn't have a phonebook you want, check the local office of
your telephone company.

REFERRAL SERVICES

Many professional organizations operate employee referral services. If you belong to the student chapter of an organization that does,
ask that it supply your name to prospective employers.

Writing the Job Application Letter

If your first contact with an organization occurs through a
campus interview, a letter of application is not required, although
you may write a brief letter to develop one or two points raised during
the interview. In all other cases, however, an application letter of the
sort described in this chapter will be needed.

A job application letter can be the most important letter you'll
ever write. If you're like many job seekers, you have a good idea of the
sort of company you'd like to work for, and you have geographical
preferences, too. Perhaps you prefer a large organization on the East
Coast. Or you may favor a medium-sized company in the South or
Southwest. A well-written application letter greatly increases your
chances of getting what you want.

Unfortunately, few job seekers know how closely most companies examine the application letters they receive and how ruthlessly
they discard those that fail to measure up. Some companies, for
instance, automatically reject any letter that is not on business-size
stationery or does not follow one of the standard business letter
formats, and no organization will accept a letter that is handwritten

rather than typed. Even a single misspelled word or insufficient information about the applicant can send a letter to the "reject" file. Obviously, you must prepare your letter with great care if you hope to compete successfully with other applicants.

Before you write an application letter, it is important to analyze the job you are seeking, and your own qualifications for it. A good way to do this is to make a list, itemizing the qualifications required for the job in one column and your own qualifications in another. Although the two columns should be very similar, they need not be identical. If you lack or partially lack one qualification, you may have another that would compensate for it.

Assuming you have the proper qualifications, you are ready to start your letter. But how can you ensure that it will make the desired impression? To begin, address your letter to a specific person, if possible. Make every effort to determine the name of the personnel manager or the supervisor who hires for the position you want. The job advertisement may state the name, you may find it out through word of mouth, or you could call the company and ask. Don't write to "personnel manager" unless securing a name is impossible.

Since your aim is to sell yourself, you should look upon your application letter as a specialized kind of sales letter. A successful sales letter, as noted on page 156, does these things:

> catches the reader's attention
>
> creates a desire for the product or service by convincing the reader of its superiority
>
> causes the reader to take some action.

By following the procedure described below, you can accomplish each of these objectives.

ATTRACTING ATTENTION

Beyond naming the position you are applying for and telling how you heard of the vacancy, the opening paragraph should interest the reader in considering you for the job. To spark interest, you should begin by stating a service you can provide or naming one of your outstanding qualifications. Three common types of openings that will catch the reader's attention are the summary opening, the name opening, and the challenging question opening.

A *summary opening* presents the required information as a direct statement.

> I feel my college training in biology and art qualifies me for the position of scientific illustrator that you advertised in the July 20 *Detroit Free Press*.

> Because of my training in chemistry and two summers of laboratory work experience, I believe I can fill any opening you may have for a chemical laboratory technician.

As the second example shows, the summary opening can be used to inquire about possible openings as well as to answer advertisements.

If you use the summary opening, be careful not to omit any pertinent information. For example, if you open your letter by saying only, "I wish to be considered for the position of laboratory technician in your firm," you have not presented a qualification or stated a service you can provide. Since it is the qualification or service that attracts the reader's attention, to omit it lessens your likelihood of success.

Above all, never let the employer think you're not serious about wanting the job. If you begin your letter by saying, "I happened to be reading the *Boston Globe* and saw that you are looking for a computer programmer," you will destroy your chances with the very first sentence.

The *name opening* mentions the name of the person who told you about the job. This opening can be especially effective because use of a name suggests a recommendation by that person.

> Ms. Loretta Naegele, head of your firm's drafting department, has told me that you plan to hire two more draftsmen next month. I believe that my B + record at Newton Technical Institute and two years of summer employment as a draftsman's assistant will enable me to meet your requirement for this position.

Note that a summary of the writer's qualifications immediately follows the opening sentence.

The *challenging question opening*, obviously, asks a question and is used most often by persons inquiring about possible job openings. This opening can also be used effectively in response to advertisements for positions.

Can your company use someone with two years' experience in designing specialized heating and air-conditioning systems for office buildings?

Would the engineer's assistant you advertised for in today's *Washington Post* be more valuable to your company if he also had worked three years as a maintenance technician in the army?

Do not use the challenging question unless you have a special qualification that the employer is likely to find useful. Mentioning a far-fetched special qualification will hurt, not help, your job chances.

ESTABLISHING SUPERIORITY

Having gained your reader's attention, you must next establish your superiority as a candidate for the position. This is done by supplying details that elaborate upon the qualifications mentioned in the opening paragraph and by presenting others that suit you for the job. Before you begin writing, think carefully about the requirements of the particular job and then stress those aspects of your background that are most relevant and that would interest the employer most. If you are a recent graduate with little job experience, you should first emphasize your course of study and your grades (if outstanding) and then turn to your work experience or extracurricular activities.

In discussing your previous employment, do not mention such specifics as the names of the organizations, the dates of employment, or the duties you performed. These will be included in the personal data sheet that will accompany your letter. Instead, try to relate your experiences to the position you are applying for. If you desire a job as a salesperson or receptionist and have worked as a cashier in a supermarket, you might indicate that this earlier job taught you to deal with the public. If the opening is for an office manager and you have worked as a bell captain at a summer resort, you might note that your previous work provided experience in supervising others. Even if you have never had directly related work experience, try to think of some aspect of a past job—even a part-time or summer job—that you can relate to the position you are seeking.

If you have paid part or all of your educational expenses or held one or more elective offices, say so. The first denotes ambition; the second, the ability to lead—both qualities that employers find highly desirable. Mentioning membership in student chapters of professional organizations shows that your interest in your profession is not just monetary. Do not feel that you must mention every job or office you have held. Rather, try to single out those that are most likely to interest the prospective employer, and take up any others only in the personal data sheet.

The following section of a job application letter establishes superiority. The writer is applying for the position of assistant manager in a plastics factory.

> I am now enrolled in the plastics technology program at Wilson College and expect to receive my Associate in Applied Science degree this May. My area of concentration is the injection molding of both thermoplastic and thermosetting resins. I am acquainted with all major types of molding machines.
>
> During the summer of 1981, I served a ten-week internship at a small plastics parts company. About half my time was spent in quality control and the other half in assisting the foreman. As an intern, I gained first-hand knowledge of testing procedures and practical experience in supervision.
>
> For the past six months, I have worked part-time as a molding machine operator in a toy factory.
>
> I am an active member of the local chapter of the Society of Plastic Engineers and am currently serving as its president. I have been active in all local seminars.
>
> *Gordon Hignite*

If you are changing jobs after several years of working, follow the general guidelines for establishing superiority but stress your employment experience rather than your educational background. In this case, name your present employer and explain why you wish to work elsewhere.

SUGGESTING ACTION

Few people, if any, are ever hired for a permanent position without first being interviewed, so the closing section of your letter should seek to obtain an interview at the employer's convenience.

If the hiring company is located nearby, you may request an interview directly, as in the following example.

> May I come in for an interview at some mutually convenient time? You can reach me at the above address or by phone at (616) 796-3962.

When the hiring company is a long way off, the expenses of an interview will be high, and there is no tactful way to request one directly. Instead, you can ask if a company representative will be in your area soon, and offer to meet with him or her at that time. Similarly, if you plan to visit the city in which the company is located, you can suggest an interview then. These approaches often lead to scheduled interviews.

Applicants for positions in journalism and the graphic arts should also offer to let employers see samples of their work.

> Should you wish to review my portfolio, please call or write and I shall send copies of my drawings.

Again, the result is often an interview offer.

THINGS TO AVOID

Job hunters often damage or destroy their chances of being hired by taking the wrong approach in their application letters. To ensure that your letter will be received favorably, there are certain pitfalls that you must avoid.

To begin, do not be long-winded. People who must read dozens of application letters naturally prefer a letter that is brief. You will improve your chances of being hired if you keep your letter to a single page. Be sure, however, that the letter contains all the information needed to sell you as a desirable applicant.

Never mention in your application letter how badly you need work. Most companies are not charitable institutions, and although your appeal may arouse sympathy, it will do little more. If you are unemployed, there is no need to say so. A brief statement to the effect that you can begin work immediately will suffice.

If you are unhappy with your present job, do not so much as hint at this in your letter. The person who airs such grievances is likely to be seen as a malcontent or a troublemaker and receive no further consideration. If you have valid reasons for wanting to change jobs, present these in terms of the positive aspects of the job you are applying for, not the negative aspects of the job you are leaving.

It is rarely a good idea to mention how eager you are to work for the particular organization to which you are writing. Such comments, unless very carefully phrased, tend to sound insincere and create an unfavorable impression. The employer, after all, wants to know how you can benefit the company, not how the company can benefit you.

If you lack on-the-job experience, do not mention this. Such an approach is negative and suggests a lack of self-confidence. Stress instead how your training has prepared you for the job, and mention the relevant aspects of any part-time or summer work.

It is best to avoid the question of salary until the job interview. By bringing it up in your letter, you run the risk of appearing to be more interested in the pay than in the job itself. If you're answering an advertisement that asks you to state your salary requirements, suggest that the matter be deferred until the job interview.

> May I suggest that the matter of salary be deferred until we have discussed the position? Once I have a fuller idea of the duties, I will be in a better position to talk about a figure.

Remember, your goal is to sell your services. Your best approach, therefore, is to ask yourself, "What can I do for this company?"—and then tell your reader as clearly and succinctly as you can.

POLISHING YOUR LETTER

Once your letter is finished, there is one more thing that you must do—carefully proofread and polish what you have written. The letter that you send must not have a single misspelled word or incorrect sentence. After all, the only way the employer can tell that you are a careful, conscientious person is by your application letter.

Be sure, too, that in typing your letter you follow either the modified block or the full block format. (These formats, and business letters in general, are discussed in Chapter 8.) If you know the format used by the company you're writing, use that format in your letters. If you don't know the format, it is best to follow the modified block, the more commonly used of the two.

EXAMPLES OF JOB APPLICATION LETTERS

```
                                        20900 Moxon Drive
                                        Mt. Clemens, MI  48043
                                        March 16, 1981


        Ms. Mary Ann Buday
        Personnel Director
        Allan Dee-Fraser Senior Citizens'
          Residential Center
        33300 Utica Road
        Fraser, MI  48026

        Dear Ms. Buday:

        Mrs. Diane Schebil, director of your activities department, has
        informed me that you intend to hire an assistant administrator
        soon.  I feel that my training in health services management
        and experience in the field of allied health qualify me for
        this position.  Please regard this letter as my formal
        application.

        On May 21, 1981, I shall receive a Bachelor of Science degree in
        health services management from Ferris State College.  This
        program offers a thorough background in health science, personnel
        and financial management, and plant operations, as well as train-
        ing in leadership techniques.  My area of concentration is
        health care for the aged.

        As an intern, I worked in the administration department of a
        public health clinic.  I have also worked as a hospital ward
        clerk for one summer and served as a counselor for a summer
        recreation program.  This experience has taught me to apply
        business practices to the operation of health care facilities
        and prepared me to hold a supervisory position.

        While in college, I have been a member of the Ferris Health
        Services Management Association.  I belong to the Clinton Town-
        ship chapter of the Goodfellows Association.  The enclosed
        resume will provide a fuller picture of my background and
        experience.

        May I have a personal interview with you to discuss my qualifi-
        cations in more detail?  You can reach me by calling (313) 468-
        4861 or writing to the above address.

                                 Sincerely,

                                 Susan M. Santine
                                 Susan M. Santine

        Enc.
```

Discussion Questions

1. What kinds of information are presented in the opening of this letter?
2. What does the writer accomplish by mentioning her specific field of concentration (health care for the aged) as well as her major field (health services management)?
3. Why doesn't the writer name the organizations for which she worked or specify her duties with them?

```
                62E West Campus Apartments
                Grolier College
                Medina, ND  58467
                February 14, 1981


                Mr. Jonas Dupree
                General Manager
                Cherry Hill Country Club
                100 Hillside Drive
                Jordan, AR  72548

                Dear Mr. Dupree:

                I believe that my formal college training, together with nearly
                one summer of management experience, has provided me with the
                skills needed to fill the position of assistant maintenance
                manager that you advertised in the December issue of Weed and
                Turf Magazine.

                My graduation this coming May will mark the completion of a two-
                year program in ornamental horticulture technology that includes
                courses in plant, grass, and vehicle maintenance, use of pesti-
                cides and herbicides, and management practices.  I have earned
                an A average in my major field.

                To help pay for college, I have worked for two summers at a
                local golf course and one summer in a small nursery.  When the
                owner of the nursery was hospitalized for ten weeks, I assumed
                its complete management for that period.  Besides providing
                maintenance and supervisory experience, these jobs have given me
                the opportunity to meet and deal with the public.

                I have played varsity golf for both Grolier College and my high
                school.  To keep abreast of developments in golf course
                management, I have become a student member of the Golf Course
                Superintendent's Association of America.

                If my qualifications interest you, I would welcome the opportu-
                nity to meet with you and discuss them in greater detail.  I will
                be visiting your area for ten days starting March 11 and can
                come in for an interview any time during that period.  Please
                call me at (701) 349-2500, extension 62, or write to the above
                address.

                Sincerely yours,

                James N. Skellinger
                James N. Skellinger

                Enc.
```

Discussion Questions

1. Which of the three types of openings discussed in the chapter does this letter illustrate?
2. Generally, a job applicant would not cite athletic accomplishments in a letter to a prospective employer. Why does this writer mention playing varsity golf in high school and college?
3. Why does the writer suggest that the job interview be held when he visits the prospective employer's area rather than asking for an interview at the employer's convenience?

216 Burnam Hall
Byron Technical Institute
Dublin, NC   28332
March 14, 1981

Mr. Reginald Washington
Manager
Ames Heating and Cooling Company
1500 Monroe Street
Durham, NC   27701

Dear Mr. Washington:

Does your company have an opening for a serviceman whose background combines academic training with extensive practical
experience? If the answer is yes, I would like to be considered
for the position.

In June, I will receive an Associate in Applied Science degree
in heating, air conditioning, and refrigeration. My chief
interest is in air conditioning.

Before starting my program at Byron Technical Institute, I
worked for two years as a service assistant of a small air
conditioning and refrigeration company. This job has given me a
solid foundation in troubleshooting air conditioning units.
While in school, I have worked part-time as a desk clerk at a
local motel, thus learning to deal with many types of people.

Would it be possible to arrange for an interview? I am
available any weekday except Thursday.

                         Sincerely,

                         Kenneth Hollingbeck —

                         Kenneth Hollingbeck

Enclosure

Discussion Questions

1. Which of the three types of openings discussed in this chapter does this letter illustrate?
2. What is the significance of the "enclosure" notation at the bottom of this letter and of the "enc." notations at the bottoms of the preceding two letters?

1357 Oak Street
Balfour, MI 48613
March 18, 1982

Mr. William Howard
Employment Manager
Union Carbide Corporation
270 Park Avenue
New York, N.Y. 10017

Dear Mr. Howard:

I have read your New York Times advertisement for a supervisor for your technical writing staff and believe my employment experience has provided me with the qualifications needed to handle the job successfully.

For twelve years, I have been employed as a technical writer by the Randall Chemical Corporation. This job has provided me with practical experience in every major aspect of preparing technical literature as well as some supervisory experience. I have helped produce more than 150 pieces of writing, ranging from one- and two-page data sheets to lengthy technical manuals. Although I enjoy my work and have an excellent relationship with my coworkers and supervisor, my prospects for promotion are very limited. It is for this reason that I wish to change jobs.

My academic background includes a Bachelor of Science degree in chemistry. To help prepare myself for a supervisory position and keep abreast of technical developments, I am taking evening classes in management and the use of computers in publishing.

I am a member of two professional associations and active in community service organizations.

I would appreciate an interview to discuss at greater length my qualifications and possible role with your company. If you wish, I will be happy to provide you with samples of publications I have written. You may write me at the above address or call me at (616) 784-1739.

Sincerely yours,

Ambrose Crawford

Ambrose Crawford

Enclosure

Discussion Questions

1. In what ways does this letter differ from the preceding three?
2. Why does Crawford mention that he is on excellent terms with his coworkers and supervisor?

257 Maple Street
Big Rapids, MI 49307
March 30, 1981

Ms. Nancy J. Newman
Personnel Director
Great Lakes Surveying, Inc.
27657 Wide Track Drive
Pontiac, MI 48402

Dear Ms. Newman:

Mr. Donald Lange, of your firm's public relations department, has told me you have several summer openings for surveyor's assistants. I believe my schooling at Ferris State College has provided me with the qualifications to fill one of these positions.

I am a junior in the surveying program at Ferris and expect to receive my Bachelor of Science degree in May 1982. My overall academic average is 3.5 on a 4.0 scale, and I have a 3.75 in my major field.

I have worked two summers as a carpenter's helper and one summer as a member of a farm crew, jobs which provided practical experience in teamwork and cooperation. I am capable, responsible, and quick to learn, and I believe I will prove an effective member of your surveying crew.

If you require further information concerning my background and qualifications, the Ferris Placement Office can supply you with copies of my placement registration form and instructor evaluations. I would be happy to come in for an interview. Just call me at (616) 796-0713. I look forward to hearing from you.

Sincerely yours,

Kermit Hulman

Kermit Hulman

Discussion Questions

1. Why does the writer note that his carpenter and farm crew jobs have given him experience in teamwork and cooperation?
2. Why does the writer mention that further information concerning his background and qualifications is available from the Placement Office?

Personal Data Sheet

Job application letters should be accompanied by a personal data sheet, sometimes called a résumé or vita. A personal data sheet summarizes, in one or two pages, the qualifications mentioned in the application letter and presents additional information that the employer will find useful. The data sheet, moreover, allows you to keep your letter brief so that it functions effectively as a sales tool.

The information included in a personal data sheet is ordinarily grouped under five headings: Employment Objective, Education, Employment Experience, Personal and Professional Interests, and References. If you wish, you may also have a Personal Data section. The arrangement of sections within the data sheet depends upon the stage of the applicant's career. Students and recent graduates, who have had little or no full-time work experience, should obviously put Education before Employment Experience. Applicants who have worked a number of years, on the other hand, should reverse the order, so that employers can read about their work experience first.

Although there is no single "correct" format for personal data sheets, any format you use must be attractive, well organized, and easy to read. The following general rules can help.

1. Underline and/or capitalize headings to make them stand out on the page.
2. Use phrases and clauses rather than complete sentences so that you can condense information.
3. List your most recent education and employment experience first and work backward so the employer can quickly and easily find what you have done most recently.
4. Don't try to cram too much material onto a page. Ample white space is important.
5. Don't reproduce a data sheet by mimeographing or xerography. Instead, retype each copy or have copies typeset and offset.

HEADING

The heading of the personal data sheet includes your name, address (including zip code), and telephone number. Generally, this information is centered at the top of the page, although there are other possible arrangements, as shown by the sample data sheets. Do not include a date. If you do, your data sheet will become obsolete much more quickly than it otherwise would.

Marie Kowalski
1239 Sunningdale Street
Philadelphia, PA   19141
Telephone: (215) 545-3194

PERSONAL DATA

This section is optional. If you decide to include it, give your date of birth, social security number, marital status, and general condition of health, if excellent. Do not include race, religion, national origin, or sex: the courts have ruled that this information cannot be used as a basis for hiring. Unless you are applying for a job that requires United States citizenship, do not mention citizenship either. Finally, do not send a photograph with the data sheet.

EMPLOYMENT OBJECTIVE

This statement indicates your immediate work goal and, if appropriate, the direction you hope your career will take. Here are two examples of employment objectives.

To learn the duties of a librarian and later qualify for the position of head reference librarian.

To begin work as a management trainee or assistant buyer and eventually become a marketing specialist or head buyer for a large department store or a mail order house.

Such a statement tells the employer that you are ambitious, have confidence in your ability, and know the avenues for advancement open to you.

In preparing your statement, avoid sounding as if you intend using this job merely as a stepping stone to a better job elsewhere or to establishing your own business.

EDUCATION

The education section of the data sheet includes both post-high-school and high-school education, in that order. Begin by giving the date of your college or technical school graduation, the degree or certificate you received and your major field of study, and the name and location of the institution.

Especially if you are a new graduate, include, in addition to these basic facts, any other details about your education that will enhance your attractiveness as a job candidate. If your academic record is noteworthy, especially in your major field, be sure to call it to your reader's attention. if you've received any academic honors, mention them also.

Extracurricular activities likewise help create a desirable image for new job seekers, so don't fail to mention some of the more significant ones you've taken part in. Belonging to one or more campus clubs, social and professional organizations, or similar groups stamps you as a person who is outgoing and has a variety of interests. Holding office in an organization denotes a capacity for leadership. These are qualities that an employer—no matter what the field—looks for in a job applicant.

The education section of a recent graduate's data sheet should look something like this:

May 1981, Associate in Applied Science degree, building construction, Ferris State College, Big Rapids, MI 49307

Academic Honors:

Upper 20% of class
3.5 G.P.A. (4.0 scale) in major field
3.2 G.P.A. overall

Extracurricular Activities:

Captain intramural baseball team one year
Member Pi Kappa Alpha, a social fraternity
Member Associated Building Construction Technologists, a campus professional organization; treasurer senior year
June 1977, graduate from Cannon High School, South Park, Pennsylvania 15102, industrial arts program.

Do not list major-field courses unless you feel employers would not be familiar with the course content of your program or unless the program includes courses not given elsewhere. Do, however, list minors and elective courses that relate to the job you're applying for. If, for example, your major field is diesel and heavy equipment service but you're applying for a job with an automobile dealership, list the courses in automobile repair that you have taken.

If you have very little employment experience, handle high school as you did your post-high-school education. Mention your academic standing if it was high. Then mention significant extracurricular activities, positions of leadership, and the like. Otherwise, treat high school as shown in the preceding example. If you have completed a program in a vocational or skill center or some comparable institution, note that fact.

If you have been out of school for several years, give only the basic facts of graduation: date, name of degree or certificate, major field of study, and name and location of the institution. Do, however, name any recent supplementary courses related to your occupation.

EMPLOYMENT EXPERIENCE

The employment experience section should include your full-time jobs and—if you have little work experience—any part-time or temporary jobs you have held. List the jobs in reverse chronological order, most recent first, and separate them clearly from one another on the sheet. Begin by telling when you held the job, and then give the job title, if any, and the name and address of the organization. Briefly specify your duties if they are similar to those of the job you're seeking. Otherwise, just provide a job title or brief job description. For example, if you are applying for a position as a highway technologist, there is no need to discuss the duties of such jobs as a gas station attendant or supermarket checkout clerk.

Whatever the job, though, be sure to mention any bonuses, raises, or promotions you have received as well as any supervisory experience you have gained. All of these things reflect superior job performance and make you more attractive to prospective employers. Here is part of the employment experience section of a data sheet.

| November 1976 to September 1978 | Sanitarian assistant, Chester County Health Department, West Chester, PA 16529 |
| | Inspected licensed establishments, swimming pools, mobile home parks; conducted mosquito surveys; collected drinking-water samples. Starting salary, $760/month; final salary, $890/month. |

Although military service can be discussed in a separate section, it is more conveniently treated under Employment Experience at the appropriate place in the chronology. When describing military experience, give the dates, the branch of service and your specialty, and the places you served. Discuss your specific duties if they relate to those of the job you're applying for. Since military promotions, like those in civilian life, indicate satisfactory performance, be sure to note your rank upon discharge. If you supervised others, mention this also.

| December 1976 to November 1980 | Electronics repairman, United States Air Force, Washington, D.C., and Wiesbaden, Germany. Supervised a five-person crew. Honorably discharged as sergeant (E-5). |

PERSONAL AND PROFESSIONAL INTERESTS

Here you should list memberships in technical and professional societies, participation in civic activities and organizations, special training such as lifesaving, and hobbies. Such information shows that you have an interest in your profession, a concern for your community, a liking for others, and a variety of interests. All of these are qualities that employers find attractive.

As a rule, it is best not to mention partisan political activity in your data sheet. Like religion, politics should play no part in the employment process.

Member National Association of Printers and Lithographers. Enjoy music, backpacking, swimming, bowling.

REFERENCES

Although the "References" heading is an essential part of the
data sheet, there may be occasions when you won't want to include
your references' names. You may, for instance, be answering a "blind"
advertisement (one that gives no company name but asks you to send
your reply to Box ——). In such a case, you probably will not want
your references to be contacted until you learn more about the
company and the position. Even when you do know the company,
you may want to be absolutely sure you are interested in the job
before your references are contacted. In either of these situations,
simply indicate, under the heading, that you will furnish references
on request. Otherwise, include a list of your references on the data
sheet.

Common courtesy requires that you obtain permission to use a
person's name *before* you list it on your data sheet. A good letter of
reference is hard to write. Anyone unexpectedly asked to supply one
might well resent the request and either refuse to comply or do a
slipshod job. Moreover, you will want to make sure that the people
you wish to list as references will speak well of you.

A list of references should include three or four names. A smaller
number might cause the employer to question your ability or character. A larger number is unlikely to provide any important additional
information.

For each reference, list name, title, and address, including zip
code. If you know the person's phone number, be sure to give this also,
including the area code. The employer can then call the reference, a
procedure that is convenient for both parties and allows the employer
to pursue any line of questioning that seems desirable.

The references you give can be of several types. In addition to
former employers, you might also include instructors, coworkers in
responsible positions, clients or customers, or prominent people in
your community who know you. Do not include relatives. Some
employers may specify the types of references they wish. If so, be sure
you include only those types.

EXAMPLES OF PERSONAL DATA SHEETS

Susan Marie Santine
20900 Moxon Drive
Mt. Clemens, MI 48043
Telephone: (313) 468-4861

PERSONAL DATA

Date of Birth: February 15, 1959
Social Security Number: 472-11-3157
Marital Status: Single
Health: Excellent

EMPLOYMENT OBJECTIVE

To become a member of the staff of a private institution or
community agency in the health care field and eventually assume
managerial responsibilities.

EDUCATION

May 1981, Bachelor of Science degree, health services management,
Ferris State College, Big Rapids, MI 49307

Academic Honors:

   3.6/4.0 G.P.A., health services and science courses

Electives Related to Major:

   Problems of Aging
   Biomedical Ethics
   Communicable Disease Control

Extracurricular Activities:

   Member of Zeta Tau Alpha, a social sorority

June 1977, graduated from Chippewa Valley High School, Mt.
Clemens, MI 48043, college preparatory program

EMPLOYMENT EXPERIENCE

   December 1980   Manager trainee (internship program)
                              Muskegon Health Center
         to   Muskegon, MI 49444
                              Assisted with accounting, purchasing,
   February 1981   personnel, and maintenance.

Summer of 1980

Ward clerk, Mt. Clemens General Hospital, Mt. Clemens, MI 48043 Answered phone, updated patients' charts and records, handled secretarial duties.

Summer of 1979

Counselor, Clinton Township Parks and Recreation Department, Mt. Clemens, MI 48043 Conducted recreation programs at area playgrounds and parks.

September 1976
    to
July 1978

Part-time theater cashier, Parkway Theater, 40335 Groesbeck Highway, Mt. Clemens, MI 48043

Volunteer work experience includes serving as an aide at East Detroit Blue Cross Center and as a Candy Striper at St. Joseph Hospital in Mt. Clemens.

PERSONAL AND PROFESSIONAL INTERESTS

Treasurer, Ferris Health Services Management Association. Member, Clinton Township Goodfellows Association. Enjoy swimming, doll collecting, racketball, softball, and reading.

REFERENCES

Mr. John Booth
Department Head
Health Services Management
Ferris State College
Big Rapids, MI 49307
Telephone: (616) 796-9971, ext. 380

Mrs. Vivian Meed, R.N.
Ward Clerk Supervisor
Mt. Clemens General
  Hospital
Mt. Clemens, MI 48043
Telephone: (313) 463-
  2241, ext. 187

Mr. Thomas Ryan
Manager
Muskegon Health Center
1301 Apple Avenue
Muskegon, MI 49444
Telephone: (616) 733-4321

Father Lawrence Jackson
St. Michael's Catholic
  Community
2008 Garfield Road
Mt. Clemens, MI 48043
Telephone: (313) 469-
  0455

Discussion Questions

1. Show that the writer has provided an adequate reference section.
2. What does the writer's volunteer work experience suggest about her?

James N. Skellinger
62E West Campus Apartments
Grolier College
Medina, ND 58467
Telephone: (701) 349-2500 Ext. 62

Employment Objective

To learn the particular maintenance and management practices of
the golf course that employs me and eventually become maintenance
manager or head greens superintendent.

Education

May 1981, Associate in Applied Science degree, ornamental
horticulture technology, Grolier College, Medina, ND 58467

Academic Honors:

   3.8/4.0 G.P.A., ornamental horticulture technology; 3.2
   G.P.A. overall.

Extracurricular Activities:

   Varsity golf team two years
   Member apartment council one year
   Treasurer senior class
   Yearbook editor junior year

June 1977, Graduated from Dwight D. Eisenhower High School,
Ryder, ND 58779, college preparatory program.

Employment Experience

Summer of 1979   Greenhouse worker, Marshall Nursery,
                            Medina, ND 58467
                            Planted and propagated flowers and
                            shrubs, waited on customers, managed
                            business while owner was hospitalized.
                            Received bonus at end of summer.

Summers of 1977   Maintenance worker, Riverview Golf
and 1978   Course, Medina, ND 58467
                            Mowing, watering, fertilizing,
                            spraying weeds, maintaining bunkers

Personal and Professional Interests

Growing flowers, swimming, bicycling, coin collecting, photography

References

Mr. Gordon Booker
Instructor, Ornamental Horticulture Department
Grolier College
Medina, ND   58467
Telephone: (701) 349-1871

Ms. Natalie Marshall
Owner, Marshall Nursery
259 Pawnee Road
Medina, ND   58467
Telephone: (701) 349-6496

Mr. Rodney Donforth
Manager, People's Savings Bank
186 Main Street
Medina, ND   58467
Telephone: (701) 349-1000

Discussion Questions

1. Why does the writer mention that he has served on his apartment council, as class treasurer, and as yearbook editor?
2. What does the Personal and Professional Interests section of his personal data sheet suggest about the writer?

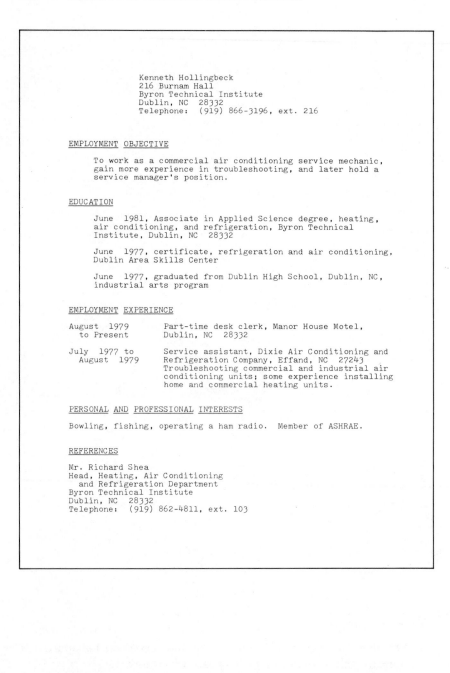

Kenneth Hollingbeck
216 Burnam Hall
Byron Technical Institute
Dublin, NC   28332
Telephone: (919) 866-3196, ext. 216

EMPLOYMENT OBJECTIVE

    To work as a commercial air conditioning service mechanic,
    gain more experience in troubleshooting, and later hold a
    service manager's position.

EDUCATION

    June 1981, Associate in Applied Science degree, heating,
    air conditioning, and refrigeration, Byron Technical
    Institute, Dublin, NC   28332

    June 1977, certificate, refrigeration and air conditioning,
    Dublin Area Skills Center

    June 1977, graduated from Dublin High School, Dublin, NC,
    industrial arts program

EMPLOYMENT EXPERIENCE

August 1979   Part-time desk clerk, Manor House Motel,
   to Present   Dublin, NC   28332

July 1977 to   Service assistant, Dixie Air Conditioning and
   August 1979   Refrigeration Company, Effand, NC   27243
                    Troubleshooting commercial and industrial air
                    conditioning units; some experience installing
                    home and commercial heating units.

PERSONAL AND PROFESSIONAL INTERESTS

Bowling, fishing, operating a ham radio.   Member of ASHRAE.

REFERENCES

Mr. Richard Shea
Head, Heating, Air Conditioning
   and Refrigeration Department
Byron Technical Institute
Dublin, NC   28332
Telephone: (919) 862-4811, ext. 103

Mrs. Hazel Kinott
Instructor, Heating, Air Conditioning
   and Refrigeration Department
Byron Technical Institute
Dublin, NC 28332
Telephone: (919) 862-4811, ext. 107

Mr. Frank Trapp
Owner, Dixie Air Conditioning
   and Refrigeration Company
828 Quinkert Street
Effand, NC 27243
Telephone: (919) 327-5333

Discussion Questions

1. Why does the writer note the wage increase he has received as a desk clerk and a service assistant?
2. What does the writer accomplish by mentioning that he has earned a certificate in refrigeration and air conditioning at a skills center?
3. Why does Hollingbeck omit mentioning his duties as a desk clerk but specify his duties as a service assistant?

Ambrose Crawford
1357 Oak Street
Balfour, MI 48613
Telephone (616) 784-1739

EMPLOYMENT OBJECTIVE

To supervise the technical writing staff of a chemical company
and eventually become assistant director or director of corporate
communications.

EMPLOYMENT EXPERIENCE

July 1968 to   Technical writer, Randall Chemical Corporation,
Present   Balfour, MI 48613
                       Write and edit data sheets, brochures,
                       manuals; obtain legal clearance for finished
                       manuscripts; arrange for production of
                       graphs, drawings, covers; help choose
                       printers. Have overseen work of other
                       technical writers while supervisor was away.
                       Starting Salary, $1,350/month; present
                       salary, $2,100/month.

August 1966 to   Part-time writer and librarian, Michigan
June 1968   Department of State Highways, East Lansing,
                       MI 48824
                       Edited research reports; organized and
                       operated Highway Testing and Research
                       Laboratory library.

EDUCATIONAL BACKGROUND

June 1968, Bachelor of Science degree in chemistry, Michigan
State University, East Lansing, MI 48824.

Current Courses: Principles of Management, computer typesetting
                  and printing.

PERSONAL AND PROFESSIONAL INTERESTS

Member Society for Technical Communication, Society of Editors
and Writers; active in Kiwanis Club, Rotary Club, Community
Chest Organization.

REFERENCES

Mr. Clinton Dreyfus
Director, Publications Department
Randall Chemical Corporation
100 Centralia Avenue
Balfour, MI   48613
Telephone: (616) 784-2500

Ms. Mildred Purcell
Technical Writer
Randall Chemical Corporation
Telephone: (616) 784-1893

Mr. Harley Fine
Director (retired)
Highway Testing and Research Laboratory
Michigan Department of State Highways
173 Hunto's Ridge Road
East Lansing, MI   48824
Telephone: (517) 351-8926

Discussion Questions

1. In what ways does this personal data sheet differ from the preceding three?
2. Why hasn't Crawford included a former instructor in his list of references?

Roberta L. Grinnell
617 Ethan Allen Lane
Willimantic, CT 06226

Employment Objective

To begin work as a programmer/analyst and gain experience that will qualify me for a position as a systems supervisor.

Education

June 1981, Bachelor of Science degree in applied mathematics and data processing, Eastern Connecticut State College, Willimantic, CT 06226

Academic Honors:

3.2 G.P.A. (4.0=A, 3.0=B, etc.) in major field

Extracurricular Activities:

Member of Alpha Gamma Delta, a social sorority

June 1977, graduated from Stratford High School, Stratford, CT 06597, college preparatory program.

Academic Honors:

3.3 G.P.A.

Extracurricular Activities:

Member Math Club
Vice-president sophomore class

Employment Experience

Summer 1980	Custodian, Dura Tools, Inc., 381 Bishop Avenue, Bridgeport, CT 06610
Summers of 1978 and 1979	Kitchen helper/busgirl, Robert's Magic Kitchen, 47 Nickols Avenue, Stratford, CT 06597

Personal and Professional Interests

Swimming, bird watching, chess, member Willimantic chapter Big Sisters organization

References

Will be furnished on request.

Discussion Questions

1. What is the probable reason why the writer has not included a list of references?
2. What does mention of membership in the Big Sisters organization tell the prospective employer about the writer?
3. Why does the writer mention her high-school academic honors and extracurricular activities?

The Interview

No matter what job you apply for, before you are hired you can expect to have a job interview. It is possible that the interview will be your first contact with the employer; for example, the interviewer may be a recruiter who visits your school or campus. Usually, however, the interview occurs on the employer's premises after the employer has received and evaluated your letter and personal data sheet. An interview may last from twenty minutes to several hours and sometimes may involve a number of persons, all of whom you must impress favorably. Obviously, you must plan and execute the interview as carefully as your application letter and personal data sheet.

ADVANCE PREPARATION

Before you appear for your interview, try to learn as much as you can about the organization or company. This information will enable you to show the interviewer that you have a real interest in his or her organization and will allow you to discuss your possible role more intelligently than you otherwise could.

To begin, go to the library and look the company up in the corporate directories (*Dun and Bradstreet's, Moody's Industrials,* and the like). From these publications, you can learn the company's credit rating, sales volume, and products, as well as the locations of its plants, the names and locations of its subsidiaries and affiliates, the names of its chief officers, and other important information.

Annual reports can also provide much information about the company. They give financial statements, discuss building programs and other projects, describe new and promising products, and outline the company's plans for the future. Increasing numbers of college libraries are now subscribing to a new service that makes available on microfiches the annual reports of some 11,000 companies whose stocks are traded on the major exchanges. A booklet accompanying the microfiches lists the companies alphabetically and provides a code number that will allow you to find the microfiche. Libraries without this service often maintain files of annual reports, as do placement offices. If an annual report is not available at your college, you can obtain a copy by writing to company headquarters or going to a brokerage firm.

Government agencies and many private institutions are not listed in the publications mentioned above. Quite often, though, such organizations issue pamphlets describing their facilities and services. Your school placement office may have copies of these pamphlets. If not, you can obtain them directly from the organizations.

DRESS AND MANNERS

A job applicant's dress and manners are weighed very carefully during an interview, so strive to make the best impression possible.

Generally, you should dress rather formally and conservatively for an interview. Even if the job you are applying for will never require you to wear a skirt or a coat and tie, you should wear such clothing to the interview. Pay particular attention, too, to the *condition* of your clothes. Their appearance—like the appearance of your application letter and data sheet—is an indicator of the care with which you approach your work. If your clothes are ripped, soiled, or in any way sloppy, the employer will naturally think that your work habits are sloppy too—and there go your chances of being hired. Personal cleanliness is viewed in the same light. If you are well groomed, you will simply make a better impression.

When the interview is held at school or on campus and you must schedule it between shop or laboratory classes, the rules of clothing are often relaxed. In this situation, it is generally acceptable to wear shop or laboratory clothing. Do not, however, wear blue jeans, cutoffs, T-shirts, or the like. Be sure to start the day with fresh clothing so you'll be as neat as possible for the interview.

The employer will also be concerned with your manners during the interview. Once you have been called into the interviewer's office, wait for him or her to shake hands and begin the conversation. Remain standing until you have been offered a seat, and then sit up straight and look directly at the interviewer. You will make a poor impression indeed if you slouch or sprawl in the chair or fuss with items on the interviewer's desk. Never chew gum during an interview, and if you must smoke, wait until the interviewer indicates that it is all right to do so. Try to appear relaxed and confident—without bragging or resorting to wisecracks—throughout the interview. When it is over, be sure to express your appreciation. Good manners can't help but leave a favorable impression.

ANSWERING QUESTIONS

The problem of how to conduct yourself during an interview is complicated by the variety of approaches interviewers use. Some do almost all the talking while carefully observing how closely and intelligently you listen. Others say almost nothing, forcing you to present your case virtually unaided. Generally, though, the interviewer obtains information by asking questions.

Advance preparation can greatly improve your ability to answer these questions. A day or so before the interview, draw up a list of questions that you might reasonably be asked to deal with. Such a list might include, among others, the following items:

Tell me something about yourself and your family background.

Why did you choose your particular field of work?

What qualifications do you have that make you feel that you will be successful in your field?

What special courses have you taken to prepare yourself for a job such as this?

What jobs have you held in the past, and how would the experience prove useful to you in this job?

What do you know about opportunities in your field?

What percentage of your college expenses did you earn? How?

What do you know about our company?

Why do you wish to work for us?

What interests you about our product(s) or service(s)?

Do you work best as part of a team or by yourself?

Do you like to travel?

Are you willing to go where the company sends you?

What future role do you hope to play in our organization?

Once the list is complete, outline an answer to each item, whenever possible expanding information contained in your letter of application and personal data sheet. Familiarize yourself with the answers and then, if a tape recorder is available, record them so that you can hear yourself as the interviewer would. If you are speaking too quickly or too softly, you will hear these flaws and be able to correct them. It is also helpful to have a friend act as interviewer and criticize your performance. Even if the interviewer's questions are phrased differently from those in your list, your efforts won't be wasted, for both sets of questions will concern the same general information.

The way you respond to questions is an important factor in determining whether or not you will be hired. To begin, always wait until the interviewer has finished the question before answering. At times, the interviewer will describe a situation and then ask a question relating to it—a procedure that can take several minutes. When this happens, resist any temptation to begin your answer before the interviewer has finished speaking. Once the question has been asked, take a moment or two to organize your thoughts, then answer. Do not stray from the subject or run on for long periods of time. Say only what you must to answer properly, then stop. At the same time, try to avoid one-word "yes" or "no" answers, which do not allow the interviewer to learn much about you. Do not be afraid to admit that you don't know the answer to a question. Chances are this won't happen frequently, but if it does, an honest "I don't know" is far better than a hastily formulated and perhaps incorrect response.

Interviewers occasionally ask "catch" questions just to see how you'll handle them. If this happens, imagine that the question has been asked by a future customer or client and then phrase your answer in a way that will neither offend the speaker nor contradict your own views. The interviewer might say, for example, "The president is certainly catching a lot of criticism these days, isn't he?" One good response to this question would be, "Yes, but I suppose any president has to expect quite a bit of that." Such an answer would offend neither a supporter nor a critic of the president, and at the same time would not compromise your own position.

ASKING QUESTIONS

Interviewing is not a one-way street. It is as important for you to know that the job, the company, and the community are right for you as it is for the company to know that you are right for it. Therefore, do not hesitate to ask questions that have not been covered by the interviewer. Some of your questions might include:

What opportunities for advancement are open to a person with my background?

Might I expect to be transferred periodically or would I work
permanently in this location?

Are the hours I would work likely to be regular or variable?

What fringe benefits does your company offer its employees and
their families?

What opportunities for furthering my education are available in
the area?

What recreational and cultural activities do the community and
surrounding areas offer?

You should leave the interview with your key questions answered so
that you will be able to make an intelligent job choice. Be sure,
though, that you avoid asking so many questions that the interviewer
doesn't have time to evaluate you.

DISCUSSING SALARY

At some point during the interview, the subject of salary will
come up. Although salary is very important to you, it is best to let the
interviewer mention it first. Otherwise, you may appear to be interested only in the money. Sometimes, however, interviewers deliberately avoid the subject to see how you will bring it up. In such a
situation wait until the interview is clearly drawing to a close and
then ask, directly and without embarrassment, "What salary are you
offering for this position?" An interview is a business transaction and
there should be candor on both sides.

Occasionally, an interviewer will ask you what salary you are
looking for. This creates an embarrassing situation unless you know
the salary range for positions like the one you are seeking. To avoid
embarrassment and the bad impression you'll create by having to
admit you don't know or by making a wild guess, investigate salaries
before the interview. You can do this by asking your instructors,
consulting literature in your school's placement office, and checking
the classified ads in newspapers and professional publications. Many
states also have annual occupational guides that list, among other
things, the national and state salary levels for all occupations in the
state. Ask your library staff whether this guide is available.

Most companies have an established salary range for each job,
and the interviewer will tell you what your starting salary would be.

In such a case, unless your qualifications are exceptional, it is unwise to try to bargain for more money. The company knows what a particular position is worth, and your attempt may well lose you the job.

KEEPING A RECORD OF THE INTERVIEW

It is unlikely that you'll receive a job offer at the time of the interview. Instead, the organization will review your qualifications, as well as those of other applicants, and then make a decision. In the meantime, what you've learned can improve your performance in other interviews.

To help you remember each interview, keep a detailed record in a notebook. Record the pertinent information as soon after the interview as you can, while it is still fresh in your mind. Include the names of the interviewers, a description of the job, a summary of the job qualifications, and the salary range. There is always a possibility that you will be called for a second interview, and the information will be very helpful. Note, too, any questions that gave you trouble or any mistakes that you made so that you can correct these weaknesses.

Postinterview Letters

There are four common types of postinterview letters: letter of thanks, job acceptance letter, job refusal letter, and follow-up letter. These are discussed below.

LETTER OF THANKS

A day or two after your interview, send the interviewer a brief note of thanks. Use the opportunity to tell the interviewer once again that you want the job and feel you can handle it. You might write something like this:

> Thank you for a very pleasant interview for the position of computer programmer. The job matches my qualifications and sounds extremely attractive. I hope that you will decide to hire me.
>
> I look forward to hearing from you.

Many job candidates neglect to write letters of thanks. Your note, therefore, will set you apart as an especially thoughtful person and increase your chances of winning the job you're after. If the interviewer has spoken to many other applicants, the note also helps ensure that you will be remembered.

JOB ACCEPTANCE LETTER

A job acceptance letter is used to accept a written job offer or to confirm the verbal acceptance of a job offered over the phone. In writing such a letter, show courtesy—even enthusiasm—but don't go overboard in expressing your thanks.

> Thank you very much for offering me the position of marketing assistant with your firm. I am happy to accept and I am sure I will be able to justify your confidence in me. As you requested, I will report for work on Monday, July 10. In the meantime, if you need to get in touch with me, I will be at my present address until July 7.
>
> I look forward to working for you.

The above letter, though brief, does much more than merely accept the job. It thanks the company for the offer, gives assurance of good future performance, confirms the starting date, tells where to reach the new employee until then, and ends by expressing pleasure. In short, its tone is pleasant, and it says everything necessary.

JOB REFUSAL LETTER

The job refusal letter is harder to write than the other types of postinterview letters. Keep in mind that the organization you are turning down has spent considerable time, effort, and money in corresponding with you, conducting your interview, and reviewing your qualifications before making its offer. It also may have counted heavily on your services. Your refusal letter, therefore, must be especially tactful and courteous.

Begin your letter with a courteous remark about the organization, job, or interview. Follow this with a polite refusal and your reasons for choosing another job. End with another pleasant comment.

I enjoyed meeting you and discussing the duties of your commercial artist position, and I was gratified to receive your job offer last Wednesday. I have given the offer serious thought but have decided to accept a position with another publisher. As you know from our conversation, I wish to concentrate on scientific illustration. The job I have chosen will allow me to spend full time doing so, while your position would not.

I appreciate the consideration you have shown me.

The preceding letter is both pleasant and thoughtful. Though it may disappoint the receiver, it should leave no trace of bitterness or resentment.

FOLLOW-UP LETTER

Ordinarily, you will be hired or rejected within a month of your job interview. If you are rejected, it may be because you lack one or more of the qualifications needed for the position. With medium-sized and large companies, however, there is always a chance that a more suitable opening will occur a few months later. For this reason, if you are still unemployed after several months, you may wish to send a follow-up letter to the companies you've previously interviewed.

On August 15, I was interviewed by Union Carbide Chemicals for the job of chemical laboratory technician. Although I was rejected because I lacked courses in organic analysis, I remember both you and your organization very favorably and hope you will consider me for any current opening that fits my qualifications.

A follow-up note could well lead to a review of your credentials and possibly to a job offer. Without such a note, it is unlikely that your application will be reconsidered.

It is also possible that you are qualified for a job but that another candidate—perhaps one with more experience—is hired instead. If the company has a number of positions like the one you applied for, there probably will be another opening before long. This time, you might be the best condidate to apply. If you are still interested in being considered for an opening of the type you applied for, you might send a follow-up letter such as this one.

Early last summer you interviewed me for a sales position with General Foods. Although I was not hired, you indicated during the interview that I was qualified for the position. General Foods remains in my mind one of the top companies to work for. Should another opening occur in your sales force, I would appreciate your reconsidering my application.

Suggestions for Writing

1. Write a letter applying for a specific job that you have seen advertised or that someone has told you about. Use whichever of the three openings you wish.
2. Write a letter applying for a specific position with a company that may or may not have a vacancy.
3. Prepare a personal data sheet to accompany your application letter. Include references.
4. Write a letter
   a. thanking an interviewer for interviewing you
   b. accepting a job offer
   c. refusing a job offer
   d. expressing interest in working for a company that has rejected you previously

APPENDIX

Grammar, Usage, Punctuation, and Mechanics

The purpose of this guide is twofold. First, it is a handy reference tool for answering questions that arise when you are writing your papers. Second, it can be used to review the fundamentals of English usage. The guide is divided into three main sections. The first section, "Sentence Elements," discusses subjects, predicates, complements, appositives, the eight parts of speech, phrases, and clauses. The second section focuses on understanding and avoiding common errors of usage. The final section covers the fundamentals of punctuation and other mechanical concerns. Although this condensed treatment cannot hope to answer all your questions, the information presented here should give you a good basic grasp of the "nuts and bolts" of English as well as help you to avoid most common writing errors.

Sentence Elements

Subject and Predicate

SUBJECT

The subject of a sentence usually names something about which a statement is made or a question is asked. The subject may carry out an action, receive an action, or simply exist. A *simple* subject consists of one or more words that name one or more persons, places, things, actions, qualities, or ideas. A *complete* subject includes the simple subject plus certain other words that describe it. Here are five simple subjects and five complete subjects.

Simple Subjects	Complete Subjects
man	the tall man
trees	the slender, leafy trees
complaint	your complaint
baby	the baby
Mr. Davis	old Mr. Davis

PREDICATE

The predicate tells something about the subject and completes the idea expressed by the sentence. A simple predicate consists of one or more words, called *verbs,* that show action or existence—what someone or something is, or will be. A complete predicate includes the simple predicate plus any other words needed to expand and modify its meaning.

Simple Predicates	Complete Predicates
laughed	laughed loudly
are swaying	are swaying in the wind
will be discussed	will be discussed next Wednesday
is	is in its crib
was	was the neighborhood grouch

Combinations like *are swaying* and *will be discussed* are called *verb phrases*—two or more *verbs* that function as a single unit.

Notice that none of the subjects and predicates can stand alone; they don't convey complete ideas by themselves. However, combining appropriate subjects and predicates gives us complete sentences and therefore complete thoughts.

> The tall man laughed loudly.
> The slender, leafy trees are swaying in the wind.
> Your complaint will be discussed next Wednesday.
> The baby is in its crib.
> Old Mr. Davis was the neighborhood grouch.

Recognizing Subjects and Predicates. Here are two of the above sentences, this time with their simple subjects underlined once and their simple predicates or verbs underlined twice.

> The tall <u>man</u> <u>laughed</u> loudly.
> The slender, leafy <u>trees</u> <u>are swaying</u> in the wind.

In each of these sentences, the main idea is expressed by the simple subject and verb—a fact that holds true for every other sentence as well.

Picking out these key parts is not difficult. Simply locate the verb part of the sentence, and then ask yourself who or what controls the verb. Consider the following sentence.

> Elmer gave the old beggar a dollar.

The answer to the question "What or who have?" is clearly *Elmer,* rather than *the beggar.* Thus, *Elmer* is the subject of the sentence.

When identifying subjects and verbs, you will find it helpful to keep a few pointers in mind. First, as already noted, the verb part of a sentence may be a verb phrase. In the following examples, the subjects are underlined once and the verbs twice.

> By tomorrow, <u>I</u> <u>will have finished</u> my report.

Sometimes one or more words may interrupt the verb phrase or come between the subject and the verb.

Joyce had completely forgotten her appointment with the dentist. (A word interrupts the verb phrase.)

Marvin has certainly not shown any talent as a writer. (Two words interrupt the verb phrase.)

Do you believe that story? (A word interrupts the verb phrase.)

Note that in the last example the interrupting word is the subject of the sentence. This verb-subject-verb pattern occurs in many sentences that ask questions.

Some sentences have compound subjects (two or more simple subjects), compound verbs (two or more individual verbs), or both.

The house and garage burned to the ground. (compound subject)

He jogs and swims for exercise. (compound verb)

The knight and the squire mounted their horses and rode off. (compound subject and compound verb)

In most sentences, the subject comes ahead of the verb. Sometimes, though, the verb comes first and may be preceded by one or more other words.

Across the river stands a lone pine tree.

Here is my house.

There goes Jack.

When is your theme due?

If a sentence begins with *here* or *there* or a question begins with *when, where, how,* or *why,* the subject is likely to follow the verb.

In sentences expressing a command or a request, the subject, which is always "you," may be unstated but understood.

(you) Come here right away!

(you) Hand me that wrench, please.

Exercise

Place a slash mark (/) between the complete subject and the complete predicate of each sentence; then underline the simple subject once and the verb or verb phrase twice. Some sentences may have more than one subject and one verb. If the subject interrupts the verb phrase, set the subject off with a pair of slash marks. If the subject is unstated, put a slash mark at the beginning of the sentence.

> My boss/is planning the agenda for the safety meeting.
> What will/you/do after graduation?
> /Return the wrench to the tool crib. (The subject *you* is understood.)

1. The new helper will finish the job soon.
2. The crew of carpenters worked all day.
3. As an apprentice, Janice will be learning the plumbing trade.
4. Miranda and her family drove to Chicago and visited the Museum of Science and Industry.
5. What did you hear about the accident?
6. I do not understand the directions for this procedure.
7. Where are the minutes of last month's meeting?
8. There are several empty shelves in the stockroom.
9. One man and two women were hired.
10. Behind the barn sat a rusty tractor.

COMPLEMENTS

A sentence may include one or more complements—words or word groups that are part of the predicate and help complete the meaning of the sentence. There are four kinds of complements: *direct objects, indirect objects, subject complements,* and *object complements.*

Direct Object. A direct object names the person, place, or thing that receives, or is the result of, the action of a verb.

> The store clerks chose *John* to represent them. (The direct object *John* receives the action of the verb *chose.*)
> The Boy Scouts built a *fire.* (The direct object *fire* is the result of the action of the verb *built.*)

Indirect Object. An indirect object names one or more persons, places, or things for whom (or which) or to whom (or which) something (the verb plus the direct object) is done. It always precedes a direct object.

Ramona Chavez sold *me* her slide rule. (The indirect object *me* tells to whom the slide rule was sold. *Slide rule* is the direct object.)

They built the *dog* a kennel. (The indirect object *dog* tells for whom the kennel was built. *Kennel* is the direct object.)

Lend *me* your tape measure. (The indirect object *me* tells to whom the tape measure should be lent. *Tape measure* is the direct object.)

Subject Complement. A subject complement follows a verb that shows existence—what something is, was, or will be. It renames or describes the subject.

Lucille is an *architect*. (The complement *architect* renames the subject *Lucille*.)

Lucille is *efficient*. (The complement *efficient* describes the subject *Lucille*.)

Object Complement. An object complement follows a direct object and renames or describes it.

The class elected Mary *president*. (The object complement *president* renames the direct object *Mary*.)

They painted the lounge *green*. (The object complement *green* describes the direct object *lounge*.)

Exercise

For each of the following sentences, identify the italicized item as a direct object (DO), an indirect object (IO), a subject complement (SC), or an object complement (OC).

I consider that suggestion *foolish*. (OC)

1. Mona and Rose were very *angry* over their low test scores.
2. I understand the *problem* and how to solve it.
3. They have offered *William* the promotion at least three times.
4. David has been *supervisor* of the stock room for two months.
5. The police checked the *airplane* for a bomb.
6. Everyone in the class thought the instructor *incompetent*.
7. I will be *ready* soon.

8. The local machine shop has donated a *lathe* to the school.
9. I'll certainly give *him* a piece of my mind.
10. Because of the rain, the road was almost *impassable*.

Parts of Speech

Traditional English grammar classifies words into eight parts of speech, based on their function in sentences. These parts are *nouns, pronouns, verbs, adjectives, adverbs, prepositions, conjunctions,* and *interjections.*

NOUNS

Nouns name. They may name persons, places, things, qualities, ideas, events, or occurrences. In the following examples, the nouns are italicized.

> *Angelo* drove to *Colorado* in his *car.* (The first noun names a person, the second a place, and the third a thing.)
> He has never shown *compassion* for anyone. (The noun names a quality.)
> *Socialism* has never appealed to me. (The noun names an idea.)
> The *party* was enjoyable. (The noun names an event.)
> Her *departure* was abrupt. (The noun names an occurrence.)

Proper Nouns. When nouns name particular persons, places, institutions, or events, their first letters are always capitalized (*John, Sacramento, American Stock Exchange, World War II*). These nouns are known as *proper nouns.*

Common Nouns. Most other nouns fall under the heading *common nouns,* which, broadly, means that they name general classes that can include a variety of examples of what is being named (*dog, business, house*). Think of common nouns as names for things, usually concrete and tangible, that can be counted (*one dog, two businesses, three houses*). Common nouns frequently add s or *es* to indicate a quantity greater than one; that is, their plurals often end in s.

Mass and Abstract Nouns. Nouns also name things that are not ordinarily counted and therefore do not often have plural forms. *Mass nouns* name formless things (*water, grass*), and *abstract nouns* name intangible objects and ideas (*courage, liberalism*).

Collective Nouns. Still other nouns, called *collective nouns*, are singular in form but stand for a group of individual units (*herd, grove*). Collective nouns also have plural forms, which indicate more than one such group.

You will notice that many nouns can fit into more than one category: a noun's type may depend on how it is used in a particular instance. In sentences, nouns can serve as subjects, objects, and complements.

Exercise

List the nouns in the following sentences.

> The new senator from North Dakota was met by a delegation that protested his conservatism. (Senator, North Dakota, delegation, conservatism)

1. The cowboys rounded up the herd for shipment to Chicago.
2. Sylvia Broom was born in Newark, Ohio.
3. Thoughtlessness has led to many industrial accidents.
4. The Acme Corporation rates aggressiveness above all other qualities in its salespeople.
5. Two members of the committee presented a report on the cost of the project.
6. Scientists believe that the surface of the planet Uranus is cold and barren.
7. In our town, the Knitwell Textile Company is the chief industry.
8. Raymond filled his tank with twenty gallons of gasoline.
9. Professor La Fontaine spent his sabbatical leave in France.
10. Sandra is conducting a survey for the Danbury Merchants' Association.

PRONOUNS

A pronoun is a word that takes the place of a noun in a sentence. There are eight types of pronouns: *personal, interrogative, relative, demonstrative, reflexive, intensive, indefinite,* and *reciprocal.*

Personal Pronouns. Personal pronouns are pronouns that refer to one or more clearly identified persons, places, or things.

Subjective	Objective	Possessive
I	me	my, mine
you	you	your, yours
he	him	his
she	her	her, hers
it	it	its
we	us	our, ours
you	you	your, yours
they	them	their, theirs

The personal pronoun forms listed under "Subjective" are used as the subjects of sentences or clauses; the forms listed under "Objective" are used as direct or indirect objects; and the forms listed under "Possessive" are used to show possession. *My, your, her, our,* and *their* always precede a noun.

I repaired the lawnmower. (pronoun as subject)
William called *him.* (pronoun as direct object)
William threw *him* the ball. (pronoun as indirect object)
The camera is *hers.* (possessive pronoun as subject complement)

Interrogative Pronouns. Interrogative pronouns begin sentences or clauses that ask questions.

who	what
whom	which
whose	

What is wrong with the dishwasher?
Which of these wrenches fits the bolt?

Relative Pronouns. A relative pronoun is a pronoun that starts a noun clause (see page 407) or an adjective clause (see page 407). Note that, with the exception of *that*, the relative pronouns in the first column below can also serve as interrogative pronouns.

who	(whoever)
whose	(whosever)
whom	(whomever)
what	(whatever)
which	(whichever)
that	

The field *that* I plan to major in is heating, air conditioning, and refrigeration.

Harvey Wilson, *whose* printing shop burned last month, is rebuilding in a new location.

Demonstrative Pronouns. A demonstrative pronoun is used to point out or identify something. There are four demonstrative pronouns.

this	these
that	those

That is the lathe to use.

I like *those*.

This and *these* are used to point out things that are recent or nearby, *that* and *those* to point out things that are farther away in time or space.

This T-square and *that* compass belong to Joan. (Compass is farther from speaker from T-square).

Reflexive and Intensive Pronouns. A reflexive pronoun turns the action of a verb back upon the doer of the action. An intensive pronoun is used to give emphasis to a noun or a pronoun. Reflexive and intensive pronouns always end with *-self* or *-selves*.

myself	oneself
yourself	ourselves
himself	yourselves
herself	themselves
itself	

The machinist cut *himself* on the metal shaving. (reflexive pronoun)

The manager *herself* answered the customer's complaint. (intensive pronoun)

Do not use a reflexive pronoun as a substitute for a personal pronoun.

John and *myself* will repair the radiator. (incorrect)

John and *I* will repair the radiator. (correct)

The following nonstandard forms should not be used in your writing: *hisself, theirself,* and *theirselves.*

Indefinite Pronouns. This group includes the many pronouns that do not refer to specifically named persons, places, or things. Among the common indefinite pronouns are the following:

all	everyone	none
another	everything	no one
any	few	nothing
anybody	many	one
anyone	most	some
anything	much	somebody
each	neither	someone
either	nobody	something
everybody		

Neither of the students wrote a good exam.

I saw *nobody* in the chemistry laboratory.

Reciprocal Pronouns. A reciprocal pronoun is used to indicate an exchange of action between two or more parties. There are two reciprocal pronouns: *each other* and *one another. Each other* is used when there are two parties involved in the action; *one another* is used when there are three or more.

Larry and I always help *each other* with chemistry problems. (two persons)

The shop employees congratulated *one another* upon winning the company's safety award. (more than two persons)

In informal speech, *each other* and *one another* are often used interchangeably. However, this practice should be avoided in formal writing.

Exercise

List the pronouns in the following sentences.

> They had convinced themselves that neither would be promoted.
> (They, themselves, neither)

1. He can afford to pay for it himself.
2. Help yourself to whatever you wish to eat.
3. Now, that is the right way to do it.
4. They themselves are to blame for the problem.
5. What is the matter with my micrometer?
6. To whom am I speaking?
7. If we help one another, everyone will find the task easy.
8. Of the two themes, yours is written better than hers.
9. These are problems we can solve by ourselves.
10. Anybody who wishes additional overtime can have it.

VERBS

A verb is a word that indicates action or existence and helps express the main idea of a sentence. Verbs may be classified as *action verbs, linking verbs,* and *helping verbs.*

Action Verbs. As its name suggests, an action verb expresses an action or occurrence. Action verbs may be classified as transitive or intransitive. A transitive verb requires a direct object, which receives the action of the verb and completes its meaning.

The mechanic *installed* the carburetor.

In this example, *carburetor* is the direct object and completes the meaning of the action indicated by *installed.*

An intransitive verb, on the other hand, does not need an object to complete its meaning.

Ellen *resigned*.
Betty *worked* for the O'Hara Electronic Corporation.

There are many verbs that can be both transitive and intransitive. Whether a verb is transitive or intransitive depends on the sentence in which it is used.

Jerry *stood* the tripod in the corner. (transitive verb)
Jerry *stood* in the doorway. (intransitive verb)

Linking Verbs. A linking verb expresses a condition or state of being rather than an action. Some linking verbs connect the subject of a sentence or clause to a noun or pronoun that identifies or renames the subject. Others connect the subject to an adjective, a word that describes the subject. (For a discussion of adjectives, see page 395.)

Ms. Kincaid *is* the chief biologist. (The subject, *Ms. Kincaid*, is linked to the noun, *biologist*, which identifies or renames the subject.)
His speech *was* excellent. (The subject, *speech*, is linked to *excellent*, which describes the subject.)

The most common linking verbs are forms of the verb *be* (*is, are, am, was, were, been*). Some other verbs that may be used as linking verbs are *seem, become, appear, remain, feel, look, smell, sound*, and *taste*. When used as linking verbs, words in the second group in effect function as forms of the verb *be*. Thus, in the sentence "The water felt cold," *felt* has the same meaning as *was*. When, however, the words in the second group stand for physical actions, they function as action verbs. For example, in the sentence "The swimmer felt the water," *felt* is an action verb.

Helping Verbs. A helping verb accompanies an action verb or a linking verb, allowing it to express shades of meaning, such as when an action takes place. Combining one or more helping verbs with an action verb or linking verb results in a verb phrase. The following list includes some of the most common helping verbs.

has	been	had (to)
have	do	shall
had	does	will
am	did	going (to)
is	used (to)	
are	may	would
was	might	should
were	must	ought (to)
be	have (to)	can
being	has (to)	could

The sentences below illustrate the use of helping verbs:

The mechanic *will install* the carburetor in the automobile. (helping verb *will* with action verb *install*)

Betty *will have worked* for the O'Hara Electronic Corporation two years this June. (helping verbs *will have* with action verb *worked*)

He *does seem* less competent than the others. (helping verb *does* with linking verb *seem*)

Tuesday *may be* the day when Belinda receives a raise. (helping verb *may* with linking verb *be*)

Several helping verbs can function as verbs by themselves. This dual function is illustrated in the following two sentences.

I *have* requested a raise. (*have* as a helping verb)

I *have* two jobs. (*have* as a verb by itself)

Principal Parts and Tense. Verbs undergo changes in form to show time distinctions, which are called *tenses*. For every verb, tenses are built from three principal parts—*present, past,* and *past participle*. For the verb *talk*, the principal parts are as follows:

Present	**Past**	**Past participle**
talk	talked	talked

The present principal part is formed from the verb's *infinitive*—its *to* form (for a discussion of the infinitive, see page 405). The "to" is dropped to leave the present principal part or stem, the form under which you would look the verb up in a dictionary. Accordingly, the present principal part of *to talk* is *talk*, and this form is the stem of the *present* and *future tenses*. Without a helping verb, the present principal part forms the present tense. As its name indicates, the present tense is used for actions or conditions occurring in the present. Note that an *s* is added to the stem when the subject is *he, she it*, or a singular noun.

Present Tense

I (you, we, they)   *talk* to them daily.

he (she, it, Henry, the parrot)   *talks* to them daily.

The future tense, used for actions or conditions that will occur in the future, is formed by using the present stem with the helping verbs *will* or *shall*.

Future Tense

I (you, he, she, it, we, they)   *shall (will) talk* to them tomorrow.

The past principal part of a verb is its *past tense*, and it is used to show that an action or condition occurred and was completed at some point in the past.

Past Tense

I (you, he, she, it, we, they)   *talked* to them yesterday.

The past participle is used in the *perfect* tenses with the present and past tenses of the helping verb *to have*. The *present perfect tense* generally shows that an action or condition begun in the past continued over a period of time or continues into the present. The present perfect is formed with the present tense of *to have* (*have* or *has*) plus the past participle.

Present Perfect Tense

I, (you, we, they)   *have* always *talked* to them about matters of policy.

he (she, it)   *has* always *talked* to them about matters of policy.

The *past perfect tense* is formed with the past participle plus the helping verb *had* (the past tense of *to have*) and shows that one past action or condition ended before another took place.

Past Perfect Tense

I (you, he, she, it, we, they)   *had talked* to them before I talked to you.

The *future perfect tense* is formed with the past participle and the helping verbs *shall have* or *will have* (the future tense of *to have*). This tense shows that an action or condition will have been completed by a specified time in the future.

Future Perfect Tense

I (you, he, she, it, we, they)   *shall (will) have talked* to them by the time I next talk to you.

Notice that both the past and the past participle principal parts of *to talk* are the same and are formed by adding the suffix *-ed* to the present principal part. This system applies to most—but unfortunately not all—verbs. The exceptions are known as *irregular verbs*, and the degree to which a verb may be irregular can vary. The three principal parts of the verb *to hit*, for example, are identical, and *-ed* appears in none of them.

I *hit* him hard whenever we box. (present)

I *hit* him hard when we boxed yesterday. (past)

I have *hit* him hard whenever we have boxed. (past participle with *have;* that is, present perfect)

On the other hand, the three principal parts of *to write* are different, and again neither the past nor the past participle is formed regularly.

I *write* a letter a day. (present)

I *wrote* a letter yesterday. (past)

I have *written* a number of letters. (past participle with have; that is, present perfect)

The most irregular verb in the language is also the one most used—the verb *to be*. The present principal part, *be*, appears only in the infinitive and not with *I, you, he, she, it, we,* or *they.*

To Be—Present Tense

I	*am*
you	*are*
he, she, it	*is*
we, they	*are*

The past tense is *was* or *were*, depending on whether its subject is singular or plural (*you* is always treated as a plural subject, even when it stands for only one person). The past participle of *to be* is *been*. For further discussion of irregular principal parts, see pages 418–420.

In addition to the tenses formed from the three principal parts, there are progressive forms that use the *present participle* with the verb *to be*. The present participle is formed from the present principal part and the suffix *-ing*. The present participle of *to talk* is *talking*.

I am talking (present progressive)

I shall be talking (future progressive)

I was talking (past progressive)

I have been talking (present perfect progressive)

I had been talking (past perfect progressive)

I shall have been talking (future perfect progressive)

Voice. Transitive verbs have two voices: *active* and *passive*. A verb is in the active voice when the subject performs the action specified by the verb.

Teresa *identified* the organic compound. (The subject performs the action.)

A verb is in the passive voice when the subject does not perform the action but is acted upon. The noun or pronoun that identifies the performer of the action either appears in a prepositional phrase or is not mentioned at all.

> The organic compound was *identified* by Teresa. (The prepositional phrase *by Teresa* identifies the performer.)
> The organic compound was identified as ethyl alcohol. (The performer is not identified.)

Technical and scientific writing commonly employs the passive voice for explanations of processes, where objectivity is desirable. Other kinds of writing should, however, avoid the passive voice except where the action rather than the actor is important. For further discussion of the passive voice, see pages 425–427.

Exercise

List the verbs in the following sentences and identify the tense and voice of each.

> Has the chisel been returned to the tool crib? (Has . . . been returned, *present perfect passive*)

1. Perry is changing the tire.
2. Can you begin the new job right away?
3. I will supervise every stage of the project.
4. I shall have finished the preparations for the speech by late afternoon.
5. Henry worked diligently on his mathematics assignment.
6. Edmond has worked for the same boss for ten years.
7. We believe that our company's products are without equal.
8. Two months after he enlisted, Neville had earned the rank of corporal.
9. I should have considered other approaches to this problem.
10. In a few days, you will feel better about this decision.

ADJECTIVES

An adjective *modifies* a noun or pronoun by describing or limiting it or in some way making its meaning more exact. Sometimes the adjective is positioned next to the word it modifies. At other times, one or more words may come between the two of them.

Mary is *beautiful.*
Grouchy men irritate me.
The *yellow* car belongs to Bob.
Three people have applied so far.

You will notice from the last example that numbers, when used to limit nouns, are adjectives. The words *a, an,* and *the,* known as articles, are also considered adjectives. Unlike most adjectives, an article *must* precede the noun it modifies.

The girl brought *an* apple and *a* sandwich to *the* picnic.

Often, two or more adjectives modify the same word.

The tall, leafy tree has *gray* bark.

Several categories of pronouns can function as adjectives.

Whose micrometer is on the floor? (interrogative adjective)
The repairman *whose* truck was stolen called the police. (relative adjective)
This shop has the best safety record. (demonstrative adjective)
Some chemists have special training in bacteriology. (indefinite adjective)
She focused *her* microscope on the rod-shaped organisms. (possessive adjective)

Some adjectives, called proper adjectives, are derived from proper nouns.

That building is a fine example of *Victorian* architecture.
An *Italian* restaurant is opening across the street.

Exercise

List the adjectives in the following sentences.

A tall, thin man wearing a red ski mask robbed the local bank yesterday. (A, tall, thin, a, red, ski, the, local)

1. Our company gives its employees three weeks of vacation each year.
2. A clean, tidy house will sell faster than a dirty one.
3. Because of the good pay, thirty people applied for the job.
4. The dishonest salesperson cheated me by selling me a defective car.
5. We shared an orange and a banana at lunch.
6. Few people live without some stress.
7. Arnold was delighted when he won the lottery after buying many tickets.
8. Before he could finish his question, the angry chairperson silenced him.
9. Five actors auditioned for the lead in the new musical.
10. The doors were locked when the first speaker began her report.

ADVERBS

An adverb is a word that modifies a verb, an adjective, another adverb, or a whole sentence. Adverbs generally modify verbs and answer the questions "how?" "when?" "where?" "how often?" and "to what extent?"

> The painter worked *rapidly*. (The adverb *rapidly* modifies the verb *worked* and answers the question "how?")
>
> The supplies arrived *yesterday*. (The adverb *yesterday* modifies the verb *arrived* and answers the question "when?")
>
> Fred drove *home* after leaving the expressway. (The adverb *home* modifies the verb *drove* and answers the question "where?")
>
> I *sometimes* watch TV in the evening. (The adverb *sometimes* modifies the verb *watch* and answers the question "how often?")

Adverbs that modify adjectives, other adverbs, and whole sentences are also common.

> The draftman's work was *extremely* precise. (The adverb *extremely* modifies the adjective *precise* and answers the question "how?")
>
> This tire is *too* worn to be safe. (The adverb *too* modifies the adjective *worn* and answers the question "to what extent?")
>
> *Perhaps* I will be promoted this year. (The adverb *Perhaps* modifies the whole sentence but does not answer any specific question.)

Most adverbs are formed by adding *-ly* to adjectives.

The sea is *calm*. (*Calm* is an adjective modifying *sea*.)
She spoke *calmly* to the dog. (*Calmly* is an adverb modifying
   spoke.)

However, a considerable number of adverbs—including some
of the most common ones— do not end in *-ly*. Here is a representative
listing.

almost	often	there
here	quite	too
never	soon	well
now	then	

I *never* imagined economics would be so difficult.
We expect our order to arrive *quite soon*.

In addition, certain words—some ending in *-ly* and some not—
can function either as adjectives or adverbs.

better	hard	only
close	late	right
cowardly	little	straight
early	much	well
far	near	wrong
fast		

There must be a *better* way to do this. (*Better* is an adjective
   modifying *way*.)
You'll work *better* after you've rested awhile. (*Better* is an adverb
   modifying *work*.)

Exercise

List the adverbs in the following sentences.

Soon you will become completely familiar with this procedure.
   (Soon, completely)

1. We went skiing yesterday, and I can barely walk today.
2. Please divide the tasks equally and finish them quickly.
3. If this speech lasts much longer, I'll fall asleep.
4. Actually, we have all made too many mistakes in this project.

5. Each day the old man moved more slowly.
6. I never thought I would be promoted so soon.
7. Alton worked fast to finish his assignment before the late movie began.
8. He tried hard to solve the problem, but it proved too hard for him.
9. Our supply of sheet steel is almost exhausted, but we expect a new shipment tomorrow.
10. The boss told us to move close to the stage and pay close attention to the demonstration.

PREPOSITIONS

A preposition links its object, which consists of a noun or noun substitute, to some other word in the sentence and shows a relation between the two. This relation is often one of location, time, possession, means, or reason or purpose.

The drillpress *in* the corner needs overhauling. (The preposition *in* links its object, *corner*, to *drillpress* and shows location.)

We will wait *until* Tuesday. (The preposition *until* links its object, *Tuesday*, to *wait* and shows time.)

The laws *of* nature sometimes contradict civil regulations. (The preposition *of* links its object, *nature*, to *laws* and shows possession.)

Sally went *by* automobile. (The preposition *by* links its object, *automobile*, to *went* and shows means.)

Wilfred bicycles *for* pleasure. (The preposition *for* links its object, *pleasure*, to *bicycles* and shows reason or purpose.)

Here is a list of common prepositions, some of which consist of two or more words.

above	by reason of	of
after	contrary to	on
against	during	onto
along with	except	out of
among	for	over
at	from	since
because of	in	through
before	instead of	to
below	into	toward
beside	like	under
between	near	with
by	next to	without

Occasionally, and particularly in questions, a preposition may be separated from its object.

> What are you looking *for*? (The object of the preposition *for* is *what*.)
>
> Whom are you selling your car *to*? (The object of the preposition *to* is *whom*.)

Prepositions, their objects, and words associated with these objects form prepositional *phrases* that may serve as adjectives or adverbs. Prepositional phrases are discussed in detail on page 403.

Exercise

List the prepositions in the following sentences and identify the object of each.

> The noise from the apartment above us made sleeping difficult.
>   (from [apartment], above [us])

1. The sign on the door said that the office was closed until noon.
2. Jethro covered the dingy walls of the room with brightly colored wallpaper.
3. The house next to ours has been for sale for six months.
4. What are you writing with?
5. After a short nap, I felt ready for an evening of bowling.
6. We have had three days of rain in the last five days.
7. Because of the flu epidemic, several factories in this town have stopped operations for the week.
8. After a term of biology, Sally decided to major in bacteriology.
9. The memorandum from the superintendent said that the productivity of the department had increased by 20 percent in the past year.
10. Over half of our employees have been with the company for a decade or more.

CONJUNCTIONS

Conjunctions join. They are used to connect the parts of sentences or to connect whole sentences. One group of conjunctions connects items of equal rank—words, word groups, and simple sentences. These conjunctions can occur singly (*and, but, or, nor, for, yet, so*) or in pairs (*either—or, neither—nor, both—and, not only—but also*). The single conjunctions are called *coordinating conjunctions;* the paired conjunctions are called *correlative conjunctions.*

> Tom *and* his brother are opening a gas station. (The coordinating conjunction connects two nouns.)
>
> Should I call you at home *or* at your office? (The coordinating conjunction connects two prepositional phrases.)
>
> Bill applied to medical school, *but* he was not accepted. (The coordinating conjunction connects sentences.)
>
> Henry *not only* works full time *but also* takes classes at night. (The correlative conjunctions connect two verbs.)
>
> You can study auto mechanics *either* at Ferris State College *or* at Delta College. (The correlative conjunctions connect two prepositional phrases.)

A second group of conjunctions (for example, *because, as if, even though, since, so that, while, whereas,* and *wherever*) is used to show unequal rank between groups of words that contain both subjects and predicates (see clauses, p. 406). These conjunctions, called *subordinating conjunctions,* introduce *subordinate* or *dependent clauses*—ideas expressed with a subject and a predicate but which cannot stand alone as sentences. Because of the introductory conjunction, these clauses are subordinate to or dependent on a group of words that can stand alone as a complete sentence—a *main clause.*

> The class was canceled *because* the instructor was ill. (The subordinating conjunction connects the subordinate clause *because the instructor was ill* to the main clause.)
>
> Lend me your typewriter *so that* I can finish this report. (The subordinating conjunction connects subordinate clause *so that I can finish this report* to the main clause.)

The *conjunctive adverb,* another type of connector, has characteristics of both conjunctions and adverbs. Like conjunctions, conjunctive adverbs serve as linking devices, connecting elements of equal rank. Like adverbs, they modify sentences and sentence elements, showing such things as similarity, contrast, result or effect, addition, emphasis or clarity, time, and example. Here are the most commonly used conjunctive adverbs, grouped according to the things they show.

Similarity	consequently	in other words
likewise	hence	indeed
similarly	therefore	that is
Contrast	thus	**Time**
however	**Addition**	afterwards
nevertheless	also	later
on the contrary	furthermore	meanwhile
on the other hand	in addition	subsequently
otherwise	in the first place	**Example**
Result or Effect	moreover	for example
accordingly	**Emphasis or Clarity**	for instance
as a result	in fact	to illustrate

The job will require you to travel a great deal; *however*, the salary is excellent.

Andrea misread the instructions for carrying out the experiment; *as a result*, she had to repeat it.

INTERJECTIONS

An interjection is an exclamatory word that expresses strong feeling or surprise. It has no grammatical relation to the rest of the sentence. An interjection is followed by either an exclamation point or a comma.

Hey! That's my coat you're taking. (strong interjection)

Oh, is it time to leave already? (mild interjection)

Exercise

List and identify the conjunctions (C), conjunctive adverbs (CA), and interjections (I) in the following sentences.

The water looked inviting; therefore, Jan and Marie decided to take a swim. (therefore, CA; and, C)

1. We employ both men and women as machinists.
2. Molly didn't like the instructor even though she earned an *A* in the class.
3. Kimberley did not feel especially energetic; nevertheless, she walked to work rather than taking the bus.
4. Because we all work in the same building, let's form a car pool and save on driving expenses.
5. I'm sure that either Gary or Jason could handle this job, so why not offer it to one of them?
6. Wow! Did you see that shooting star or were you looking the other way?
7. This experiment requires a one-liter erlenmeyer flask and two small beakers.
8. Renée not only has a full-time job but also does her own housework.
9. Neither her boss nor her fellow employees know why Elaine has asked for a transfer.
10. Audrey has always been interested in navigation; consequently, she eagerly accepted the invitation to see the airport control tower.
11. Hey, will you wait for me while I finish this assignment?
12. Jim breezes through our math problems; however, I have to puzzle over them for hours.

Phrases

A phrase is a group of related words that lacks a subject and a predicate and that serves as a single part of speech. There are five types of phrases: *verb phrases, prepositional phrases, participial phrases, gerund phrases,* and *infinitive phrases.* The last three are built around gerunds, participles, and infinitives, which are known as verbals. Verb phrases have already been discussed on page 380; this section will deal with the four other types of phrases.

PREPOSITIONAL PHRASES

A prepositional phrase is made up of a preposition, one or more objects of that preposition, and any words associated with the object. Prepositional phrases can function as adjectives or adverbs.

> The student *at the microscope* is examining a fly's wing. (prepositional phrase as adjective)
>
> I ran *into the laboratory.* (prepositional phrase as adverb)

PARTICIPIAL PHRASES

A participial phrase is made up of a participle plus associated words. Participles are verb forms (see pp. 391–394) which, when used in participial phrases, function as adjectives and therefore modify nouns or noun substitutes. A present participle ends in *-ing* and indicates an action being carried out by the noun or noun substitute it modifies. A past participle regularly ends in *-ed*, although there are many verbs with irregular past participles (see p. 419). It indicates that the noun or noun substitute it modifies has been acted upon or has carried out an action.

> The typesetter *operating the linotype* is my sister. (present participial phrase)
>
> Mr. Wilson, *disturbed by the noise,* called the police. (past participial phrase)
>
> The typewriters, *worn beyond repair,* are being replaced. (past participial phrase)
>
> *Finished with the operation,* the surgeon removed her gloves. (past participial phrase)

A perfect participial phrase consists of *having* or *having been* plus a past participle and any associated words. It denotes that an action has been carried out by or upon the noun or noun substitute it modifies.

> *Having warned the student to stop talking,* the instructor resumed his lecture. (perfect participial phrase)
>
> *Having been warned to stop talking,* the student fell silent. (perfect participial phrase)

Participial phrases may be restrictive or nonrestrictive. A restrictive participial phrase distinguishes the person or thing modified from others in the same class. A nonrestrictive participial phrase provides more information about someone or something that has previously been identified. The difference between restrictive and nonrestrictive elements is discussed fully on pages 463–464.

GERUND PHRASES

A gerund phrase is made up of a gerund plus associated words. Gerunds are verb forms that—like present participles—end in *-ing* but serve as nouns rather than as adjectives. Like ordinary nouns, gerund phrases can function as subjects, direct objects, indirect objects, subject complements, appositives, and objects of prepositions.

> *Running the X-ray spectrograph* requires specialized chemical training. (gerund phrase as subject)
>
> John enjoys *swimming in the ocean.* (gerund phrase as direct object)
>
> Felice gave *writing the report* her full attention. (gerund phrase as indirect object)
>
> Henrietta's hobby is *collecting stamps.* (gerund phrase as subject complement)
>
> He devoted every spare moment to *overhauling the car.* (gerund phrase as object of preposition)

INFINITIVE PHRASES

An infinitive phrase is built around the present principal part of a verb preceded by *to (to run, to see, to laugh)*—the infinitive—plus its objects and modifiers. Infinitive phrases can function as adjectives, adverbs, or nouns.

> The student had a project *to complete by Friday.* (infinitive phrase as adjective)
>
> Lenore worked *to earn money for college.* (infinitive phrase as adverb)
>
> Her goal was *to major in environmental health.* (infinitive phrase as noun)

When used as nouns, infinitive phrases can serve as subjects, direct objects, subject complements, and objects of prepositions.

A gerund can often be substituted for an infinitive and vice versa.

> *To identify the chemical compound* took two hours. (infinitive phrase as subject)

> *Identifying the chemical compound* took two hours. (gerund
> phrase as subject)

At times, the *to* in an infinitive may be omitted following verbs
such as *make, dare,* and *let.*

> He made the engine (to) *run again.* (*To* is omitted but understood.)
> She didn't dare (to) *challenge the instructor's statement.* (In this
> sentence, *to* can be kept or omitted.)

Exercise

Identify the italicized words as prepositional, participial, gerund, or infinitive phrases, and tell whether each is used as a noun, an adjective, or an
adverb.

> My purpose in taking this trip is *to conduct a job interview.*
> (infinitive, noun)

1. *Flying a crop-dusting plane* is an exciting job.
2. Helen's goal was *to major in ornamental horticulture.*
3. The rain *predicted for tomorrow* will prevent us from completing our
   surveying assignment.
4. The bus *to the Deere Agricultural Museum* will leave in five minutes.
5. Anyone *needing a ride tomorrow* should call 784-4183.
6. *Having worked a double shift,* Jim wanted only to rest.
7. His hobby is *restoring old cars.*
8. Madge studied interior decorating *through an extension course.*
9. Acme Auto Sales has built an enviable reputation by *treating its
   customers fairly.*
10. Jeremy studied every minute *to make the dean's list.*
11. *Swollen by the spring floods,* Sulter's Creek rushed angrily past us.
12. The boss has given me two reports *to abstract this afternoon.*

Clauses

A clause is a group of related words that includes both a subject
and a predicate. There are two types of clauses—independent and
dependent (subordinate). An independent clause expresses a complete thought and can stand alone as a sentence. A dependent clause

has a subject and a predicate, but it does not express a complete thought and therefore cannot stand alone as a sentence. A dependent clause can function within a sentence as a noun, adjective, or adverb.

NOUN CLAUSES

A noun clause is a dependent clause that functions as a noun. Thus it may serve in any of the ways that other noun substitutes serve.

> *What I am working toward* is a degree in avionics. (noun clause as subject of sentence)
>
> I'll award first prize to *whoever has the highest average in my course.* (noun clause as object of preposition.)
>
> His greatest hope was *that he would graduate with high honors.* (noun clause as subject complement)

Noun clauses normally begin with one of the following words:

who	what	when
whom	whoever	why
whose	whomever	where
that	whatever	how
which	whichever	whether

The words in the first two columns are relative pronouns; the words in the third column are subordinating conjunctions. The relative pronoun *that* at the beginning of a dependent clause is sometimes left out when the clause is used as a direct object.

> Marybelle hoped *(that) she would graduate with honors. (That* is omitted but understood.)

ADJECTIVE CLAUSES

An adjective clause is a dependent clause that functions as an adjective, modifying a noun or a pronoun.

> Mr. Martin, *who now works as a mechanic,* used to sell insurance. (Adjective clause modifies noun.)
>
> Our company is looking for someone *who has a background in data processing.* (Adjective clause modifies pronoun.)

Adjective clauses usually begin with one of the following words:

who	when
whom	where
whose	why
that	after
which	before

The words in the first column are relative pronouns; the words in the second column are subordinating conjunctions. Sometimes, a relative pronoun at the beginning of an adjective clause can be omitted.

> The woman *(whom) he hired as a bacteriologist* has her master's degree. (The relative pronoun *whom* is omitted but understood.)
>
> The parts *(that) we ordered six weks ago* have not arrived. (The relative pronoun *that* is omitted but understood.)

Sometimes, too, a preposition comes ahead of the relative pronoun.

> The gauge *with which Norman measured the pressure* was faulty. (The preposition *with* is used before the relative pronoun *which.*)

Some adjective clauses are restrictive; that is, they distinguish the person or thing that they modify from others in the same class. Other adjective clauses are nonrestrictive, providing information about someone or something that has already been clearly identified. Restrictive clauses are not set off by commas, but nonrestrictive clauses are. Page 463 provides a detailed discussion of restrictive and nonrestrictive elements.

ADVERB CLAUSES

An adverb clause is a dependent clause that functions as an adverb; thus it may modify a verb, an adjective, another adverb, or an entire clause (or sentence).

> You may go *whenever you wish.* (Adverb clause modifies verb.)
>
> The shop looked cleaner *than I had ever seen it before.* (Adverb clause modifies adjective.)

She worked rapidly *so that she could leave early.* (Adverb clause modifies adverb.)

Unless everyone cooperates, we have little chance of success. (Adverb clause modifies entire main clause.)

Some words that commonly introduce adverb clauses are listed below, according to the questions that the clauses answer. The words that signal adverb clauses are always subordinating conjunctions.

When?
while
when
whenever
as
as soon as
before
after
since
until

Where?
where
wherever

How?
as if
as though

Why?
because
since
as
so that
now that

Under What Conditions?
if
once
unless
though
although
provided that

To What Extent?
than

Occasionally, an adverb clause will omit one or more words that are not needed for an understanding of its meaning. Such a construction is called an *elliptical clause.*

While (he was) watching TV, Richard stuffed himself with potato chips. (*He was* can be omitted but understood.)

Unlike noun and adjective clauses, adverb clauses can often be moved about in their sentences.

Richard stuffed himself with potato chips *while (he was) watching TV.*

Exercise

Identify the italicized clauses as noun, adjective, or adverb.

> I'm switching to Dr. Jekyll *because I don't like Dr. Fell.* (adverb clause)

1. *Whether Melvin passes the course* depends upon his score on the final.
2. Harriet Thomas, *who has just been promoted to vice-president,* started work in this company as a secretary.
3. I wish *I could persuade my boss to raise my salary.*
4. Nick fractured his thumb *while fixing the dented fender.*
5. Give me one reason *why you think that the experiment won't work.*
6. I'll hire anyone *Dr. Stone recommends.*
7. George spoke loudly *because he wanted everyone in the room to hear him.*
8. The candidate *for whom I'm working* is well qualified for the office.
9. Have you heard *why the company failed?*
10. Tell me *where the instruction manuals are filed.*

Avoiding Common Errors of Usage

Avoiding Sentence Fragments

A sentence fragment is a part of a sentence that is capitalized and punctuated as if it were a complete sentence. To be considered a sentence, a word group must pass two tests. First, it must have a subject and a verb. Second, it must express a complete thought. Following are two examples of fragments.

> If *you* decide to go. (The fragment has a subject and verb but does not make sense by itself; *if* makes the clause dependent.)
>
> An accident in the shop. (The fragment lacks a verb.)

Types of Fragments. Word groups mistakenly written as fragments include phrases, dependent clauses, verbs with their associated words, the second half of compound predicates, and nouns or noun substitutes with their associated words. The following examples illustrate these kinds of fragments. In each case, the fragment is italicized.

> *Having been warned about the washed-out road.* We took another route. (participial phrase)
>
> I went to class. *Although I was not prepared.* (adverb clause)
>
> John washed the windows. *And cleaned out the basement.* (second half of compound predicate)
>
> *The old gentleman sitting on the park bench and feeding the pigeons.* (noun clause with modifying phrase)
>
> *Was once the president of our largest bank.* (verb with complement and modifying phrase)

Eliminating Fragments. Getting rid of a sentence fragment in your writing is not difficult. Often, a fragment belongs either to the sentence that precedes it or to the sentence that follows it. In such cases, simply combine the fragment with the appropriate sentence. Sometimes you can convert a fragment into a sentence by adding or changing a word or phrase. Observe how the example fragments presented just above have been corrected.

411

Having been warned about the washed-out road, we took another route. (The fragment has been joined to the following sentence.)

I went to class *although I was not prepared.* (The fragment has been joined to the preceding sentence.)

John washed the windows *and cleaned out the basement.* (The fragment has been joined to the preceding sentence.)

John washed the windows. *He also cleaned out the basement.* (The fragment has been changed into a complete sentence.)

The old gentleman sitting on the park bench and feeding the pigeons was once the president of our largest bank. (The fragments have been joined together.)

When combining a fragment and a sentence, put a comma between them if the first element is a long phrase or long adverb clause or if there is a distinct pause between the two elements. Note the use of a comma in the first sentence above.

Appropriate Uses for Fragments. Fragments are commonly used in everyday conversation as well as in writing that reproduces it. They also occur in the works of professional writers, who use them to create special moods or effects. In general, though, fragments should be avoided except in dialogue or for special emphasis.

Exercise

Ten main clauses paired with fragments are presented below. In each case identify the sentence and the fragment, then eliminate the fragment.

Stanley has made plans. To retire in August. (Sentence, fragment)
Stanley has made plans to retire in August.

1. In just about a minute. I'm going to lose patience with this task.
2. Harrigan discussed the procedure for checking the tolerances on the part. While the apprentices listened.
3. Because I couldn't find my car keys. I had to take the bus.
4. While in Chicago, I visited the Sears Tower. The tallest building in the world.
5. Living in an apartment house is pleasant. Unless one requires a great deal of privacy.
6. Gail and Olive have gone to Armour Technical Institute. To take a summer course in special education.
7. Dennis bought a pound of peanuts. And ate them in one evening.

8. Frustrated by a boss he could never please. Clayton quit the company.
9. If I leave for Cleveland in the next hour. I'll arrive at the auditorium for the opening of the midwestern electronics suppliers' convention.
10. Gasping and red-faced. The worker stumbled from the smoke-filled building.

Avoiding Run-On Sentences and Comma Splices

A run-on sentence occurs when one complete sentence is run into another without the proper end punctuation and beginning capital letter to separate them. A comma splice occurs when there is only a comma between two complete sentences.

> The millwrights voted to strike the electricians decided to stay on the job. (run-on sentence)
> The millwrights voted to strike, the electricians decided to stay on the job. (comma splice)

These two types of errors can be corrected in several ways. First, the sentences may be separated by using a period and capital.

> The millwrights voted to strike. The electricians decided to stay on the job.

Second, the sentences may be separated by using a semicolon.

> The millwrights voted to strike; the electricians decided to stay on the job.

Third, the sentences may be separated with a comma plus a coordinating conjunction.

> The millwrights voted to strike, *but* the electricians decided to stay on the job.

Fourth, one of the sentences may be changed into a subordinate clause introduced by a subordinating conjunction.

> *Although* the millwrights voted to strike, the electricians decided to stay on the job.

Finally, the sentences can be separated by means of a semicolon and a conjunctive adverb.

> The millwrights voted to strike; *however,* the electricians decided to stay on the job.

The method of correction to use will depend upon the particular sentence pairs. When the two ideas are not closely related, using a period and capital letter—or a semicolon—is often preferable, unless a choppy effect results. For more closely related ideas, use the method of correction that best shows the relationship between them. If, for example, examination shows one idea to be subordinate to the other, then the sentence expressing it can be converted to a subordinate clause introduced by a subordinating conjunction. In some cases, several or all of the methods may be used interchangeably.

Exercise

Indicate whether any of the following sentences is a run-on sentence or contains a comma splice; then correct the faulty sentences.

> Teach me a few magic tricks, I want to surprise my friends. (comma splice) Teach me a few magic tricks, for I want to surprise my friends.

1. Ramón lost his part-time job he couldn't continue in school.
2. Joe is a college senior, his sister runs a beauty shop.
3. I believe that chemistry is an overcrowded profession many experts agree with me.
4. Wesley worked all night that's why he's sleeping now.
5. Harvey worked in Ecuador for five years, consequently, he is very fluent in Spanish.
6. Our employment incentive plan is simplicity itself, make one mistake and you're fired!
7. The card catalog is an important library research tool every student should know how to use it.
8. Gideon wanted to become a doctor Hector chose engineering as his profession.
9. He didn't work hard his boss didn't promote him.
10. Industrial accidents are a serious problem, both management and labor must look for ways to reduce the number of injuries that occur each year.

Making Subjects and Verbs Agree

A verb should agree in number with its subject. If the subject is singular, the verb should be singular. If the subject is plural, the verb should be plural.

Ordinarily, making subjects and verbs agree causes no problems. However, the following special situations can lead to difficulties.

Subject and Verb Separated by a Word Group. Sometimes the subject is separated from the verb by a word group that includes a noun. When you write this sort of sentence, be sure that the verb agrees in number with the subject of the sentence, not a noun in the word group.

> Our supply of nails *was* inadequate. (The verb agrees with the singular subject *supply.*)
>
> Several courses required for my major *are* not being offered this term. (The verb agrees with the plural subject *courses.*)

Phrases beginning with words such as *along with, as well as, in addition to, like,* and *with* that follow the subject do not affect the number of the verb. The verb agrees with the subject of the sentence.

> Mr. Jones, along with his son and daughter, *operates* a repair shop. (The verb agrees with the singular subject *Mr. Jones.*)
>
> The walls, as well as the ceiling, *were* freshly painted. (The verb agrees with the plural subject *walls.*)

Two Singular Subjects. Singular subjects joined by *and* usually require a plural verb.

> The drafting board and T-square *were* initialed by the owner.
>
> Grading papers and preparing lectures *take* up most of my evening.

Few of us would use *was* in the first of these two examples. However, when the subjects are word groups like *grading papers* and *preparing lectures,* singular verbs are often mistakenly used.

When two singular sentences joined by *and* are preceded by *each* or *every,* use a *singular,* rather than a plural verb.

> Every cup and saucer *was* badly chipped. (*Every* makes a singular verb necessary.)
>
> Each watercolor and etching *has* been signed by the artist. (*Each* makes a singular verb necessary.)

Singular subjects joined by *or, either—or,* or *neither—nor* require a singular verb.

> A doctor or a nurse *is* always on hand.
>
> Neither his house nor his yard *was* in very good shape.
>
> Either Dr. Miles or Ms. Reynolds *is* the speaker for tonight.

One Singular and One Plural Subject. When one singular and one plural subject are joined by *or, either—or,* or *neither—nor,* the verb agrees in number with the subject that is closer to it.

> Neither the secretaries nor the office manager *was* there. (The verb agrees with the singular subject, *manager,* which is closer to the verb.)
>
> Neither the office manager nor the secretaries *were* there. (The verb agrees with the plural subject, *secretaries,* which is closer to the verb.)

Pronouns as Subjects. When the following pronouns are used as subjects, they take singular verbs:

each	anyone	someone
each one	anybody	somebody
either	anything	something
either one	everyone	no one
neither	everybody	nobody
neither one	everything	nothing

> Somebody *has* stolen the car.
>
> Neither *was* told about the meeting.

Collective Nouns as Subjects. Collective nouns are nouns that are singular in form but stand for a group or collection of individuals or things. In most instances, collective nouns are regarded as single units and therefore require singular verbs.

> The class *is* in the library. (*Class* is considered a unit.)
>
> The convoy *was* headed for the harbor. (*Convoy* is considered a unit.)

Occasionally, though, a collective noun is regarded as a group of individuals acting separately. In such cases, the collective noun takes a plural verb.

> The Thurston family are hard workers. (*Family* is considered a group of individuals.)

Sentences in Which the Verb Comes Ahead of the Subject. Sentences in which the verb comes ahead of the subject may begin with a phrase or such words as *here, there, how, what,* and *where.* In each case, the verb must agree in number with the subject that follows it.

> Where *is* my book? (The verb agrees with the singular subject *book.*)
>
> Where *are* my books? (The verb agrees with the plural subject *books.*)
>
> There *are* several ways of checking the acidity of a solution. (The verb agrees with the plural subject *ways.*)
>
> There *is* no battery in that flashlight. (The verb agrees with the singular subject *battery.*)

Sentences with Linking Verbs and Subject Complement. A linking verb agrees with its subject, not with the subject complement that follows it.

> My favorite fruit *is* bananas. (The verb agrees with the singular subject *fruit.*)
>
> Bananas *are* my favorite fruit. (The verb agrees with the plural subject *bananas.*)

Exercise

Choose the correct verb form from the pair in parentheses.

We are looking for applicants who (holds, hold) degrees in accounting. (hold)

1. Either Kevin or Harley (is, are) sure to win this race.
2. All of the tools (needs, need) replacing.
3. The student committee, together with two faculty members, (is, are) drafting a final report.
4. Either the cats or the dog (has, have) been digging in the flower bed.
5. There (is, are) a quick solution to this problem.
6. A completely different set of results (has, have) been obtained this time.
7. Each sword and pistol in my collection (has, have) been owned by a famous person.
8. Neither Penelope nor her brothers (plans, plan) to join the photography club.
9. Where (is, are) the books we got from the library?
10. Each of our employees (owns, own) stock in the company.
11. My favorite breakfast (is, are) ham, eggs, and toast.
12. The team (has, have) all signed contracts for next season.

Choosing the Right Verb Form

Using a verb that does not agree in number with its subject is not the only kind of error involving verb forms. Several other types of verb errors occur so frequently that they merit special attention. These errors include using the wrong *principal part*, confusing *lie* with *lay* and *sit* with *set*, omitting the final -*d* from certain verbs, and using *nonstandard verb forms*.

Using Wrong Principal Parts. As noted on page 391, all verbs have three principal parts—the *present*, the *past*, and the *past participle*. The present form may occur without a helping verb or with *shall* or *will*. The past form always occurs without a helping verb, while the past participle form occurs with one or more helping verbs (*has, have, had, shall have, will have*).

Most verbs have the same past and past participle forms (for example, I *walked*, I have *walked*; she *heard*, she has *heard*). However, a sizable number have different past and past participle forms, and many usage problems result from confusing these forms (for example, I have *went* for I have *gone*). Following are forty common verbs that are especially likely to cause this sort of difficulty.

Present	**Past**	**Past Participle**
arise	arose	arisen
bear	bore	borne
become	became	become
begin	began	begun
bite	bit	bitten
blow	blew	blown
break	broke	broken
choose	chose	chosen
come	came	come
do	did	done
draw	drew	drawn
drink	drank	drunk
drive	drove	driven
eat	ate	eaten
fall	fell	fallen
fly	flew	flown
forget	forgot	forgotten
freeze	froze	frozen
give	gave	given
go	went	gone
grow	grew	grown
know	knew	known
ride	rode	ridden
ring	rang	rung
rise	rose	risen
run	ran	run
see	saw	seen
shake	shook	shaken
sing	sang	sung
sink	sank	sunk
speak	spoke	spoken
spring	sprang	sprung
steal	stole	stolen
swear	swore	sworn
swim	swam	swum
take	took	taken
tear	tore	torn
throw	threw	thrown
wear	wore	worn
write	wrote	written

Memorizing the principal parts of any verb that gives you trouble will help prevent this kind of error. Until you have the parts down pat, check this list or consult a good desk (not pocket) dictionary whenever you can't decide which form is right.

Confusing "Lie" and "Lay" and "Sit" and "Set." The use of *lay* for *lie* is very common in informal spoken Engish ("I'm going to lay down."). Nonetheless, this usage is incorrect and when you write or speak in formal situations, you must distinguish carefully between these verbs.

To *lie* means "to be or to remain in a horizontal position." Because we can't "remain" things, this verb never takes a direct object. The following sentences illustrate the three principal parts of *lie*.

> I *lie* down for a nap each afternoon. (present)
>
> I *lay* down for a nap yesterday afternoon. (past)
>
> I have *lain* down for a nap every afternoon this week. (past participle)

To *lay* means "to place." Because we do "place" things, this verb always takes a direct object.

> Those two men *lay* bricks for a living. (present)
>
> Those two men *laid* over twelve hundred bricks yesterday. (past)
>
> Those two men have *laid* an average of twelve hundred bricks every day this month. (past participle)

Notice that the past principal part of *lie* and the present principal part of *lay* are identical—a fact that goes a long way toward explaining the confusion between the two verbs.

Sit and *set* do not cause as much trouble as *lie* and *lay*. Nevertheless, they too are often confused, as shown by such errors as "Come in and set awhile" and "I sat the dish on the sideboard."

To *sit* means "to rest on one's haunches" as in a chair. Like *lie*, it does not take a direct object.

> Sometimes I *sit* on the floor when I watch TV. (present)
>
> We *sat* on the floor when we ate at that Japanese restaurant. (past)
>
> I have *sat* through some pretty terrible movies in my time. (past participle)

To set means "to place in position." It almost always takes a direct object. Notice the verb's three principal parts are identical.

> I *set* my briefcase on the desk when I come home at night. (present)
> I *set* my briefcase on the desk when I came home last evening. (past)
> I have *set* the package on the desk. (past participle)

When used with the subject *sun, set* does not take a direct object.

> The sun *set* behind the hills.

The same is true when *set* has the meaning "to become hard or firm" or "to begin or get started."

> The cement has *set*.
> The crew *set* to work.

Whenever you have trouble choosing between *lie* and *lay* or *sit* and *set,* check to see whether the sentence has a direct object. If there is none, use the proper form of *lie* or *sit* except in those special cases that call for *set*. If there is a direct object, use the proper form of *lay* or *set*.

Omitting Endings from Certain Verbs. Omitting endings involves dropping the *-d* or *-ed* from verbs that have the same past and past participle principal parts. The most common errors include the use of *ask* for *asked, prejudice* for *prejudiced, suppose* for *supposed,* and *use* for *used*.

> I *ask* my roommate yesterday to lend me his tweed jacket.
> The governor's reputation as an alcoholic *has prejudice* his chances for reelection.
> Lucinda mistakenly *suppose* that she would receive an invitation to the party.
> Henry *use* to work for General Motors.

The correct verb forms for these sentences are as follows:

I *asked* my roommate yesterday to lend me his tweed jacket.

The governor's reputation as an alcoholic *has prejudiced* his chances for reelection.

Lucinda mistakenly *supposed* that she would receive an invitation to the party.

Henry *used* to work for General Motors.

Use of Nonstandard Verb Forms. Some usages are considered nonstandard and should be avoided whenever you speak or write. Common errors include the use of *busted* for *broke, broken,* and *burst; drownded* for *drowned; swang* for *swung;* and *throwed* for *threw* and *thrown.* Here are four examples of these errors.

The balloon *busted* when Sam tried to blow it up.

My typewriter is *busted.*

When ten years old, I nearly *drownded.*

The children *swang* all afternoon in the park.

The correct verb forms are as follows:

The balloon *burst* when Sam tried to blow it up.

My typewriter is *broken.*

When ten years old, I nearly *drowned.*

The children *swung* all afternoon in the park.

Exercise

Choose the right verb form from the pair in parentheses.

It was so cold that the car battery had (froze, frozen). (frozen)

1. The price of gasoline has (rose, risen) every year since the Arab oil embargo.
2. Because of the subzero weather, our water pipes have frozen and (burst, busted).
3. She has (forgot, forgotten) her keys.
4. After mowing the lawn, I (lay, laid) down for an hour.
5. In the morning, (sit, set) the trash out by the curb.
6. A man (come, came) into the gas station and asked for directions to the research center.

7. Manfred (suppose, supposed) that he would be promoted.
8. He said he had (lain, laid) very still in his hiding place while the killers looked for him.
9. You have (set, sat) around long enough; get up and go to work.
10. For his summer job, Rupert (lay, laid) pipe for a building contractor.
11. They (lay, laid) the hero to rest last Friday.
12. The foundations of the electrical generation building (sank, sunk) three inches last year.

Avoiding Errors in Showing Time

Errors in showing time include unwarranted shifts in time and failure to make clear the order in which two past events occurred.

Unwarranted Shifts in Tense. When describing a series of events or a past situation, student writers sometimes make unwarranted and confusing shifts from past tense to present and vice versa. Such shifts are especially likely in summaries of the plots of plays, movies, and stories. The following paragraph contains two unwarranted shifts in tense.

> When Framton Nuttel first *arrives* at Mrs. Sappleton's home, he *is greeted* by her niece, Vera, who *announces* that she *will entertain* him until her aunt *comes* downstairs. Vera, a compulsive storyteller, *proceeded* [shift from present to past tense] to tell Framton a beautifully tragic but completely false tale about the death of her aunt's husband and two brothers. She *said* that three years before, the three *had gone* hunting and *perished* in a bog, and that their bodies *were* never *recovered*. Framton *believes* [shift from past back to present tense] her.

To prevent such shifts, you must pay close attention to the time frame of the events or situation you are describing and shift time only when the narrative time changes. Here is a corrected version of the above paragraphs, in the present tense.

> When Framton Nuttel first *arrives* at Mrs. Sappleton's home, he *is greeted* by her niece, Vera, who *announces* that she *will entertain* him until her aunt *comes* downstairs. Vera, a compulsive storyteller, *proceeds* to tell Framton a beautifully tragic but completely false tale about the death of her aunt's husband and two

brothers. She *says* that three years before, the three *went* hunting and *perished* in a bog, and that their bodies *were* never *recovered*. Framton *believes* her.

The future *will entertain* in the first sentence is correct because the entertainment must follow the announcement. The next-to-last sentence retains the past tense because it deals with an event that supposedly occurred before Framton's visit to Mrs. Sappleton.

Sequence of Past Tenses. Often you will need to indicate that one past action or condition ended before or after another past action or condition occurred. To do so, use the past tense of one verb and the past perfect tense (*had* plus the past participle) of the other verb, as in the following sentence.

Bob *bought* a new lamp because he *had broken* the old one.

Failure to do so can cause you to misstate the time relationship of the events, as in the following sentence.

The team *scored* two touchdowns when the first quarter *ended*.

This sentence indicates that the team scored two touchdowns at the moment the first quarter ended. Such a situation is impossible. When misstatements of this sort occur in your writing, you must decide which verb needs to be changed in order to correct the situation. Usually, it will be the verb for the earlier event.

The team *had scored* two touchdowns when the first quarter ended. (The verb indicating the earlier action has been changed.)

If two past events occurred at the same time or nearly the same time, then use the past tense for both verbs.

When the bell *rang*, the students *rushed* out the door.

Exercise

Indicate whether each sentence is correct (C), contains an unwarranted shift in time (S), or shows past times improperly (I).

When I made the coffee, I sat down and drank a cup. (I) When I had made the coffee, I sat down and drank a cup.

1. General Gung Ho decorated his walls with weapons he captured during his last campaign.
2. I have been working as a landscape architect this summer, and I found the work very interesting.
3. Because I heard so much about Houston, I was delighted when the company transferred me there.
4. Have you received the bonus the company will give its employees?
5. Once the instructor had worked the problem, I saw my mistake.
6. The assembly line starts operating at 7 A.M. and usually ran until 6 P.M.
7. After Tammie has carefully read the instructions for assembling the swing, she got her tools and set to work.
8. Marilyn worked for Ames Products six months when she got her first promotion.
9. After he rested awhile, he began studying again.
10. Students who wish to save money on books will find lower prices at the off-campus bookstore.

Avoiding Overuse of the Passive Voice

Transitive verbs have two *voices: active* and *passive.* A verb is in the *active voice* when the subject of the sentence performs the action named by the verb. A verb is in the *passive voice* when the subject receives the action. The noun or pronoun that tells who performed the action may appear in a prepositional phrase or remain unmentioned.

Joan *planned* the sales meeting. (active voice)

The sales meeting *was planned* by Joan. (passive voice; prepositional phrase *by Joan* identifies performer)

The sales meeting *was held* last week. (passive voice; performer not identified)

Drawbacks of the Passive Voice. The passive voice gives writing a flat, impersonal tone and almost always requires more words than the active voice. Consider the following paragraph, written largely in the passive voice.

Graft becomes possible when gifts are given to police officers or favors are done for them by persons who expect preferential treatment in return. Gifts of many kinds may be received by officers. Often free meals are given to officers by the owners of restaurants on their beats. During the Christmas season, officers may be given liquor, food, or theater tickets by merchants. If favored treatment is not received by the donors, no great harm is done. But when traffic offenses, safety code violations, and the like are overlooked by the officers, corruption results. When such corruption is exposed by the newspapers, faith is lost in the law and law enforcement agencies.

Note the livelier tone of the following revised version, which is written largely in the active voice.

Graft becomes possible when police officers accept gifts or favors from persons who expect preferential treatment in return. Officers may receive gifts of many kinds. Often restaurant owners provide free meals for officers on local patrol. During the Christmas season, merchants make gifts of liquor, food, or theater tickets. If donors do not receive favored treatment, no great harm is done. But when officers overlook traffic offenses, safety code violations, and the like, corruption results. When the newspapers expose such corruption, citizens lose faith in the law and law enforcement agencies.

This version has twenty-three fewer words than the earlier version, and is livelier as well.

Situations Where the Passive Voice Is Preferable. Because of its livelier, more emphatic tone, the active voice is usually the more effective. Nonetheless, there are certain situations where the passive voice is better. Occasionally, for instance, it may be desirable to conceal someone's identity. Consider this memorandum from a supervisor to a group of employees who have consistently taken overly long coffee breaks.

At the monthly supervisors' meeting, a suggestion was adopted that coffee breaks be suspended permanently unless employees immediately limit them to ten minutes. Please observe the ten-minute limit from now on so that such action will not be necessary.

To prevent hostile comments and harassment, the supervisor deliberately uses the passive voice to conceal the name of the person who
made the suggestion.

Technical and scientific writing commonly makes use of the
passive voice to explain how processes are or were carried out. In such
descriptions the action, not the actor, is important, and an objective,
impersonal tone is desirable.

> To obtain a water sample for dissolved oxygen analysis, a
> B.O.D. bottle is completely filled and then capped so no air is
> trapped inside. Next, 2 ml of manganese sulfate solution is added,
> well below the surface of the sample, and this is followed by 2 ml of
> alkali-iodine-oxide agent. The bottle is then stoppered carefully, so
> as to exclude air bubbles, and the contents are mixed by inverting
> the bottle at least 15 times.

There are times when the passive voice is preferable in everyday
writing.

> The garbage is collected once a week—on Monday.
> The aircraft carrier was commissioned last August.

In these sentences, just as in the scientific example above, what was
done, rather than who did it, is the important thing. Omitting the
name of the doer gives the action the necessary emphasis.

Except in such special situations, however, you should try to use
the active voice.

Exercise

Indicate whether each sentence is in the active voice (A) or the passive voice
(P); then convert each passive-voice sentence to the active voice.

> If we are lucky, the drill press will have been repaired by this time
> tomorrow. (P) If we are lucky, they will have repaired the drill
> press by this time tomorrow.

1. The switch is attached to the wall with four screws.
2. By 7 P.M., I will have finished my term paper.
3. Additional fire extinguishers have been purchased for the building.
4. The high rate of employee absenteeism was discussed by the supervisors.

5. For twenty years, I have admired your work in genetics.
6. She has not learned how to be assertive.
7. Witnesses said the getaway car had been driven by Chester Stark.
8. We have scraped all the old putty from the window frame.
9. Wendy's parents gave her a new calculator for her birthday.
10. Our new sales office will be opened in just two weeks.
11. Your suggestion has been adopted by the committee.
12. Copper is being replaced by aluminum as an electrical conductor for high temperature service.

Making Pronouns and Antecedents Agree

The noun or noun substitute that a pronoun refers to is called its antecedent. Like verbs with their subjects, pronouns should agree in number with their antecedents. If the antecedent is singular, the pronoun should be singular. If the antecedent is plural, the pronoun should be plural. The following pointers will help in the special situations that are most likely to cause problems.

Indefinite Pronouns as Antecedents. Indefinite pronouns are pronouns that do not refer to specific persons or things. When the following indefinite pronouns are used as antecedents, the pronouns that follow them should be singular.

each	anyone	someone
each one	anybody	somebody
either	anything	something
either one	everyone	no one
neither	everybody	nobody
neither one	everything	nothing

Anyone who has finished *his* test may leave.
Neither of the salesmen had met *his* quota.

Recently, the use of *his or her* has become common when the sex of the antecedent is unknown, as in the first sentence above.

Anyone who has finished *his or her* test may leave.

Don't, however, use the *his or her* construction so often that your writing becomes awkward and distracting to your reader. The use of *he* as a general reference is standard in English and should not necessarily be considered sexist. However, sometimes one can rewrite the sentence in the plural and avoid apparent sexism.

> *Those* who have finished *their* test may leave.

Occasionally, a ridiculous result occurs when a singular pronoun refers to an indefinite pronoun that is obviously plural in meaning.

> Everybody complained that the test was too hard, but I didn't agree with *him*.
> Everyone was talking, so I told *him* to quiet down.

In such cases, recast the sentence to eliminate the problem.

> Everybody complained that the test was too hard, but I didn't think so.
> Everyone was talking, so I asked for silence.

In informal writing and speaking, there is an increasing tendency to use plural pronouns with indefinite pronoun antecedents.

> Someone has left *their* muddy footprints on the floor.

However, because many people object to this practice, you should avoid it in your own writing and speaking.

Two Singular Antecedents. Two or more antecedents joined by *and* usually require a plural pronoun.

> His car and boat were left in *their* usual places.
> Harold, Norman, and Lucinda finished *their* joint presentation ten minutes early.

However, when the antecedents are preceded by *each* or *every*, the pronoun should be singular.

> Every family and business must do *its* part to conserve energy. (*Every* makes a singular pronoun necessary.)

Each college and university sent *its* budget request to the legislature. (*Each* makes a singular pronoun necessary.)

Singular antecedents joined by *or, either—or,* or *neither—nor* require singular pronouns.

Has either John or Bill finished *his* report?

Neither Margaret nor Jane has completed *her* preparations for the trip.

Applying this rule will sometimes result in an awkward or ridiculous sentence. In such cases, recast the sentence to avoid the problem.

Neither Sharon nor Robert has written *his* or *her* thank-you note. (The sentence is awkward.)

Sharon and Roger have not written thank-you notes. (The sentence has been recast.)

Neither Sharon nor Robert has written a thank-you note. (The sentence has been recast.)

Singular and Plural Antecedents. If one singular and one plural antecedent are joined by *or, either—or,* or *neither—nor,* the pronoun agrees in number with the closer antecedent.

Either Jim Forbes or the *Mastersons* will lend us *their* car. (The pronoun *their* agrees with the plural antecedent *Mastersons.*)

Either the Mastersons or *Jim Forbes* will lend us *his* car. (The pronoun *his* agrees with the singular antecedent *Jim Forbes.*)

Sometimes you must write the antecedents in one particular order to express the desired meaning.

Neither the superintendent nor the *workers* recognized their peril. (The pronoun *their* agrees with the plural antecedent *workers.*)

Neither the workers nor the superintendent recognized *his* peril. (The pronoun *his* agrees with the singular antecedent *superintendent.*)

Notice that the meaning is different in these sentences. In the first, the peril is to everyone. In the second the peril is to the superintendent only.

Collective Nouns as Antecedents. Collective nouns (see page 385) are singular in form but stand for a group of individuals or things. If a collective noun is regarded as a single unit, the pronoun that refers to it should be singular. If the collective noun is regarded as a group of individuals acting separately, then the pronoun should be plural.

> The group presented *its* resolution. (The group is acting as a unit.)
> Yesterday the team signed *their* contracts for the coming season. (The team is acting as a group of individuals.)

Exercise

Choose the right form of the pronoun for each of the following sentences.

> The graduating class was unanimous in (its, their) choice of Ralph Nader for commencement speaker. (its)

1. If anyone objects to this proposal, now is the time for (him or her, them) to speak up.
2. Each foreman and superintendent agreed that (he, they) would contribute to the Red Cross drive.
3. Anyone wanting a successful college career must devote much of (his, their) time to studying.
4. The board will announce (its, their) decision next week.
5. When asked to make statements, Doris and Zula insisted on (her, their) right to remain silent.
6. I'm told that neither Betty Myers nor the Engels filed (her, their) income tax on time.
7. No one should force (his or her, their) interests on other members of the family.
8. To cope with the tornadoes, each town and city set up (its, their) special warning system.
9. We watched the crowd leaving the theater and heading toward (its, their) homes.
10. Either the Borom brothers or Ronald Drag will show (his, their) travel slides at the meeting.

Avoiding Faulty Pronoun Reference

A pronoun reference is faulty if the pronoun refers to more than one antecedent, to a hidden antecedent, or to no antecedent at all.

More Than One Antecedent. The following sentences are unclear because they include more than one possible antecedent.

Take the radio out of the car and sell *it*. (It is unclear whether the radio or the car should be sold.)

The supervisors told the sheet-metal workers that *they* would receive a bonus. (It is unclear whether supervisors or workers will receive a bonus.)

Sometimes writers will produce a sentence like the one below.

If the fans don't buy all the pennants, pack *them* away until next season. (In this case, *pennants* is clearly the antecedent, but the presence of *fans* makes the sentence ridiculous.)

You can correct both of these kinds of faults by substituting a noun for the pronoun or by rephrasing the sentence.

Take the radio out of the car, and then sell the car. (A noun has been substituted for the pronoun.)

The supervisors told the sheet-metal workers to expect a bonus. (The sentence has been rephrased to make its meaning clear.)

The supervisors told the sheet-metal workers that they were expecting a bonus. (The sentence has been rephrased to make its meaning clear.)

Pack away any unsold pennants, and save them for the next game. (The sentence has been rephrased so that it is no longer ridiculous.)

Hidden Antecedents. An antecedent is hidden if it is serving as an adjective rather than as a noun. Here are two sentences with hidden antecedents.

When I removed the table's finish, *it* proved to be oak. (*It* ought to refer to *table*, which in this sentence appears as the adjective *table's*.)

The popcorn bowl was empty, but we were tired of eating *it* anyhow. (*It* ought to refer to *popcorn*, which in this sentence is an adjective.)

To correct this error, substitute a noun for the pronoun, or switch the positions of the adjective and the pronoun and then make whatever changes are required by correct English.

When I removed its finish, the table proved to be oak. (The adjective and the pronoun have been switched and their forms have been changed accordingly.)

The popcorn bowl was empty, but we were tired of eating popcorn anyhow. (The noun has been substituted for the pronoun.)

No Antecedent. A no-antecedent sentence is one without any noun to which the pronoun can refer. Sentences of this sort are common in informal speech, but you should avoid them in formal writing or speaking. The following sentences show this error.

The shop is humming with activity because *they* are working hard.
It says in this article on leukemia that many cases are now being cured.

To correct such a sentence, substitute an appropriate noun for the pronoun, or reword it to avoid the problem.

The shop is humming with activity because the *employees* are working hard. (A noun has been substituted for the pronoun.)
This article on leukemia says that many cases are now being cured. (The sentence has been reworded to avoid the problem.)

Sometimes a *this, that, it,* or *which* will refer not to a single noun but to a whole idea. This usage is perfectly acceptable as long as the writer's meaning is obvious, as in the following sentence.

The instructor lost our midterm exams, *which* meant we had to take the test again.

Problems can arise, however, when the reader can't figure out to which of two or more ideas the pronoun refers.

Harry called Bert two hours after the agreed-upon time and canceled their next-day's fishing trip. *This* made Bert very angry.

Here, we cannot tell whether the late call, the cancellation of the fishing trip, or both caused Bert's anger. Again, the problem can be corrected by the addition of a clarifying word or phrase or by rewording.

Harry called Bert two hours after the agreed-upon time and canceled their next-day's fishing trip. This *tardiness* made Bert very angry. (The clarifying word *tardiness* has been added.)

Harry called Bert two hours after the agreed-upon time and canceled their next-day's fishing trip. *Harry's change of plans* made Bert very angry. (The sentence has been reworded to avoid the problem.)

Exercise

Indicate whether each sentence is correct (C) or contains a faulty pronoun reference (F), and correct any faulty sentences.

Millie asked Suzanne how she liked her new hat. (F) Millie, sporting a new hat, asked Suzanne how she liked it.

1. Move the car out of the garage and paint it.
2. Caught cheating on the examination, Pam tried to lie her way out of it.
3. Jack's father felt proud when he received a promotion to manager.
4. As the wolf approached the sheep paddock, they moved to its far side.
5. Alvin found that the Craftwell Corporation had excellent fringe benefits and paid its employees very well, which improved his morale greatly.
6. When Malcolm walked into the employees' lounge, they burst out laughing.
7. Because my parents like oysters, I served them as an appetizer.
8. When Charles poked the snake's cage, it hissed.
9. They say that the sales force will receive a bonus this year.
10. Albert told Sue that she was tired and needed to rest.
11. The locker room was very noisy because the players were celebrating their victory.
12. The receptionists told the typists that they should be making more money.

Avoiding Unwarranted Shifts in Person

Pronouns can be in the first person, second person, or third person. First person pronouns (for example, *I, me, mine, we, us, ourselves*) identify people who are speaking or writing about themselves. Second person pronouns (*you, your, yours, yourself, your-*

selves) identify people who are being addressed directly. Third person pronouns (for example, *he, she, it, his, hers, its, they, theirs, himself,* and any indefinite pronoun) identify people or things that are being spoken or written about.

Student writers often shift needlessly from one person to another, usually from the third person to the second. The following examples illustrate unwarranted shifts.

> If an employee works hard, *he* has many opportunities for advancement, and eventually *you* might become a department supervisor. (The shift is from third to second person.)
>
> An understanding roommate is one *you* can tell *your* personal problems to. This kind of roommate knows when *I* want to be alone and respects *my* wish. (The shift is from second to first person.)
>
> After working as a cashier for six months, *I* welcomed a promotion to bookkeeper with *her* own office. (The shift is from first to third person).

You can avoid such errors by paying careful attention to the pronouns you use in each sentence and by making sure that no shifts occur as you go from one sentence to the next. Notice the improved smoothness and clarity of the corrected examples.

> If an employee works hard, *he* has many opportunities for advancement, and eventually *he* might become a department supervisor. (The sentence uses the third person only.)
>
> An understanding roommate is one *you* can tell *your* personal problems to. This type of roommate knows when *you* want to be alone and respects *your* wishes. (The sentence uses the second person only.)
>
> After working as a cashier for six months, *I* welcomed a promotion to bookkeeper with *my* own office. (The sentence uses the first person only.)

Not all shifts in person are unwarranted. Consider, for example, the following correct sentences.

> *I* would like *you* to take this sales report to Ms. Carter's office. *She* asked to borrow it.

Here the speaker identifies himself or herself (*I*) while speaking directly to a listener (*you*) about someone else (*she*). In such cases, shifts are necessary in order to get the message across.

Exercise

Indicate whether the sentence is correct (C) or contains an unwarranted shift in person (S) and correct any faulty sentences.

> I believe you should buy a set of snow tires for your car this winter.
> (C)

1. Would you ask John whether he will lend me his biology book for the afternoon?
2. Participants in the meeting should come prepared to discuss the items on the agenda and to bring up any other matters you consider important.
3. When I ask Rochelle to help me with my homework, sometimes she turns you down.
4. Our house was situated in a grove of trees, and you couldn't see the highway from our front window.
5. Once we are committed to a course of action, it is often difficult for people to change their views.
6. When we weren't on duty, employees could use any recreational facilities at the resort.
7. Anyone wishing to attend the department luncheon should sign your name on this sheet.
8. The company must realize that its greatest asset is our employees.
9. We think our boss is wonderful; he is always ready to help you with problems that arise on the job.
10. Unless you have good grounding in grammar, no one can hope to succeed as a technical writer.

Using the Right Pronoun Case

The term "case" refers to the changes in form that a noun or a pronoun undergoes to show its function in a sentence. There are three cases in English: the *subjective*, the *objective*, and the *possessive*. The subjective case is used for subjects and subject complements. The objective case is used for direct objects, indirect objects, and objects of prepositions. The possessive case shows ownership or possession.

Nouns and most indefinite pronouns (*anyone, someone, no one, everyone,* and the like) undergo changes in form for the possessive case only.

> *John* knows *Douglas. Douglas* knows *John.* (The forms are identical in both the subjective and objective cases.)
>
> *John's* college program is very difficult. (The *'s* is added to *John* to show possession.)
>
> *Anyone's* guess is as good as mine. (The *'s* is added to *anyone* to show possession.)

However, several of the most common problems have different forms for each case.

Subjective	Objective	Possessive
I	me	my, mine
you	you	your, yours
he	him	his
she	her	her, hers
we	us	our, ours
they	them	their, theirs
who	whom	whose

"We" and "Us" Preceding Nouns. Nouns that serve as subjects take the pronoun *we.* Those that serve as objects take the pronoun *us.*

> *We* managers set a good example for the employees. (The pronoun *we* precedes the subject of the sentence, *managers.*)
>
> The guide took *us* visitors through the nuclear installation. (The pronoun *us* precedes the object of the sentence, *visitors.*)

If you have difficulty choosing the right pronoun, mentally omit the noun and read the sentence to yourself, first with one pronoun and then with the other. The incorrect pronoun will sound wrong, and the correct one will sound right.

> Father gave (we, us) girls two large chocolate hearts for Valentine's Day.

Omitting *girls* reveals at once that *us* is the correct choice.

Compound Subjects, Objects, and Appositives. Pronouns in the compound subjects of sentences and of dependent clauses should be in the subjective case. Those in compound objects should be in the objective case.

Sam and *I* plan to work in public health. (The pronoun *I* is part of the compound subject.)

The school awarded Marcia and *her* certificates of academic excellence. (The pronoun *her* is part of the compound indirect object.)

Between John and *me*, we finished the job in one hour. (The pronoun *me* is part of the compound object of the preposition.)

An appositive is a noun or noun substitute—and any associated words—that follows another noun or noun substitute and tells something about it. When the appositive accompanies the subject of the sentence, the pronoun should be in the subjective case. When it accompanies an object, the pronoun should be in the objective case.

The superintendent selected two people, Loretta and *me*, to receive merit increases. (The pronoun *me* is the appositive of the noun *people*, which functions as the direct object.)

Two people, Loretta and *I*, received merit increases. (The pronoun *I* is the appositive of the noun *people*, which functions as the subject.)

Again the technique of mental omission can help you to pick the right pronouns.

Pronouns in Dependent Clauses. A pronoun that serves as the subject of a dependent clause must be in the subjective case. A pronoun that serves as an object must be in the objective case.

The recruiter will see all students *who* request a job interview. (The pronoun *who* is the subject of the dependent clause.)

Sheila is the student *whom* we voted most likely to succeed. (The pronoun *whom* is the direct object of the dependent clause.)

Once again there is a simple trick to help you decide whether *who* or *whom* is correct. First, mentally isolate the dependent clause. Second, block out the pronoun in question, and then insert *he* and *him* at the appropriate spot in the remaining part of the clause. If *he* sounds better, *who* is the correct case form. If *him* sounds better, *whom* is correct. Now let's apply this trick to the following sentence, in which the clause has been italicized.

> The man *who(m) I met last night* is a well-known art critic.
> I met (he, him) last night.

Clearly, *him* is correct, and therefore *whom* is the proper form.

Pronoun as Subject Complement. In formal writing and speaking, the subject complements should always be in the subjective case.

> It is *I*.
> It is *he* who is most responsible for this company's success.

However, this rule is often ignored in conversation and informal writing.

> It's *me*.
> That's *him* working in the garden.

Comparisons Using "than" or "as . . . as." Sentences that make comparisons and include the expressions *than* or *as . . . as* often provide no direct statement about the second item of comparison. When the second naming word is a pronoun, you may have trouble choosing the proper one.

> She is taller than (they, them).
> The explanation amazed my classmates as much as (I, me).

If such a problem arises, expand the sentence by mentally supplying the omitted material. Next read the sentence with one pronoun and then the other, and see which sounds right.

> She is taller than (they, them) are.
> The explanation amazed my classmates as much as it did (I, me).

Applying this test to our two examples shows that *they* is the right choice for the first sentence and *me* is the right choice for the second one.

Pronouns Preceding Gerunds. A pronoun that precedes a gerund should be in the possessive case.

> I don't understand *his* failing the course.
> I dislike *her* constant bickering.

Use of the possessive case shows that it is the *failing* that you don't understand and the *bickering* that you dislike, rather than the person who failed and the person who bickers. *Failing* and *bickering* are gerunds, or verbal nouns, and are the direct objects of *understand* and *dislike*. We can say that the emphasis is on the actions rather than on the actors.

Now consider the following sentence.

> William caught *them* sneaking out of the house.

Here, the use of the objective rather than the possessive case shows that William caught the persons doing the sneaking rather than the sneaking itself. *Sneaking* is a participle modifying the direct object *them*. The emphasis is on the actors rather than on their actions.

Whenever you have trouble deciding between the objective and the possessive cases in such sentences, check to see whether the emphasis is on the action or on the actor. When the emphasis is on the action, the word ending in -*ing* will be a gerund and will require a possessive; when the emphasis is on the actor, the word ending in -*ing* will be a participle modifying the object—a pronoun in the objective case.

Exercise

Choose the right form of the pronoun for each of the following sentences.

> Joseph and (they, them) are officers in the employees' credit union.
>   (they)

1. Although all three of us worked equally hard, our boss praised Sam more than (we, us).
2. There are several reasons for (me, my) leaving school temporarily.
3. The high cost of gasoline is causing (we, us) commuters a great deal of concern.
4. Mary is the sort of person (who, whom) excels at whatever she does.

5. (We, Us) laboratory workers should form a union.
6. The recruiter said that (we, us) fellows would like working for U.S. Steel.
7. Do you think I'll be able to finish this test as quickly as (they, them)?
8. I regret to announce that Mr. Martinez, with (who, whom) most of you are well acquainted, has decided to retire this summer.
9. High interest rates have forced our neighbors and (we, us) to postpone buying new homes.
10. (Who, Whom) do you wish to see?

Avoiding Errors with Adjectives and Adverbs

As noted before, adjectives modify nouns and noun substitutes, whereas adverbs modify verbs, adjectives, and other adverbs. Ordinarily, adjectives and adverbs cause little trouble when we speak and write. Three kinds of errors do crop up with some frequency, however. These errors are misusing adjectives for adverbs, misusing adverbs for adjectives in subject complements, and using the wrong forms to make comparisons.

Misusing Adjectives for Adverbs. Although almost any adjective can mistakenly be used for the corresponding adverb, the word pairs listed below are most likely to cause problems. For each pair, the adjective comes first.

awful—awfully	good—well
bad—badly	real—really
considerable—considerably	sure—surely

The following faulty sentences illustrate the sorts of errors that can occur.

His explanation for the mistake seems *awful* weak to me. (The adjective *awful* is used mistakenly to modify the adjective *weak.*)

We came *real* close to having a bad accident. (The adjective *real* is used mistakenly to modify the adverb *close.*)

In each of these cases, the adverb is needed. Here are the above sentences rewritten in correct form.

His explanation for the mistake seems *awfully* weak to me.

We came *really* close to having a bad accident. (In this case, *very* might be used in place of *really.*)

Whenever you don't know whether an adjective or adverb is needed, check the word being modified. If the word is a noun or a pronoun, use an adjective. If it is a verb, adjective, or adverb, use an adverb.

Misusing Adverbs as Adjectives in Subject Complements. An adjective used as a subject complement follows a linking verb and describes the subject of the sentence. Linking verbs fall into two groups. The first group includes the different forms of the verb *be (is, are, am, was, were, be, been)*. The second group includes such words as *seem, remain, feel, look, smell, sound,* and *taste*—words that can also function as action verbs.

When used as linking verbs, words in the second group, in effect, function as forms of the verb *be*. They must, therefore, be followed by an adjective rather than an adverb.

Wanda felt *uncertain* about changing her job.

My boss looked *angry.*

When the linking verbs in the second group stand for physical actions, they function as action verbs and must be followed by adverbs.

Wanda felt *uncertainly* in the grass for her lost ring.

My boss looked *angrily* at me.

The verb *feel* presents complications. First, it can be transitive or intransitive; second, it may be used properly with either *good* or *well,* as in the sentences below.

I feel *good* about giving ten dollars to the Red Cross.

I feel *well* today; I was sick yesterday.

The first of these sentences indicates that the speaker is morally and spiritually satisfied. The second sentence means, "I am in good health"; *well* here is an adjective meaning *healthy* rather than the adverb corresponding to the adjective *good. Feel* is also commonly used with *badly,* rather than *bad,* in such sentences as these:

I am feeling *badly* today.

Sheila feels *badly* about her parents' divorce.

Although such usage is acceptable in informal speech, it is incorrect in formal speaking and writing. Use *bad* instead.

Using the Wrong Forms to Make Comparisons. Adjectives and adverbs change form to show comparison. When one thing is compared with another, short adjectives usually add *-er;* longer adjectives and most adverbs add *more* (for example, *high, higher; defective, more defective; slowly, more slowly*). When something is compared with two or more other things, *-est* is added to short adjectives, and *most* is used with longer adjectives as well as with adverbs (*highest, most defective, most slowly*). A few adjectives and adverbs—for example, those shown below—have irregular forms.

Adjectives	**Adverbs**
good—better—best	well—better—best
bad—worse—worst	badly—worse—worst
much—more—most	much—more—most

In making comparisons, a person may mistakenly use a double form, as illustrated by these two faulty sentences.

My lamb chop seems *more tenderer* than yours.

That is the *most stupidest* idea he's ever had!

Here are the sentences written correctly.

My lamb chop seems *more tender* than yours.

That is the *stupidest* idea he's ever had!

A second problem involves using the form for three or more things when only two things are being compared.

Eva is the *smartest* of the two girls.

Although such usage sometimes occurs in informal writing, it is incorrect. Use *-est* and *most* only when you actually compare something with two or more other things, as in these sentences.

Wendell is the *richest* of the three brothers.

Exercise

Choose the proper word for each of the following sentences.

> You have done an (awful, awfully) good job restoring this printing.
> (awfully)

1. If I do (good, well) on this assignment, I'll get a good grade for the course.
2. As the body becomes (healthier, more healthier), the emotions improve.
3. The bouquet of flowers smelled very (fragrant, fragrantly).
4. I feel (good, well) about my performance in the seminar.
5. We are (real, really) pleased to have you working for us.
6. Fred groped (awkward, awkwardly) along the wall until he found the light switch.
7. Killer McGurk clearly proved the (better, best) fighter in that bout.
8. Don't feel (bad, badly) about failing to get that order.
9. This skit is (cleverer, more cleverer) than the one we saw last week.
10. His voice sounded (harsh, harshly) because of his cold.

Avoiding Misplaced Modifiers

A misplaced modifier is a word, phrase, or clause that is improperly separated from the word it modifies. Because of the separation, sentences with this fault often sound awkward, ridiculous, or confusing. Furthermore, they can be downright illogical.

Misplaced modifiers can be corrected by shifting the modifier to a more sensible place in the sentence, generally next to the word modified. Occasionally, small changes in phrasing are also necessary. The following sections illustrate the different kinds of misplaced elements and tell how to correct them.

Misplaced Adjectives and Adverbs. Misplaced adjectives almost always distort the meaning the writer intends to convey. Consider, for example, this incorrect sentence.

> I ate a *cold* dish of cereal for breakfast today.

The sentence conveys the idea that the *dish*, not the *cereal*, was cold. Positioning the adjective next to the noun it modifies clears up the difficulty.

I ate a dish of *cold* cereal for breakfast today.

Although an adjective must be positioned as closely as possible to the word it modifies, an adverb can often be shifted around in a sentence without causing a change in meaning.

Nervously, he glanced upward at the shaky scaffolding.
He glanced *nervously* upward at the shaky scaffolding.
He glanced upward *nervously* at the shaky scaffolding.

Such flexibility is not always possible, though, as the following sentences show.

Just John was picked to MC the first half of the program. (No one else was picked.)
John was *just* picked to MC the first half of the program. (John was recently picked.)
John was picked to MC *just* the first half of the program. (John will not MC the second half of the program.)

Each of these sentences says something logical but quite different, and its correctness or incorrectness depends upon what the writer had in mind.

Often, misplacing an adverb not only alters the intended meaning but also yields one that is highly unlikely, as in the following examples.

I *only* brought ten dollars with me.
John has *almost* eaten the whole pie.

Like adjectives, adverbs should be precisely positioned in any writing you do. Proper positioning yields sentences that accurately reflect the meaning you intend.

I brought *only* ten dollars with me.
John has eaten *almost* the whole pie.

Misplaced Phrases and Clauses. Like single words, phrases and clauses can be misplaced. The following sentences illustrate this kind of fault.

The dealer sold the Mercedes to the banker *with leather seats.* (The banker appears to have leather seats.)

There is a fence behind the house *made of barbed wire.* (The house appears to be made of barbed wire.)

Here are corrected versions of the above sentences.

The dealer sold the Mercedes *with leather seats* to the banker.
Behind the house, there is a fence *made of barbed wire.*

There is a *barbed wire* fence behind the house. (Note the change of wording in this corrected version.)

In attempting to make a correction, don't reposition the modifier so as to create a second erroneous or ridiculous meaning.

I found a photograph in the attic that Father had given to Mother. (Father appears to have given Mother the attic.)

I found a photograph that Father had given to Mother in the attic. (The photograph appears to have been given to Mother in the attic.)

In the attic, I found a photograph that Father had given to Mother. (This version is correct.)

Squinting Modifiers. A squinting modifier is a modifier that is positioned so that the reader can't tell whether it is intended to modify the part of the sentence that precedes it or the part that follows it.

The teacher said *on Monday* she would return our tests.

As this sentence is written, we can't tell whether the teacher made the statement on Monday or intends to return the tests on Monday.

This kind of error can be corrected by repositioning the modifier so that the sentence has just one meaning.

On Monday, the teacher said she would return our tests.
The teacher said she would return our tests *on Monday.*

Exercise

Indicate whether each sentence is correct (C) or contains a misplaced modifier (MM), and correct any faulty sentences.

Dr. Mitty only needed ten minutes to remove the brain tumor.
(MM)   Dr. Mitty needed only ten minutes to remove the brain
tumor.

1. I have made nearly fifty dollars this week.
2. My boss told me after the meeting to stop by his office.
3. Shelley read an interesting article in the *New York Times* about cerebral palsy.
4. The instructor told the students that they would only have to write three papers that term.
5. The man who had entered noisily tripped over the carpet.
6. Clayton uses a pen with a gold cap to write his reports.
7. A stranger came to the house where we lived asking directions.
8. The job took scarcely an hour to complete.
9. I've only watched that TV show three times.
10. The president made some vigorous comments about inflation during the news conference.

Avoiding Dangling Modifiers

A dangling modifier is a phrase or clause that is not clearly and logically related to the word or words it modifies. In most cases, the modifier appears at the beginning of the sentence, although it can also come at the end. Sometimes the error occurs because the sentence fails to specify anything to which the modifier can logically refer. At other times, the modifier is positioned next to the wrong noun or noun substitute.

Looking toward the horizon, a funnel-shaped cloud was stirring up the dust.

Tossing the candy wrapper on the sidewalk, a policeman ticketed me for littering.

The first of these sentences is faulty because the looker is not identified in any way. As the sentence is written, the funnel-shaped cloud seems to be looking toward the horizon. In the second sentence, the modifier is incorrectly positioned next to *policeman,* and thus the policeman appears to have tossed the wrapper away—and then ticketed the writer for doing so! As these examples show, dangling modifiers result in inaccurate and sometimes ludicrous statements. Other examples of dangling constructions are shown below.

Walking to the movies, a cloudburst drenched me. (The *cloudburst* appears to be walking to the movies.)

A string broke *while playing the cello*. (The *string* appears to have been playing the cello.)

Fatigued by the long walk, the lemonade was refreshing. (The *lemonade* appears to have been fatigued by the long walk.)

When nine years old, my mother enrolled in medical school. (*Mother* appears to have enrolled when she was nine years old.)

Dangling modifiers may be corrected in two general ways. First, the modifier may be left as it is and the main part of the sentence rewritten so that it begins with the term actually modified. Second, the dangling part of the sentence can be expanded into a complete dependent clause with both a subject and a verb. With certain sentences, either method will work equally well. With others, one of the two will be preferable, or only one will be feasible. Here are corrected versions of the above set of sentences.

Walking to the movies, *I was drenched by a cloudburst*. (The main part of the sentence has been rewritten.)

While I was walking to the movies, a cloudburst drenched me. (The modifier has been expanded.)

A string broke *while Lana was playing the cello*. (The modifier has been expanded.)

Because I was fatigued by the long walk, the lemonade was refreshing. (The modifier has been expanded.)

Fatigued by the long walk, I found the lemonade refreshing. (The main part of the sentence has been rewritten.)

When I was nine years old, my mother enrolled in medical school. (The modifier has been expanded into a dependent clause with an expressed subject.)

Exercise

Indicate whether each sentence is correct (C) or contains a dangling modifier (DM), and correct any faulty sentences.

Rewritten for the third time, the essay received a much higher grade. (C)

1. From under a rock, a snake appeared suddenly.

2. At the age of ten, my parents took me to Disney World.
3. When born, we know a baby can't care for itself.
4. Standing on the corner, I watched the fire engines race by.
5. Rubber fins are necessary when skin diving.
6. In order to repair this engine, a special wrench is needed.
7. The mercury in the thermometer must be shaken down before taking the patient's temperature.
8. By inserting a nail in a baked potato, the time required to bake it can be reduced.
9. Because of inexperience, Priscilla lost the job.
10. As a secretary, certain responsibilities were delegated to me.

Avoiding Nonparallelism

Nonparallelism results when different grammatical forms are used to express two or more equivalent ideas. This error can occur with elements in pairs or in series as well as with elements following correlative conjunctions.

Elements in Pairs or in Series. Elements in pairs or in series may include words, phrases, and clauses. The following faulty sentences illustrate some of the many possible nonparallel combinations.

We called the meeting *to present* our new vacation policy, *to discuss* last week's accident, and *for reporting* on the status of our XR-1 project. (The phrases are different in form.)

James's outfit was *wrinkled, mismatched,* and *he needed to wash it.* (The adjectives do not parallel the main clause.)

The instructor complimented the student *for taking part in classroom discussions* and *because she had written a superb library research paper.* (The phrase does not parallel the subordinate clause.)

Note the improvement in smoothness and clarity when the sentences are revised so that the ideas in them are expressed by parallel structure.

We called the meeting *to present* our new vacation policy, *to discuss* last week's accident, and *to review* the status of our XR-1 project. (All the phrases begin with infinitives.)

James's outfit was *wrinkled, mismatched,* and *dirty.* (Three adjectives describe the noun *outfit.*)

The instructor complimented the student *for taking part in class-room discussions* and *for writing a superb library research paper.* (The two phrases begin with the preposition *for.*)

Parallelism is achieved in the first and third examples with phrases that are identical in form and in the second example with the same part of speech repeated throughout a series.

Another type of nonparallelism results when items are wrongfully included in a single series.

This estimate includes the cost of constructing the driveway, foundation, building, carpeting, light fixtures, plumbing, and furnace.

This sentence appears to be referring to the cost of constructing the carpeting, light fixtures, plumbing, and furnace. The problem can be corrected by rewriting the sentence so that it includes two series.

The estimate includes the cost of constructing the driveway, foundation, and building, as well as the cost of the carpeting, light fixtures, plumbing, and furnace.

Elements Following Correlative Conjunctions. Correlative conjunctions (p. 401) emphasize the ideas that they link. Nonparallelism occurs when the correlative conjunctions are followed by unlike grammatical elements. Once again, awkwardness and decreased effectiveness are the result. Here are three sentences that show nonparallelism. In each case the conjunctions are underlined once, and the elements that follow them are underlined twice.

He is either sick or he is drunk. (adjective, main clause)

When asked whether she would pledge a sorority, Edith replied that she neither had the time nor the inclination. (verb plus direct object, noun)

The play was both well-acted and had beautiful stage sets. (adjective, verb plus direct object)

Ordinarily, repositioning one of the correlative conjunctions will eliminate the problem. Sometimes, however, one of the grammatical elements must be rewritten. Here are revised versions of the four sentences shown above.

<u>Either</u> <u>he is sick,</u> <u>or</u> <u>he is drunk</u>. (two main clauses)

When asked whether she would pledge a sorority, Edith replied that she had <u>neither</u> <u>the time</u> <u>nor</u> <u>the inclination</u>. (two nouns)

The play was <u>both</u> <u>well-acted</u> <u>and</u> <u>beautifully staged</u>. (two past participles modified by adverbs)

The first two sentences were corrected by repositioning the first correlative conjunction; the last one was corrected by rewriting the part following the second correlative conjunction.

Exercise

Indicate whether each sentence is correct (C) or nonparallel (NP), and correct any faulty sentences.

He was tall, broad-shouldered, and had red hair. (NP)

He was tall, broad-shouldered, and red-headed.

1. Edith could neither recall the purse snatcher's height nor build.
2. The shop was dark, gloomy, and dusty.
3. Uncle Solomon not only flies planes but he also fixes them.
4. Some good reasons for going to college are to gain an education, to learn independent living, and getting a better job.
5. He wishes either to major in industrial hygiene or environmental health.
6. She performs her tasks quickly, willingly, and with accuracy.
7. Professor Jensen was neither a good lecturer nor a careful grader.
8. The novel's chief character peers through a tangle of long hair, slouches along in a shambling gait, and gets into trouble constantly.
9. Joel's problem is not that he earns too little money but spending it foolishly.
10. While working for the health department, I inspected marinas, children's day camps, public water supplies, and various nuisance complaints.

Avoiding Faulty Comparisons

A faulty comparison results when a writer fails to mention one of the items being compared, omits words needed to clarify the relationship, or compares unlike items.

Failure to Mention Both Items. Writers of advertisements often produce sentences like the following:

Snapi-Krak Cereal is a better nutritional value.

Such sentences, however, have no place in formal writing because they fail to specify exactly what their writers mean. With what other cereal or cereals is Snapi-Krak being compared, for example? Mentioning the second term of a comparison eliminates guesswork and ensures that the reader receives the intended message.

Snapi-Krak Cereal is a better nutritional value than any competitive sweetened cereal.

Omission of Clarifying Words. Two words, *other* and *else*, are especially likely to be omittted from comparisons. Doing so results in illogical sentences like these two examples.

Mr. Smothers, my history instructor, is more conscientious than any instructor I have had.
Grigsby has more merit badges than anyone in his scout troop.

The first sentence is illogical because Smothers is one of the writer's instructors and, therefore, cannot be more conscientious than any instructor the writer has had. Similarly, because Grigsby is a member of his scout troop, he cannot have more badges than anyone in the troop. Adding *other* to the first sentence and *else* to the second clears up these logical difficulties.

Mr. Smothers, my history instructor, is more conscientious than any *other* instructor I have had.
Grigsby has more merit badges than anyone *else* in his scout troop.

Another common error of omission is the failure to include the second element of the word pair *as . . . as* in sentences that make double comparisons.

> The house looked just *as* decrepit, if not more decripit than, the barn.

The two comparisons in this sentence are *as decrepit as* and *more decrepit than*. Because of the omission of the second *as*, however, the first comparison reads as follows: "The house looked just as decrepit the barn." Supplying the missing *as* corrects this error and gives us the following sentence:

> The house looked just *as* decrepit *as*, if not more decrepit than, the barn.

Sentences of this sort are often smoother when written so that the second comparison follows the name of the second item.

> The house looked just as decrepit as the barn, if not more decrepit.

Comparison of Unlike Items. To make a sentence of comparison logical, we must compare similar items. We can compare two or more insurance policies, cereals, instructors, Boy Scouts, or buildings; but we can't logically compare Boy Scouts and insurance policies or cereals and buildings. Nevertheless, student writers often unintentionally compare unlike items. The following sentences illustrate this error.

> Beth's *photography* is like *a professional*. (The sentence compares *photography* and *professional*.)
> The electronics *graduates* from Acme College get better job offers than *Apex College*. (The sentence compares *graduates* and *Apex College*.)

This problem can be corrected by changing the sentences so that things of the same kind are compared.

> Beth's photography is like that of a *professional*.
> Beth's photography is like a *professional's*. (The word *photography* is omitted but understood.)

The electronics *graduates* from Acme College get better job offers than do electronics *graduates* from Apex College.

Exercise

Indicate whether the sentence is correct (C) or contains a faulty comparison (FC), and correct any faulty comparisons.

A hardcover novel published today costs much more than one published twenty years ago. (C)

1. Compared with her sister Maxine, Sybil has a better sense of humor.
2. Unlike my job at the restaurant, I received two weeks' vacation when I worked in Grady's Department Store.
3. American business has invested much more heavily in the Far East.
4. This physics class beats anything I'm taking this term.
5. Kimberly works as hard as, if not harder than, the other trainees.
6. The students at Passwell College earn better grades than Flunkwell University.
7. The industry in Port Arthur is much more varied than Crestburg.
8. Suzanne is more talented than any dancer in her ballet troupe.
9. The offset printing process is more widely used than any other printing process.
10. Studies show that children whose parents smoke are much more prone to respiratory ailments than nonsmoking families.

Avoiding Wordiness

Wordiness can result because a paper contains deadwood or gobbledygook. Such papers are long-winded, boring, and often difficult to read.

Deadwood. This term refers to words and phrases that do nothing but take up space and clutter writing. In the following passage, the deadwood is enclosed in brackets.

Responsible parents [of today] do not allow their children [to have] absolute freedom [to do as they please], but neither do they severely restrict their children's activities. For an illustration, let's see how one set of responsible parents, the McVeys, react to their son's request for permission to attend a party at a friend's house.

When he asks [his parents] whether he can attend [the party], his parents say that he may [do so] but tell him that he must be home by a particular time. [By telling their son to be home by a particular time, the parents place restrictions on him.] If he does not [pay] heed [to] the restrictions and comes home late, he is punished: [to punish him,] his parents refuse to let him go out the next time he asks.

Deleting the paragraph's deadwood not only reduces the length by 30 percent—from 135 words to 94—but also increases the clarity of the writing.

The following list includes twenty-eight common wordy expressions and corrections for them.

Expression	Correction
absolutely essential	essential
at this point in time	at this time, now
audible to the ear	audible
combine together	combine
commute back and forth	commute
completely eliminate	eliminate
completely unanimous	unanimous
in the vicinity of	near
in the modern world of today	today
in this day and age	today
in view of the fact that	because, since
large in size	large
personally, I believe	I believe
red in color	red
due to the fact that	because, since
final outcome	outcome
four different times	four times
four in number	four
important essentials	essentials
in my opinion, I believe	I believe
in the event that	if
repeat again	repeat
round in shape	round
true facts	facts
usual custom	custom
very unique	unique
visible to the eye	visible
with the exception of	except for

Gobbledygook. Gobbledygook, a special form of wordiness, is characterized by the unnecessary use of long words and technical terms. Gobbledygook is usually the result of an attempt to make writing sound impressive or to conceal the lack of anything to communicate. Here are some sentences written in gobbledygook. Revised versions in good, plain English are given in parentheses.

> The fish exhibited a 100 percent mortality response. (All of the fish died.)
>
> Implementation of this policy will be effectuated on January 2, 1982. (The policy will take effect on January 2, 1982.)

Technical terms in writing are justified only if (1) they save words *and* (2) the reader knows their meaning. Biologists, for instance, know that *symbiotic relationship* means "a mutually beneficial relationship between two unlike organisms," and so the term poses no problems in technical journals published for biologists. Such a term should not, however, be employed in an article aimed at nontechnical readers unless it is clearly defined the first time it is used. As a general rule, technical terms should be used very sparingly in articles for general audiences.

Exercise

Indicate whether each sentence is correct (C) or wordy (W), and correct the wordy sentences.

> It is essential that we completely eliminate this problem within a time span of two days. (W) We must eliminate this problem within two days.

1. As a rule, I am usually up and about by 7 A.M. in the morning.
2. We have been made cognizant of the fact that the experiment will be terminated in the near future.
3. After crawling over a fence and through a tunnel, the boys found themselves in a small garden.
4. At this point in time, I am planning to pursue a major in the field of environmental health.
5. Fillmore's proposal that a committee study the proposed merger was adopted unanimously.
6. Last summer I engaged in the repair of railroad cars.

7. Illumination is required to be extinguished on the premises on termination of daily activities.
8. Disturbed by the screaming jets, the animals fled into the wilderness surrounding the airport.
9. At the present time, I am preparing for a business trip that I will soon be going to make to Buffalo.
10. The sarcastic remarks that Linda delivered had the effect of causing everyone to become quite angry.

Punctuation and Mechanics

Apostrophes

Apostrophes (') are used to show possession; to mark contractions (the omission of letters or numbers in a word or date); and to form plurals of letters, figures, symbols, and words used in a special sense.

Possession. Ordinarily, possessive apostrophes show ownership (*John's book*). Sometimes, however, they are used to identify (*Shakespeare's plays*) or to indicate an extent of time or space (*one day's time, one mile's distance*).

Possessive apostrophes are used with nouns as well as with pronouns like *anyone, no one, everyone, someone, each other,* and *one another.* They way possession is shown depends upon how the word ends. If the noun is singular or if it is plural and does not end in an *s,* add an apostrophe followed by an *s.*

> My *friend's* car was stolen. (possessive of the singular noun *friend*)
>
> The *children's* toys were stolen. (possessive of the plural noun *children*)
>
> *Anyone's* guess is as good as mine. (possessive of the singular pronoun *anyone*)
>
> The *boss's* orders must be obeyed. (possessive of the singular noun *boss*)

Although you will often see such forms as *boss'* used as singular possessives, this usage is no longer considered correct.

Plural nouns that end in an *s* form the possessive by adding only an apostrophe at the end.

> The *workers'* lockers were moved. (possessive of the plural noun *workers*)

At times you may wish to let your reader know that two or more people own something jointly. To do so, use the possessive apostrophe with the last-named person only. At other times, you may want to indicate individual ownership. In this case, use an apostrophe with each name.

> Ben and *Martin's* project took them a month to complete. (joint possession)
> *Madeline's* and *Mary's* notebooks were lying on the laboratory bench. (individual possession)

Some businesses and other organizations with names that show possession write the names without the apostrophe.

> The Veterans Administration
> Citizens Bank and Trust Company

Do not, however, do this in your own writing. Use an apostrophe whenever the name of a company or organization calls for one.

Although the pronouns *his, hers, whose, its, ours, yours,* and *theirs,* show possession, a possessive apostrophe is never used with them.

> This car is *hers;* the other car is *theirs.* (No apostrophe is needed.)

Contractions. Contractions of words or numbers are formed by omitting one or more letters or numerals. The omission is shown by placing an apostrophe exactly where the deletion is made.

> *Isn't* our report longer than theirs? (contraction of *is not*)
> *I'm* a University of Delaware graduate, class of '76. (contraction of *I am* and *1976*)

The contraction *it's,* meaning *it is* or *it has,* presents a special problem, as it can be confused with the possessive pronoun *its,* which has no apostrophe. However, there's an easy way to tell whether you should use an apostrophe with an *its* you've written. Just expand the *its* to *it is* or, if necessary, to *it has,* and see whether the sentence still makes sense. If it does, the *its* is a contraction and needs the apostrophe. If the sentence becomes nonsense, the *its* is a possessive pronoun, and no apostrophe should be used.

Plurals. For the sake of clarity, the plurals of letters, numbers, symbols, and words used in a special sense—that is, singled out for particular attention rather than used for their meaning—are formed by adding an apostrophe and an *s*. In addition, an apostrophe is often used to form the plurals of abbreviations.

Your *i*'s look like *e*'s and your *a*'s look like *o*'s. (plurals of letters)

Your 2's and 3's should be spelled out. (plurals of numbers)

Your &'s should be written as *and*'s. (plural of symbol and word referred to as word)

The furnace has a capacity of 250,00 *Btu*'s. (plural of abbreviation)

When there is no danger of confusion, however, an *s* alone is sufficient.

This turbine was installed in the *1960s.*

The president gave a reception for the *VIPs.*

Exercise

Supply apostrophes where necessary to correct the following sentences.

Arent you glad that they invited us to the party? (Aren't)

1. Both meetings will be held at Jake and Charlottes house.
2. When transcribing what you hear, you must be careful to distinguish the *ors* from the *oars.*
3. The Browns relatives from the Twin Cities are visiting them for two weeks.
4. When everybodys special, nobody is special.
5. Susans and Ryans safety suggestions won company awards.
6. I always do my laundry at Burtons Washeteria.
7. The algebraic equation included two πs and three Δs.
8. Its apparent that my car is on its last legs—or should I say wheels?
9. For pitys sake, havent you heard that expression before?
10. All persons viewpoints will be aired at the meeting.

Commas to Separate

Commas (,) are used more often than any other mark of punctuation. One important use of commas is to separate one sentence element from another. The elements thus separated include main clauses, items in a series, coordinate adjectives, and introductory words and word groups.

Main Clauses. When two independent clauses are connected by a coordinating conjunction (*and, but, or, for, yet*, or *so*), the conjunction should be preceded by a comma.

> The side of the heater cracked, *and* Elise stood staring glumly at the ruined experiment.
>
> Alvin is majoring in electronics, *but* his sister is studying dental hygiene.

Writers sometimes omit commas between short independent clauses, but it is safer to avoid this practice because the reader may be at least temporarily confused.

> No one spoke *but* the instructor appeared surprised.
>
> No one spoke but the instructor . . . (initial confusion)
>
> No one spoke, but the instructor appeared surprised. (confusion eliminated by comma)

Do not mistake a simple sentence with a compound predicate for a compound sentence.

> Harry washed the dishes, and Doreen sliced the carrots. (compound sentence)
>
> Harry washed the dishes and sliced the carrots. (simple sentence with compound predicate)

Items in a Series. A series consists of three or more words, phrases, or clauses grouped together. When words, phrases, or clauses are in a series, these items are separated by commas.

> *Tom, Manuel*, and *Roberta* earned two-year degrees in television servicing. (words in series)
>
> He walked *through the door, down the hall*, and *into the engine room*. (phrases in series)
>
> The employment director said *that his company had openings for chemists, that it was actively recruiting*, and *that a representative would visit the school soon*. (clauses in series)

When a coordinating conjunction comes between each successive pair of items, no commas are used.

> Feuding and fussing and fighting are our pastimes.

Coordinate Adjectives. Commas are used to separate coordinate adjectives—adjectives that modify the same noun or noun substitute and that can be reversed without changing the meaning of the sentence.

> Sam was a sympathetic, intelligent listener.
> Sam was an intelligent, sympathetic listener.

When the word order cannot be reversed, the adjectives are not coordinate, and no comma is used to separate them.

> Many advanced models of computers were on display.

In this sentence, *many* and *advanced* cannot be reversed without making the sentence meaningless.

A second way of testing whether or not adjectives are coordinate is mentally to insert an *and* between them. If the meaning does not change when *and* is inserted, the adjectives are coordinate, and a comma is used to separate them.

Introductory Elements. Introductory elements separated from the rest of the sentence by commas include words, phrases, and clauses. When an introductory element is very short and there is no chance the sentence will be misread, the comma can be omitted.

> *Soon* I will retire.
> *Below*, the river threaded its way through the valley.
> *By 1982* we expect to double our sales.
> *In all*, the task was very difficult.

Omitting the commas from the second and the fourth sentences might temporarily confuse the reader.

With longer introductory elements, commas should always be used.

After changing the oil and checking the tire pressure, Albert started his journey.

Whenever she finished a laboratory report, Pamela treated herself to a sundae.

Exercise

Supply commas as necessary to correct the following sentences. If a sentence is correct, write a C.

In all the directions were very confusing. (In all, . . .)

1. Get your work done or I'll have to fire you.
2. Few short men ever become movie idols.
3. The rewards of hard work include financial security peace of mind and self-respect.
4. To win Mae practiced her violin three hours each day.
5. Wilma expected to attend the meeting but fell ill the day it was held.
6. In April the company will move to Tennessee.
7. When she finishes writing the report Mary will start typing it.
8. Ralph is a careful accurate worker.
9. On Saturday I'll buy Dad a birthday gift.
10. Moe jumped violently when he heard the sharp high scream.

Commas to Set Off

A second important use of commas is to set off sentence elements. These elements include nonrestrictive expressions, geographical items, dates, and various kinds of parenthetical expressions.

Nonrestrictive Expressions. A nonrestrictive expression provides added information about the persons, places, and things that it modifies. This additional information, however, is *not essential* to the meaning of the sentence. A nonrestrictive expression is set off by commas from the rest of the sentence in which it appears. Here are two sentences that include nonrestrictive expressions.

The inspector, *engrossed in her work*, did not hear the fire alarm. (The nonrestrictive phrase adds information about the inspector.)

> Dr. McKay, *our laboratory director,* will address the seminar. (The nonrestrictive appositive adds information about Dr. McKay.)

The nonrestrictive expressions in these sentences are not essential to the sentences' basic meanings. If we delete the phrase *engrossed in her work* from the first example, we still know that the inspector didn't hear the alarm. Similarly, removing the appositive from the second example does not interfere with the main idea of the sentence—that Dr. McKay will address the seminar.

Restrictive expressions—which are *not* set off with commas—single out the person, place, or thing that they modify from other persons, places, or things in the same cateogry, thus *restricting,* or limiting, the noun modified. Unlike their nonrestrictive counterparts, they are almost always essential to the main idea of the sentence. When a restrictive expression is removed, the meaning of the sentence changes, and the sentence that results may make no sense.

> Anyone *running for governor in this state* must file a report on his campaign contributions within one month after the election.

Omitting the italicized material in this sentence changes its meaning entirely. The sentence now makes the absurd statement that everyone, not just candidates for governor, must report campaign contributions. Applying this meaning test will tell you whether an expression needs to be set off with commas.

Geographical Items and Dates. Geographical items include mailing addresses and locations. The sentences below show where commas are used.

> I live at 2497 Jarrett Court, Westbury, New York 11590.
> Skiing at Aspen, Colorado, is my idea of a perfect way to spend a winter vacation.

Note that although commas appear after the street designation and the city and state, they are not used to set off zip codes.

Dates are punctuated by placing commas after the day of the week, the day of the month, and the year.

On Monday, June 9, 1975, I began working for the Bennett Corporation.

With dates that omit the day of the month, you have the option of
using or not using commas.

In April, 1865, the Civil War ended.
In April 1865 the Civil War ended.

Although both of these examples are correct, the second is preferable.

Parenthetical Expressions. A parenthetical expression is a word
or word group that is added to a sentence to link it to the preceding
sentence, gain emphasis, or clarify the meaning in some way. Like a
nonrestrictive expression, it can be omitted without affecting the
basic meaning of the sentence. Parenthetical expressions include:

incidental, interrupting, and clarifying phrases
names and titles of persons being addressed directly
degree titles and abbreviations of junior and senior following a
person's name
echo questions
adjectives that follow, rather than precede, the words they modify

The following sentences illustrate the use of commas to set off such
expressions.

Leo's whole life seems taken up with sports. Randy, *on the other
hand*, is totally uninterested in athletics. (phrase linking a sentence to the one before it)
He knows, *of course*, that his decision to become a free-lance writer
may cause him financial hardship. (phrase adding emphasis)
Cake, *not pie*, is my favorite dessert. (a clarifying phrase)
You know, *Sally*, that your attitude is hurting your chances for
promotion. (name of person being addressed directly)
Marcia Mendel, *M.D.*, is tonight's lecturer. (degree title following
name)
Tom realizes, *doesn't he*, that his research report is due this Friday?
(echo question)
The kittens, *playful and energetic*, chased each other wildly
through the house. (adjectives out of usual order)

Exercise

Supply commas as necessary to correct the following sentences. If a sentence is correct, write a C.

> I don't believe dummy that you'll ever become a ventriloquist. (I don't believe, dummy, . . .)

1. This company it is clear never intends to install pollution-control equipment.
2. His wife whom he first met on vacation works as an air-traffic controller.
3. Sherry Davis 230 Archer Boulevard Morristown Oklahoma won the grand prize.
4. The slacks not the sweaters are on sale.
5. Look Senator at these horrible figures on inflation.
6. Jens Hansen our new classmate from Norway is an expert skier.
7. Any mother who mistreats her children should lose custody of them.
8. The boss told you didn't he that you're being considered for promotion?
9. On Sunday June 15 1975 Shirley received her degree in civil engineering.
10. John Asterbilt Sr. made ten million dollars during his lifetime; John Asterbilt Jr. spent it all in two years.

Semicolons

The semicolon (;) is used to mark especially pronounced pauses in the flow of sentences. Its chief use is to separate main clauses. These clauses may have no connecting word, or they may be connected with a conjunctive adverb. In addition, semicolons are used to separate two or more series of items, items containing commas in a single series, and main clauses that contain commas and are separated by a coordinating conjunction.

Main Clauses. The following sentences illustrate the use of semicolons to separate main clauses.

> John apologized for being late; he said he had been caught in rush hour traffic. (No conjunctive adverb is used.)

Noreen didn't want to be chairperson; *however,* she agreed to accept the position. (A semicolon precedes the conjunctive adverb.)

Every conjunctive adverb except *then* is ordinarily followed by a comma.

Two or More Series of Items. With sentences that contain two or more series of items, semicolons are often used to mark the end of each series and thus reduce the chances of misreading.

The table was cluttered with pens and pencils; newspapers, magazines, and books; and plates, cups, and saucers.

Because of the semicolons, this sentence is clearer and easier to read than it would be if only commas were used.

Comma-Containing Items Within a Series. When one or more of the items within a series contains commas, the items are preferably separated by semicolons rather than commas.

The judges of the Homecoming floats included Jerome Kirk, Dean of Men; Elwood Barnes, the basketball coach; and Elsie La Londe, the president of the student council.

Again, using semicolons improves clarity and reduces the chance that the sentence will be misread.

Independent Clauses with Commas and a Coordinating Conjunction. Ordinarily, a comma is used to separate independent clauses joined by a coordinating conjunction. However, when one or both of the clauses contain commas, a semicolon will provide clearer separation.

The short, serious student wanted to explain the experiment; but the visitor, nervous and impatient, would not stay to listen.

Using the semicolon in a sentence like the one above makes it easier to see the two main divisions.

Exercise

Supply semicolons wherever they are necessary or desirable in the following sentences. If a sentence is correct, write a C.

> The meeting will start in thirty minutes meanwhile, I'll read this magazine. (The meeting will start in thirty minutes; meanwhile, I'll . . .)

1. The president of the college did not oppose vocational education, on the contrary, he strongly supported it.
2. For recreation the Smiths golf, hike, and play tennis, the Browns swim, water ski, and fish, and the Greens attend plays, movies, and concerts.
3. He wanted employees who were completely loyal, totally dedicated, and outstandingly brilliant, and so, after trying many humans, he turned to computerized robots.
4. The scouts, tired and discouraged after two days of rain, asked to go home, and the scoutmaster, yielding to their pleas, cut the trip short.
5. Noreen didn't want to be discussion leader, however, she agreed to accept the task.
6. The table closet contained carpenters' saws, hammers, and planes, draftmen's T-squares, drawing boards, and triangles, and machinists' calipers and micrometers.
7. Nearly all our graduates find jobs, for example, 93 percent of this year's printing technology students have found newspaper jobs.
8. Pollution is not new to the human race it destroyed the Sumerian civilization and plagued the Romans.
9. When I was a child, my favorite comedians were Curly, Larry, and Moe of the Three Stooges, Spanky, Alfalfa, and Buckwheat of Our Gang, and the three Marx Brothers, Groucho, Chico, and Harpo.
10. He refused to write a term paper, and therefore he failed the course.

Colons, Dashes, Parentheses, and Brackets

Like commas and semicolons, colons, dashes, parentheses, and brackets are used to separate and enclose: they clarify the relationships among the various parts of the sentences in which they appear.

Colons. One important use of the colon (:) is to introduce appositives, formal lists, and formal explanations when they are preceded by material that could serve as complete sentences.

All her efforts were directed toward one goal: earning a degree in civil engineering. (appositive)

Four occupations were represented by those in attendance: electrician, carpenter, plumber, and sheet-metal worker. (formal list)

To determine if the product is suitable, do as follows: (1) select random samples of six-inch angle irons, (2) mount each sample in the testing machine, and (3) test for deformation tensile strength. (formal explanation)

Unless the introductory material can stand alone, *don't* use a colon. The following sentence is incorrect because of the colon.

My courses for next semester include: algebra, economics, English, and history.

Here's how the sentence should look.

My courses for next semester include algebra, economics, English, and history.

A colon is often used instead of a comma to introduce a long, formal quotation, particularly if the quotation consists of more than one sentence.

The candidate arose, faced his audience, and said: "Ladies and gentlemen, we are living in troubled times. Millions of Americans are out of work, food prices are soaring, and we face critical fuel shortages. The present administration is doing nothing to solve these problems. We need new leadership."

With long quotations, the material preceding the colon may be a complete sentence or just part of one, as in our example.

Colons are also used to separate hours from minutes, titles of publications from subtitles, salutations of business letters from the body of the letters, and numbers indicating ratios.

The second show begins at 9:15 P.M. (The colon separates the hour from the minutes.)

Our textbook for this course is entitled *The Short Story: Fiction in Transition.* (The colon separates the title from the subtitle.)

To make French dressing, start by combining salad oil and wine vinegar in a 4:1 ratio. (The colon separates numbers indicating a ratio.)

Dashes. Like colons, dashes (—) are used to set off appositives, lists, and explanations, but they are employed in less formal writing.

> Only one person could be guilty of such an oversight—William! (appositive)
>
> The workroom was very sparsely equipped—a workbench, a small tool cabinet, and a single lathe. (list)
>
> There's only one plausible reason why your level has disappeared—it was stolen. (explanation)

A sudden break in thought is generally set off by two dashes—one preceding the interrupting material and the other following it.

> Her TV set—she bought it just last month, didn't she?—is at the repair shop.

Dashes also set off parenthetical expressions that contain commas.

> The speaker—poised, articulate, and well informed—made a pleasing impression on her audience.

Finally, dashes are used to set off comments following a list.

> A set of crescent wrenches, pliers, and a screwdriver—these are what he bought.

In typing, a dash consists of two hyphens, one after the other with no space between them and the words that come before and after. The dash emphasizes the material it sets off.

Parentheses. Parentheses—( )—are used to enclose numbers or letters that accompany formal listings in sentences and to set off examples and other supplementary information or comments that would interrupt the main sequence of ideas.

> Each paper should contain (1) an introduction, (2) a number of paragraphs developing the thesis sentence, and (3) a conclusion.
>
> Some vocational programs (auto service, for example) are filled months before the new semester begins.

John's first promotion came as a surprise. (He had been with the company only three months.) But his second promotion left all of us astounded.

James Watt (1736–1819) helped pioneer the development of the steam engine.

Parentheses de-emphasize rather than emphasize the material they enclose. If the material in parentheses appears within a given sentence, it is not necessary to use an initial capital letter or a period even if the parenthetical material is itself a complete sentence.

The development of nuclear energy (one cannot foresee where it will lead) is a controversial issue today.

If, however, the material in parentheses takes the form of a separate sentence, punctuate it as you would a sentence. In such sentences, the closing parenthesis follows the final punctuation.

John's first promotion came as a surprise. (He had been with the company only three months.)

If the material in parentheses appears at the end of a sentence, the closing parenthesis precedes the final punctuation.

The development of nuclear energy is a controversial issue today (one cannot foresee where it will lead).

Brackets. Brackets—[ ]—are used with quoted material to enclose words or phrases that have been added or changed for clarity. They are also used with the word *sic* (Latin for "thus") to identify errors in the material being quoted.

"The founder of the school [Woodbridge Ferris] also served as governor of Michigan." (The bracketed name is added to the original.)

"[Margaret Mead's] years of study have made her one of the foremost experts on culturally determined behavior." (The bracketed name replaces "her" in the original.)

"The accused man dennied [*sic*] all charges." (The word "denied" is misspelled in the original.)

As the third sentence illustrates, when a writer notices an error in material being quoted, he or she inserts the word *sic*, in brackets, directly after the error. The reader who sees this knows that the error was not made by the writer but is being accurately reproduced from the original.

Exercise

Supply colons, dashes, parentheses, and brackets wherever they are necessary. If a sentence is correct, write a C.

> Representative Guy Emmett Democrat, Texas announced yesterday that he would not seek reelection. (Representative Guy Emmett (Democrat, Texas) . . .

1. My bus leaves for Chicago at 850 A.M.
2. The procedure for taking a blood sample requires 1 a sterile syringe, 2 a sterile cotton ball, 3 alcohol, and 4 a tourniquet.
3. He ate just four things all week hot dogs, hamburgers, peanut butter sandwiches, and chocolate cake.
4. Our own findings see Table 3 clearly support the state's conclusions that this lake is contaminated.
5. Mary writes textbooks for two reasons to gain professional recognition and to make money.
6. The report concluded with this sentence "These statistics clearly show that drunk driving is the principle *sic* cause of auto accidents."
7. Whitman's outburst I never dreamed he was capable of such anger stunned everyone in the office.
8. Our school has a 4 2 1 ratio of technical, business, and liberal arts students.
9. Rubber aprons, chemical workers' goggles, and hard hats all these are needed for this job.
10. "His Charles Darwin's book touched off a religious controversy that hasn't yet died," said the review.

Periods, Question Marks, and Exclamation Points

Periods, question marks, and exclamation points serve primarily to mark the ends of sentences, and thus they are sometimes called *end marks*. In addition, periods may indicate abbreviations and omissions and are used in certain numerical designations, whereas question marks are used to indicate uncertainty.

Periods. Periods (.) are used to end sentences which state facts, make requests that are not in the form of questions, give instructions, or ask indirect questions—that is, questions that have been rephrased to form part of a statement.

> Monty works for Northgate Tool and Die Company. (Sentence states fact.)
>
> Please lend me your protractor. (Sentence makes request.)
>
> Do your assignment before you leave. (Sentence gives instruction.)
>
> She asked whether I had attended last wek's sales presentation. (Sentence includes indirect question as part of a statement.)

Periods also follow common abbreviations as well as a person's initials.

Mr.	B.C.	Ave.
Mrs.	A.D.	Inc.
Ms.	A.M.	etc.
Dr.	P.M.	i.e.
Jr.	c.o.d.	vs.

> Harvey H. Borden, Jr., will address the Rotary Club this evening.

Today, periods are often omitted after abbreviations for the names of organizations or governmental agencies. Some abbreviations commonly written without periods are these:

AFL-CIO	TVA	FHA
ROTC	IBM	PTA
FDIC	CBS	NAACP
VA	FBI	CIA

If you don't know whether a particular abbreviation should be written with periods, check an up-to-date collegiate dictionary.

Periods are used to precede decimal fractions and to separate numeral designations for dollars and cents.

0.39 percent	$6.29
4.39 percent	$0.76

Question Marks. A question mark (?) is used after a whole sentence or a part of a sentence that asks a direct question (one that repeats the exact words of the person who asked it).

> Will you show me how to focus this laser beam? (The whole sentence asks a question.)
>
> Have you checked the oil? cleaned the windshield? replenished the battery water? (A series of sentence parts asks questions.)
>
> Mrs. Kendall—wasn't she your teacher once?—has retired after thirty-five years of service. (An interrupting clause between dashes asks a question.)
>
> The inspector asked, "Why is the guard missing from this gear box?" (A quotation asks a question.)

Exclamation Points. Exclamation points (!) are used after words, phrases, or clauses to denote a high degree of fear, anger, joy, or other emotion or to express an emphatic command.

> William! It's been years since I've seen you!
>
> Walter! Get back to work immediately!
>
> Ouch! That hurts!

Don't overuse the exclamation point. If you do, it will soon fail to produce the intended effect.

Exercise

Supply periods, question marks, or exclamation points wherever they are necessary. If a sentence is correct, write a C.

> Our new neighbor, Dr Jerome Beardsley, Sr, moved here from North Carolina. (. . . Dr. Jerome Beardsley, Sr., moved . . .)

1. If your temperature is 1002° F., you are running a low fever.
2. When are you scheduled to begin the project.
3. The president asked her assistant which of the district sales managers was most qualified for the position of sales director.
4. Dr. Winkler asked, "What do you plan to do this summer?"
5. Please don't dangle your arm out the car window.
6. For the love of Pete, watch what you're doing there.
7. Stepanski's Grocery Shoppe—didn't it begin as a meat market—is moving to its new location next week.

8. The program begins at 9 PM and lasts about an hour.
9. This year, the budget for the VA was increased just 123 percent—scarcely any gain at all.
10. While you were in New York, did you see the Statue of Liberty visit Radio City Music Hall take a carriage ride through Central Park.

Quotation Marks

Quotation marks (" ") are used to set off direct quotations, titles of shorter works and subdivisions of books, and to identify expressions used in a special sense.

Direct Quotations. A direct quotation repeats a person's written or spoken comments in his or her own words.

> The placement director announced, "The Aeolian Heating and Air Conditioning Corporation's recruiter will be on campus this Thursday." (spoken comments)
>
> "Coffee prices are expected to increase by ten cents a pound in the next three months," the first sentence of the newspaper story said.
>
> Sally described her job as "a total bust."

As these examples show, the commas that come before direct quotations are positioned outside the quotation marks. Commas and periods that come at the end of direct quotations are positioned inside the marks. Quotations that are sentence fragments are not preceded by commas.

Titles of Shorter Works and Subdivisions of Books. Besides setting off written and spoken quotations, quotation marks also are used to denote titles of

magazine articles	chapters and sections of books
essays	short poems
short stories	songs
other short pieces of prose	television and radio programs

> The article was titled "Results of Testing Willow Creek for Coliform Organisms." (article)

> Next week we will discuss Chapter 8, "Letters and Memoran-
> dums." (chapter of a book)

With titles, as with direct quotations, commas and periods that
directly follow the quoted material are positioned inside the quotation marks. Commas that precede the quoted material are outside the
quotation marks.

Expressions Used in a Special Sense. Words, letters, numerals,
and symbols used in a special sense—that is, singled out for particular
attention rather than used for their meaning—are sometimes set off
by quotation marks.

> "Bonnets," "valves," and "lifts" are British terms for car hoods,
> radio tubes, and elevators.
> It's hard to tell whether this letter is a "G" or a "C."

Often, however, such expressions are printed in italics (see page 490).
Note that the commas and periods in our examples again come
inside the quotation marks.

Quotation Marks Within Quotation Marks. Occasionally, a
direct quotation or the title of a shorter work will occur within a
direct quotation. In such cases the inner quotation or title is set off
with single quotation marks (' ').

> The witness told the court, "I heard the defendant say, 'Let's rob
> Peterson's Party Store.' "

Notice that the period and the comma at the end of these double
quotations come ahead of both the single mark and the double mark.

**Quotation Marks That Accompany Semicolons, Colons, Excla-
mation Points, and Question Marks.** Unlike periods and commas,
semicolons and colons that come at the end of quoted material are
always placed outside the quotation marks.

> He said, "I want to study drafting"; however, his placement test
> indicated a low aptitude for that field.

A question mark or exclamation point may be placed either inside or outside the quotation marks, depending upon what it applies to. If, for example, only the quoted part of a sentence asks a question, the question mark goes inside the quotation marks. If the entire sentence, but not the quoted material, asks a question, the question mark goes outside the quotation marks. If the entire sentence asks one question and the quoted material asks another, then the question mark goes inside the quotation marks.

> He asked, "When will your laboratory project be finished?" (The quoted material, but not the whole sentence, asks the question.)
>
> Why did Irma suddenly announce, "I've quit my job"? (The whole sentence, not the quoted material, asks the question.)
>
> Where did he get the nerve to ask, "How much money did you earn last year?" (The whole sentence and the quoted material ask separate questions.)

Exercise

Supply properly positioned quotation marks wherever they are necessary. If a sentence is correct, write a C.

> Tomorrow, we'll discuss the article The ABC's of Supply-Side Economics. (. . . article "The ABC's of Supply-Side Economics.")

1. Harry called the following my favorite English authors: Jane Austen, Charles Dickens, and George Orwell.
2. If you say I told you so one more time, I'll scream, Penny snapped angrily.
3. The interviewer asked the applicant, Why do you want to work for this company?
4. Sidney told everyone, I spend two hours each night studying this course; nevertheless, he could never answer his instructor's questions.
5. In Baskerville type, the bottom loop of the g is not completely closed.
6. In the Eastern part of the country, a carbonated drink is called a soda.
7. What made my father ask me, Don't you think you're acting awfully foolish?
8. The 7 in my house number isn't lined up with the other numbers.
9. Who said, A little inaccuracy sometimes saves tons of explanation?
10. Elsie called the article on genetic engineering a scientific bombshell.

Hyphens

Hyphens (-) are used to separate compound adjectives and nouns, two-word numbers and fractions, numerals followed by units of measurement, and certain prefixes and suffixes from the words with which they appear. In addition, they are employed to prevent misreadings and awkward combinations of letters or syllables.

Compound Adjectives and Nouns. Perhaps the most widespread use of hyphens is to join separate words that function as single adjectives and come before nouns. The use of these hyphenated, or compound, adjectives is very common, allowing a wide range of ideas to be expressed. Two typical examples of hyphenated adjectives are:

> The *deep-blue* sea was beautiful.
> The *cane-shaped* tube measures both vacuum and pressure.

Note that the meaning of the first sentence would change if the hyphen were replaced with a comma or simply omitted. With the hyphen, we are referring to a sea that is deep blue in color. If the hyphen were replaced with a comma, we would be referring to a sea that is deep and blue. With neither a hyphen nor a comma, there would be no way to tell which is deep, the color blue or the sea itself.

When the first word of the compound is an adverb ending in *-ly* or when the compound adjective comes after the noun it modifies, the hyphen is omitted.

> The *deeply* embarrassed man apologized for his comment.
> The sea was *deep blue*.

In a series of two or more compound adjectives that all have the same term following the hyphen, the term following the hyphen need not be repeated throughout the series. It is often briefer and smoother to use the term only at the end of the series. However, the hyphens preceding omitted parts are retained:

> Several *six-* and *eight-cylinder* engines were overhauled yesterday.

Hyphenated nouns include such expressions as the following:

editor-in-chief	go-between
father-in-law	jack-of-all-trades

Here is a sentence with hyphenated nouns.

Denton is *editor-in-chief* of the largest newspaper in this state.

Two-Word Numbers, Fractions, and Numerals with Units of Measurement. Hyphens are used in two-word numbers from twenty-one to ninety-nine and in fractions when these are written out.

The company's *seventy-eighth* year saw its sales exceed $800 million.
Three-fourths of the class will receive Cs.

Similarly, hyphens are used to separate numerals followed by units of measurement.

The *40-hour* workweek was the exception, not the rule, fifty years ago.

Prefixes and Suffixes. Prefixes and suffixes are words or a group of letters attached to words to expand or change their meaning. A prefix is attached at the beginning of the word; a suffix is attached at the end of the word. Although most prefixes are not hyphenated, the prefixes *self-* and *all-* and the suffix *-elect* are set off with hyphens, as is the prefix *ex-* when it precedes a noun.

The founder of this magazine is a *self-made* woman.
The timing of this announcement is *all-important*.
Norbert is *president-elect* of our club.
The *ex-governor* gave a speech.

A prefix used before a term that begins with a capital letter is always hyphenated.

The *anti-CIA* speaker received little applause.

Preventing Misreadings and Awkward Combinations of Letters and Syllables. Hyphens are also used to prevent misreadings of certain words that would look like other words if they were not hyphenated, as well as to prevent awkward combinations of letters or syllables between some prefixes and suffixes and their core words.

> The *un-ionized* salt precipitates from the solution. (Without the hyphen, the word, meaning *not ionized,* might be misread as *unionized.*)
>
> The worker *re-covered* the exposed pipe. (Without the hyphen, the word might be misread as *recovered.*)
>
> The committee is determined to *de-emphasize* sports at Franklin Pierce High School. (The hyphen prevents the awkward repetition of the letter *e* in *de-emphasize.*)

Exercise

Supply hyphens wherever they are necessary. If a sentence is correct, write a C.

> Three fourths of the directors missed the last meeting of the farmers' coop. (Three-fourths . . . co-op.)

1. The villain tried to whisper sweet nothings into the shelllike ear of the pure young maiden.
2. Wouldn't it be nice to have a six or seven figure income?
3. About one third of our work force will lose their jobs if this recession continues.
4. The transCanadian pipeline brings Alaskan oil to the United States.
5. The president's antiinflationary measures seem woefully inadequate to me.
6. I like the pea green blouse better than the one that's navy blue.
7. Within the next month, we will start offering 90 day guarantees on our Fasklik line of cameras.
8. Mr. Gonzales, our chairman elect, has served on the board of directors for twelve years.
9. This drawing is a recreation of the scene of the accident.
10. At the age of twenty three, Sidney was graduated from MIT with a doctorate in physics.
11. Our new neighbor, an excolonel in the army, feels that this country's military budget is inadequate.
12. Maxwell is truly a jack of all trades.

Capitalization

The first letter of any sentence, including any sentence that appears as a quotation within another sentence, is always capitalized, as is the pronoun *I*, both by itself and in contractions.

He said, "When *I* finish this job, *I*'ll watch television with you."

In addition, capitals are used with proper nouns, adjectives derived from proper nouns, certain abbreviations, personal titles preceding names, and titles of literary and artistic works.

Proper Nouns. Proper nouns refer to one particular person, group of persons, place, or thing, and their first letters are always capitalized. They includes names of the following:

persons
organizations and institutions
racial, national, political, and religious groups (but not *black* and
   white)
countries, states, cities, streets, and buildings
geographical locations and geographical features
days, holidays, and months (but not seasons)
trademarked products (and slogans that are trademarked)
languages
ships, trains, and airplanes
academic and professional degree designations and their abbreviations

The following sentences illustrate the capitalization of proper nouns.

He attends *Ferris State College*, a college that has pioneered in
   offering health-related programs.
Lolita Martinez, our class valedictorian, was born in *Matamoras,
   Mexico*.
Next *Monday, June 5*, I begin work as a supervisor for the *Bradley
   Company*.
To protect the food, she covered it with *Reynolds Wrap* aluminum
   foil.
I have a *Bachelor of Science* degree, and my brother is a *C.P.A.*

Terms such as "building," "street," and "company" are not capitalized unless they form part of a proper name. Thus, in the first sentence in the preceding list, "college" is not capitalized when it is written by itself. Similarly, the names of nonlanguage courses are not capitalized unless they are followed by a course description or begin a sentence.

> This term, Geology 101 is my worst course, but algebra is causing me no difficulty at all.

Proper Adjectives. Adjectives created from proper nouns are called proper adjectives. Like the nouns themselves, they should be capitalized.

> Lolita Martinez, our class valedictorian is of *Mexican* ancestry. (*Mexican* is derived from the proper noun *Mexico*.)

Certain usages of proper nouns and words derived from them have become so well established that the expressions are regarded as common nouns and are written without capitals. Here are a few examples:

chinaware	plaster of paris
frankfurters	turkish towel
india ink	volt
italics	watt

Abbreviations. Abbreviations are capitalized if the words they stand for would be capitalized; otherwise, they are not.

> Stanley Kolinski is an *FBI* agent. (*FBI* is capitalized because "Federal Bureau of Investigation" would be.)
>
> The shaft revolved at 1,500 *rpm*. (The abbreviation *rpm* is not capitalized because "revolutions per minute" would not be.)

Personal Titles. Capitalize the first letter of a personal title that immediately precedes a name. A personal title not followed by a name is ordinarily left uncapitalized unless it is used in place of the name.

The banquet for graduating chemical technologists was addressed
by *Dean* Arthur Swanson.

Tell me, *Dean*, will this year's enrollment exceed last year's?

The *dean* of our Special Education Division is Dr. Helen McConnell.

With persons of high rank, titles used in place of names are often
capitalized as a mark of respect.

I plan to watch the President on TV tonight.

I plan to watch the president on TV tonight.

Either of these usages is acceptable, although the second is preferred.

Titles of Literary and Artistic Works. Literary and artistic works
include books, magazines, newspapers, articles, short stories, poems,
reports, films, television programs, musical compositions, pictures,
sculptures, and the like.

When you write such titles, capitalize the first and last words as
well as all other words except *a, an, the,* coordinating conjunctions,
and prepositions with fewer than five letters.

He used a study guide, *Solving Problems in Chemistry and Physics,*
when he did his homework.

For tomorrow, read the handout article "New Trends in Preparing
Aluminum Alloys."

Note that the titles of longer publications are italicized, and the titles
of shorter publications are set off with quotation marks. In typed or
handwritten papers, indicate italics by underlining.

Exercise

Identify any word or abbreviation in the following sentences that should
be capitalized. If the sentence is correct, write a C.

Paul gleason, one of the most prominent blacks in this city, holds a
graduate degree from the wharton school of finance. (Gleason,
Wharton School of Finance)

1. Each account at people's savings bank is insured by the Federal Deposit Insurance Corporation (fdic).
2. tom's family doctor referred him to dr. Leland F. Hilton, who specializes in eye surgery.
3. Negotiations for a new contract between general motors and the uaw will begin next week.
4. In our part of the country, it's not wise to manifest marxist beliefs.
5. Do you believe that the popular image of politicians has improved, senator?
6. Our office has a new xerox copying machine.
7. *The wall street journal* and *business week* keep me posted on the latest business trends.
8. This article "after the me generation" offers a fine analysis of modern social trends.
9. Professor bacon is one of the world's foremost shakespearean scholars.
10. We are fortunate to have as our speaker mayor jerry manders.

Abbreviations

Abbreviations are used for certain personal titles, names of organizations and agencies, Latin terms, and for scientific and technical terms. Names of persons, streets, geographical locations, days, months, and school and college courses should be spelled out.

Personal Titles. *Mister, doctor,* and similar titles of address are always abbreviated when they immediately precede a name.

> *Mr.* John Williams and *Dr.* Sandra Barkon operate a small medical testing laboratory.

Junior, Senior, Esquire, and degree titles are abbreviated when they immediately follow proper names.

> The company was founded by Anthony Cappucine, *Jr.*
> The sign on the office identified its occupant as Elizabeth Williams, *M.D.*

Names of Organizations and Agencies. Some organizations or agencies are commonly referred to by their initials. Here are some typical examples.

FBI	AMA	NASA
GOP	UN	HUD

Latin Terms and Abbreviations with Dates. Certain Latin terms are always abbreviated, and other terms, mostly Latin, are abbreviated when they occur with dates or numerals.

e.g. (*exempli gratia:* for example)

etc. (*et cetera:* and [the] others)

i.e. (*id est:* that is)

vs. (*versus:* against)

B.C. (before Christ)

A.D. (*anno Domini:* In the year of our Lord)

A.M. (a.m.) (*ante meridiem:* before noon)

P.M. (p.m.) (*post meridiem:* after noon)

I'll pick you up around 7 P.M.

Certain diseases (e.g., measles and polio) are no longer serious childhood threats.

Scientific and Technical Terms. Science and technology make use of many terms of measurement. When these terms occur repeatedly in a single article or report, they are generally abbreviated. Whenever the meaning of the abbreviation might not be known to every reader, the term is written out the first time it is used and its abbreviation, in parentheses, put immediately after it. (This procedure can also be used with unfamiliar organizations and agencies that are mentioned repeatedly.)

The heater was a 250,000 British thermal unit (Btu) model.

Ordinarily, such an abbreviation is written without periods. However, if it has the same spelling as another word, a period is generally used after the last letter to distinguish the abbreviation from the word. Thus, *inch* is abbreviated *in.* to distinguish it from *in*, and *fig.* rather than *fig* is used for *figure*.

Exercise

Supply abbreviations wherever they are necessary or customarily used. If the sentence is correct, write a C.

> This engine is now operating at 5,000 revolutions per minute. (. . . 5,000 rpm.)

1. I think 8:00 *ante meridiem* is too early to begin a marketing seminar.
2. Tell me more more about those noises you've been hearing, Mister Usher.
3. It's about time the Environmental Protection Agency established and enforced strict rules for toxic waste disposal.
4. Please hand me that 30 milliliter syringe.
5. Ten years ago, I sold all my stock in International Business Machines, and now I couldn't be sorrier.
6. If that pain in your chest doesn't go away, make an appointment with Doctor Abraham Goldberg, Senior.
7. Terence didn't know that 212° Fahrenheit is the same as 100° Celsius.
8. The Interstate Commerce Commission is investigating the Central States Trucking Company.
9. The expression *et cetera* should be used very sparingly in one's writing.
10. Gail Birnhausen, Master of Arts, has joined the faculty at Grove Community College.

Numbers

Figures are usually used for numbers larger than ninety-nine. Numbers smaller than one hundred are usually written as words. This is not a hard-and-fast rule, however, and some writers prefer to spell out numbers through nine and use figures for all others. No matter which general practice your instructor prefers, there are several specific exceptions. These are discussed below.

Numbers in a Series. Numbers in a series should be written in the same way, regardless of their size.

> We have 150 salesmen, 52 research engineers, and 7 laboratory technicians.
> Harley owns three cars, two motorboats, and one hundred and fifteen motorcycles.

Dates. In dates that include the year, figures are always used.

January 3, 1975 (not January 3rd, 1975)

When the year is not given, the number may be spelled out or figures may be used.

August 5
August fifth
the fifth of August

Page Numbers and Addresses. Figures are used for page numbers of publications and most numbers in street addresses.

The diagram is open on page *223* of the text.
Her photographic studio is located at *139* Powell Street.

If the name of the street is also a number, spell out the name unless it is preceded by a word like "North" or "South." The following examples are both correct.

175 Fifth Avenue
203 West 48th Street

Numbers Beginning Sentences. Any number beginning a sentence should be spelled out. If this would require too many words, the sentence should be rewritten so that the number occurs within the sentence.

Forty thousand voters went to the polls.
A crowd of *115,394* people attended the game. (If this number began the sentence, eight words, an excessive number, would be needed to write it out.)

Units of Measurement, Decimals, Percentages, Expressions of Time. In business and technical writing, figures are used for units of measurement; for decimals, percentages, and other mathematical expressions; and for expressions of time with P.M. or A.M.

The metal is *0.315* inch thick.
The project has been *35* percent completed.

This constant, multiplied by 3, gives *12.424.*

The plant's work day starts at 9 A.M. and ends at *4:30* P.M.

Fractions, Two Consecutive Numbers. Ordinarily, fractions are spelled out unless (1) they occur in a mathematical expression or with a unit of measurement, (2) they have denominators larger than 10, or (3) they occur in a series that includes four or more fractions.

> Of the students in highway technology, three-fourths have received job offers.
>
> Multiply $3/4$ by $3/16$ to obtain the answer. (mathematical expression)
>
> A $5/16$ -inch crescent wrench is needed for the bolt. (unit of measurement)
>
> The new machine performs the operation in $1/20$ th the time required by the old. (denominator larger than ten)

When two numbers occur one immediately after the other, spell out the first one and use numerals for the second one. Exception: if the first number is larger than 100, use numerals for the first one and spell out the second one.

> The parts are held together by *six* 2-inch bolts.
>
> Hanson's Hardware sold *125 sixty-watt* light bulbs last week.

Exercise

Identify any miswriting of numbers in the following sentences, and rewrite these numbers correctly. If a sentence is correct, write a C.

> We must increase the diameter of the hole by two one-hundredths of an inch. (. . . by 0.02 inch.)

1. Jay has twenty-four suits, eighty-seven shirts and 114 ties.
2. The *Directory of Publishers*, page seven, lists the address of the Dowling Company as eleven J Street, Modesto, California 95355.
3. He graduated June 8th, 1957, from Northeastern College.
4. Fifty ten-foot beams will be required for this job.
5. Lend me a one-sixteenth inch drill bit, please.
6. During the last two years, Jerry has worked 7 months in a grocery store, 3 months in a car wash, and four months as a carpenter.
7. The seminar will start promptly at ten A.M. next Thursday.

8. You can find the John Kennedy quotation on page nineteen of your text.
9. Pam isn't thrilled about her fourteen and a half percent mortgage, but at the time she got it, no better rate was available.
10. October twenty 9, 1929, the day the stock market crashed, is sometimes known as "Black Monday."

Italics

Italics are used for the titles of longer publications and of artistic works, the proper names of vehicles and vessels, foreign words and phrases, and expressions used in a special sense—that is, called to the reader's attention rather than used for their meaning. In handwritten and typed papers, use underlining to indicate italics.

Titles of Longer Publications and of Artistic Works. Italics are used to designate the titles of the following:

books	full-length movies
magazines	long musical works and poems
newspapers	plays
journals	sculptures
bulletins	paintings

Titles of articles, newspaper columns, short stories, short poems, one-act plays, and the like are set off with quotation marks.

His paper included quotations from the *New York Times*, the *Journal of Business Education*, and a U.S. Office of Education bulletin entitled *Business School Enrollments, 1965–1975*. (newspaper, journal, bulletin)

Names of Vehicles and Vessels. Proper names of individual airplanes, ships, trains, and spacecraft are italicized (but not their model designations, such as DC-7 or Boeing 747, or abbreviations preceding them, such as S.S.).

He flew to Oslo on the *Star of the North*. He sailed back on the *Queen Elizabeth II*. (plane, ship)

Foreign Words and Phrases. Many foreign words and phrases have made their way into English over the centuries. At any one time there are many that have not been completely absorbed, and these are italicized.

> He committed a terrible *faux pas.* (a social blunder)
> I have a strange feeling of *déjà vu.* (a sensation that something has been experienced before)

When a foreign word is completely absorbed into the English language, the italics are dropped. For example, the word *employee,* originally a French word, used to be italicized but no longer is. Collegiate dictionaries use a special symbol such as an asterisk (*) or a dagger (†) to mark words or phrases that should be italicized. Check the introductory part of your dictionary to see what symbol it uses, and italicize any items marked with the symbol.

Expressions Used in a Special Sense. Expressions used in a special sense—that is, singled out for special attention, rather than used for their meaning—include words, letters, numerals, and symbols.

> The English word *thou* is related to the German word *du.*
> My handwriting is hard to read because each *r* looks like an *s,* and each *4* looks like a *9.*
> The symbol *&* is called an ampersand.

As we noted on page 476, quotation marks are sometimes used instead of italics for words, letters, numerals, and symbols.

Exercise

Supply italics wherever they are necessary. If a sentence is correct, write a C.

> Mark is a noun in the first sentence and a verb in the second. (*Mark* is a noun . . .)

1. Detective Holmes tried to piece together a modus operandi for the series of robberies in Pinehurst Subdivision.
2. One whole wall of our basement is lined with my father's back copies of the quarterly bulletin Business Barometer.

3. Voyager II is the second in a series of unmanned spaceships that this country will launch.

4. I mistook that M for an N; that's why I marked the word as misspelled.

5. "My Turn," a column by Felix Farnsworth, appears five days a week in the Columbia Post Gazette.

6. A copy of Van Gogh's painting Sunflowers hangs in my sister's living room.

7. Gone with the Wind, starring Clark Gable and Vivien Leigh, is my all-time favorite movie.

8. The sudden coup de main took the enemy completely by surprise.

9. The May, 1980, issue of Today's Backpacker contains an article on avoiding blisters.

10. The passenger train that passes through this town is called the Peoria Pearl.

Index

Revision Symbols
for Student Papers

Symbol	Problem	Page
ab	improper abbreviation	484-486
adj	wrong adjective form	441-444
adv	wrong adverb form	441-444
agr / pa	faulty agreement of pronoun and antecedent	385-389, 428-434
agr / sv	faulty agreement of subject and verb	415-417
apos	missing or misused apostrophe	458-460
awk	awkward phrasing	
[ ]	missing or misused brackets	471-472
cap	capital letter needed	481-483
case	wrong case	436-440
cl	cliché	
col	missing or misused colon	468-469
com	missing or misused comma	460-466
cs	comma splice	413-414
comp	faulty comparison	452-454
dm	dangling modifier	447-448
dash	missing or misused dash	470
ellip	missing or misused ellipses	277-278
excl	missing or misused exclamation point	474
frag	sentence fragment	411-413
hy	missing or misused hyphen	478-480
ital	missing or misused italics	489-490
lc	lowercase letter needed	481-483
log	faulty logic	